Gender and Slave

Emancipation in the Atlantic World

D0063293

Gender and Slave

Emancipation in the Atlantic World

edited by PAMELA SCULLY and DIANA PATON

Duke University Press Durham and London

2005

© 2005 Duke University Press

Printed in the United States of

America on acid-free paper ∞

Designed by C. H. Westmoreland

Typeset in Quadraat

by Keystone Typesetting, Inc.

Library of Congress Cataloging-in-

Publication Data appear on the

last printed page of this book.

Contents

Acknowledgments

This book originated in e-mail conversations between Pamela and Diana in 1998. Since then, many individuals and institutions have provided support. Most important, we would like to thank the contributors for their hard work, their timeliness in submitting and revising chapters, and their patience with the production process. Several of them also read and provided important comments on the introduction and bibliographic essay.

Versions of the introduction were given as papers at Warwick University, Newcastle University, the Women's History Seminar at the Institute for Historical Research, and the University of London. We would like to thank the audiences at those occasions, as well as the audience and participants at our round table at the Berkshire Women's History Conference in 2002, "Gendering the History of Slave Emancipation," for their encouraging and helpful feedback. Denison University, Queens' College, Oxford, and Newcastle University provided research support. Pamela completed this project at Emory University and would like to thank her colleagues for welcoming her so warmly to Atlanta. We extend our thanks to Frederick Cooper, Laura Edwards, Gad Heuman, Jocelyn Olcott, Robert Ross, Rebecca Scott, Mrinalini Sinha, Mary Turner, Kerry Ward, and Nigel Worden for their ongoing interest in our work. Kate Chedgzoy and Clifton Crais read the introduction at several critical moments. We thank them for their insightful comments as well as their support throughout the project. At Duke University Press, we have been fortunate to work with Valerie Millholland. We thank her, Miriam Angress, and the anonymous readers for the press, who helped us make this a better book. Woody Hickcox did the maps.

We dedicate this volume to Pamela's father, Larry Scully, and to Diana's grandmother, Polly Epstein, who both died while we were working on this project.

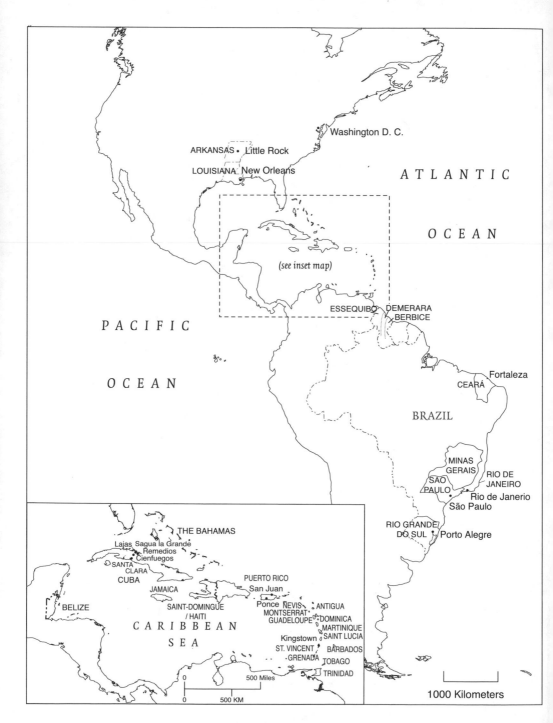

ATLANTIC

OCEAN

Washington D. C.

ARKANSAS • Little Rock
LOUISIANA •New Orleans

(see inset map)

PACIFIC

OCEAN

ESSEQUIBO DEMERARA
BERBICE

Fortaleza
CEARÁ

BRAZIL

MINAS
GERAIS
SAO
PAULO
RIO DE
JANEIRO
Rio de Janerio
São Paulo

RIO GRANDE
DO SUL • Porto Alegre

THE BAHAMAS
Lajas Sagua la Grande
Remedios
Cienfuegos
SANTA
CLARA
CUBA
JAMAICA
PUERTO RICO
San Juan
Ponce
BELIZE
SAINT-DOMINGUE
/ HAITI
NEVIS ANTIGUA
MONTSERRAT
GUADELOUPE DOMINICA
CARIBBEAN MARTINIQUE
SAINT LUCIA
SEA Kingstown
ST. VINCENT BARBADOS
GRENADA TOBAGO
TRINIDAD

0   500 Miles

0   500 KM

1000 Kilometers

The Atlantic World in the Age of Emancipation

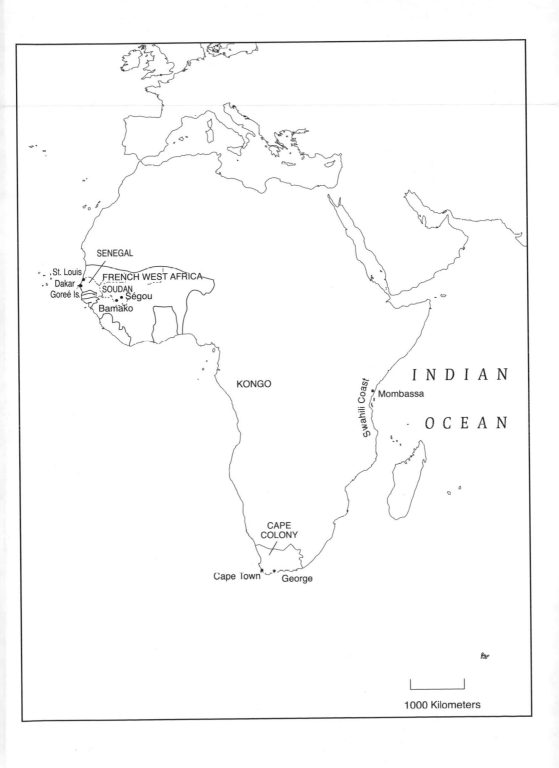

SENEGAL

St. Louis
Dakar
Goreé Is.
FRENCH WEST AFRICA
SOUDAN
Ségou
Bamako

KONGO

Swahili Coast
Mombassa

INDIAN

OCEAN

CAPE
COLONY

Cape Town
George

1000 Kilometers

Gender and Slave

Emancipation in the Atlantic World

DIANA PATON AND PAMELA SCULLY

Introduction: Gender and Slave Emancipation in Comparative Perspective

From Brazil to Cuba to the U.S. South, from Jamaica to the British Cape Colony, from Martinique and Haiti to French West Africa, gender was central to slave emancipation and to the making of the nineteenth-century Atlantic world. For many participants in emancipation, including abolitionists, state authorities, and freedpeople themselves, the transformation and restabilization of gender relations and identities was a key component of the process. Ideas of masculinity and femininity shaped slaves' and abolitionists' understanding of the wrongs of slavery, consolidated notions of contract and liberalism, contributed to the organization of postemancipation wage labor and political economies, and influenced freedpeoples' dreams of freedom and family in racially charged postemancipation landscapes.

A gendered approach to the study of emancipation helps to answer more fully many of the questions about labor, contract, and formal politics that have traditionally been at the heart of comparative emancipation studies. It also raises important new questions. Women and men accessed and experienced citizenship, labor, and bodily freedom in different ways in postemancipation societies. We would argue that the transition from slavery to regimes more compatible with free wage labor ideologies was crucially dependent on the gendered organization of "free" labor which made women's work invisible. As we shall see, the claims to masculine entitlement forged through revolutionary struggles to end slavery, as in Haiti, as well as abolitionist and liberal assumptions that the individual freed from slavery was male, ensured the persistence of gender inequality in postslave societies.

Recognizing how gender shaped slave emancipation requires that we rethink narratives that have dominated the scholarship in this area. A gendered reading of emancipation that makes false claims to universality may itself drive the centrality of particular topics, such as labor and politics, to emancipation studies. For example, for women the ending of slavery may have involved a challenge to a particular patriarchal order in which they often had been sexually abused as much as a transition to a new form of labor. Reflecting on emancipation from the point of view of women, and on how emancipation confirmed or disrupted existing gender relations, places issues such as violence, sexuality, and the gendered politics of public space at the heart of emancipation studies. Slave emancipation was not only experienced differently by men and women, it also served to reconstruct the very categories "man" and "woman."

The essays in this book draw on feminist theory which shows that gender involves "doing" rather than "being." Scholars such as Judith Butler and Jane Flax have argued that there are no presocial gendered essences. There are no "women" and "men" who have different experiences, only people whose bodily differences are, through social and discursive processes, fixed and categorized into two opposed groups: male and female. As Butler puts it, gender is not "the cultural inscription of meaning on a pregiven sex," but rather the "very apparatus of production whereby the sexes themselves are established."[1] For historians, this insight requires us to ask not only how women's experience of a process such as emancipation differed from that of men, but also how this and other processes work to produce and naturalize gendered categories and identities. The chapters in this book examine how those involved in emancipation also produced and reproduced gender difference. This could be expressed, for example, in the allocation of work, the organization of sexual relationships, the reconstruction of households, and freedpeople's political action.

Gender both helped construct and was itself constructed through class and racial categories.[2] For instance, increasingly from the late eighteenth century, race was being consolidated as a self-evident category in European thought. Both scientific discourse and European and colonial popular cultures came to see femininity as well as blackness as pathological.[3] Ideas about women as both marginal and threatening mirrored and came to enhance emergent racist ideologies about people of African descent.[4]

Discourses of race and their articulation with gendered ideologies and practices underwent transformations in the emancipation period. While tensions within slave societies predated the nineteenth century, the emancipation period coincided with a renewed attention by many slaveholding classes to the elaboration of the ideal of white womanhood. Individuals were gendered and raced in intertwined ways. Abolitionist gender politics, with its twin rhetorical questions "Am I not a woman and a sister?" and "Am I not a man and a brother?" worked to fix black people within the newly defined versions of femininity and masculinity. But abolitionist rhetoric was ambivalent about whether it was the condition of slavery or slaves' "blackness" which produced their perceived divergence from the normative rules of abolitionist morality. Indeed some of the conflicts at the moment of emancipation involved struggles over the meanings of black or white womanhood.

The gendering of slave emancipation in the nineteenth-century Atlantic world arose from three main sources. It arose out of enslaved people's ideas of masculinity and femininity, that is, the gender ideals that they brought to emancipation. The destruction of slavery through military force in many places also tended to masculinize the emancipation process by granting men title to citizenship on the basis of military service, thus rendering women political minors in the postslavery landscape. Finally, gendered assumptions and exclusions were central to abolitionist discourses, whether these were produced from below as in Haiti or through the liberal ideals of freedom held by many of those who oversaw and participated in emancipation. Despite the diversity of processes and outcomes in the Atlantic world, slave emancipation everywhere took gendered forms, restructuring relationships between men and women and making men's entitlement to leadership of a family a central feature of postemancipation societies.

Rethinking the Atlantic World

This book begins the work of creating a comparative gendered analysis of slave emancipation, using the analytic construct of "the Atlantic world" as a framework. The literature on the British experience in North America has dominated the emerging scholarship on "the Atlantic world."[5] Implicit in much of this work is the notion that ideas and activity flow westward from Europe to the Americas, with Africa joining the Atlantic world primarily as a source of slaves. Paul Gilroy's influential work on the black Atlantic, as well as that of Peter Linebaugh and Marcus Rediker on the creation of an eighteenth-century working class, suggests instead that the Atlantic world emerged from the engagement of different communities on all sides of the ocean.[6] Where many conceptions of the Atlantic world are primarily concerned with movement from East to West, our understanding implies the circulation of people, knowledge, and goods in all directions around the Atlantic littoral.[7] An "Atlantic" approach to history is more useful when it examines a set of processes rather than an object.[8]

Indeed there were many Atlantic worlds, not a unitary and singular Atlantic world. They were made through the reiterative tracing of multiple and overlapping routes of communication and trade, and in particular by slavery and the slave trades. The imaginary Atlantic of a merchant in Luanda in 1750 might focus on Bahia and Lisbon; that of an enslaved person in Virginia in the 1790s could encompass Saint-Domingue along with the Gold Coast; while a London-born sailor's Atlantic would be different again. Furthermore, we would argue that people did not themselves have to move to be drawn into a broader Atlantic system.[9] The expansion of slavery in West and West-Central Africa in the era of the Atlantic slave trade is perhaps the clearest example of what might be called the "Atlanticization" of people who never themselves crossed the ocean.[10]

The ending of the slave trade, and later of slavery in the course of the nineteenth century, helped construct another Atlantic experience, one that created circuits of knowledge and practice that did not automatically flow east to west. For instance, the ending of the British slave trade and later the emancipations in the Americas initiated a movement from west to east into other parts of West Africa. The Saro community of Port Harcourt in Nigeria, for example, was made up of individuals the British recaptured off other countries' slave ships, as well as ex-slaves and people of African descent from the Americas who initially settled in Sierra Leone. These emancipations also witnessed the consolidation of the Afro-Brazilian Aguda communities in the Bight of Benin.[11]

The hybrid worlds around the Atlantic make particularly visible differences in gender ideologies and practices which, when analyzed in isolation, have a tendency to be naturalized, biologized, or pathologized.[12] Attention to the work of gender in the making of postemancipation societies demonstrates the extent to which emancipation was linked to wider histories of migration and nation building that dominated the nineteenth century. Slave emancipation was one strand of a wider long-nineteenth-century process of transformation of mercantilist empires into global markets. The new world of free trade was underpinned by explicit ideologies of liberalism and free labor, in which the ownership of persons was unacceptable, although in practice the elaboration of new forms of unfree labor was an important part of the transition. Taken together, the essays in this book demonstrate that gender ideologies were central to the reformulation of citizenship and labor relations that took place in this period, in both slave and nonslave societies.

The Experience of Slavery and the Gendering of Emancipation

Recent literature on slavery and emancipation in the Atlantic World has emphasized the connections between freedpeople's aspirations for autonomy in economic and personal life. We argue that this widespread desire for autonomy, often manifested in attempts to access land and to reunite family members, can be better understood if we recognize that transformations in gender relations were an important part of what former slaves wanted from freedom. Enslaved people drew on a variety of sources for the elaboration of ideas about masculinity and femininity, including the gender conventions and ideologies of their particular African backgrounds,[13] the organization of gender in the specific slave society in which they lived, and their encounter with European gender ideologies.

The concept of the patriarchal household ordered slave societies throughout the Atlantic world.[14] Even in those plantation zones where owners were mainly absentees, the law and ideology of slave societies figured slaves as subordinate and inferior members of male-headed households. Some women did head slaveholding households, but they could only do so as widows or unmarried women, and they were almost always marginal and small-scale slaveholders.[15] In addition, maternity in most slave societies constituted the basis of slavery: the status of the mother determined if an individual was born free or enslaved. This practice was intrinsic to the patriarchal nature of slavery as an institution. The refusal of the social rights of fatherhood to enslaved men emphasized that slaves could not form their own households for the purpose of transmitting names or property but were incorporated into their owners' households.[16] Gender, as well as race, was thus fundamental to the continuation of slave societies.

In most of West Africa, from where many slaves in the Atlantic world came, gender was a crucial principle of social organization. Among the Yoruba and Igbo in the area of present-day Nigeria, for example, a sharp separation between men and women existed in daily life, and one's gender centrally determined one's social, economic, and political experience. The "dual-sex system" gave men and women specific and discrete social, economic, and political functions.[17] Women, especially elder women, had substantial institutional authority and political roles, as well as social autonomy.[18]

In contrast, in many of the societies of the South East African coast from which slaves were taken to Cuba and Brazil in the mid-nineteenth century, women were more clearly subordinated to men.[19] Women did primarily agricultural and household work while men engaged in seasonal heavy labor, trade, warfare, and politics. Women were subject to the authority of their husbands and husbands' kin and enjoyed little formal political power, although widows and divorced women on the Swahili coast seem to have enjoyed some independence.[20] Women's status increased with age and with the production of children, but it did not equal that of men. In these regions women generally did not enjoy the degree of respect and autonomy experienced by women in many West African societies. Nevertheless, the spiritual arena gave women access to political power in East Africa, as mediums between ancestors and the living.[21]

The importance of spirituality as an avenue to power for women was shared across much of the subcontinent. Women also gained status by becoming wealthy, by joining women's title groups, by filling niche roles such as *griottes* (community singers and historians in parts of West Africa), and particularly by advising kings through the status of sister, wife, or mother.[22] Sandra Barnes has argued that women in Africa were "one of history's most politically viable female populations."[23] We still need more research to discover how enslaved people used their experience of women's roles in Africa to shape their understanding of gender in the Americas.

In plantation economies in the Americas, the status of slave entailed a reworking of gender roles. In contrast to labor regimes in both Europe and Africa, plantation work did not crucially depend on a gendered division of labor. Although plantation managers generally reserved specialized, artisanal, and managerial tasks for men, both women and men did agricultural work.[24] From the planters' perspective, women's performance of agricultural labor involved a denial of their femininity and thus emphasized both racial difference and inferiority. African men felt more acutely the transgression of gender roles when slaveholders forced them to do agricultural labor, which was often a predominantly female occupation in their original African societies.[25] Meanwhile, enslaved people on plantations across the Americas organized labor within their own communities along gender lines, with women in most places taking on the primary responsibility for domestic and reproductive tasks. Work in what has been called the "slaves' economy" made use of gender as an organizing principle, although in complex and varying ways in different slave societies.[26]

In much of Africa into the nineteenth century, domestic slavery, in which a family owned few slaves, was the dominant experience for most enslaved people, and the majority of slaves were women. Slavery took place within the existing gendered division of labor, with many female slaves sharing a great deal with free women, especially in patrilineal societies.[27] They could marry, and often married their owners, although not necessarily by choice; their children were often free, and enslaved women worked with free women in agricultural and other labor.

In towns and cities in Atlantic societies, enslaved people's work roles were more closely tied to gender than in rural areas. While most enslaved people on plantations worked at tasks which might be done by men or women, enslaved people in urban settings almost always performed gender-specific labor: women were laundresses, marketers, cooks, prostitutes, and looked after children; men were porters, stevedores, household servants, and sometimes artisans. Urban communities required large numbers of women to perform conventionally feminine jobs. As a result, the numerical predominance of male over female slaves was less pronounced in urban than in rural settings, and in many cities enslaved women outnumbered enslaved men.[28]

Particularly in Protestant areas of the nineteenth-century Atlantic world, slaves also forged their gender ideologies through encounters with missionaries and agents of colonial states. These individuals encouraged enslaved people to organize gender according to European bourgeois conventions. Protestant missionaries and preachers in the British Caribbean, the Cape Colony, and the U.S. South from the late eighteenth century actively encouraged slaves to transform their organization of sexual and family life by adopting monogamous marriage. They allied with "progressive" planters who hoped that transformations in sexual behavior would lead to increased reproduction and thus greater profitability.[29] Yet one should be wary both of flattening out enslaved people's gender ideologies and of overestimating the effects of missionary activity on them. Missionaries were keen to produce Christian subjects as evidence of their success. Documentation about converts who embraced monogamy and the Christian nuclear family is thus easily found in many missionary publications. Slaves who did not embrace such visions tend to fall out of the documentary record.

The pattern in the Catholic Atlantic world was somewhat different, both because the Catholic Church placed less emphasis on proselytizing and conversion than did evangelical Protestantism, and because the slave trade to the largest Catholic slave societies, Brazil and Cuba, only ended in the mid-nineteenth century. Slave communities in these regions had greater cultural autonomy, and also repeatedly had to integrate newly arrived Africans who brought with them African ideologies and cultural practices.[30] As a result, even though the Brazilian, Spanish, and French states tried to influence the marital and reproductive behavior of the enslaved people in their empires, for instance, through imperial slave codes that rewarded monogamy, African gender ideologies were less thoroughly ideologically challenged.[31]

The Course of Emancipation: A Brief Overview

While "slave emancipation" is usually taken to mean those dramatic moments of the full abolition of slavery with which this book is primarily concerned, these were almost everywhere preceded by smaller-scale emancipations resulting from self-purchase and manumission. In the Iberian colonies, imperial slave codes facilitated such processes, making them especially widespread. As several essays in this volume emphasize, self-purchase and manumission were gendered processes, accessible to men and women in different ways. For women, manumission was most likely if they had a child by their owner. Some women thus turned the male slaveholder's power to rape into a complex bid for freedom. Self-purchase and manumission were also ideologically gendered: women's acquisition of freedom through what became known as "concubinage" was in many places extremely important to the construction of the racist stereotype of the licentious black woman.

These smaller emancipations had crucial consequences for later postslavery societies, providing as they did the basis for the formation of substantial free populations of color, which in parts of the Atlantic world, especially Brazil and Spanish America, equaled or outnumbered the enslaved population by the time slavery was abolished.[32] A minority of free people of color became successful slave-owning planters. In some areas, perhaps most notably Saint-Domingue/Haiti and most of the small societies of the Eastern Caribbean, this minority went on to form a significant fraction of the postemancipation ruling class, while in others, such as Brazil, newly freed people joined an already large free population of color to form a postemancipation group with diverse experiences of becoming free. Emancipation was not simply a binary process in which black freedpeople confronted their white former owners. The relationship between freedpeople and former slave owners was also complicated by the presence of other significant groups such as indentured laborers from India and China in Trinidad, British Guiana, and Cuba; indigenous people in many parts of Africa and the Americas; and working-class southern-European immigrants in Brazil, Cuba, and Louisiana.[33] Different formations of "race" and "ethnicity" in postslave societies may have been responsible for different gender norms and conventions among working people and in sexual and labor relations across such societies.

As slaves became freedpeople they thus drew on complex and multiple sources for understanding gender. Indeed, many of the conflicts of the postemancipation era, whether over marriage and family life, the use of public space, or labor, resulted from the different visions of manhood, and in particular of womanhood, constructed by these different groups.

Slavery ended in the Atlantic world over the course of more than a hundred years, beginning with the Haitian Revolution and ending with the halting and uneven emancipations in Africa under colonial rule in the late nineteenth and early twentieth centuries.[34] The first great emancipation took place in Haiti in the 1790s, creating the first state ever to completely abolish slavery, and (after the United States) the second independent state in the Americas. During roughly the same period, many northern states in the newly established United States began cautious and gradual emancipation, mainly using "free birth" laws that left all current slaves still in bondage. Similar forms of emancipation took place in Spanish South America in the early nineteenth century. All these emancipations were in some way linked to anticolonial struggles.[35]

The next substantial emancipation took place in the British Empire in the 1830s, where the imperial state imposed abolition on slaveholding elites. Emancipation in most parts of the empire proceeded gradually, with a four-year intermediary period of "apprenticeship." This form of emancipation consolidated rather than challenged colonial rule. The same was true in the remaining French colonies, where immediate emancipation was achieved in the wake of the 1848 revolution. The impact of emancipation in the French colonies was felt in other parts of the Caribbean. Slaves in both the Danish and Dutch West Indies were inspired by disturbances in Martinique and Guadeloupe. In the Dutch colonies (excepting Suriname) planters were unable to sustain the coercive power necessary to maintain slavery, and the system effectively, although not legally, came to an end in 1848. In Saint Croix in the Danish Virgin Islands, slaves rebelled in 1848, and in response the governor decreed emancipation. By 1860, the remaining slave societies in the Americas were the United States, Brazil, Suriname, and the Spanish colonies that had not yet won independence. Nevertheless there were still millions of slaves in the Atlantic world, augmented by the illegal slave trade to Cuba and Brazil, by the natural increase of the U.S. enslaved population, and by the expansion of plantation slavery in West Africa as a result of the abolition of the Atlantic slave trade.

In the United States, slavery was destroyed through the Civil War of 1860–65. Suriname ended slavery in 1863, but former slaves there had to serve a period of "apprenticeship," as they had in the British colonies. Cuban abolition was a protracted process, begun in the Ten Years' War (1868–78) but not completed until 1886. In Puerto Rico, where slavery was less economically significant than in Cuba, the system was abolished in 1873. Brazil's abolition process was also gradual, extending from the "Free Womb Law" of 1871 to the final emancipation decree in 1888, with which Brazil became the last American society to abolish slavery.

There were still large numbers of slaves in many African societies by the time of the "Scramble for Africa" in the 1880s and 1890s. Emancipation in Africa was, with the exception of the British Cape Colony, a much slower process than in the Americas, imposed by colonial powers that wanted to abolish slavery while maintaining access to unfree labor. In practice, colonial authorities in Africa moved very slowly against slavery. While all powers made trading in people illegal, most did not enforce these laws for many years.[36] In French West Africa, slavery was formally abolished in 1848, but as Klein and Roberts argue in this volume, in the second half of the nineteenth century more people were being enslaved than were being freed. The recent revitalization of slavery in some parts of Africa under the pressures of neoliberal globalization reminds us that slave emancipation is not a historical process with a neat endpoint.

Haiti as Precedent: Militarism and Citizenship

The process of emancipation in Haiti demonstrates many of the key characteristics of the gendering of emancipation in other parts of the Atlantic world. Haitians achieved emancipation through an anticolonial struggle that made powerful connections among military service, citizenship, and the nation. Similar connections were made in other places where the ending of slavery was tied to attacks on colonial rule. Saint-Domingue had been the jewel in the French imperial crown, the annual importer of thirty thousand African slaves, and the producer of two-fifths of the world's sugar and more than half the world's coffee in the 1780s.[37] This society, founded on massive violence and exploitation, began to unravel as its members participated in the upheavals precipitated by the French Revolution. The slave uprising of 1791 put the complete abolition of slavery on the agenda; the actions of the French Jacobin Léger Félicité Sonthonax and the Haitian revolutionary general and former slave Toussaint Louverture formalized abolition. Toussaint's revolutionary army defeated the imperial armies of Napoleon (who aimed to restore slavery), Britain, and Spain, creating a new nation whose achievements were, in Michel-Rolph Trouillot's words, "unthinkable history."[38]

While the revolution swept away white privilege, it reinscribed gender inequality. All Haitian citizens were defined as black, but not all black Haitians were citizens. The 1805 constitution reserved voting, for instance, for men. The founding fathers of the Haitian nation, Toussaint, Jean-Jacques Dessalines, Henri Christophe, and Alexandre Pétion, all contributed to the construction of a masculinist and patriarchal nationalism. Haiti here showed its ideological links to the Enlightenment and to the French Revolution, which made the same connection between revolutionary citizenship and masculinity.[39]

Part of the reason for this association in Haiti was the deep connection among military participation, masculinity, and nationalism. The revolutionary army conscripted men in massive numbers, both during the revolution and in independent Haiti, maintaining a large standing army in case of renewed French attempts to retake the former colony. Soldiers were seen as the founders of Haitian freedom. The 1805 constitution declared that "no one is worthy of being a Haitian if he is not a good father, a good son, a good husband, and above all a good soldier." But women could not be soldiers, and this had more than symbolic consequences. Under Dessalines and Christophe, the non-militarized sector of the population, of which women formed a substantial majority, had to undertake compulsory fieldwork on the plantations, many of which were now owned by the state. Pétion embarked on a policy of land distribution in 1809, in which each soldier received fifteen acres from state lands. As a result, women received no land in this founding act in the formation of the Haitian peasantry.[40] In addition, the heavily militarized politics of nineteenth-century Haiti left little space for women to participate in government.

Other societies where slavery ended as part of an assault on colonialism similarly linked citizenship, military participation, and national identity. Thus in mainland Latin America, Simón Bolívar's republican army included many conscripted male slaves. Those who survived the military campaign were freed. Conscription and manumission of male slaves was also a significant part of the emancipation process in the rest of Spanish South America. According to Robin Blackburn, after independence the coastal haciendas of Peru "were left with slave crews containing disproportionate numbers of women, children, and old people."[41] In Cuba, male slaves participated extensively in the Ten Years' War and the Guerra Chiquita. Here too, as Michael Zeuske notes in his contribution to this volume, the participation of black men in the revolutionary army became a crucial sign of their citizenship. The discourse of the independence movement constructed Spain as decadent and feminized and the insurgent forces as manly and virile. The inclusion of black men within this concept of manliness defined the nation as antiracist, but at the cost of excluding women from the national story.[42] Similarly, in French West Africa, military participation was a long-standing route to emancipation for men but one that was denied to women.[43]

Societies where slave emancipation occurred through military campaigns and/or revolutionary violence articulated the linkages between masculinity and citizenship very explicitly. But the connection of citizenship to masculinity was germane to all postemancipation societies, as we shall see later in our discussion of contract theory and citizenship in the postemancipation Atlantic world.

The Conservative Road to Emancipation

In Haiti, and in most places where emancipation took place as a result of an acute political crisis, the precise way slavery would end was obviously not planned in advance. In contrast, other emancipations, of which those in the British Empire and Brazil are the most notable, were relatively managed. Of course, these emancipations emerged out of complex struggles among different contending groups; they were not top-down processes. In the British Empire even the precise terms of emancipation—for example, the timing of the ending of apprenticeship—emerged from former slaves' actions.[44] In Brazil, emancipation was proclaimed through the "Golden Law" of 1888, but only after thousands of slaves had taken their freedom, making slavery unsustainable. Nevertheless, in contrast to the anticolonial and revolutionary contexts of emancipations in Haiti and Cuba, for instance, the British and Brazilian ruling classes were able to seize the day: to present emancipation as a gift bestowed from above.[45]

In both the British Empire and Brazil, slave emancipation came at a point when gender relations were in flux due to the changes resulting from the development of capitalism, and when they were the subject of much anxiety and debate.[46] As a result, the ending of slavery in the British Empire was explicitly ideological in its approach to gender relations. A central goal of British imperial emancipation was to transform colonial gender relations. Slaves, imperial officials and others believed, had been degendered by their enslavement. Emancipation, then, should make them properly into men and women.

British imperial visions of freedom had been heavily gendered long before the passage of the Emancipation Act in 1833. As Moira Ferguson has shown, the practice of criticizing slavery by attacking its impact on gender relations reached back to the seventeenth century.[47] In the nineteenth century this critique was written into colonial policy. Gendered assumptions were evident in British policy toward "liberated Africans"—those rescued from illegal slave-trading ships—in the 1810s and 1820s. These individuals were subject to work regimes that countered their expectations of how labor should be organized by gender. The British imperial authorities barred women from most agricultural labor.[48] Brazilian debates about slavery also frequently invoked gender. In 1871, for instance, debates around slavery focused in particular on the prostitution of enslaved women as a symbol of the corrupt relationship between slave owner and slave.[49]

The moment of full emancipation in the British Empire in 1838 saw a widespread effort by both missionaries and colonial officials to persuade freedpeople to organize their family lives around monogamous Christian marriage and domesticity. Characteristic of this effort was a newspaper article published in the Cape Colony, praising emancipation in the following terms: "Freedom . . . offers something in addition to personal enjoyments. The Freeman becomes the Head of a Family. . . . The Father, however poor, however overlooked or despised by the world, is now an object, in one place at least, not only of love but reverence. There is now a circle where, if he chooses, he may reign as a King."[50] This vision of emancipation conceptualized the meaning of freedom as patriarchal authority for freedmen. Women were to be released from slavery, but into a new kind of subordination and dependence.

In postemancipation Brazil, similar goals were expressed in a more authoritarian way. Elites' concern to "civilize" racially mixed urban populations led to police crackdowns on prostitutes and to campaigns to persuade the urban poor to marry and to adopt bourgeois gender norms. The authorities suspected poor women of immorality and prostitution when they did not adhere to the new standards of "civilization" but instead remained present in public space. While such campaigns were directed at the lower orders as a whole, regardless of their status prior to abolition, in practice many of the targets were freedpeople, including those who had migrated to the cities in the wake of emancipation.[51]

Throughout the Atlantic world, state officials and reformers encouraged freedpeople to adopt monogamous patriarchal marriage and female domesticity as a mark of their civilization. Like Brazil, postemancipation Puerto Rico saw campaigns to "moralize" and "civilize" the poor, including attacks on prostitutes and consensual unions.[52] In Martinique the Société des Femmes Schoelcheristes, named after the French abolitionist Victor Schoelcher, was founded in 1849, one year after emancipation. It aimed to promote religiosity and marriage among the freed population, and in doing so it particularly directed its attention to those women engaged in "concubinage" with white men.[53] In the United States, the Freedmen's Bureau circulated a book titled *John Freeman and His Family*, which was intended to teach freedpeople how to adapt to their new situation. In the book, the former slave John Freeman took a new name and made a contract for his labor. His wife, Mrs. Freeman, had to learn to keep a clean house.[54] The similarity of efforts to establish patriarchal families and attempts to curtail women's independence across a range of societies suggests a deeply embedded conception of gender within the liberal idea of freedom.

Such efforts worked in parallel with attempts to reform the gender relations of other subordinate groups across the Atlantic world. Immigrant laborers, indigenous peoples, and working classes were subjected in the nineteenth century to both moralism and legal forces that aimed to transform their gender relations. In the United States, for instance, the General Allotment Act (Dawes Act) of 1887 imposed a system of private landholding on Native American tribes, distributing what had been communally held land to male "heads of families" and single people. The process meshed with efforts of missionaries and reformers to "civilize" native peoples in many societies in the Atlantic world by persuading them to adopt male-dominant nuclear family structures alongside private property.[55] Efforts to impose a different understanding of gender on former slaves were thus part of the wider formation of liberal capitalist societies in which a particular form of bourgeois patriarchy was seen as appropriate. In this process, proponents of liberalism attacked "old-fashioned" forms of patriarchy such as the slaveholding household, the aristocratic patriarchy of the European and Latin American great landed estates, and the honor codes of Latin American elites. While these attacks opened up spaces in which women were able to claim new rights, the main outcome was the reconfiguration, rather than the overturning, of gender inequality.

Gender and Postemancipation Freed Communities

Emancipation created spaces for struggle to define the meaning of freedom in ways that rarely perfectly matched the visions of liberty participants brought to the experience. Nevertheless, freedwomen and freedmen could order their lives with greater autonomy than they had been able to as slaves. The extent of this change, of course, depended on where they lived. Where the plantation system and the planter class remained strong, as in the Cape Colony, Barbados, Southeast Brazil, and parts of the United States and French West Africa, states subjected freedpeople to harsh controls intended primarily to enforce their participation in "free" wage labor, and to prevent their becoming "dependent" on state support. Such controls assumed and thus sought to impose a particular construction of gender. For instance, vagrancy, poor relief, and bastardy legislation all worked toward the goal that men should act as heads of households and provide for their families.[56]

Planter classes were less successful in imposing gendered class legislation when freedpeople had wider opportunities. For instance, in societies such as Jamaica and Dominica, where freedpeople managed to secure some land for themselves and engage in peasant farming, they were less subject to, although not completely free from, colonial or plantocratic intervention.[57] In this sense, state and ruling-class control of gender is one aspect of a wider set of questions about the degree to which freedpeople were able to control their own lives.

Former slaves constructed postemancipation communities that drew powerfully on visions of extended and fictive families.[58] Men and women's connections to and roles within these families sometimes confirmed and sometimes were in tension with the visions of male authority and female domesticity contained in official blueprints for emancipation. Child rearing was probably universally allocated to women, but much else seems to have been variable. The precise content of these gendered ideologies is only just beginning to be unpacked, but as the essays in this book show, marriage, politics, land, and family are emerging as central areas for examination and comparison. At least as substantial as the overlaps were the ways in which the gender conventions of former slaves differed from those that were imposed upon them. Substantial evidence demonstrates freedwomen's active engagement in the politics of their communities, including efforts to control their men's votes. Laura Edwards has shown that in North Carolina, for instance, freedpeople had distinctive understandings of the meaning, rights, and obligations associated with marriage and other sexual relationships.[59] Similarly, the work of Jean Besson on the pan-Caribbean institution of family land—that is, land that is passed down to all descendants, male and female, of an original ancestor, who may also be male or female—demonstrates a very different idea of property to those embedded in legal inheritance practices.[60] The challenge for research is to investigate the gender norms in play in situations where they did not match the norms of white observers.

The similarities and differences between the gendered conventions of freedpeople and the ruling classes they confronted are not, however, the only issues that need discussion. Such an analysis of the gendering of emancipation risks understanding gender as merely an aspect of class and/or race formation and relations, rather than a contradiction and power relation in its own right. We cannot assume the existence of a coherent and conflict-free set of gender norms within each class group, in which ruling classes seek to impose one set while former slaves adhere to another. Both feminist theory and empirical evidence point to the conclusion that relations between men and women of the same "race" and/or class involve power and conflict.[61] For instance, a number of scholars have documented cases in which freedwomen experienced and resisted domestic violence and other forms of abuse from their husbands and partners.[62]

Yet freedmen's power over freedwomen was limited. The widespread African diasporic pattern of separate and autonomous control of property by men and women, along with the prominence of female-headed households throughout the diaspora, meant that relatively few freedmen were in a position to use economic power to dominate freedwomen.[63] The model of domesticity assumed that men would be able to provide for their wives and children, but this was rarely even a realistic possibility in most of the postslave societies discussed here. In many areas, most significantly Barbados and small islands in the Eastern Caribbean, lack of jobs led to male migration, leaving behind a predominantly female population.[64] In other areas it simply meant that women had to perform some kind of income-generating work, whether that was waged work, household manufacture, or peasant farming. As a result, even had they wanted to do so, it was impossible for all but a few of the most economically successful former slaves to adopt in full the ideology that was supposed to mark their transition to freedom and civilization. This had obvious costs in terms of impoverishment, but it also prevented the consolidation of a family-wage or peasant-based patriarchy among former slaves.

Liberalism, Gender, and Citizenship

Throughout the Atlantic world, the late eighteenth and nineteenth centuries witnessed the consolidation of liberal political economy as the dominant model of social and economic organization. Liberalism was inflected differently in its French, Anglophone, Hispanic, and Lusophone iterations, but it always countered the image of slave society with the ideal of a society in which each person was an autonomous individual able to make contracts. As David Brion Davis has demonstrated, the processes that led to slave emancipation in the Atlantic world involved the intellectual and moral rejection of human bondage in favor of an ideology of free waged labor that stressed the value of the contract.[65]

Liberalism was, of course, a contradictory and protean ideology. Liberals' commitment to formal equality and to contract-making everywhere coexisted with hierarchies and exclusions based on race and class.[66] Such exclusions were particularly marked in postslave societies, where a wide range of unfree and semifree labor systems prevented ex-slaves and other workers from acting as the contract makers of liberal theory. Many of these systems, which included sharecropping, *métayage*, convict labor, indenture, debt bondage, and coercive vagrancy legislation, were intrinsically connected to gender hierarchies within familial relationships. Meanwhile, varying combinations of racial violence, racist laws, and poverty prevented freedpeople from exercising political rights.

These race- and class-based exclusions were integrated with liberalism's gendered premise. As Carol Pateman has shown, the model of liberal individualism implicitly assumed that the individual making contracts was a man whose right and ability to do so arose from his status as head of a family of dependents.[67] It was the marriage contract that rendered men and women's relationship to the family so different. Marriage made a man head of a family or potential family. It defined him as having the independent status required of a contract-making individual. In contrast, marriage rendered a woman permanently the subordinate of her husband. Through marriage, women became minors. The father's right to make contracts on behalf of his daughter was in essence transferred to the husband.

Married women's position in contract theory was, of course, echoed by the legal position of slaves. Slaves were also legally unable to make contracts. In the transition to emancipation, then, the acquisition of the right to make contracts was symbolically crucial. Emancipation's propagandists always stressed this point, even when the actual social relations created by emancipation allowed former slaves little space to make contracts. For freedwomen, the ability to contract was even more tenuous than it was for their male peers. If they married, as moralists and missionaries wanted them to do, they were in danger of losing a capacity that was represented to them as the essence of their freedom. No wonder women did not always show great enthusiasm for married life.

The promise of emancipation was, to some extent, a gendered one: that is, men were promised the entitlement of masculinity, of being head of a household. Women, in contrast, were liberated into dependence. What was to change for women was that they would be dependents of the right person, their husband or father, rather than the wrong one, their master.[68]

Visions of patriarchal authority vested in the family thus girded many plans for emancipation. Male dominance was legally enshrined throughout many ex-slaveholding societies. For instance, in many places, freedmen gained suffrage at or soon after emancipation. Casting a vote became freighted as a symbol of freedom and citizenship in the United States, the French colonies, and many of the British colonies (where it was somewhat less significant because of property qualifications, but still important).[69] No postemancipation state allowed freedwomen to vote. To have done so would have been an extraordinarily radical step, given that women did not vote anywhere in the Atlantic world at this time. Nevertheless, the explicitness with which the vote was allowed to men and not to women was a significant statement about who was a citizen and who a dependent in these new societies. Even in places like Brazil which excluded most freedmen along with all freedwomen from citizenship—the Brazilian republican constitution of 1891 limited "active citizenship" to literate males aged twenty-one and over—women's exclusion *because they were women* emphasized the postemancipation state's deep commitment to gender hierarchy.[70]

The inscription of male authority into the legal discourses of many postemancipation societies was the product of a momentary union of popular and bourgeois male interests in managing emancipation. In a process similar to that described by Eileen Suárez Findlay in her study of late nineteenth-century Puerto Rico, emancipation created a short-lived alliance between men, which helped to confirm masculinity as a key criterion of the fully emancipated individual.[71] For freedmen, this alliance came at a price. Emancipation, as envisaged by its planners, involved an ideological move whereby freedmen were to trade their visions of economic independence for power over the family. By emphasizing the authority and independence of freedmen within the family, their lack of authority and continued dependence outside of it was de-emphasized.

Yet freedwomen and freedmen shaped gender systems that were far more complex than abolitionist rhetoric allowed for. While states may have intended to grant citizenship only to freedmen, freed communities and in particular freedwomen did not always accept this limitation. Studies of Louisiana and of Richmond, Virginia, indicate that freedwomen believed that they could and should play a role in formal politics.[72] Similarly, Mimi Sheller has shown that in Jamaica women were actively involved in the political life of the postemancipation black community, while Gilbert Pago describes the participation of freedwomen in political rallies for all the candidates in the 1848 elections in Martinique.[73] Similar work remains to be done on many of the other postslave societies of the Atlantic world, but it seems likely that citizenship rights were widely reinterpreted by freedpeople along more inclusive lines than authorities had intended. Despite the theoretical inability of the married woman to contract, married women in many situations did in fact sell their labor, making implicit and explicit contracts to do so. Their work was essential to the functioning of the capitalist economy, both in industrializing regions and in postemancipation plantation societies.[74]

In practice, the wage labor demands on freedwomen in postslave societies frustrated both the sexual contract of liberal political economy and the masculine promise of emancipation. Even while abolitionists and missionaries, along with planters in some regions such as the French ex-slave colonies and the U.S. South, promoted patriarchal families as a way of maintaining order and lessening ex-slaves' dependence on the state, perceived labor shortages after emancipation also led to calls for freedwomen to labor. The problem faced by colonial legislators, planters, and factory owners was how to keep the model of the masculine provider intact while not only allowing but strongly encouraging freedwomen as well as freedmen to engage in wage labor.

The tensions surrounding freedwomen's ability to contract expose the interrelations of class, racial, and gendered identities. In many slave and postslave societies, white women's possession of both whiteness and femininity became linked to their ability to avoid labor outside the home. Elite whites expected that freedwomen, on the other hand, would work outside of as well as within their own households. This work confirmed for many whites the racially subordinate status of freedwomen, as well as their tenuous claim to womanhood. Freedwomen's membership in ex-slave communities, and/or in an emergent working class, trumped their status as women. Meanwhile the ambiguous position of poor white, indentured, formerly free black, and "mixed-race" women (named variously colored, brown, *métisse, mulata, sang-mêlé*, etc.) could both challenge and confirm these raced and gendered equations with regard to labor. Race and gender statuses were thus protean, circumstantial, and highly political.

Themes

This book addresses enduring themes in the historiography of slave emancipation: how the emancipations of the long nineteenth century involved new visions about what it meant to work, to be a citizen, and to engage in politics.

The chapters show that those new ideals derived some of their contemporary power from their affirmation of deeply held gender norms. This combination of factors helped inscribe ideas about men's supremacy into postemancipation societies.

The chapters also address newer historiographical themes, such as the mutual constitution of racial and gendered identities and the politics of sexuality. The contributors begin to address questions of representation and epistemology, of how historians know what we claim to know. Can archives compiled by slaveholding regimes or through the lenses of postemancipation ruling classes' preoccupations with crime and labor yield truths about the experiences of slaves and freedpeople? Slavery and postslavery studies have been surprisingly silent on this quandary. Foregrounding questions about the constitution of the archives allows historians to understand the limits of historical documents even as we seek to make them speak. Attending to this is particularly important, because women's experiences as well as questions of gender are often silenced and oblique in the sources.[75]

The chapters that follow offer detailed analyses of slave emancipation in specific societies or groups of societies. Collectively, they demonstrate the gains that a gendered approach can provide in understanding the complex processes and representations of emancipation. Slave and postemancipation societies were diverse. The work presented here discusses all the main players in emancipation: enslaved and freedpeople, abolitionists, free people of color, state officials, and slave owners.

Part 1, "Men, Women, Citizens," explores the importance of gender ideologies for processes of emancipation as well as for the construction of citizenship in postemancipation societies. Pamela Scully's chapter argues that historians of emancipation need to grapple more explicitly with how power relations constructed the colonial archives: she asks if historians can confidently interpret freedpeople's reported speech as easily accessible and self-evident in meaning. In order to fully appreciate the agency of freedpeople we must develop a wider understanding of politics and citizenship in the postemancipation era than that promoted by the colonial state and abolitionists. This concern to problematize the transparency of sources, as well as to develop broader understandings of political behavior and ideas is a point generalizable across many postslave societies. Likewise, Sue Peabody's analysis of initiatives by women slaves to obtain manumission in the French Caribbean, and of the way that gender was implicated in the general emancipations of the late eighteenth and mid–nineteenth century, confirms a central theme of this book: that emancipation tended to benefit men more than women, particularly in the political sphere.

Mimi Sheller discusses the importance of masculinity to Jamaican emancipation, analyzing the interplay of racial with gendered ideas about the individual and society. Showing that the discursive reconstruction of freedmen's masculinity was also, and inextricably, a reconstruction of blackness, she argues that a postslavery masculine subjectivity was produced not only in contrast to ideas about whiteness and femininity, but also through the exclusion of indentured migrants, termed "Coolies," from claims to citizenship.

The last two chapters in part 1 deal with abolitionism, in Brazil and the United States, respectively. Roger Kittleson shows how the success of the abolitionist movement in Brazil depended not just on women's activism but also on mobilizations of particular representations of femininity as virtuous and moral. Kittleson's chapter echoes, but also modifies, historiographies of British and North American abolitionism. He suggests that the Brazilian abolitionist movement's use of representations of traditional femininity emphasized its claim to the moral high ground, enabling it to mobilize wide public support. Unlike abolitionism in Britain and the United States, Brazilian antislavery did not produce wider claims to women's rights as citizens.

Carol Faulkner similarly emphasizes the intersection between the role of actual women and of gendered ideologies in abolitionism, focusing on the work of two white U.S. abolitionist women with the Freedman's Bureau after the Civil War. Josephine Griffing and Julia Wilbur, she argues, used their experience as women struggling against their own gender subordination to develop an understanding of economic and political dependence among former slaves which was much less negative than that of the dominant Freedman's Bureau.

Part 2, "Families, Land, and Labor," charts the relationship between women, the household, gendered labor ideologies, and postemancipation political economy. Scholars of the British Caribbean have long noted freedwomen's "flight" from plantation labor in the postemancipation period. Bridget Brereton's chapter suggests that women's withdrawal from labor must be contextualized by paying attention to women's choices and to the context of struggle over women's and children's labor in the years before full emancipation in 1838. In addition, she shows that the "withdrawal" has been exaggerated: many women did continue to work for wages. Her chapter reiterates the need for historians to scrutinize the bias of the historical record. The master narrative of women's flight owes as much to the perceptions of the people who wrote the records as to the experiences of the people being written about.

Martin Klein and Richard Roberts's contribution examines the meaning of a different form of women's flight and speaks to the specificity of West African emancipations. Focusing on French West Africa from the mid-nineteenth century to 1914, they demonstrate that domestic slavery of women increased alongside colonial conquest of the region. In 1905 the French outlawed the sale of people, although they did not make real efforts to enforce the law. Women slaves ultimately forced the hand of the French by fleeing their husbands, who were also sometimes their owners, and using colonial courts to achieve freedom by obtaining divorces. But, as Klein and Roberts show, after 1910 courts tended to make women return to their husbands, even if these husbands were also former masters.

Michael Zeuske's close study of material processes of class formation in Cuba examines the interdependence of class, race, and gender formation. He shows the difference in men's and women's routes to acquiring land and suggests that paying attention to women's participation in the construction of freed communities will require rewriting the narrative of Cuban emancipation. Ileana Rodríguez-Silva argues that, despite elite efforts to define them out of the category of "worker," freedwomen in Puerto Rico managed both to write themselves into that category and to bargain at least as effectively as freedmen over the conditions of their labor.

Slave emancipation instigated a dramatic expansion of the public sphere. Colonial and postcolonial authorities depicted former slaveholding households as sites for the illegitimate exercise of private authority and tried to replace such authority, at least theoretically, with contractual relations. The contributors to part 3, "The Public Sphere in the Age of Emancipation," examine the implications of these transitions for freedpeople, former slaveholders, and the larger communities of postemancipation society.

Focusing on the relationship between free people of color and the white plantocracy in Barbados, Melanie Newton shows that both groups redefined gender in the wake of emancipation. The philanthropic activity widespread among elite whites and free people of color, she argues, played a crucial role in the generation of a new form of masculinity, defined in contrast to the figure of the debauched planter-rake. Philanthropic movements were thus at least as much about the disciplining of the gender behaviors of members of their own class as they were about regulating or supporting the lower orders to whom their efforts were officially directed. The philanthropic associations of free people of color, meanwhile, worked to produce male dominance within that community at the same time as they asserted its respectability.

Emancipation set in train the reformation of class and race as well as gender, and these reformations took place in complex interrelated ways. Examining urban culture in St. Vincent, Sheena Boa demonstrates the importance of women's reputation as a marker of class status: the ability—or desire—to maintain the "proper" domestic role of women became a key means of distinguishing among the elite, the "middle," and the poor. Poor women, she argues, had a complex relationship to ideas of "proper" femininity, seeking to emulate its standards even while subverting many of its codes. Class and race, in effect, came to be symbolized by women's public use of their bodies. Martha Abreu also analyses popular culture and the public sphere in her chapter on the gendered representations of different racially defined categories of person in Brazilian popular culture. Analyzing the lundu form of popular song, she shows that representations of the mixed race woman, the mulata, changed depending on the performer and the context of performance. She demonstrates that apparently racist images could also be used satirically to undermine contemporary ideas about blackness and femaleness.

Gender was both at stake and a weapon in a range of struggles in slave and postemancipation societies, whether these took the form of violent slave rebellions or the polite but charged words of the debating chamber. In the context of the post–Civil War Arkansas constitutional convention discussed by Hannah Rosen, political debates about suffrage became intimately linked to discussions of sexuality and gender, and in particular to the possibility of marriage between white women and black men. As Rosen shows, for southern whites both suffrage and marriage to white women, as signs of black male citizenship, had the potential to undermine racial categories and hierarchies. The fact that the Fourteenth Amendment made it illegal to ban the former made attacks on the latter all the more necessary. African American delegates, meanwhile, were prepared to accept a resolution deeming all interracial sexual relationships inappropriate, an acceptable compromise from their point of view because it included condemnation of white men's rape of black women.

The formal political debates analyzed by Rosen are played out in practice in the horrifying case of Eliza Pinkston of Louisiana discussed by Marek Steedman. Here we have an example of an intimate relationship between a black woman and a white man, a relationship that could not, by the norms of its time and place, lead to marriage. Pinkston was one of the women about whom the black Arkansas delegates could have been talking. She later chose to marry a man of "her own color," a decision that created tension between her black husband and her white former lover, expressed through political conflict as well as labor disputes, leading ultimately to extreme violence. Steedman's analysis of the case emphasizes the complex reformulations of the idea of the household in the Reconstruction South, as Eliza Pinkston and her husband tried to assert the autonomy of their own household against whites who believed that former slaves should remain part of plantation households.

Toward a Gendered History of Slave Emancipation

The essays in this book focus on a wide range of societies and present an important series of arguments which collectively demonstrate the importance of gender to understanding many of the questions with which scholars of postemancipation societies have long been concerned, as well as raising new questions. They do not however, attempt to provide a complete and fully gendered comparative and transnational history of slave emancipation in the Atlantic world. Such a history remains to be written, but the research published here and elsewhere allows us to begin to imagine what it will look like.

A fully gendered comparative history of slave emancipation would uncover the involvement of gender in many of the struggles during and after emancipation, including those that have traditionally been interpreted as primarily about race and/or class. This would include, for example, recognition of the ways that struggles among competing ruling groups to achieve hegemony in postemancipation society involved contested gender conventions. Examples would include the challenge to the dominant hard-drinking, sexually promiscuous masculinity of Caribbean planters by more "polite," bourgeois metropolitan masculinities, as well as the important gendered dynamic of struggles over freedpeople's labor, at the heart of which was the issue of whether women would or would not become plantation wage workers in the new society. A gendered comparative history of emancipation would recognize that, while all freedpeople faced the enormous difficulties of attempting to make new lives as unpropertied people in a capitalist world, postemancipation societies were structured in certain legal, institutional, political, and economic ways that made these difficulties more severe for freedwomen than for freedmen. It would need, however, to explain not only the subordination of women but also the relationship of that subordination to the specific targeting of freedmen *as men* for hostility and violent attack in some societies, seen most notably in the history of lynching in the postemancipation United States.

Such a history would have to come to terms with freedwomen's contradictory experience of the doubleness of gender, as both symbol of freedom and source of oppression. Because slavery had denied all enslaved people the autonomy to organize gender according to their own understandings, both freedmen and freedwomen had reasons to support the maintenance and even strengthening of gender divisions among them. And yet for freedwomen emphasizing differences between men and women was problematic, because their position as women also served as a site of oppression, experienced through, for example, wage discrimination, lack of access to citizenship, sexual violence, and disproportionate responsibility for reproductive labor.

A gendered history of emancipation would reveal difference as well as similarity in societies across the Atlantic world. Probably the biggest differences would be found between the experience of the Americas and the Cape Colony on the one hand, and the rest of Africa on the other. European bourgeois gender conventions did not dominate among the rulers of African societies as they did, to varying degrees, in other parts of the Atlantic world. The end of slavery in the Americas and the Cape led to reconstructions of racial hierarchy, often linked to debates about "miscegenation" and/or "whitening," which were always in part about sexuality. In contrast, in much of the rest of Africa "race" was connected to emancipation primarily because the latter was imposed on African societies by European colonial regimes, which construed African slavery as evidence of African barbarism. The consolidation of plantation slavery in parts of West Africa and East Africa in the nineteenth century also helped affirm and create racial and religious difference, as Muslim Africans used religious difference to justify their enslavement of Africans who practiced indigenous religions.

Nevertheless, the gender dynamics of emancipation in American societies should not be homogenized. As we suggested above, the means by which emancipation was achieved had major implications for gendered claims to citizenship and gendered understandings of the nation. Other important differences could, we suspect, be traced between societies in which postemancipation ruling classes brought in large numbers of predominantly male laborers to maintain plantation production, and those where this did not occur; between urban and rural spaces; between plantation and nonplantation societies; and so on.

Throughout Atlantic societies, slave emancipation involved, and to some extent ignited, struggles over access to land, resources, and political power, as well as over definitions of freedom, labor, and culture. Gender was always at stake in these battles. Individuals entered the postemancipation world already gendered and with understandings of masculine and feminine personhood already in place. The essays that follow suggest that the battles and conflictual processes that shaped the world of freedom provide a moment in which such understandings about gender and their connection to race and class were made transparent. Emancipation both drew on existing ideas about the meaning of manhood and womanhood, about the content of the categories "man" and "woman," and contributed to new ideologies and practices of gender.

Notes

1 Judith Butler, *Gender Trouble: Feminism and the Subversion of Identity* (New York: Routledge, 1990), 7; Jane Flax, "Postmodernism and Gender Relations in Feminist Theory," *Signs* 12, no.4 (1987): 621–43; Denise Riley, *"Am I That Name?" Feminism and the Category of "Women" in History* (Minneapolis: University of Minnesota, 1988).

2 See Evelyn Brooks Higginbotham, "African-American Women's History and the Metalanguage of Race," *Signs* 17 (1992): 251–74.

3 Nancy Stepan, "Race and Gender: The Role of Analogy in Science," *Isis* 77 (1986): 261–77.

4 This paragraph is based on Pamela Scully, "Race and Ethnicity in Women's and Gender History in Global Perspective" in *Women's History in Global Perspective: Themes*, ed. Bonnie G. Smith (Urbana: University of Illinois Press, 2004).

5 E.g., Bernard Bailyn, *The Peopling of British America* (London: Tauris, 1987); Jack P. Greene, *Pursuits of Happiness: The Social Development of Early Modern British Colonies and the Formation of American Culture* (Chapel Hill: University of North Carolina Press, 1988); and Bernard Bailyn and Philip D. Morgan, *Strangers within the Realm: Cultural Margins of the First British Empire* (Chapel Hill: University of North Carolina Press, 1991).

6 Paul Gilroy, *The Black Atlantic: Modernity and Double Consciousness* (Cambridge: Harvard University Press, 1993); Peter Linebaugh and Marcus Rediker, *The Many Headed Hydra: Sailors, Slaves, Commoners and the Hidden History of the Revolutionary Atlantic* (Boston: Beacon, 2000).

7 For an East-to-West version of Atlantic history, see Bailyn, *Peopling of British America*.

8 For a thoughtful exploration of the many meanings of Atlantic histories, see David Armitage, "Three Concepts of Atlantic History," in *The British Atlantic World, 1500–1800*, ed. David Armitage and Michael J. Braddick (Basingstoke, U.K.: Palgrave Macmillan, 2002), 11–27. In an otherwise subtle discussion, Armitage argues that the Atlantic world was a European creation (16–17).

9 For an innovative reconceptualization of Atlantic history, see Kristin Mann and Edna G. Bay, "Shifting Paradigms in the Study of the African Diaspora and of Atlantic History and Culture," in *Rethinking the African Diaspora: The Making of a Black Atlantic World in the Bight of Benin and Brazil*, ed. Kristin Mann and Edna G. Bay (London: Frank Cass, 2001), 3–21.

10 Paul E. Lovejoy, *Transformations in Slavery: A History of Slavery in Africa* (Cambridge: Cambridge University Press, 1983).

11 Mac Dixon-Fyle, *A Saro Community in the Niger Delta, 1912–1914: The Potts-Johnsons of Port Harcourt and Their Heirs* (Rochester, N.Y.: University of Rochester Press, 1999); Robin Law, "The Evolution of the Brazilian Community in Ouidah," in Mann and Bay, *Rethinking the African Diaspora*, 22–41.

12 We are grateful to an anonymous reader for Duke University Press for this observation.

13 Scholarly debate about the significance of African "origins" and "continuities" in slave cultures and societies originates with the work of Melville Herskovits, who argued for continuity between African and African diasporic cultures in response to claims that slavery had wiped out any cultural links with or memory of Africa; see his *The Myth of the Negro Past* (Boston: Beacon, 1967 [1958]). Sidney Mintz and Richard Price placed more emphasis on the elaboration of culture in New World societies; see their *The Birth of African-American Culture: An Anthropological Perspective* (Boston: Beacon, 1992 [1976]). Recent work on the slave trade traces concrete historical rather than speculative connections between slaves in different regions of the Americas and specific African societies. See Michael A. Gomez, *Exchanging Our Country Marks: The Transformation of African Identity in the Colonial and Antebellum South* (Chapel Hill: University of North Carolina Press, 1998); David Northrup, "Igbo and Myth Igbo: Culture and Ethnicity in the Atlantic World, 1600–1850," *Slavery and Abolition* 21, no. 3 (2000): 1–20; and João José Reis, *Slave Rebellion in Brazil: The Muslim Uprising of 1835 in Bahia*, trans. Arthur Brakel (Baltimore: Johns Hopkins University Press, 1993).

14 Elizabeth Fox-Genovese, *Within the Plantation Household: Black and White Women of the Old South* (Chapel Hill: University of North Carolina Press, 1998); Laura F. Edwards, *Gendered Strife and Confusion: The Political Culture of Reconstruction* (Urbana: University of Illinois Press, 1997); Robert C.-H. Shell, *Children of Bondage: A Social History of the Slave Society at the Cape of Good Hope, 1652–1838* (Hanover, N.H.: Wesleyan University Press, 1994); Stuart B. Schwartz, *Sugar Plantations in the Formation of Brazilian Society: Bahia, 1550–1835* (Cambridge: Cambridge University Press, 1985), 287–94.

15 Kathleen Mary Butler, *The Economics of Emancipation: Jamaica and Barbados, 1823–1843* (Chapel Hill: University of North Carolina Press, 1995), chap. 6, esp. 95; Hilary McD. Beckles, "White Women and Slavery in the Caribbean," *History Workshop Journal* 36 (1993): 66–82.

16 Of course, this was true primarily in legal and ideological rather than practical terms. In practice slaves did form coresidential units, have a socially recognized place for fatherhood, and transmit property.

17 The term "dual-sex system" is widely used in the historiography of gender in West Africa. For a discussion of the political empowerment of women in this system, see Beverly Stoeltje, "Asante Queen Mothers: A Study in Female Authority," in *Queens, Queen Mothers, Priestesses, and Power: Case Studies in African Gender*, ed. Flora

Edouwaye Kaplan, Annals of the New York Academy of Sciences, vol. 810 (New York: New York Academy of Sciences, 1997).

18 Niara Sudarkasa, "The 'Status of Women' in Indigenous African Societies," in *Women in Africa and the African Diaspora*, ed. Rosalyn Terborg-Penn, Sharon Harley, and Audrea Benton Rushing (Washington, D.C.: Howard University Press, 1987), 25–41; Ifi Amadiume, *Male Daughters, Female Husbands: Gender and Sex in an African Society* (London: Zed, 1988); Agnes Akosua Aidoo, "Asante Queen Mothers in Government and Politics in the Nineteenth Century," in *The Black Woman Cross-Culturally*, ed. Filomina Chioma Steady (Rochester, Vt.: Schenkman, 1981), 65–77; Edna G. Bay, *Wives of the Leopard: Gender, Politics, and Culture in the Kingdom of Dahomey* (Charlottesville: University of Virginia Press, 1998).

19 David Eltis, "The Export of Slaves from Africa, 1821–1843," *Journal of Economic History* 37, no. 2 (1977): 409–33; Elizabeth Schmidt, *Peasants, Traders and Wives: Shona Women in the History of Zimbabwe, 1870–1939* (Portsmouth, N.H.: Heinemann, 1992); Marcia Wright, *Strategies of Slaves and Women: Life Stories from East/Central Africa* (New York: Lillian Barber, 1993); Holly Hanson, "Queen Mothers and Good Government in Buganda: The Loss of Women's Political Power in Nineteenth-Century East Africa," in *Women in African Colonial Histories*, ed. Jean Allman, Susan Geiger, and Nakanyike Musisi (Bloomington: Indiana University Press, 2002), 219–36.

20 Jonathon Glassman, *Feasts and Riot: Revelry, Rebellion, and Popular Consciousness on the Swahili Coast, 1856–1888* (Portsmouth, N.H.: Heinemann, 1995); Margaret Strobel, *Muslim Women of Mombasa, 1890–1975* (New Haven, Conn.: Yale University Press, 1979).

21 See Terence Ranger, "Connexions between 'Primary Resistance Movements' and Modern Mass Nationalism in East and Central Africa," part 1, *Journal of African History* 9, no. 3 (1968): 437–53, and part 2, *Journal of African History* 9, no. 4 (1968): 631–41.

22 Allman, Geiger, and Musisi, *Women in African Colonial Histories*.

23 Sandra T. Barnes, "Gender and the Politics of Support and Protection in Precolonial West Africa," in Kaplan, *Queens, Queen Mothers, Priestesses, and Power*, 2.

24 See, e.g., Marietta Morrissey, *Slave Women in the New World: Gender Stratification in the Caribbean* (Lawrence: University Press of Kansas, 1989), chap. 5; Ira Berlin and Philip D. Morgan, eds., *Cultivation and Culture: Labor and the Shaping of Slave Life in the Americas* (Charlottesville: University Press of Virginia, 1993), esp. Berlin and Morgan's introduction and the essays by Richard S. Dunn and Lorena S. Walsh; and David Eltis, *The Rise of African Slavery in the Americas* (Cambridge: Cambridge University Press, 2000), 100–101.

25 Hilary McD. Beckles, *Centering Women: Gender Discourses in Caribbean Slave Society* (Kingston: Ian Randle, 1999), 6–10; Mona Etienne, "Women and Men, Cloth and Colonization: The Transformation of Production-Distribution Relations among the Baule (Ivory Coast)," in *Women and Colonization: Anthropological Perspectives*, ed. Mona Etienne and Eleanor Leacock (New York: Praeger, 1980), 214–38.

26 "The slaves' economy" refers to provision ground and kitchen garden agriculture, the raising of livestock, hunting and fishing, household production, and the marketing of surpluses produced through these activities. See Betty Wood, *Women's Work, Men's Work: The Informal Slave Economies of Lowcountry Georgia* (Athens: University of Georgia Press, 1995); Josephine A. Beoku-Betts, " 'She Makes Funny Flat Cakes She Call Saraka': Gullah Women and Food Practices under Slavery," in *Working toward Freedom: Slave Society and Domestic Economy in the American South*, ed. Larry E. Hudson Jr. (Rochester, N.Y.: University of Rochester Press, 1994), 211–31.

27 Martin Klein, *Slavery and Colonial Rule in French West Africa* (Cambridge: Cambridge University Press, 1998); Suzanne Miers and Igor Kopytoff, eds., *Slavery in Africa: Historical and Anthropological Perspectives* (Madison: University of Wisconsin Press, 1977), 28; Claire Robertson and Martin Klein, eds., *Women and Slavery in Africa* (Madison: University of Wisconsin Press, 1983).

28 Mieko Nishida, "Manumission and Ethnicity in Urban Slavery, Salvador, Brazil: 1808–1888," *Hispanic American Historical Review* 73, no. 3 (1993): 361–91; Kimberly S. Hanger, *Bounded Lives, Bounded Places: Free Black Society in Colonial New Orleans, 1769–1803* (Durham, N.C.: Duke University Press, 1997), 22–23; B. W. Higman, *Slave Populations of the British Caribbean, 1807–1834* (Mona, Jamaica: University of the West Indies Press, 1995), 118–19.

29 Catherine Hall, *White, Male and Middle Class: Explorations in Feminism and History* (New York: Routledge, 1992), chap. 9; Melanie Newton, " 'New Ideas of Correctness': Gender, Amelioration and Emancipation in Barbados, 1810s–50s," *Slavery and Abolition* 21, no. 3 (2000): 94–124.

30 Reis, *Slave Rebellion in Brazil*; Franklin W. Knight, *Slave Society in Cuba during the Nineteenth Century* (Madison: University of Wisconsin Press, 1970), esp. chap. 3.

31 Knight, *Slave Society in Cuba*, 129–30.

32 For comparative population figures, see David W. Cohen and Jack P. Greene, eds., *Neither Slave nor Free: The Freedmen of African Descent in the Slave Societies of the New World* (Baltimore: Johns Hopkins University Press, 1972).

33 This "presence" should not, of course, be naturalized: indentured laborers and immigrant European workers alike came to postslave societies as a direct consequence of former slave owners' manipulation of state policy to serve their economic interests. See Madhavi Kale, "Making a Labour Shortage in Post-Abolition British Guyana," *Itinerario* 21, no. 1 (1997): 62–72.

34 The most comprehensive comparative study of emancipation is Robin Blackburn, *The Overthrow of Colonial Slavery, 1776–1848* (London: Verso, 1988), which does not, however, discuss emancipation in the Cape Colony, Cuba, Brazil, or West Africa. For a short overview of emancipations, see Stanley L. Engerman, "Emancipation in Comparative Perspective: A Long and Wide View," in *Fifty Years Later: Antislavery, Capitalism and Modernity in the Dutch Orbit*, ed. Gert Oostindie (Leiden, the Netherlands: KTLV Press, 1995), 223–41. The literature on individual emancipation processes is too extensive to cite here. For full references see the bibliographic essay in this volume.

35 Frederick Cooper, Thomas C. Holt, and Rebecca J. Scott make a similar point in the introduction to their *Beyond Slavery: Explorations of Race, Labor, and Citizenship in Postemancipation Societies* (Chapel Hill: University of North Carolina Press, 2000), 13.

36 Suzanne Miers and Richard Roberts, "The End of Slavery in Africa," in *The End of Slavery in Africa*, ed. Suzanne Miers and Richard Roberts (Madison: University of Wisconsin Press, 1988), 20.

37 David Geggus, *Slavery, War, and Revolution: The British Occupation of Saint-Domingue, 1793–1798* (Oxford: Clarendon, 1982), 6. Figure for slave imports is from Jaime E. Rodríguez O., "The Emancipation of America," *American Historical Review* 105, no.1 (2000): 135.

38 Michel-Rolph Trouillot, "An Unthinkable History," in *Silencing the Past: Power and the Production of History* (Boston: Beacon, 1995). For a recent short overview of the Haitian Revolution and its scholarship, see Franklin W. Knight, "The Haitian Revolution," *American Historical Review* 105, no.1 (2000): 103–15.

39 Joan Landes, *Women and the Public Sphere in the Age of the French Revolution* (Ithaca, N.Y.: Cornell University Press, 1988); Joan Wallach Scott, *Only Paradoxes to Offer: French Feminists and the Rights of Man* (Cambridge: Harvard University Press, 1996); Lynn Hunt, *The Family Romance of the French Revolution* (Berkeley: University of California Press, 1992).

40 Mimi Sheller, "Sword-Bearing Citizens: Militarism and Manhood in Nineteenth-Century Haiti," *Plantation Society in the Americas* 4, nos. 2–3 (1997): 233–78; James Leyburn, *The Haitian People* (New Haven, Conn.: Yale University Press, 1966 [1941]), 56.

41 Blackburn, *Overthrow of Colonial Slavery*, 342–60; quote on 360.

42 Ada Ferrer, *Insurgent Cuba: Race, Nation and Revolution, 1868–1898* (Chapel Hill: University of North Carolina Press, 1999).

43 Klein, *Slavery and Colonial Rule*, 104.

44 Michael Craton, "The Transition from Slavery to Free Wage Labour in the Caribbean, 1780–1890: A Survey with Particular Reference to Recent Scholarship," *Slavery and Abolition* 13, no. 2 (1992); Diana Paton, *No Bond but the Law: Punishment, Race, and Gender in Jamaican State Formation, 1780–1870* (Durham, N.C.: Duke University Press, 2004), chap. 3.

45 Richard D. E. Burton, *Afro-Creole: Power, Opposition, and Play in the Caribbean* (Ithaca, N.Y.: Cornell University Press, 1997), 103–8; Catherine Hall, *Civilising Subjects: Metropole and Colony in the English Imagination, 1830–1867* (Chicago: University of Chicago Press, 2002), 120.

46 Sonya O. Rose, "Protective Labor Legislation in Nineteenth-Century Britain: Gender, Class, and the Liberal State," in *Gender and Class in Modern Europe*, ed. Laura L. Frader and Sonya O. Rose (Ithaca, N.Y.: Cornell University Press, 1996), 193–210; Mary Poovey, *Making a Social Body: British Cultural Formation, 1830–1864* (Chicago: University of Chicago Press, 1995); Sueann Caulfield, *In Defense of Honor: Sexual Morality, Modernity, and Nation in Early Twentieth-Century Brazil* (Durham, N.C.: Duke Univer-

sity Press, 2000); Susan K. Besse, *Restructuring Patriarchy: The Modernization of Gender Inequality in Brazil, 1914–1940* (Chapel Hill: University of North Carolina Press, 1996); Magali Engel, *Meretrizes e doutores: saber médico e a prostituição no Rio de Janeiro (1840–1890)* (Sao Paulo: Brasiliense, 1989).

47 Moira Ferguson, *Subject to Others: British Women Writers and Colonial Slavery, 1670–1834* (New York: Routledge, 1992). Ferguson's focus, and that of other scholars, such as Clare Midgley, who have attended to the gendering of antislavery ideology, is on representations produced by women. However, the antislavery discourse of male abolitionists and missionaries was equally inflected by gender, although in somewhat different ways. See Hall, *Civilising Subjects*, 112–13; Diana Paton, "Decency, Dependence, and the Lash: Gender and the British Debate over Slave Emancipation, 1830–1834," *Slavery and Abolition* 17, no. 3 (1996): 162–84.

48 Rosanne Marion Adderley, " 'A Most Useful and Valuable People?' Cultural, Moral, and Practical Dilemmas in the Use of Liberated African Labour in the Nineteenth-Century Caribbean," *Slavery and Abolition* 20, no.1 (1999): 59–78.

49 Sandra Lauderdale Graham, "Slavery's Impasse: Slave Prostitutes, Small-Time Mistresses, and the Brazilian Law of 1871," *Comparative Studies in Society and History* 33, no. 4 (1991): 669–94.

50 *South African Commercial Advertiser*, 1 Dec. 1838.

51 Caulfield, *In Defense of Honor*, 55–63; Teresa Meade, *"Civilizing" Rio: Reform and Resistance in a Brazilian City, 1889–1930* (University Park: Penn State University Press, 1997), esp. 37–42; Martha de Abreu Esteves, *Meninas perdidas: Os populares o cotidiano do amor no Rio de Janeiro da belle époque* (São Paulo: Companhia das Letras, 1989).

52 Eileen J. Suárez Findlay, *Imposing Decency: The Politics of Sexuality and Race in Puerto Rico, 1870–1920* (Durham, N.C.: Duke University Press, 1999), chap. 3.

53 Myriam Cottias, "La séduction coloniale: Damnation et stratégies—Les Antilles, XVIIe–XIXe siècle," in *Séduction et sociétés: Approches historiques*, ed. Cécile Dauphin and Arlette Farge (Paris: Seuil, 2001), 125–40.

54 Amy Dru Stanley, *From Bondage to Contract: Wage Labor, Marriage, and the Market in the Age of Slave Emancipation* (Cambridge: Cambridge University Press, 1998), 38–39. State officials directed similar propaganda at freedpeople during emancipation in the French colony of Réunion in the Indian Ocean. The official who brought the emancipation decree to the island in 1848 declared, "Work elevates man in God's eyes; it makes him a citizen; it calls him to found a family." Françoise Vergès, *Monsters and Revolutionaries: Colonial Family Romance and Métissage* (Durham, N.C.: Duke University Press, 1999), 58–68; quote on 59.

55 Jane E. Simonsen, " 'Object Lessons': Domesticity and Display in Native American Assimilation," *American Studies* 43, no.1 (2002): 75–99; Natasha Erlank, " 'Raising up the Degraded Daughters of Africa': The Provision of Education for Xhosa Women, Mid-nineteenth Century," *South African Historical Journal* 43 (2000): 24–38; Deborah Gaitskell, "At Home with Hegemony: Coercion and Consent in African Girls' Education for Domesticity in South Africa before 1910," in *Contesting*

Colonial Hegemony: State and Society in Africa and India, ed. Dagmar Engels and Shula Marks (London: British Academic Press, German Historical Institute, 1994), 110–30; On similar anxieties about the gender relations of immigrants in Argentina, see Donna Guy, Sex and Danger in Buenos Aires: Prostitution, Family, and Nation in Argentina (Lincoln: University of Nebraska Press, 1990).

56 Amy Dru Stanley, " 'We Did Not Separate Man and Wife, but All Had to Work': Freedom and Dependence in the Aftermath of Slave Emancipation," in Terms of Labor: Slavery, Serfdom, and Free Labor, ed. Stanley L. Engerman (Stanford, Calif.: Stanford University Press, 1999), 188–212; Edwards, Gendered Strife and Confusion, 95–96; Newton, " 'New Ideas of Correctness' "; Ileana Rodríguez-Silva, "Libertos and Libertas in the Construction of the Free Worker in Postemancipation Puerto Rico," this volume; Hebe Maria Mattos, Das cores do silêncio: Os significados da liberdade no Sudeste escravista—Brasil, século XIX (Rio de Janeiro: Nova Fronteira, 1998), 248. For similar arguments in relation to England's 1834 Poor Law—passed in very close proximity to slave emancipation—see Marjorie Levine-Clark, "Engendering Relief: Women, Ablebodiedness, and the New Poor Law in Early Victoria England," Journal of Women's History 11, no. 4 (2000); and Lisa Forman Cody, "The Politics of Illegitimacy in an Age of Reform: Women, Reproduction, and Political Economy in England's New Poor Law of 1834," Journal of Women's History 11, no. 4 (2000): 131–56.

57 Thomas C. Holt, The Problem of Freedom: Race, Labor and Politics in Jamaica and Britain, 1832–1938 (Baltimore: Johns Hopkins University Press, 1992); Michel-Rolph Trouillot, Peasants and Capital: Dominica in the World Economy (Baltimore: Johns Hopkins University Press, 1988).

58 Jean Besson, "Freedom and Community: The British West Indies," and Raymond T. Smith, "Race, Class, and Gender in the Transition to Freedom," both in The Meaning of Freedom: Economics, Politics, and Culture after Slavery, ed. Frank McGlynn and Seymour Drescher (Pittsburgh, Penn.: University of Pittsburgh Press, 1992), 183–219 and 257–90.

59 Edwards, Gendered Strife and Confusion.

60 Jean Besson, Martha Brae's Two Histories: European Expansion and Caribbean Culture-Building in Jamaica (Chapel Hill: University of North Carolina Press, 2002).

61 See, e.g., Eudine Barriteau, The Political Economy of Gender in the Twentieth-Century Caribbean (Basingstoke, U.K.: Palgrave, 2001); M. Jacqui Alexander and Chandra Talpade Mohanty, eds., Feminist Genealogies, Colonial Legacies, Democratic Futures (Routledge: New York, 1997); and Patricia Mohammed, ed., "Rethinking Caribbean Difference," special issue of Feminist Review 58 (1998).

62 Leslie A. Schwalm, A Hard Fight for We: Women's Transition from Slavery to Freedom in South Carolina (Urbana: University of Illinois Press, 1997), 261–66; Newton, " 'New Ideas of Correctness' "; Pamela Scully, Liberating the Family? Gender and British Slave Emancipation in the Rural Western Cape, South Africa, 1823–1853 (Portsmouth, N.H.: Heinemann, 1997), 131–33.

63 Sidney Mintz, "Black Women, Economic Roles and Cultural Traditions," in

Caribbean Freedom: Economy and Society from Emancipation to the Present, ed. Hilary Beckles and Verene Shepherd (Kingston, Jamaica: Ian Randle, 1993); Diana Paton, "The Flight from the Fields Reconsidered: Gender Ideologies and Women's Labor after Slavery in Jamaica," in Reclaiming the Political in Latin American History: Essays from the North, ed. Gilbert Joseph (Durham, N.C.: Duke University Press, 2001), 175–204.

64 Janet Henshall Momsen, "Gender Ideology and Land," in Caribbean Portraits: Essays on Gender Ideologies and Identities, ed. Christine Barrow (Kingston: Ian Randle, 1998), 115–32.

65 David Brion Davis, Slavery and Human Progress (New York: Oxford University Press, 1984).

66 Uday S. Mehta, "Liberal Strategies of Exclusion," in Tensions of Empire: Colonial Cultures in a Bourgeois World, ed. Frederick Cooper and Ann Laura Stoler (Berkeley: University of California Press, 1997), 59–86.

67 Carole Pateman, The Sexual Contract (Stanford, Calif.: Stanford University Press, 1988).

68 This is the argument of Scully, Liberating the Family?. See the introduction for a discussion of the implications of Pateman's analysis for studies of emancipation.

69 On suffrage in the United States, see Eric Foner, Reconstruction: America's Unfinished Revolution, 1863–1877 (New York: Harper and Row, 1988); Julie Saville, The Work of Reconstruction: From Slave to Wage Laborer in South Carolina, 1860–1870 (Cambridge: Cambridge University Press, 1994), 172–77. On the French colonies, where male ex-slaves acquired the vote in 1848 only to lose it in 1851, see Blackburn, Overthrow of Colonial Slavery, 496–500; on the British colonies, see Gad Heuman, Between Black and White: Race, Politics, and the Free Coloreds in Jamaica, 1792–1865 (Westport, Conn.: Greenwood, 1981); Swithin Wilmot, "Race, Electoral Violence and Constitutional Reform in Jamaica, 1830–1854," Journal of Caribbean History 17 (1982), 1–13; Holt, Problem of Freedom, chap. 7.

70 Caulfield, In Defense of Honor, 26; Besse, Restructuring Patriarchy, 14.

71 Findlay, Imposing Decency.

72 Marek Steedman, "Gender and the Politics of the Household in Reconstruction Louisiana, 1865–1878," this volume; Elsa Barkley Brown, "Negotiating and Transforming the Public Sphere: African American Political Life in the Transition from Slavery to Freedom," Public Culture 7 (1994): 107–46.

73 Mimi Sheller, "Quasheba, Mother, Queen: Black Women's Public Leadership and Political Protest in Post-emancipation Jamaica, 1834–65," Slavery and Abolition 19, no. 3 (1998): 90–117; Gilbert Pago, Les femmes et la liquidation du système esclavagiste à la Martinique, 1848–1852 (Petit-Bourg, Guadeloupe: Ibis Rouge, 1998), 169–86.

74 Sonya O. Rose, Limited Livelihoods: Gender and Class in Nineteenth-Century England (Berkeley: University of California Press, 1992); Mary Poovey, Uneven Developments: The Ideological Work of Gender in Mid-Victorian England (Chicago: University of Chicago Press, 1988).

75 Natalie Zemon Davis, *Fiction in the Archives: Pardon Tales and Their Tellers in Sixteenth-Century France* (Stanford, Calif.: Stanford University Press, 1987); Joan Wallach Scott, "Gender: A Useful Category of Historical Analysis," *American Historical Review* 91, no. 5 (1986): 1053–75; Scott, "The Evidence of Experience," *Critical Inquiry* 17 (1991): 773–97.

PART I

Men, Women, Citizens

 PAMELA SCULLY

Masculinity, Citizenship, and the Production of Knowledge in the Postemancipation Cape Colony, 1834–1844

In December 1834 the British government ended slavery in their Cape Colony and replaced it with a four-year period of apprenticeship. In February 1835, the widow Meers, a settler living in straitened circumstances, came to the office of the local justice of the peace in Caledon village. The widow complained about what she perceived as the outrageous behavior of an apprentice, Cobus. The widow lived in the rural district of Swellendam, some sixty miles from Cape Town, a district which had a long history of slaveholding dating back well over a hundred years. Meers lived on the farm of John Phil. Marais, the former owner of Cobus. The justice of the peace recorded that Meers said the following: "Cobus has used great liberties such as saying that he is now no more Slave [sic]—is as good as She is, and will have her daughter a Girl of about 14 years also for his wife—nay he even insisted on it, that he would have a white wife."[1] Marais also laid a complaint about both Cobus and another of his former slaves, saying he was "in bodily fear." He stated that Cobus and the other apprentice, a woman called Sena, "would not perform their work, were very insolent and have made use of many unbecoming words." The justice noted that he would report the issues to the special magistrate on the weekend. On 12 March, the justice recorded that Cobus and Sena had been sentenced to four days in prison for insolence and neglect of their duties.[2]

The story of Cobus is located at the interstices of multiple histories and struggles in the postemancipation era. In this case we have a combination of two apparently transgressive acts by apprentices: the one a refusal to labor, the other a personal affront to a white woman by a freedman. In fact the case forces us, I argue, to reconsider how we conceptualize "the political." Slave emancipation flagged such a conflation of the personal and the political by making the private sphere of slaveholding a sphere of public interest. Most clearly, the case is part of a larger history of slaves' and settlers' reactions to the ending of slavery in 1834.

Cobus and Sena saw the beginning of apprenticeship as the ending of unconditional subservience. Cobus also asserted his equality with the widow. Understanding precisely that the personal is perhaps the most political, Cobus pressed for the most explicit manifestation of such equality: his ability to marry the daughter of a white woman whom he knew. Meers found such claims so outrageous and hostile as to be actionable. Marais, the former owner, also reacted with alarm to the apprentices' slowdown at work and to what he perceived as insolence.

The two settlers' efforts to lay a complaint some distance from their abode, is evidence of their outrage at the actions of Cobus and Sena. The fact that the justice sent the case to the special justice also suggests that he felt some sympathy with the widow Meers and her landlord Marais. These whites seem to have shared a sense that the ending of slavery was unraveling historic patterns of deference and that freedpeople already threatened the social fabric of settler life.

The case also is an important site for examining the local making and remaking of ideas and practices of masculinity and citizenship in different communities in the aftermath of emancipation.[3] Men living in Khoikhoi mission communities articulated most clearly a discourse of citizenship that corresponded with the emergent political discourse of rights and civic entitlement newly legitimated by the ending of Khoi bondage in 1828 and the abolition of slavery in 1834. The Khoi, Africans indigenous to the Cape, had labored for whites often in conditions very akin to slavery.[4] After a long campaign led by John Philip of the London Missionary Society, the Cape government passed Ordinance 50 in 1828. The Ordinance emancipated the Khoi from having to carry a pass to show employment status and it severed their obligation to work in indentured labor. A number of missionary societies encouraged Khoi to move to missions where they were given access to plots of land in return for living in accordance with Christian values. As we shall see, freedmen, of both indigenous Khoi and slave descent, at the Kat River Settlement in the Eastern Cape Colony, for example, conceptualized being a fully free person as opposed to a slave in the language of selfhood and citizenship. They made little use of the language of masculine entitlement to rights.

In other settings, some Khoi men affirmed their rights as citizens in a language of masculinity that stressed men's responsibilities as fathers and husbands. They represented themselves and familial relationships in ways that effectively reproduced the gender ideologies promoted by abolitionists. In requests to the government for land, Khoi men echoed what Mimi Sheller suggests in this volume for Jamaica. They "resorted to a Christian discourse of 'manhood' in order to insert themselves into British political discourses that emphasized a kind of active masculine citizenship."[5]

Men freed from legal slavery shared with Khoi men the sense that emancipation created them as new masculine individuals entitled to new rights and expectations of both the state and of settlers. But, for many freedmen, as in the case of Cobus, the world of politics was the world of daily life emanating from the farms, rather than the discourse of liberalism that missionaries inculcated on the stations. Freedmen made political statements in the more prosaic language of daily social interaction. Across the Cape, freedmen also shared the association made by Cobus between freedom and marriage. Cobus's insistence that he could marry a white woman, however, is by all accounts unique. This case is the only record I found in the archives of three rural Cape slaveholding districts where a freedman explicitly states that he sees marriage to a white woman as a feature of his emancipation. Cobus is possibly the only freedman in Worcester, Swellendam, and Stellenbosch districts to state explicitly to a settler a connection between freedom and marrying a white woman. We can imagine that other freedmen might have made similar statements to their peers, or thought this to themselves, but the archives do not easily reveal such histories outside the purview of settlers.

An investigation into freedmen's understanding and representations of citizenship necessarily involves us in a consideration of the production of knowledge in the postemancipation era. Freedmen's discussions of the significance of freedom constitute a central site for our understanding of political discourse in the postemancipation period. Taking seriously such political discussions means that we sometimes need to look beyond the formal claims and debates about citizenship if we are to adequately engage with and identify subaltern political discourses. The language of liberal political economy and the civil society that seemingly underwrote claims to citizenship were not always available to men freed from rural slavery. Part of the challenge is to map political discourse across different arenas: both those that emulated British colonial politics and those in which men articulated a political ideology not rendered in the language of high liberal political discourse. This is the challenge posed both by the statements of Cobus about the meanings of freedom and by the world that freedpeople participated in shaping after the ending of slavery in 1834. How do we write of masculine citizenship in a nonbourgeois world in which individuals spoke out in highly unequal and cross-cultural contexts? How do we chart the languages of citizenship and the formation of political identity among colonized people?

The central case of Cobus with which this chapter is concerned is representative of the kinds of cases on which the historian relies when writing about Cape emancipation. It mirrors many in other British colonial archives in which the ideas of slaves and freedpeople are refracted through the words and languages of missionaries, officials, and settlers. Cobus was not present when the widow Meers and Marais laid complaints against him before the justice of the peace. The justice relied solely on Meers's and Marais's testimony when he decided to take their case to the special magistrate in Swellendam. As far as one can tell, the justice did not interview either Cobus or Sena to ascertain the truth of the settlers' testimony. Our only access to the case and indeed to the thoughts of the apprentices is therefore through the words of their employer, Marais, and of a white woman, the widow Meers. The case is, in fact, at least triply mediated: what we have in the archives is the justice's report in English on the settlers' allegations, which were probably initially made in Dutch, or a combination of Dutch and English. We do not know if the report is accurate, nor can we verify the settlers' complaints.[6]

The justice's official verdict was that Cobus was guilty of refusing to work. Yet other perspectives also seem to have shaped the official interpretation of the case. The widow's complaint that Cobus had been insolent and his former owner's statement that he was in fear of his life seem to have moved the justice of the peace to direct the case to the attention of the special magistrate. Perhaps Cobus had engaged in rhetoric designed to irritate and possibly strike fear into the whites on the farm. Cobus perhaps also genuinely desired Meers's daughter, or desired to marry a white woman as a sign of independence. The chapter explores the implications of these multiple possibilities for understanding the case.

For the historian of the Cape Colony, the problems posed by the paucity of many kinds of information, and the necessity to rely on certain forms of archival material, are particularly vexing. The historian trying to uncover or analyze slaves' perspectives on slavery, emancipation, and gender and racial ideologies has to press the limits of the evidence. In comparison to historians of emancipation in the United States, for example, who can consult a relatively ample archive of oral history and literature, Cape historians can draw on very few interviews with former slaves, and no diaries of slaves. People at the center of bureaucratic, political, and economic power created the vast majority of the records available to the historian. Methodologically it will always be difficult to tell, at least in the public sphere of the Cape, when a freedman articulated his own opinion and when he strategically invoked dominant discourses to secure other rights or advances.

The postemancipation reconstruction of the political economy of the slave-holding districts of the Cape Colony made the speech acts of freedmen highly charged political and cultural endeavors. Freedmen appear in the archives already to some extent bound and constructed by power relations of colonial knowledge. The colonial officers and settlers who adjudicated freedmen's statements "knew" that the men had been slaves, that they were from the margins of Cape colonial society. And freedmen knew this was how they were perceived, and their place in the socioeconomic order.

Embracing the ambiguity of the archives means acknowledging our limitations as historians. It also means acknowledging the political agency of freedpeople. Seeing freedmen as political actors helps reshape our understanding of the colonial encounter. Some of the more influential writings on colonialism in nineteenth-century South Africa have stressed the hegemony of colonial ideologies. Authors have concentrated on examining the ways that Africans adopted the cultural values of British mission culture in the nineteenth century.[7] If we accept the political and cultural agency of the subaltern, then this hegemony of British culture seems a lot less secure, at least in the case of the Western Cape.

Historians of colonial societies in Africa and the Indian subcontinent have long recognized the bias of the archival record toward the activities and perspectives of the colonizer.[8] They have uncovered different perspectives of the colonized through attention to practices, through the use of oral history, and through skillful reading between the lines to find evidence of subaltern views. This reading across the grain has resulted in some fine studies that take seriously indigenous perspectives and which refuse to resolve ambiguity.[9]

This refusal to resolve the tensions in the evidence still needs to be more fully explored in studies of slavery and emancipation. Historians need to wrestle more explicitly with the problems posed by the apparent transparency of archival sources, rendering more problematic the claim implicit in "primary evidence" that it neutrally documents reality. We also have to engage with the increasing recognition that historical actors (that is, both historians and the people they study) engage in various forms of rhetoric and self-representation in different spheres.[10] We cannot confidently proclaim a truth, for example, in postemancipation settings where freedmen became free in a political economy still dominated by their former owners. Rather we might ask, how did the colonized, and in this case, ex-slave men, employ a variety of discourses to gain a measure of security in the colonial order? How did freed-men engage politically in the postemancipation world? And, how do we as historians negotiate the ambiguity of the archival information?

Attention to the messiness of history, and to freedmen as agents rather than as subjects of history, forces us to recast the sites of political economy. Struggles over land, over who will own land and who will farm it on the share, become arenas for the elaboration and articulation of cultural and gendered identities. The speech acts of ex-slaves become crucial sites for examining both the social and political agency of freedmen and for investigating the limits of what we may say with any certainty. The speech act that primarily occupies us here is Cobus's statement to the widow Meers. Cobus had told the widow that he was no longer a slave, that he was "as good as she" and that he wanted to marry her daughter; he allegedly insisted "that he would have a white wife." This statement contains various features emblematic of eman-cipation relating to the meaning of liberty and new identities that it engen-dered. These include freedpeople's stress on the importance of marriage; abolition's creation of a new public sphere; and the significance of race in the emerging discourse of rights in the postemancipation setting.

One might interpret the statement as demonstrating Cobus's understanding of the ending of slavery in 1834 as a tremendous and significant event. While Cobus was legally now an apprentice, bound to work for his former owner for a period of four years, he knew that his status had forever changed with the ending of slavery. Full emancipation only came to the Cape on 1 December 1838. In saying that he was no longer a slave, for example, Cobus commented explicitly on his previous slave status and marked the transition between slavery and apprenticeship. He invoked his earlier status as a person without legal and social rights. In telling Meers that he was now "no more Slave . . . as good as She is," Cobus contrasted his former status of being socially dead, in Orlando Patterson's phrase, with his new status as a free man.[11]

Lineages of Masculinity

Multiple sources of historical experience and social understanding informed freedmen's understanding of masculinity in the rural Western Cape in the nine-teenth century.[12] These contexts included the African societies on the west and east coasts of Africa; the experiences of bondage; as well as the quasi-European slaveholding culture of the Dutch-speaking settlers, with its strong ideologies of patriarchal control. While up to the late eighteenth century, the Dutch East

India Company had predominantly sought slaves in the Dutch East Indies, increasingly the Dutch turned also to East and West Africa. From 1808, the British also introduced Africans "rescued" off other countries' slave ships. The British brought some 2,100 Africans, known as "Prize Negroes," to the Cape between 1808 and 1816, most of them from Madagascar and Mozambique.[13]

For now, we can only guess at what Mozambican men and women might have contributed to the gendered ideologies of Cape slave society, but they probably incorporated some ideas about men's power over women. In the societies of the east and west-central African coasts women were generally subordinated to men, at least in contrast to the relative economic and social independence enjoyed in many parts of West Africa.[14] Men participated in politics and trade and had authority over women, who engaged primarily in agricultural and domestic work. In Khoi society, too, at least of an earlier period, men appear to have enjoyed authority over women in the political and household spheres. Men and women also did different work: men tended to cattle and sheep, while women gathered berries and other wild foods.[15] Some understanding of a gendered division of labor, and perhaps of men's superiority, might have resonated still in the culture of the unfree at the time of emancipation.

For slaves living in conditions of bondage, the gender underpinnings of Cape slavery resonated in daily life. Masculinity helped define the very structure and system of Cape slavery. Slave men resisted slavery in part by fighting for recognition as men, precisely because slaveholders had denied slave men's masculinity as a source of authority. The slaveholding household legally incorporated slaves under the status of children subject to the patriarchal authority of the senior male slaveholder.[16] The inheritance of slave status through the mother explicitly denied slave men the rights of fatherhood. Slavery thus rested on the slaveholder's ideological defense of the sole rights to masculinity. Cape slavery denied slave men the right to be recognized as husbands or as fathers.[17] Perhaps more important, the legal denial of these rights hindered the slave man from claiming the rights to masculinity deriving from being the head of a family, with authority over his wife. Slaveholders perceived the slave man's assertion of paternity as a threat to their power as men and heads of the slaveholding household.[18] Many slaveholders sought to prevent men from supporting their children or sustaining "abroad marriages"—that is, relationships with women off the farm.[19]

In ideological terms, and in practical ways arising from that, such as the lack of recognition given to slave men's relationships with both wives and children, Cape slavery denied slave men the right to be men. In daily life on the farms, slave men might have been able to see themselves as superior to women, but conditions of labor mediated this sense of masculine superiority. No strict gendered division of labor existed since both women and men worked as herders and in the fields, although women were most likely to be employed in domestic chores.[20] However, when a slave was put in a position of authority over both slave men and women, this position was held by a man. Sparse evidence also suggests that slaveholders accorded slave men superior status in the provision of food.[21]

Freedmen like Cobus thus expected emancipation to confer on them special rights and responsibilities as men. Indeed, from the perspective of abolitionists and the colonial office, emancipation did inaugurate the rightful marriage of masculinity and patriarchal authority in the family. The slave liberated into citizenship was a man.[22] Abolitionist discourse affirmed ideas that the new citizen would be a man who achieved his place in society by virtue of his freedom and his dominant, if caring, relationship to women and children in his family. The male nonracial property franchise of the Cape Constitution of the 1850s encouraged freedmen to aspire to become voters and participants in the formal political sphere.

The symbolic weight of marriage in the era of emancipation helped bolster the authority of freedmen over freedwomen. The form of Christian marriage promoted by colonial officials gave additional legitimacy to those men who perceived freedom as entailing responsibility for looking after a wife and children. Being free, for Cobus, like many freedmen and women in the British Atlantic world, meant being free to marry. Freedwomen and men in a variety of postemancipation settings married to affirm intimate relationships that slaveholders had often denied them under slavery, and to legitimate their children.[23] For many freedpeople Christian marriage also became an important cultural marker of liberation into respectability.[24]

The meanings of marriage were different for women and men. Legal Christian marriage rendered a woman a minor, under the authority of the man. In the decade after emancipation freedwomen did marry in part to affirm their relationships with men, but perhaps also in part because postemancipation labor law undermined women's maternal role by passing to the father the authority to apprentice children.[25] Being married made women somewhat more respectable in the eyes of court officials.[26] Such respectability was important for women who lodged complaints with local magistrates in the postemancipation period. They protested the treatment of their children apprenticed to employers and sometimes asked for judgment against decisions made by their husbands with respect to their children's indentures.[27]

For freedmen such as Cobus, the legal benefits of marriage were unambiguous. The marriage contract enabled freedmen's entry into the public sphere of civic rights and responsibilities. Marriage reduced a woman to the status of a minor who could not make contracts without her husband's permission. The denial of civic rights to women in part by virtue of their gender, but effected through the institution of marriage, was thus implicit in the incorporation of freedmen into the body politic in the late 1820s and 1830s: Khoi men through Ordinance 50 in 1828, and slave men in 1834 and 1838.

Freedmen, Masculinity, and Politics in the Era of Emancipation

Khoi men, in particular, seem to have used the rhetoric of a paternal Christian respectability to address the government in the aftermath of emancipation. Their public discourse with the Colonial Office seems to have assumed that fathers had responsibility to look after their families.[28] Requests for land become important sites to examine the coordinates that freedmen thought would convey most clearly to the state their qualification as useful, productive citizens deserving of government aid.

Emancipation freed ex-slaves and Khoi into conditions of long-standing and enduring political and economic inequality in which whites had taken virtually all the good land and controlled economic life. Few opportunities existed for rural free blacks, in an economy of relatively low skill specialization, to carve out economic independence. Freedmen's applications for land generally involved areas of waste or marginal land. Thus the Western Cape did not offer the kind of opportunities for the creation of a free peasantry as one sees in Jamaica, for example.

From 1834 freedpeople moved to villages such as Caledon, Stellenbosch, and Swellendam, and to the city of Cape Town, to the slopes of Table Mountain, in an area that later became part of District Six. People also looked to the lands of the mission communities as places they could farm independently. Stellenbosch and Swellendam districts also witnessed great movements of freedpeople to the mission stations established by the Moravians and the London Missionary Society to cater to indigenous people. But, neither the missions nor the villages could provide sufficient economic security and opportunities for enterprise to enable freedpeople to avoid farm labor. As early as the 1840s, freedmen from the missions were primarily working as farm laborers, although freedwomen often tried to do only seasonal work on the farms. However, for many of the people freed from slavery in 1838, emancipation was not a fundamental break in their experience of socioeconomic relations.[29]

In 1839, the magistrate from Worcester, a large rural district on the eastern border of the Western Cape, wrote to the government on behalf of Khoi men who had appealed to him for land. The men said that they wanted land primarily "to have an opportunity of sending their children to the Missionary School." The men wanted to own land also because of fights with employers over the value of family labor. The men, in this case, acting indeed as heads of families, had engaged themselves and their wives and children to the farmers. The farmers, however, apparently refused to pay fair wages, claiming that since they also had to feed the children, they could not afford to pay money, too.[30] The Khoi men's need to stress that they were trying to protect their wives and children from unfair practices, and that they wanted to send their children to missionary school, spoke to the power of the opposite images. Freedmen had to counter settler stereotypes of slaves and Khoi as being irresponsible and lacking religious dedication. These Khoi men also had to counter the very widespread negative settler stereotypes of Khoi as lazy and unreliable workers. In the above case, the petitioners emphasized to the magistrate that, in his words, they wanted their children to attend "the Missionary School, and to attend Divine Service in the Missionary Chapel." Those men, who were not members of the mission in the area, also told the magistrate that they would be joining that religious community.

A case in Cape Town in the same year, 1839, involved one Peter David, a "liberated African" taken by the British from a slave ship some thirty years before and indentured at the Cape. He, too, used his role as head of a family to emphasize his credentials in applying for land near Cape Town. His memorial stated that he was forty-four years old, employed by the government, was "lawfully married according to the Established church," and had five children. David asked for land so that he could be "enabled to support a growing family, thus keeping them from want and bringing them up honest and respectable."[31]

These petitioners invoked their status as Christian men, as fathers, and as husbands to demonstrate that they were worthy of consideration. What we cannot know is perhaps what is most important. We can only guess at the desires and landscapes of family that freedmen could not articulate within colonial discourses of labor and respectability. For example, we hear nothing here of grandchildren, foster children, second wives, and wider familial responsibilities. Although we know that such wider networks of intimacy and responsibility existed, these very public documents do not echo such social relations. In these engagements in the public sphere ex-slave men bowed to the colonial state, if symbolically, and asked for help.

The linkage that freedmen made between their responsibility for family members and their rights to land ownership and other rights is clearest in these sparse archival sources. Regional differences might have existed between the rural Western Cape, where slaves and free blacks had lived under a dominant colonial culture since the last decades of the seventeenth century, and other regions in the colony. In the Western Cape, colonial rule stretched back to the mid-seventeenth century: freedmen would have been very familiar with the colonial authorities. They thus knew what elements to emphasize in order to get redress. In contrast, in the Eastern Cape settlers and the colonial state were still trying to conquer African chiefdoms well into the 1870s.[32] There, discourses of respectability were perhaps not as entrenched among the freedpeople.

Men at a public meeting in the Kat River Settlement in the Eastern Cape in 1834, for example, spoke tellingly about their desire for inclusion in political life but did not explicitly link this new status as free men to responsibilities for family members. In 1829, the colonial government had set land aside for freed Khoi at Kat River. The commissioner general of the Eastern Cape allotted land only to those people whom he considered most "deserving." These men had already embraced Christianity and shown loyalty to the government. The commissioner general argued that only in a Christian community would Khoi have " 'the sufficient check upon them' " to make sure they progressed.[33] The men of Kat River represent a select group of Khoi and mixed-race people who already shared some of the premises of emancipation. The Kat River community publicly affirmed that Ordinance 50 had freed them to be citizens of a new British colonial world that would reward their loyalty to Britain and to the idea of free wage labor.

On 5 August 1834, men convened a meeting at Philipton to discuss whether to write a memorial to the governor and the legislative council to protest a proposed Vagrancy Act, which would have forced every person of color to show evidence of being employed. Without such evidence they would be forced to engage in wage labor. Only men seem to have attended the meeting, although one cannot be sure. Certainly the note taker only recorded men's words. The meeting itself is a document of freedmen's self-conscious participation in colonial politics. The meeting had a chair and speakers, who introduced, discussed, and then voted on various resolutions. The structure of the meeting affirmed British models of debate as the legitimate form of public political discourse. The participants' words, however, exposed the tangled histories of the Cape, including memories of independence and then bondage, and finally a new kind of liberation couched in Christian terms.[34]

In this meeting, while men referred to wives and children, they did not invoke such relationships as a justification for citizenship or land ownership.

Rather, and here they shared some of Cobus's perceptions, they argued that law had made them free, and it was that free status in itself which gave them rights to demand land and protection. The men primarily spoke of how settlers had reduced the Khoi to slavery by taking their land. Speakers affirmed the presence of missionaries who had been able to secure land for the Khoi and who had taught them to write so people could appeal to the government.

The first resolution of the meeting identified the participants as "a small part" of the "remnant of the Hottentot Nation who originally possessed the Country streatching [sic] from the Cape of Good Hope to the Kay [sic] River and who were rich in sheep and cattle . . . but who were reduced to a state of want, servitude etc, and in some respects worse than Slavery itself."[35] Participants spoke movingly of the significance of freedom. They used ideas about respectability and Christianity to anchor their claims to citizenship. Cobus Ulbricht identified the passing of Ordinance 50 as the event that gave the Khoi "an equal footing with other of His Majesty's Subjects." For Andries Stoffels, Ordinance 50 initiated a new form of identity, that of British subject, and like the Khoi men of Worcester, he seems to have linked freedom from settler domination to independent access to land. He said that when Ordinance 50 "first came out then did we first taste freedom . . . that other men eat so sweet—We rejoiced at the very word Freedom and Free labour even before it was mingled with Water and Ground—and now that it is mingled with Water and Ground it is 20 times sweeter than forced labour."

The participants embraced the power of the law to redefine them as free. They adopted the idea, exemplified by abolition, that law could change and create political identity. In this setting, men's domination over wives and children do not emerge as foundational categories on which the men built the notion of emancipation. Oerson suggested, for example, that one of the responsibilities that came with being free was for parents to pass on history and knowledge to their children. Oerson included both men and women as having that responsibility: here we do not see a clearly gendered understanding of the different roles of men and women in the postemancipation era. He urged parents: "teach your children compassion for their fellow men, and tell them how their forefathers were treated." On the other hand, perhaps Oerson's participation in a public meeting consisting only of men shows that he also believed that men had the exclusive right to participate in politics. Andries Stoffels did implicitly invoke a husband's responsibility for his wife. He said that it was after Ordinance 50 that "we began to buy more clothes for ourselves and our wives." He did not say that women bought their own clothes. This suggests, perhaps, that men felt some need to pay for their wives' clothes and felt some pride in being able to do so: marriage showed that one had crossed from bondage to freedom.

Race and Freedom

Cobus's statements to the widow Meers and Marais evoke these different aspects of freedmen's consciousness. Cobus spoke to the widow and his former master in rhetoric appropriate to the intimacy of the slavery in which they had all been implicated. While Cobus did not speak about freedom in the language of civic rights readily identifiable in the case of the men from Kat River, his statements should be interpreted as political acts. Like the many men and women who made their political statements by leaving the farms of their enslavement and moving to missions, villages, and Cape Town after 1838, Cobus also rendered a judgment on slavery.

Cobus affirmed his new status as a free person. He also withheld his labor, thus showing his employer, Marais, that work was a choice and no longer a bonded duty. With regard to the widow, Cobus exploited probably the most explosive element implicit in emancipation: that it liberated slave men into full male participation in a patriarchal but nonracial world. In the archival records for the rural districts of Stellenbosch, Worcester, and Swellendam, Cobus is alone in explicitly seeking access to whiteness through connection to a white woman. He appears to have seen freedom as permitting a new arena of sexual and racial relationships that centered on men's rights over women, not slave-holders' rights over slaves. This freedman sought to stamp his interpretation of liberty onto the consciousness of the white woman and her daughter who had witnessed his experiences of bondage and now freedom.

Theoretically at least, Cobus, on full emancipation in 1838, would be able to marry any woman of his choosing, a contract which would render that woman legally his minor. By saying to the widow Meers that he could now marry her daughter, Cobus affirmed in the most telling way possible to this white woman with whom he had long been in contact that he was now her equal. Further, through marriage to her daughter he would become more than her daughter's equal: he would become her husband, her legally sanctioned "master."

That Cobus felt emboldened to make such a statement to Meers suggests certain features of his experience of slavery and apprenticeship. The justice points out in his report that Meers and Marais were too poor even to afford a cart. The poverty of the widow might have given Cobus the courage to voice his intentions. Her low status on the rung of settler society might also have made it seem more feasible that Cobus could marry her daughter. Another perspective on the case, and the one that seems to accord most with the settlers' interpretations, is that Cobus, in fact, attempted to intimidate the widow by asserting his desire to marry her daughter. Meers's role in the case is also worth considering. Cobus presumably said these words in the context of a conversation or argument, but we do not know the precise circumstances. That Meers saw these particular phrases as actionable says much about how she perceived her identity as a poor settler, about the coming of emancipation, and her relations to former slaves.

For poor settlers, emancipation threatened economic ruin. Into the late nineteenth century, Western Cape farmers expressed anxiety about their ability to secure cheap farm labor.[36] It also ended a key distinction that had marked them as superior to people with whom they otherwise shared very similar conditions. During slavery many slaveholders had lived alongside their slaves and Khoi servants, often sharing hearths, and sometimes rooms. That Meers saw these words of Cobus as a major insult tells us something of her attempt to cling to the status of race in the absence of slave/free distinctions.

After 1838 race became invested with greater symbolic and cultural economic weight. While ideas of racial identity were to some extent muted under the Dutch, who ruled the Cape from 1652 into the early nineteenth century, race assumed greater importance as a social and political marker after emancipation.[37] Identities formed more explicitly around skin color and cultural heritage emerged particularly from the period of British rule as the British sought to bring order to what they perceived as the riotous unorthodoxy of the Dutch colonial order. Emancipation freed ex-slaves into the category *free black*. This term had hitherto referred primarily to both people manumitted from slavery and people of color descended from Muslim convicts and political prisoners brought to the Cape by the Dutch. From the 1840s, the colonial bureaucracy started creating a more generalized and larger racial category. Government documents collapsed a variety of previous distinct status groups such as *Bastard* and *Bastard Hottentot*, referring to people of mixed race and free black heritage, into the category *coloured*. As I have suggested elsewhere, slaveholders and colonial officials initially imposed this categorization after emancipation in part because the markers of slavery no longer clearly marked the boundaries of power.[38] Only in the latter part of the century did descendants of slaves and free blacks embrace colouredness as a form of political identity.

It is difficult, if not impossible, to know if Cobus's expression of a desire to marry a white wife was a form of intimidation, and a political criticism. Desire in the end is at the heart of this case: desire to regulate one's labor, desire for social status, sexual desire. It is also difficult to tell whether one is dealing with a discrete instance or one that represents a larger, yet hidden, subaltern discourse. But Cobus's longing to marry a white wife rings true as an aspiration that other freedmen might have shared given what we know of Cape slavery and emancipation. The postemancipation Cape was so clearly weighted in favor of whites that freedmen might well have seen marriage to a white woman as providing an entry into greater security and wealth.

One interpretation we can offer of Cobus's statement is that it is about his understanding of the power of whiteness in the rural Cape. If we believe the widow Meers—since Cobus was not present at the time of the complaint—Cobus had a very clear idea of the importance of whiteness in signifying status in the immediate postemancipation era. Cobus understood that settlers had already consolidated the link, if only implicitly, between whiteness and power in the slaveholding era and that this connection would solidify after emancipation.

The men of Kat River, who had suffered dispossession, forced labor on white farms, and had interacted with a particularly virulent settler consciousness, fully shared Cobus's perception of the importance of race in shaping postemancipation culture. Esau Prins, for example, said that he was a settler's child: "although I had to sit behind the chairs and stools, as my Mother was a Hottentot woman and therefore I consider myself a Hottentot also . . . I have Christian blood in me; [sic] but I know only of one blood that God has made and the so called 'Christeman' steals the name." Prins here casts serious doubt on the power of Christian identity to help freedpeople secure equality and land. Instead, he charges that settlers have stolen the identity, racialized it in a sense, and removed it from appropriation by freedpeople. A number of men at the Kat River meeting spoke of how their white fathers had violently rejected them. Mr. Magerman spoke of being very badly treated by his white father and of having to "ly [sic] among the dogs in the ashes."[39]

Conclusion

The evidence of men's responses to emancipation tells us multiple stories. This evidence is too ambiguous for us to write a tight narrative of emancipation and masculinity. All historical narratives suffer to some extent from this ambiguity. They are always made into narratives at many levels: both by the circumstances under which events were recorded, by the tales which had currency in a particular time period, and by the narrative the authors of historical documents constructed to make sense of events. Even if we had a first-person account from Cobus we would still not have clear or transparent insight into "what he really thought." The best we can do as historians is to resist the temptation to resolve ambiguity and to tidy up a narrative. In the case of the Cape at least, such resistance is perhaps the most we can offer in echoing the tangled histories of the postemancipation era.

Accepting that Cobus engaged in a variety of rhetorical political strategies helps us to recognize him as having his own agenda. If we politicize the meanings of history, we also accept that people in the past were political agents, engaging in rhetoric and forms of representation to advance their cause, particularly in the public sphere of civic discourse. Slaves and freedmen positioned themselves within various debates and contexts in which the meanings of emancipation were up for grabs. The public sphere also gave freedmen an opportunity to engage in various rhetorical strategies in order to articulate or process ideas about the meanings of independence, identity, and anger in the postemancipation era. Maybe it is enough that as historians of this particular slave setting, we give up the search for clarity and rather expose the opacity of our understanding of the worlds and discourses of freedmen.

Notes

I am particularly indebted to Clifton Crais, Joanna Grabski, Thom McClendon, Diana Paton, Jonathan Sadowsky, Mrinalini Sinha, and the participants at the Gender History Workshop at Penn State University for their help with this chapter.

1 Cape Archives (hereafter CA), I/CAL 21, Diary or Record of Proceedings of Justice of the Peace, Caledon, 1832–1839, 16 Feb. 1835. For an earlier and brief discussion of this case, see Pamela Scully, "Private and Public Worlds of Emancipation in the Rural Western Cape, 1830–1842," in Breaking the Chains: Slavery and Its Legacy in Nineteenth Century South Africa, ed. Nigel Worden and Clifton Crais (Bloomington: Indiana University Press, 1995), 201–23.

2 CA, I/CAL 21, 19 Feb. 1835.

3 On masculinity in South African history more generally, see Robert Morrell, "Masculinity in South African History: Towards a Gendered Approach to the Past," South African Historical Journal 37 (1997): 167–77; Morrell, "Of Boys and Men: Masculinity and Gender in Southern African Studies, Journal of Southern African Studies 24, no. 4 (1998): 605–30; Keith Breckenridge, "The Allure of Violence: Men, Race and Masculinity on the South African Gold Mines, 1900–1950," Journal of Southern African Studies 24, no. 4 (1998): 669–93; and Dunbar Moodie, with Vivienne Ndatshe, Going for Gold: Men, Mines, and Migration (Berkeley: University of California Press, 1994).

4 For an excellent analysis of changing Khoi identities in the mid-nineteenth century, see Elizabeth Elbourne, " 'Race,' Warfare, and Religion in Mid-nineteenth-century Southern Africa: The Khoikhoi Rebellions against the Cape Colony and Its Uses, 1850–58," *Journal of African Cultural Studies* 13, no.1 (2000): 17–42.

5 Mimi Sheller, "Acting as Free Men: Subaltern Masculinities and Citizenship in Postslavery Jamaica," in this volume.

6 I am grateful to Diana Paton for helping me to work through these issues.

7 For elegant investigations into the cultural history of colonialism, see Jean Comaroff and John Comaroff, *Of Revelation and Revolution*, vol. 2, *The Dialectics of Modernity on a South African Frontier* (Chicago: University of Chicago Press, 1997); and Robert Ross, *Status and Respectability in the Cape Colony, 1750–1850: A Tragedy of Manners* (Cambridge: Cambridge University Press, 1999).

8 Gayatri Spivak, "Can the Subaltern Speak?," in *Colonial Discourse and Postcolonial Theory: A Reader*, ed. Patrick Williams and Laura Chrisman (New York: Columbia University Press, 1994), 66–111. For a more recent work, see Gayatri Chakravorty Spivak, *A Critique of Postcolonial Reason: Toward a History of the Vanishing Present* (Cambridge: Cambridge University Press, 1999).

9 For a particularly remarkable study, see Luise White, *Speaking with Vampires: Rumor and History in Colonial Africa* (Berkeley: University of California Press, 2000).

10 If we heed Dominick LaCapra's call to take the work of rhetoric much more seriously in history, we can no longer be as confident in proclaiming what it was that freed men wanted. La Capra, "Rhetoric and History," in *History and Criticism* (Ithaca, N.Y.: Cornell University Press, 1985), 15–44.

11 Orlando Patterson, *Slavery and Social Death: A Comparative Study* (Cambridge: Harvard University Press, 1982).

12 Khoi and ex-slaves should be included in the category of freed men since they shared very similar working conditions, intermarried with both slave and Khoi women, and, by the ending of slavery, had come to identify with one another as a class of the unfree. See Pamela Scully, *Liberating the Family? Gender and British Slave Emancipation in the Rural Western Cape, South Africa, 1823–1853* (Portsmouth, N.H.: Heinemann, 1997).

13 James Armstrong and Nigel Worden, "The Slaves," in *The Shaping of South African Society*, ed. Richard Elphick and Hermann Giliomee (Middletown, Conn.: Wesleyan University Press, 1989), 120.

14 Elizabeth Schmidt, *Peasants, Traders and Wives: Shona Women in the History of Zimbabwe, 1870–1939* (Portsmouth, N.H.: Heinemann, 1992); Marcia Wright, *Strategies of Slaves and Women: Life Stories from East/Central Africa* (New York: Lillian Barber, 1993).

15 Women and children, for example, were only allowed to drink sheep milk and eat meat, whereas men ate beef and drank cow's milk. The landmark historical study of the Khoikhoi remains Richard Elphick, *Khoikhoi and the Founding of White South Africa* (Johannesburg: Ravan, 1985), 31, 60.

16 Women did own slaves at the Cape, but slaveholding as an institution was conceptually organized around the rights and entitlements of the male slaveholder. The patriarchal household was the bedrock of Cape slavery. Robert C.-H. Shell, *Children of Bondage: A Social History of the Slave Society at the Cape of Good Hope, 1652–1838* (Hanover, N.H.: Wesleyan University Press, 1994).

17 Until amelioration in the 1820s, slaves were not allowed to marry legally, and even then few were able to do so in practice. See Scully, *Liberating the Family?*, ch. 1.

18 See, e.g., CA, 1/WOC, 19/24, Daybook of Assistant Protector of Slaves, 1826–1831, 20 May 1831.

19 Evidence from the records of the protector of slaves in the 1820s and 1830s, and of the special magistrates appointed during the apprenticeship period, shows that slave men engaged in ongoing struggles to assert their rights over their families. They attempted to look after family members on different farms, protested bad treatment of their wives and children, and asserted their rights to name their children and claim authority over them. See Scully, *Liberating the Family?*, chap. 3, for examples.

20 On the hiring of women as herders, see CA, 1/WOC, 16/37, Contract of Hiring and Service, 31 May 1833; CA, 1/STB 2/34, Documents in the Trial of Jan Hermanus . . . for Rape, 4 March 1834.

21 For example, Philippus Rudolph Botha of Worcester provided men with rations of meat each morning whereas women had to do without. CA, 1/WOC, 1924, Daybook of Assistant Protector of Slaves, 1826–1831, 8 Oct. 1827.

22 Scully, *Liberating the Family?*

23 William A. Green, *British Slave Emancipation: The Sugar Colonies and the Great Experiment, 1830–1865* (Oxford: Clarendon, 1976), 131; see also Martin Klein and Richard Roberts, "Gender and Emancipation in French West Africa," in this volume.

24 The components of respectability were unstable. In Cape Town, Islam had long attracted slaves and free blacks. A distinctive community, self-identified as Malay, had emerged by the time of emancipation. In the Western Cape, the Moravians and the London Missionary Society had greater success in drawing freedpeople to the mission lands that functioned more or less autonomously until the 1850s. They helped shape an emergent postemancipation discourse that promoted patriarchal nuclear families. On missions and marriage, see Scully, *Liberating the Family?*, chaps. 6 and 7. As Robert Ross has shown, in the middle of the nineteenth century respectability increasingly became tied to notions of Englishness and middle- or upper-working-class status. Ross, *Status and Respectability*.

25 The Masters and Servants Ordinance of 1842 stated that only in cases where a father was absent or dead could a mother indenture her children.

26 For the United States, see Laura Edwards, " 'The Marriage Covenant Is at the Foundation of All Our Rights': The Politics of Slave Marriages in North Carolina after Emancipation," *Law and History Review* 14, no.1 (1996): 81–124.

27 See also, e.g., CA, 1/WOC, 16/37, Contract of Hiring and Service, 30 July

1858; CA, 1/STB 4/1/1/4, Criminal Record Book, no. 2217, 29 Jan. 1849; also no. 2411, 29 Nov. 1849.

28 Before emancipation, Khoi men appealed to the government for land rights in part by claiming to protect their families' rights. See CA, CO 362, 17 Jan. 1829, Memorial of Inhabitants of Bethelsdorp.

29 A more fundamental transformation of the rural economy only happened in the 1870s and 1880s with the coming of the railways; the later discovery of gold to the north further restructured the region's economy. See Pamela Scully, *The Bouquet of Freedom: Social and Economic Relations in the Stellenbosch District, South Africa, 1870–1900.* Communications, no. 17 (University of Cape Town: Centre for African Studies, 1989).

30 CA, CO 2788, no. 31, 2 Feb. 1839.

31 CA, CO 4000, no. 144, 29 July 1839.

32 Clifton Crais, *White Supremacy and Black Resistance in Pre-industrial South Africa: The Making of the Colonial Order in the Eastern Cape, 1770–1865* (Cambridge: Cambridge University Press, 1992).

33 Stockenstrom cited in Crais, *White Supremacy and Black Resistance.*

34 For an extended discussion of the meanings of nationhood among the Khoi, see Elbourne, " 'Race,' Warfare, and Religion." Elbourne also briefly discusses the fact that women played a part in the 1851 rebellion, which suggests that women perhaps had a greater role in Khoi society than the evidence from the meeting indicates.

35 CA, Accessions 50, "Report of a Meeting Held at Philipston," 5 Aug. 1834, by James Clark.

36 Scully, *Bouquet of Freedom.*

37 A fluidity of colonial identities marked Dutch Cape colonial society and the early years of British rule. An overlapping series of hierarchies based on Christian or heathen status, lineage, free or slave status, and, to some extent, color, determined a person's place in society. On colonial identity up to the late eighteenth century, see Richard Elphick and Robert Shell, "Intergroup Relations: Khoikhoi, Settlers, Slaves and Free Blacks, 1652–1795," in Elphick and Giliomee, *Shaping of South African Society.* For the nineteenth century, see Ross, *Status and Respectability.*

38 Pamela Scully, "Rape, Race and Colonial Culture: The Sexual Politics of Identity in the Nineteenth-Century Cape Colony, South Africa," *American Historical Review* 100 (1995): 335–59.

39 See also the statement by Windvogel Smit.

SUE PEABODY

Négresse, Mulâtresse, Citoyenne:
Gender and Emancipation in the French
Caribbean, 1650–1848

The history of black, brown, or, for that matter, white women in France's slaveholding colonies has received very little attention from historians. This is for several reasons. First, until very recently, colonial history has been marginalized in both Francophone and Anglophone French studies, which have focused instead on the metropole. Second, French republican ideology has fostered the myth of a color-blind nation of indiscriminate equality, in the face of widespread evidence to the contrary, shifting attention away from the varied experiences of immigrants, slaves, and religious minorities.[1] Third, while many historians in the United States and elsewhere have come to embrace gender as a useful category of historical analysis, much Francophone scholarship tends to ignore these contributions or to dismiss them as the product of a foreign—and thus irrelevant—feminism. Therefore, while the historiography of slavery and gender relations has matured over many decades in American scholarship to the point where emancipation and the contest over freedom and the rights of citizenship for women and former slaves have become central problems for study, systematic and critical inquiry into these areas for Francophone regions is relatively new.[2]

In this essay, then, I offer a synthesis of previous scholarship and suggest promising possibilities for future research. My chronological and geographical scope is large, covering two centuries of French colonization in the Antilles and France's three largest island colonies—Martinique, Guadeloupe, and Saint-Domingue—each of which has its own unique demographic, economic, and political history.[3] However, as each of these colonies vied with the same royal metropolitan administration and some of the same legal initiatives, they can be usefully compared. I will explore how gender shaped the avenues by which slaves might achieve their freedom: individually, through manumission, and more generally during the two large-scale emancipations of 1793–94 and 1848. The general emancipations theoretically improved the conditions of all former slaves in French-controlled territories, without regard to gender. However, I argue that postemancipation societies created more opportunities for advancement and exercise of political agency by newly freed men than women, thus minimizing many of the advantages that universal freedom should have brought to women.[4]

Gender and Manumission in the Old Regime

Throughout the slaveholding period of France's Caribbean colonies, from the 1630s until 1848, female slaves and children were manumitted significantly more often than males.[5] This is usually ascribed to demographic imbalances in the sex ratio in the free population.[6] From the earliest days, white men outnumbered white women, initially by as much as three to one.[7] Despite Minister Colbert's strategy of shipping boatloads of orphan girls from France to the colonies in the 1680s, the first full census of the French islands in 1687 showed that adult white men outnumbered white women by more than two to one. The sex ratio of the enslaved population was somewhat more balanced, ranging from 80 to 175 men for every 100 women.[8] Saint-Christophe maintained the most balanced sex ratio among slaves in 1687 (102:100) due to the colony's relative maturity and highly creolized (island-born) population. Martinique, with immediate access to shipping lanes and a booming economy in the late seventeenth century, had 153 enslaved men for every 100 women slaves. Guadeloupe (86:100) and Saint-Domingue (93:100), by contrast, were in this period secondary ports that received slaves rejected at the Martinique markets, which may explain their higher proportion of women to men.[9]

The Code Noir (1685) as well as the imbalance in the white sex ratio created special opportunities for slave women and their children to achieve free status in the early days of colonial slavery. When free men consented to a Catholic marriage with their slave concubines the Code Noir automatically manumitted the women and freed and legitimized their children; free men who refused to marry the enslaved mothers of their children were subject to heavy fines and confiscation of the slaves for royal profit (article 9). Other provisions automatically manumitted slaves who had been named as universal beneficiaries of a master's will, executor of the testament, or guardian of his children (article 56). These slaves were more likely to be women than men, given the history of sexual relations between masters and slave women. According to the authoritative study of the Code Noir's origins, these articles were based on customary practices in the colonies that predated their codification into law.[10] Several commentators observed that the Code Noir's provisions led to marriages between white colonists and black or brown women.[11] Unlike the laws of Spanish and Portuguese America, the Code Noir did not explicitly spell out a right to self-purchase (known in Spanish as *coartación*).[12] However, it did regulate slaves' participation in markets (articles 7, 18–21). Further, slaves were authorized the means to accumulate savings (a *peculium*) that could be used for self-purchase or the purchase of family members, though always subject to the master's permission (article 29). As the so-called *marché des nègres* [negro market] was dominated by female hucksters, women's commercial activity created additional potential avenues to freedom.

Slave men's routes to freedom were more limited. Though the Code Noir did not specify any blanket conditions that would apply solely to men, those who performed military duties won their freedom throughout the eighteenth century. There are also a handful of recorded instances of slaves—usually men—who were freed for saving their owners' lives.[13] Finally, one might presume that slave owners without legitimate children might be more likely to manumit their sons than their daughters, so as to have a male heir for their estate. After 1726, however, all slaves and free people of color were prohibited from inheriting from whites, though this royal decree was apparently not registered or enforced in Saint-Domingue.[14]

One case from the early eighteenth century shows the complexity of determining agency in the manumission process.[15] Three black sisters, Marie Castolet, Catin Lamy, and Babet Binture ran a tavern and inn in Saint-Pierre, Martinique, in the first decade of the eighteenth century. Castolet had already achieved her freedom and in 1704 Lamy successfully petitioned the superior council, a judicial body comprised of the colony's most prominent male citizens, to recognize her freedom.[16] The following year Binture decided to petition for her freedom from the widow La Palu as well. However, the acting intendant, [Jean Jacques] Mithon, ruled that Binture had not furnished sufficient evidence of her free birth and sentenced her to a month in prison in chains for her "temerity."[17] A new possibility opened for Binture in 1706 when Mithon was replaced by Nicolas-François Amoult de Vaucresson and the previous governor-general died in office. Binture and Lamy appealed directly to Intendant Vaucresson, who upheld both their claims to free birth. Following her manumission, Binture was accosted and beaten by a member of the La Palu family—a militia officer—with a baguette-sized stick. Vaucresson, their new champion, had the man arrested and imprisoned.

Unfortunately, the story did not end there. Binture's and Lamy's former owners, the La Palu family, appealed to the Council of State in France, which ruled that Vaucresson had overstepped his authority. What is more, the slave-holders obtained a powerful ally in the deceased governor's replacement, Raimond Balthazar Phélypeaux. Phélypeaux composed a scathing attack on the sisters and Vaucresson, alleging that the women's tavern not only served alcohol and food, but also buccaneers' pirated booty, while encouraging gambling and prostitution and harboring runaway slaves. According to Phélypeaux, Binture (whom he renamed "Babet La Palu")[18] and her sisters had bribed Vaucresson's mistress, Madame de Begue, with expensive gifts in order to gain access to the intendant. He claimed that the three sisters had spent so much time lobbying Vaucresson that ranking officials "had to wait three or four hours before the closed door of his office opened and the three *negresses* emerged to murmurs and whispers of scandal."[19] Under pressure, Vaucresson finally reversed his decision and returned Binture to slavery.

This incident illustrates several significant points with regard to the manumission process and the status of free and enslaved women of color in the French Antilles. First, the three sisters, though allegedly enslaved, had significant wealth as well as social poise—to the point where they won the support not only of one of the highest ranking officials in the colony but also his wealthy mistress, identified by one historian as the wife of one of the king's lieutenants.[20] Their wealth was earned through independent urban commercial activity in a thriving colonial port.

The fact that the sisters were able to accumulate such wealth and status through their business while still enslaved raises the question of why they formally sought free status. The answer might seem obvious—freedom was cherished for its own intrinsic value—yet free status brought considerable risks as well as benefits.[21] Semi-independent slaves like Castolet, Lamy, and Binture enjoyed a degree of autonomy in their working lives despite their enslaved status as well as protection by slave owners, in case of swindling or violence on the part of customers. Free blacks, on the other hand, faced unscrupulous predators alone, without assurance that they would be backed up by their masters or, in court, by civil authorities. Indeed, one way that this case can be read is as the story of three women who had enjoyed de facto free status yet who fell prey to whites who saw a legal opportunity to submit them to slavery.

Binture and her sisters invested both time and money for the better part of a decade to challenge the La Palus' claims to ownership. While the surviving documents are silent on the sisters' specific motives, several possibilities emerge. First, slavery meant that the women's peculium technically belonged to the La Palu family and could be confiscated at any time. Second, they lived under the threat of being sold to a new master, perhaps outside of the community. Third, both Lamy and Babet were mothers; perhaps the La Palu family, which had let them work more or less undisturbed in the tavern business, threatened to confiscate and sell the children.[22] Finally, slavery itself carried stigma and the women who had achieved such local success may have felt that they earned the respect due anyone else of their rank in society.

This case also highlights France's long, difficult, and expensive manumission procedures, whose result ultimately depended on the whims of administrators. Unlike slaves in most Spanish and Portuguese colonies, who enjoyed the right to initiate self-purchase at a fair price, with or without the master's consent (*coartación*), slaves in the French colonies were largely dependent on their master's will. French, Spanish, and Portuguese law permitted appeals through local channels all the way to the king. But unlike the Spanish and Portuguese Crowns, which sought to reinforce the allegiance of slaves and freedmen to royal authority by permitting a handful of "just" manumissions over the objections of colonial masters, Louis XVI and his successors tended to rule against individual slaves in the colonies as a way to reinforce the patriarchal authority on which the monarchy was based.

Most important, this case highlights the growing friction between France's older, ruling order of estates and a new colonial, merchant-class ethic of upward mobility through accumulation of wealth. Binture, Lamy, and Castolet, having achieved considerable success through commerce, sought to legitimize their status by formally removing the stigma of descent from slaves. The intendant Vaucresson, a representative of Colbert's royal bureaucratic functionary system, approved of the women's achievements and sanctioned their claim to free status. But Phélypeaux, a representative of the old noble order based on inherited military titles, would brook no such destabilization of the social order and employed the classic technique of tarnishing both the women and their allies' reputations through sexual smear.

During the eighteenth century, the free nonwhite segment of society, comprised almost entirely of manumitted slaves and their descendents, increased both in absolute numbers and as a proportion of the free population on all of the major French islands. In Guadeloupe, the poorest of the three major French Antillean colonies, the free colored population rose slowly from 10 percent to 18 percent of all free persons between 1687 and 1789.[23] In wealthy, populous Martinique, the number of free people of color grew from 7 percent to 33 percent of the free population during the same period. Saint-Domingue's free people of color rapidly eclipsed those of the other islands; though this population amounted to only 5.6 percent of the free population of that colony in 1687, by 1789, 40 percent of the population was considered "of color," making these individuals' loyalties a key factor in revolutionary politics.[24]

The growth of the free nonwhite population paralleled two key developments in the legal framework regulating free status. The first is that, following the Binture case, colonial administrators instituted a series of laws restricting slaveholders' rights to manumit their slaves, requiring the governors' permission for each manumission and the owner's payment of a hefty manumission tax, sometimes equivalent to the purchase price of a slave.[25] Some of these laws had an inherent gender differential. For example, the French minister set a tax of one thousand livres for the manumission of male slaves but only six hundred livres for females in Martinique in 1745 (these amounts correspond roughly to the average purchase price for each sex).

The royally appointed administrators' regulations did not always reflect the interests of all members of the slaveholding class. Some slaveholders attempted to avoid the manumission tax by registering the brown children of enslaved women as free in baptismal records.[26] Others simply permitted their slaves to live as free, without formally declaring their status. This created a subclass known as the *soi-disant libres* (so-called free) or *libres de savanne* (freedmen of the savanna), who generally continued to live on the plantations of their former masters, but with reduced labor obligations and more freedom of movement.[27]

A second change in the legal structure regulating free status in the eighteenth century was a series of laws establishing racial segregation, or—in its inverse—the privileges of whiteness. These laws reflect the growing size and, in some cases, status of free people of color in the Francophone Caribbean and their consequent competition with French colonists. The period following the Seven Years' War (1756–63) was especially important in consolidating these privileges. The Code Noir of 1685 had guaranteed that manumitted slaves would have the same "rights, privileges, and liberties enjoyed by persons born free" (article 59). Yet, immediately following the Babet Binture case, colonial administrators chipped away at this fundamental assurance of equality through manumission. Certain trades were successively forbidden to free people of color, from working in cabarets and taverns (1711) to employment as clerk of court, notary, or bailiff (1765).[28] Other laws sought to prohibit the accumulation of property through inheritance (1726). During the privations of the Seven Years' War, bakers in Cap Français faced stiff fines for selling bread or flour to *gens de couleur* (1761). Following the war, many new laws were enacted to prevent free people of color from flaunting any sign of elevated status. In

Martinique (1763), and a decade later in Guadeloupe and Saint-Domingue (1773), local ordinances prohibited people of any African ancestry from using the last names of whites. In 1777 the French government created the Police des Noirs, which sought to prevent the arrival of all blacks, mulattoes, and other gens de couleur in France. This was followed by a prohibition on marriages between whites and any person of color (1778) and a sumptuary law forbidding gens de couleur from dressing or wearing their hair in the manner of whites (1779). The laws were often backed with state terror.[29] The character of these laws testifies not only to increasing restrictions on the class of free coloreds, but also, implicitly, to the upward social mobility of *some* of these individuals and families. Saint-Domingue had the largest and wealthiest free colored population of any eighteenth-century slave society in the Americas.[30]

A legal case from this period, where the privileges of whiteness were being asserted and defined, suggests how tenuous the status of freedom might be. Before he died in 1771, Philippe Morisseau, a Saint-Domingue planter, left a will stating his intention to free six of his slaves, a twenty-three-year old mulatto woman named Marie-Victoire, her daughter, and four mulatto men. Upon his death, all six left the plantation. Philippe's brother and heir, sieur Morisseau d'Ester, went to colonial administrators to get an order requiring the slaves to return to work on the plantation. They would not legally be freed until the heir and the administrators gave their permission. Sieur Morisseau claimed that he intended to free them if their actions merited it; but first he wanted to make them "feel their ingratitude and to see that their lot depended on him." By forcing the provisionally manumitted slaves to acknowledge his authority, the new master sought not only to discipline them, but also to set an example for the rest.

The four men returned to the plantation, applied for and received their freedom.[31] But Marie-Victoire, "the most insolent toward the heir and his wife . . . remained in revolt." She was arrested and chained in the stocks for several days, whereupon she was returned to the plantation to give her the chance to "merit" her manumission. She fled a second time, and the *maréchaussée* police brought her back to the plantation again. According to the heir, she was not maltreated and she stayed "free and was tranquil" for about three years. However, in 1774, she fled for a third time and brought her case to new colonial administrators. She showed them a notarized act certifying her mother's manumission and a notarized extract of her baptismal record, signed by her father and godfather, stating that she was born free. After reviewing the evidence, the administrators declared that Marie-Victoire and her daughter were free and prohibited sieur and dame Morisseau from interfering with her in any way.

Marie-Victoire's victory was short-lived. Sieur Morisseau decided to go over the heads of the new administrators and straight to the new king, Louis XVI. In his appeal, Morisseau emphasized "the dangers that result when the public revolt of a slave against her master" is allowed to stand. Morisseau based his case on an apparent contradiction in the written evidence: If Marie-Victoire was baptized as free, then why would the deceased colonist have granted her freedom in his will? In December 1775, the new king, Louis XVI, gave a sign of his future stance toward those who challenged lines of authority in his kingdom. He ruled that Marie-Victoire and her daughter be returned as slaves to sieur Morisseau, perhaps—since they were apparently baptized as free—for the first time in their lives.

There are interesting parallels between this case and Babet Binture's some sixty years earlier. Both women asserted their free status based on their free birth but found these claims difficult to sustain in face of unsympathetic or unscrupulous administrators. Both women faced male adversaries who stood to inherit the women as slaves if their legal cases failed. One of these beat Binture brutally with a stick. It is not unreasonable to presume that Marie-Victoire was also violated as sieur Morisseau asserted his domination. Both women cannily watched for opportunities in the changing of administrative personnel and achieved temporary success, only to be undermined by appeals to the royal Council of State in Versailles. This underscores the personal—one might say arbitrary—nature of the justice system.

There are important differences as well. Babet Binture, a black woman, aided by her sisters, used their business profits to influence powerful patrons to uphold her claim to free status. Marie-Victoire, a mulatto woman, was very likely the daughter or the sexual partner of the man who authorized her freedom. It is significant that the heir to the estate, allegedly satisfied with the submission shown by the freedmen, allowed them to go their way, while focusing his efforts to dominate on the two female charges. In a society where men of all colors outnumbered all women, Marie-Victoire and her daughter were probably valued for their actual and potential sexual availability to their master.[32]

Marie-Victoire's case is emblematic of the prerevolutionary decades when white colonists and royal administrators established a racially segregated society in law as well as in their actions. While Marie-Victoire struggled to assert her free status, the meaning of freedom itself was increasingly circumscribed for all free people of color. Other significant changes were under way for

Saint-Domingue as well. Between 1770 and 1789, the size of the enslaved population of Saint-Domingue approximately doubled to 465,000.[33] While the sex ratio had somewhat stabilized in the more creolized populations of Martinique and Guadeloupe, a great portion of Saint-Domingue's predominantly male society was born in Africa and only recently enslaved through warfare.[34]

Revolutionary Disjunctures

The brutal conditions of plantation production and forced immigration of African prisoners of war, along with instabilities among the slaveholding class and indeed the whole Atlantic colonial system, exploded during the final decade of the eighteenth century. Slave insurrections in Saint-Domingue, the French Revolution, and war between the European colonial powers provided the context for the first general emancipation of slaves in the transatlantic world. In 1793 the beleaguered republican commissioners of Saint-Domingue offered freedom first to any slaves who would fight for the Republic. Commissioner Léger Félicité Sonthonax, in the North, extended the offer to the new soldiers' wives and children, provided that the marriages were registered with civil authorities. He justified the extension of freedom to women and children as a means to tie the soldiers to families, "the first link of political societies." In a letter to the Convention in Paris he wrote:

> Having declared free all the Negroes enrolled in the service of the Republic, it was necessary to free their wives and children as well, and, to turn this measure to the advantage of public decency and morals, we ordered that the warriors who wanted to free their women would have to marry them according to the forms established by the decrees of the National Assembly. The municipal office of Cap Français, successor to the old *municipalité*, is receiving at least thirty declarations daily. The weddings then follow, and the marriage festivals become festivals of liberty. I do not doubt that the civilization of this people will be very rapid.[35]

Thus, for a radical republican like Sonthonax, recently freed soldiers were to be reconnected to the body politic through the "civilizing" influence of marriage and family. Republican ideologies of womanhood, beginning with Rousseau, held that a woman's relationship to the state was mediated through her husband.[36] Sonthonax's proclamation, authorizing the recruitment of black men as soldiers and the consequent manumission of their wives and children, anticipated both the U.S. militia act of 1795 and similar U.S. federal legislation of 1862 as well as the rhetoric and the efforts of reformers in the United States immediately after the Civil War.[37]

Slave marriages, though technically permitted under the old Code Noir, were rarely performed because they interfered with slaveholders' property rights (it was difficult to sell one half of a married couple).[38] The revolutionary government's tactic to secure the new soldier's loyalties to the state bears interesting similarities to the Code Noir. In both cases, enslaved women could achieve free status through marriage to a free man, and thus be reinscribed under the authority of a patriarchal head of household. According to Sonthonax, soldiers responded to the proclamation in droves, suggesting that many men and women embraced the revolution's policy both as a formalized recognition of manumission and a public dedication of conjugal relations, as did many newly freed men and women in other postemancipation societies.[39]

Soon after these individual manumissions, Sonthonax unilaterally abolished all slavery in northern Saint-Domingue, an action that was later repeated by Etienne Polverel for the West and the South. According to one account, Sonthonax was moved to declare general emancipation by a petition signed by 882 field workers of Saint-Domingue, presented to him in a public ceremony in Cap Français where, "women, carrying their children or holding them by the hand . . . , threw themselves at his feet, while calling for the triumph of the Republic and liberty."[40] The former slaves who signed this petition and the thousands of men, women, and children who assembled to meet Sonthonax clearly saw the republican commissioner as a viable guarantor of emancipation. General emancipation was consistent with Sonthonax's and Polverel's republican ideology. However, this first large-scale emancipation in an Atlantic plantation society was ultimately an act of military and political desperation, for the commissioners needed the support of the rebellious slaves to retain France's most prosperous colony on the side of the Republic, and against the foreign and monarchist foes.

To legitimize this precipitous act, Sonthonax sent a delegation to the Convention in Paris, where the legislature obliged by issuing the Act of 16 Pluviôse, An II (4 Feb. 1794). The act extended abolition to all French colonies and declared that "all men, without distinction of color, domiciled in the colonies, are French citizens and enjoy all rights assured under the constitution." Thus general emancipation was brought to Saint-Domingue and Guadeloupe. Martinique, however, remained occupied by British forces until 1802 and thus maintained slavery for the duration of the Revolution.[41]

What are the gender implications of France's first general emancipation? At first glance, it would seem that the abolition of slavery benefited both men and women and, indeed, both male and female slaves in Guadeloupe and Saint-Domingue now found themselves "free." But in several ways general emancipation left *nouvelles citoyennes* [new female citizenesses], as they came to be known, worse off than their brethren, husbands, fathers, and sons.[42] First, the initial, liberal phase of the Revolution in France asserted equal rights for women and the inclusion of working-class women in the political process. However, the backlash against women's political action during the Terror and the codification of patriarchal law in Napoleon's Civil Code ensured that women, as a whole, lost effective political voice and civil autonomy as a result of the Revolution. So, when we examine the freedom into which the "new citizens" stepped, we must be aware that it was structured so as to create a second-class status for white, French women, let alone women of color.[43]

Second, with regard to the colonies in particular, the fact that emancipation was enacted in a state of war, and that soldiering—at least as Europeans conceived it—was a masculine enterprise,[44] meant that in practice emancipation created more opportunities for advancement by men than by women.[45] Women were more likely to be coerced into returning to agricultural labor on plantations now depleted by adult men. In both Saint-Domingue and Guadeloupe, former slaves actively resisted the forced labor that accompanied emancipation. And, in both colonies, while military service (admittedly dangerous, but with considerable opportunities for advancement in status) was open to male slaves, women were left disproportionately to the tasks of planting, weeding, and harvesting. In Guadeloupe, women who objected to agricultural work on the grounds that they were formerly employed as domestics rather than field hands were confiscated and made to work in the arsenals, presumably the most dangerous "home front" duty.[46]

Yet the legal status of emancipated women was not identical in Saint-Domingue and Guadeloupe. Polverel's 1794 work codes for Saint-Domingue, which followed the emancipation acts of 1793, paid women lower wages than men.[47] Women protested this inequality but were unable to change the policy: Polverel responded that the women did "not want any consideration to be given to the inequality of strength that nature has placed between them and men, to their habitual and periodic infirmities, to the intervals of rest that their pregnancies, their childbirth, [and] their nursing oblige them to take."[48] By contrast, in 1798 Guadeloupe's commissioner, General Edme Étienne Borne-Desfourneaux introduced equal wages for male and female plantation workers. In addition, Guadeloupean women's fertility was encouraged with fifty days' paid maternity leave and bonuses for each child born.[49] Thus, like their European counterparts who were urged to reproduce in order to replenish populations decimated by war, emancipated women of the colonies were supposed to bear and raise children for the good of the state.[50] At the same time, individual women sometimes found opportunities for self-advancement in these moments of emancipation. For example, some urban women of color in Guadeloupe, already freed before general emancipation, used the social upheaval of the Revolution to consolidate rental properties and gain proprietorship over them.[51]

Napoleon restored slavery in all slaveholding colonies in 1802, though among the Antilles only Guadeloupe effectively enforced this edict. Martinique had maintained slavery throughout British occupation and, in Saint-Domingue, Toussaint-Louverture refused to reinstitute slavery as such, though his land reform policies were designed to resurrect plantation production for export markets.[52] Guadeloupe's *nouveaux citoyens* [new citizens] did not acquiesce to the restoration of slavery peaceably. Women of color—along with men—actively opposed French forces, carrying ammunition, singing the "Marseillaise" and occasionally participating in direct combat.[53] But French forces crushed the resistance in Guadeloupe and reimposed slavery. Colonial officials cracked down on the free colored population, declaring thousands of manumission papers improper and returning their bearers to slavery.[54]

Despite Napoleon's restoration of the slave regime, not all masters sought to revoke the freedom of their former slaves. In anticipation of the restoration of slavery in Guadeloupe, some tried to assure the continued freedom of their nonwhite domestic servants through notarial acts; these were former slaves whom the masters had manumitted for "good and faithful service." Of the former slaves discussed by Laurent Dubois, the majority were women.[55] For example, in 1801 one Guadeloupean colonist, André Laroche, went to a notary to draw up papers affirming the free status of Sophie, the female domestic who had been his slave prior to 1794, along with the daughter who had been born since general emancipation.[56] Since slavery was still illegal in Guadeloupe in 1801, but likely to be reinstated, the act tried to prevent her reenslavement with this language:

> Infinitely satisfied with the good and loyal services always rendered to him by the black *citoyenne* Sophie, his servant, 28, and wishing to be just and thankful toward her, [Laroche] has felt that there is no better way to fulfill this obligation than by sheltering her from being, in the future, disturbed by the police regulations concerning domestics, on the subject of the duties and services that they constrain them to provide, in return for a salary, to the people to whom they were attached before the abolition of slavery in the colonies.[57]

The rest of the document is unique in its attempt to define the obverse of slavery: the rights of freedom that Sophie and her daughter were to enjoy. The declaration specifies Sophie's right (and the future right of her daughter) to dispose of her "services, time and industry . . . forever, as she judges appropriate, and for her personal profit . . . [such that neither Laroche, his inheritors, nor other representatives could] in any time, investigate, trouble or disturb [Sophie and her daughter] on this subject."[58]

Thus, the republican rhetoric and legal policies of the revolutionary era, while favoring general emancipation for slaves, maintained the Old Regime's patriarchal submission of women and children to male heads of household. Mimi Sheller's insightful argument that because of Haiti's difficult circumstances of state formation, the image of the male warrior became central to the construction of Haitian national identity parallels a similar transformation in the notion of citizenship in France under the Directory and the Napoleonic era.[59] The revolutionary and Napoleonic wars increasingly justified male political participation in terms of military service and women's citizenship status was formally subsumed under male heads of household, or patresfamilias.[60]

Restoration of Slavery and the 1848 Emancipation

Strategies for maintaining the workforce in the French Antilles in the post-revolutionary era differed from those of the Old Regime. Whereas the planters' primary strategy in Saint-Domingue before the Revolution had been to import massive numbers of new slaves from Africa, the abolition of the French slave trade in 1814 (though not fully enforced until 1830) led French administrators to expand policies to ameliorate conditions for slaves, and especially women, so as to increase natural reproduction. For example, in addition to increasing maternity leave for slave mothers, administrators and individual owners began to offer manumission to women who successfully bore six children into slavery.[61] The long shadow of the slave revolts and Haitian independence also tempered some of the most extreme working conditions, such as the night-shift system, which was abolished. At the same time, however, colonial authorities and planters were exceedingly anxious to prevent large-scale revolts, which led to increasing vigilance and persecution of resistance and insubordination.[62]

Nineteenth-century manumission patterns follow those of the previous century, with women and children freed significantly more often than men. The size of the white populations of Martinique and Guadeloupe became static or declined while the free colored population grew, largely as a result of these manumissions. In the 1830s, under the July Monarchy and in the face of British abolition, the French government introduced ameliorative policies, designed to ease the conditions of slavery and facilitate the gradual emancipation of slaves. For example, the French legislature voted 650,000 livres in 1839 to support a program to instruct and "moralize" the slaves, including promoting slave marriages.[63] It also reversed the century-old restrictions on manumission in all slave colonies, allowing owners to manumit their slaves without government permission or taxes.[64] From out of the woodwork came thousands of individuals who had either been already freed informally by their masters without government authorization (the soi-disant libres or libres de savane) or to be freed formally for the first time. Women and children clearly outnumbered men, by nearly three and a half to one.[65] A new law, enacted on 18 July 1845 and modeled on Spanish and Portuguese coartación forced slaveholders to free those slaves who could buy their own freedom. They were to be given parcels of land (of unspecified size) by their owners. Yet the specific implementation of this law was left to the local colonial councils, who undermined its progressive intentions.[66]

General and permanent emancipation finally came about during the Revolution of 1848.[67] As during the first emancipation of 1793–1802, authorities and planters tried to compel newly emancipated slaves to continue working in the fields for their former masters. In Martinique, women resisted and protested these requirements alongside men. After emancipation, those who had achieved free status prior to 1832 sought to shore up their elevated status by distinguishing themselves from the noueaux affranchis, or "newly freed," in part through endogamy. And, although colonial women—like their metropolitan counterparts—were ineligible to vote, wives and daughters of the free colored elite of Martinique created voluntary political associations, organized election events, and even campaigned on behalf of candidates. However, Louis Napoleon's 1851 coup removed all colonial subjects from political participation and women were further distanced from formal execution of power.[68]

Conclusion

While the patriarchal model of France's Old Regime favored upward mobility for a few female slaves, the republican model tended to create increased avenues of upward mobility for black and brown men. Yet, even under the Old Regime, only a small percentage of the hundreds of thousands of enslaved women were able to rise in status.[69] The vast majority of female slaves were as exploited and abused as their male counterparts—in terms of labor, food rationing, and regulation—and many suffered the additional burdens of sexual exploitation by masters and overseers. Moreover, many of those women who did escape slavery through manumission did so at the high price of making themselves sexually available to their benefactors. These circumstances created an environment whereby free women of color were prized and rewarded for their sensuality and calculated passion. These images would then be used against them—and against men of color as well.[70]

While Saint-Domingue, Martinique, and Guadeloupe were all subject to French imperialism, their distinct histories have yielded different formulations of gender and citizenship for former slaves and their descendents. The martial stereotype for black men in the Caribbean was invented at great personal risk to men and, if Sheller is correct with regard to Haiti, contributed to an autocratic and brutal political regime that has yet to be completely undone. In Martinique, one sees the emergence of a brown bourgeois civic society, forging new gendered political relations that parallel (but are not identical with) those in France. Guadeloupe, with its poverty, smaller size, greater proportion of women, and predominantly black population has received the least attention by historians from beyond its shores, especially for the period following the 1848 emancipation.

Despite the important differences in class and locale, gender relations in France's Caribbean slave regimes can be fruitfully compared to those in the French metropole. Under the Old Regime, women's sexual and familial alliances created limited avenues for upward social mobility for some women in both the colonial slave system and within the bourgeoisie and the nobility in France.[71] Republican interventions abolished slavery and extended the notion of citizenship to men of all classes but excluded women from formal and direct political participation. The autocratic regimes that followed the early French republics and independent Haiti formally codified the ideology of separate spheres, which was buttressed for men by the overwhelming militarization of Europe and the Caribbean, and for women by pronatalist policies designed to restore populations devastated by disease, toil, and war. By interrogating the processes of state formation and gender relations comparatively, as a truly Atlantic phenomenon, new insights into the global and local manifestations of power become clear.

Notes

I am greatly indebted to the generous and insightful readers who have critiqued earlier versions of this work, including Philip Boucher, Elizabeth Colwill, Robert Duplessis, John Garrigus, David Geggus, Lawrence Jennings, Steven Kale, Melanie Newton, Diana Paton, Rhoda Reddock, Pamela Scully, Blanca G. Silvestrini, and a very insightful anonymous reader.

1 See *The Color of Liberty: Histories of Race in France*, ed. Sue Peabody and Tyler Stovall (Durham, N.C.: Duke University Press, 2003).

2 Several recent works have begun to examine colonial gender relations more critically. For references see the section on the French Caribbean in the bibliographic essay in this volume; of particular interest are the works by Myriam Cottias, Arlette Gautier, John Garrigus, David Geggus, Bernard Moitt, and Gilbert Pago.

3 Even so, I have omitted research on Francophone Louisiana, Guiana, the Mascarene Islands, and slaveholding French settlements in India, Africa, and Canada, as well as smaller French Caribbean colonies, such as Sainte-Lucie, Marie-Galante, and Tobago.

4 Pamela Scully makes a similar argument for postemancipation South Africa in *Liberating the Family? Gender and British Slave Emancipation in the Rural Western Cape, South Africa, 1823–1853* (Portsmouth, N.H.: Heinemann, 1997).

5 In southern Saint-Domingue, women slaves were more than twice as likely to be manumitted as men. Comparable rates can be shown for eighteenth-century Guadeloupe. See Arlette Gautier, *Les soeurs de Solitude: La condition féminine dans l'esclavage aux Antilles du XVIIe au XIXe siècle* (Paris: Caribéennes, 1985), 174–75; and John Garrigus, "A Struggle for Respect: The Free Coloreds of Pre-revolutionary Saint Domingue, 1760–1769" (PhD diss., Johns Hopkins University, 1988), 422–23. Females constituted two-thirds of those manumitted in the entire colony of Saint-Domingue in the five years leading up to the French Revolution; David Geggus, "Slave and Free Colored Women in Saint Domingue," in *More than Chattel: Black Women and Slavery in the Americas* (Bloomington: Indiana University Press, 1996), 268. For comparative figures, see Kathleen Higgins, *"Licentious Liberty" in a Brazilian Gold-Mining Region: Slavery, Gender and Social Control in Eighteenth-Century Sabará, Minas Gerais* (University Park: Penn State University Press, 1999), 145–74; Mary Karasch, *Slave Life in Rio de Janeiro: 1808–1850* (Princeton, N.J.: Princeton University Press, 1987), 346; Rosemary Brana-Shute, "Approaching Freedom: The Manumission of Slaves in Suriname, 1760–1828," *Slavery and Abolition* 10, no. 3 (1990): 46–47; and Robert C.-H. Shell, *Children of Bondage: A Social History of the Slave Society at the Cape of Good Hope, 1652–1838* (Hanover, N.H.: Wesleyan University Press, 1994), 384–85.

6 However, women were manumitted more often than men in Barbados even though white women outnumbered white men, suggesting that these patterns reflect a sexual double-standard more than mere demographics; see Hilary Beckles,

"White Women and Slavery in the Caribbean," in *Caribbean Slavery in the Atlantic World*, ed. Verene Shepherd and Hilary Beckles, 663–64.

7 Adrien Dessalles, *Histoire générale des Antilles*, 5 vols. (Paris: Libraire-èditeur, 1847–48), 1:559–61.

8 Dessalles, *Histoire genérale*, 2:453–54. The census numbers include both enslaved and free blacks, though the proportion of the latter is assumed to be quite low.

9 On the hierarchy of slave markets and their impact on sex, age, and ethnic distribution, see David Geggus, "The French Slave Trade: An Overview," *William and Mary Quarterly* 58, no.1 (2001): 125–31.

10 Vernon V. Palmer, "The Origins and Authors of the *Code Noir*," in *The Louisiana Purchase Bicentennial Series in Louisiana History*, vol. 13, *An Uncommon Experience, Law and Judicial Institutions in Louisiana, 1803–2003*, ed. Judith Kelleher Schafer and Warren M. Billings (Lafayette: University of Southwestern Louisiana, 1997), 331–59.

11 "Relation des Isles de Sainct-Christofle, Gardelouppe et la Martinicque," published by Louis Philippe May in "La plus ancienne relation de voyage aux colonies françaises des Antilles," *Terre, air, mer: La géographie* (Jul.–Aug. 1932): 8–27; "Extrait des opinions de Mess. Blénac et Patoulet," 3 April 1681, Archives Nationales, Colonies (hereafter AN Col.) F^3 248, pp. 685–88.

12 Kimberly S. Hanger, "Greedy French Masters and Color-Conscious Legal-Minded Spaniards in Colonial Louisiana," in *Slavery in the Caribbean Francophone World: Distant Voices, Forgotten Acts, Forged Identities* (Athens: University of Georgia Press, 2000), 108–9; Keila Grinberg, "Freedom Suits and Civil Law in Brazil and the United States," *Slavery and Abolition* 22, no. 3 (2001): 66–82; Elsa Goveia, "West Indian Slave Laws of the Eighteenth Century," *Revista de ciencias sociales* 4 (Mar. 1960): 78–80. Rebecca Scott shows that though the legal right existed in Spanish Cuba, as the prices of slaves escalated in the late nineteenth century, self-purchase became functionally inaccessible for most slaves (*Slave Emancipation in Cuba: The Transition to Free Labor, 1860–1899* [Princeton, N.J.: Princeton University Press, 1985], 13–14, 74–75, 82).

13 Some colonial fathers enrolled their mulatto sons in the militia for eight years to guarantee their manumission while evading heavy taxes on manumission promulgated after 1710, Gabriel Debien, "Les affranchissements aux Antilles françaises aux XVIIe et XVIIIe siècles," *Annuario de estudios americanos* 24 (1967): 1187–88; Lucien Peytraud, *L'esclavage aux Antilles françaises avant 1789 d'après des documents inédits des Archives coloniales*, ed. Emile Désormeaux (Paris: E. Dèsormeaux, 1973 [1897]), 408–9; Lucien René Abenon, *La Guadeloupe de 1671 à 1759: Etude politique, économique et sociale*, 2 vols. (Paris: L'Harmattan, 1987), 2:10; Garrigus, "Struggle for Respect," 328; Pierre Baude, *L'affranchissement des esclaves aux Antilles françaises, principalement à la Martinique du début de la colonisation à 1848* (Fort-de-France, Martinique: Imprimerie du Gouvernement, 1948), 23.

14 "Déclaration du Roi touchant les Libres qui recèlent des Esclaves et les Dona-

tions faites aux Gens de couleur par les Blancs du 8 février 1726," in M. L. E. Moreau de Saint-Méry, *Loix et constitutions des colonies françoises de l'Amérique sous le vent*, 6 vols. (Paris: Chez l'auteur, 1784–[1790]), 3:159–60; Garrigus, "Struggle for Respect," 144.

15 The case is discussed in Léo Elisabeth, "Europe, Afrique, Nouveau Monde: Femmes d'antan aux origines de la femme créole," *Bulletin de la Société de la Martinique* 27 (1988–91): 79–81; and Bernard Moitt, *Women and Slavery in the French Antilles, 1635–1848* (Bloomington: Indiana University Press, 2001), 153–54.

16 The details of Lamy's claim are a little fuzzy. The Superior Council declared Catin and all her children free and "affranchis d'origine" [which might be translated as "free at birth"] yet nevertheless ordered that Catin had to pay to sieur La Cosse, the guardian of the minor children of Sir Robert Lamy and Marie Lamotte 165 *piastres*, plus costs associated with the trial (Extract of the registers of the Superior Council of Martinique, 9 May 1708, AN Col., F³ 250, p. 567).

17 AN Col. F³ 250, p. 301 (8 April 1705). The intendant was one of two royally appointed administrators who ran the island, the other being the governor-general. Authority was carefully divided between them and each was expected to police the other for corruption and errors of judgment.

18 The early documents in the case refer to her as Babet Binture (AN Col. F³ 250, p. 301 [8 April 1705]; AN Col. F³ 250, pp. 305–7 [25 Aug. 1708]). Documents surrounding the widow La Palu's appeal to Vaucresson and the French minister (1708, 1710) omit any last name, referring to her as "Babé, Catin's sister" or "the Negress Babet" (AN Col. F³ 250, pp. 309–11; AN Col. F³ 250, p. 891). By 1713, the new governor Phélypeaux was designating the woman in question as "the Negress Babet, named La Palu from the name of the lady whose slave she was" (AN Col. C⁸ A 19, f. 75–85v). Vaucresson reprises the name "Babet Binture" in his letter of 10 Sept. 1714 (AN Col. C⁸ A 20, f. 87v–89). All the historians who have previously written about this case have retained Phélypeaux's designation of Babet as "La Palu."

19 Phélypeaux to minister, 6 April 1713 (AN Col. C⁸ A 19, f. 81v).

20 Elisabeth, "Europe, Afrique, Nouveau Monde," 81.

21 In France, slaves typically did not seek to challenge their status unless faced with abuse, sale, or the threat of being returned to the colonies, sometimes after many years' service as slaves in the metropole (Sue Peabody, *"There Are No Slaves in France": The Political Culture of Race and Slavery in the Ancien Régime* [New York: Oxford University Press, 1996], 53, 58, 88–90).

22 Several of the original documents mention Lamy's and Binture's children (AN Col. F³ 250, pp. 305–7 [25 Aug. 1708]; AN Col. C⁸ A 20, f. 87v–89 [10 Sept. 1714]).

23 Marriage between blacks and whites was prohibited in Guadeloupe beginning in 1711. Myriam Cottias, "La séduction coloniale: Damnation et stratégies—Les Antilles, XVIIe–XIXe siècle," in *Séduction et sociétés: Approches historiques*, ed. Cécile Dauphin and Arlette Farge (Paris: Seuil, 2001), 131.

24 Sue Peabody, " 'A Dangerous Zeal': Catholic Missions to Slaves in the French Antilles, 1635–1800," *French Historical Studies* 25, no. 1 (2002): 75.

25 Moreau de Saint-Méry, *Loix*, 4:798, 822–24; 5:18–19, 149–50, 152–53, 190–92, 581, 610–13. These laws were repeatedly reissued and revised, suggesting that colonists were reluctant to comply.

26 The attorney general of Cap Français, representing slaveholders' interests, castigated members of the Jesuit order for refusing to accept some colonists, presumably the fathers of mulatto children, as godparents for their slaves ("Arrêt de réglement du conseil du Cap, sur les abus, en matière de la religion, de la part des gens de couleur du 18 février 1761," in Moreau de Saint-Méry, *Loix*, 4:354).

27 Geggus, "Slave and Free Colored Women," 268.

28 Phélypeaux to minister, 6 April 1713 (AN Col. C⁸ A 19, f. 84v).

29 For example, Moreau de Saint-Méry lists the case of a free mulatto who was whipped, branded, and sold for the king's profit for having fought a white man in 1767 (*Loix*, 5:84).

30 On the development of legal racial segregation in the French colonies, see Yvan Debbasch, *Couleur et liberté: Le jeu de critère ethnique dans un ordre juridique esclavagiste* (Paris: Dalloz, 1967), 53–71; and for Saint-Domingue, John Garrigus, "Blue and Brown: Contraband Indigo and the Rise of a Free Colored Planter Class in French Saint-Domingue," *Americas* 50, no. 2 (1993): 233–63; Léo Elisabeth, "The French Antilles," in *Neither Slave nor Free: The Freedmen of African Descent in the Slave Societies of the New World*, ed. David W. Cohen and Jack P. Greene (Baltimore: Johns Hopkins University Press, 1972), 157; Garrigus, "Struggle for Respect," 330–67.

31 This is according to Morisseau's account, which is the only documentation I have found for this case. The documents are reproduced in Moreau de Saint-Méry, *Loix*, 5:653–56.

32 The year following the decision in Marie-Victoire's case, the colonist Hilliard d'Auberteuil published a hypothetical census of Saint-Domingue in his *Considérations sur l'état présent de la colonie française de Saint-Domingue, ouvrage politique et législatif*, 2 vols. (Paris: Grangé, 1776). Its estimated figures show a clear preponderance of free men (25,900) over women (13,400).

33 Charles Frostin, *Les révoltes blanches à Saint-Domingue aux XVIIe et XVIIIe siècles (Haïti avant 1789)* (Paris: L'Ecole, 1975), 28.

34 Geggus, "French Slave Trade," 130–31.

35 Commissioner Sonthonax, 30 July 1793, quoted in Robert Louis Stein, *Léger Félicité Sonthonax: The Lost Sentinel of the Republic* (London: Associated University Presses, 1985), 86.

36 Joan B. Landes, *Women and the Public Sphere in the Age of Revolution* (Ithaca, N.Y.: Cornell University Press, 1988), esp. 66–89. There is a wide literature on republican notions of women's citizenship in the United States, e.g., Linda K. Kerber, *No Constitutional Right to Be Ladies: Women and the Obligations of Citizenship* (New York: Hill and Wang, 1998), esp. 11–15; and Rosemarie Zagarri, "The Rights of Man and

Woman in Post-revolutionary America," *William and Mary Quarterly*, 3d ser., 55 (1998): 203–30.

37   Public Act no. 166, extracted in General Orders, no. 91, War Department, 29 July 1862, *The War of the Rebellion: A Compilation of the Official Records of the Union and Confederate Armies*, ser. 3, 128 vols. (Washington, D.C.: 1880–1901), 2:281. Leslie Schwalm notes that in the United States northern liberal bourgeois reformers similarly represented marriage as "a means of raising freedpeople to a new level of civilization" (*A Hard Fight for We: Women's Transition from Slavery to Freedom in South Carolina* [Urbana: University of Illinois Press, 1997], 239). See also Elizabeth Ann Regosin, *Freedom's Promise: Ex-Slave Families and Citizenship in the Age of Emancipation* (Charlottesville: University of Virginia Press, 2002), 8–10.

38   Peabody, " 'Dangerous Zeal,' " 68.

39   Herbert G. Gutman, *The Black Family in Slavery and Freedom, 1750–1925* (New York: Vintage, 1976), 363–431. For more recent work, see Schwalm, *Hard Fight for We*, 243–48; and Laura Edwards, *Gendered Strife and Confusion: The Political Culture of Reconstruction* (Urbana: University of Illinois Press, 1997), 145–83; Noralee Frankel, *Freedom's Women: Black Women and Families in Civil War Mississippi* (Bloomington: Indiana University Press, 1999), 80–92. For South Africa, see Scully, *Liberating the Family?*, 116–25.

40   J. Ph. Garran-Coulon, *Rapport sur les troubles de Saint-Domingue*, 4 vols. (Paris: Imprimerie Nationale, 1797–99), 4:55–57.

41   Carolyn E. Fick, *The Making of Haiti: The Saint Domingue Revolution from Below* (Knoxville: University of Tennessee Press, 1990), 159–61; David Geggus, "Racial Equality, Slavery and Colonial Succession during the Constituent Assembly," *American Historical Review* 94, no. 5 (1989): 1290–1308; Robin Blackburn, *The Overthrow of Colonial Slavery, 1776–1848* (London: Verso, 1988), 161–264; C. L. R. James, *The Black Jacobins: Toussaint L'Ouverture and the San Domingo Revolution*, 2nd rev. ed. (New York: Vintage, 1963), 118–42.

42   Laurent Dubois, "Inscribing Race in the Revolutionary French Antilles," in Peabody and Stovall, eds., *The Color of Liberty*, 99.

43   The intersection of gender and the French Revolution has been studied for several decades, beginning with Olwen Hufton, "Women in Revolution, 1789–1796," *Past and Present* 53 (1971): 90–108. My analysis here follows Landes, *Women and the Public Sphere*, though Landes has been challenged by more recent scholarship. Many notable recent contributions are ably summarized in Jack Censor, "Social Twists and Linguistic Turns: Revolutionary Historiography a Decade after the Bicentennial," *French Historical Studies* 22, no. 1 (1999): 144–48. See also Geneviève Fraisse, *Reason's Muse: Sexual Difference and the Birth of Democracy*, trans. Jane Marie Todd (Chicago: University of Chicago Press, 1994); Dominique Godineau, *The Women of Paris and Their French Revolution*, trans. Katherine Streip (Berkeley: University of California Press, 1998); and James F. McMillan, *France and Women, 1789–1914: Gender, Society and Politics* (London: Routledge, 2000), 15–44.

44 Gautier, *Soeurs de Solitude*, 236. In some West African societies, women regularly engaged in warfare during this period. See Edna G. Bay, *Wives of the Leopard: Gender, Politics, and Culture in the Kingdom of Dahomey* (Charlottesville: University of Virginia Press, 1998), 134–39; Agnes Akosua Aidoo, "Asante Queen Mothers in Government and Politics in the Nineteenth Century," in *The Black Woman Cross-Culturally*, ed. Filomina Chioma Steady (Rochester, Vt.: Schenkman, 1981), 65–77. Olaudah Equiano asserts that in his Ibo homeland, today southern Nigeria, "even our women are warriors and march boldly out to fight along with the men"; Equiano, *Equiano's Travels*, ed. Paul Edwards (Oxford: Heinemann, 1967), 8.

45 Mimi Sheller, "Sword-Bearing Citizens: Militarism and Manhood in Nineteenth-Century Haiti," *Plantation Society in the Americas* 4, nos. 2–3 (1997): 233–78.

46 Laurent Dubois, *A Colony of Citizens: Revolution and Slave Emancipation in the French Caribbean* (Chapel Hill: University of North Carolina Press, 2004), 246–48.

47 Fick, *Making of Haiti*, 168–170; Judith Kafka, "Action, Reaction and Interaction: Slave Women in Resistance in the South of Saint Domingue, 1793–94," *Slavery and Abolition* 18, no. 2 (1997): 53.

48 "Règlement sur les proportions," A.N. DXXV; quoted in Fick, *Making of Haiti*, 170.

49 Dubois, *A Colony of Citizens*, 336. These measures are representative of a concerted pronatalism in both France and the colonies at the end of the eighteenth century; see Gautier, *Soeurs de Solitude*, 94–121.

50 I am aware of at least one proposed law in France that would have rewarded French women who bore large families for the nation: Guillaume Poncet de la Grave, *Considérations sur le célibat relativement à la politique, à la population et aux bonnes mœurs* (Paris: Moutardier, an IX [1801]). One wonders, however, whether the promised bonuses and maternity leave ever materialized for colonial women.

51 Dubois, *A Colony of Citizens*, 249–50.

52 Fick, *Making of Haiti*, 207–10.

53 Dubois, *A Colony of Citizens*, 393–94.

54 Elisabeth, "French Antilles," 150; Dubois, *A Colony of Citizens*, 411–12.

55 Dubois, *A Colony of Citizens*, 374–78.

56 *Sophie*, an extremely unusual name in Old Regime Catholic France, is a tantalizing echo of the idealized mate for Rousseau's perfect republican man, Emile, in the didactic 1762 novel, *Emile, ou l'éducation*, and likely reflects the republican sympathies of the slaveholder.

57 Laurent Dubois, "A Colony of Citizens: Revolution and Slave Emancipation in the French Caribbean, 1789–1802" (PhD diss., University of Michigan, 1998), 533–34.

58 Ibid.

59 Sheller, "Sword-Bearing Citizens."

60 Jennifer N. Heuer, "Foreigners, Families and Citizens: Contradictions of Na-

tional Citizenship in France, 1789–1830" (PhD diss., University of Chicago, 1998), 128–29, 172–75, 221–28. Aside from Heuer, and Jo Burr Mardagant, "Gender, Vice, and the Political Imaginary in Postrevolutionary France: Reinterpreting the Failure of the July Monarchy, 1830–1848," *American Historical Review* 104, no. 5 (1999): 1461–96, works on the history of gender relations in revolutionary and postrevolutionary France have tended to ignore the importance of military conscription and service for male identity. See, e.g., Lynn Hunt, *The Family Romance of the French Revolution* (Berkeley: University of California Press, 1992); and Robert Nye, *Masculinity and Male Codes of Honor in Modern France* (New York: Oxford University Press, 1993).

61 Gautier, *Soeurs de Solitude*, 132–37.

62 Christian Schnakenbourg, *Histoire de l'industrie sucrière en Guadeloupe aux XIXe et XXe siècles*, vol. 1, *La crise du système esclavagiste (1835–1847)* (Paris: L'Harmattan, 1980), 54. Slaves revolted in Martinique in 1822 and 1831 and in Guadeloupe in 1827; Josette Fallope, *Esclaves et citoyens: Les noirs à la Guadeloupe au XIXe siècle dans les processus de résistance et d'intégration (1802–1910)* (Basse-Terre: Société d'Histoire de la Guadeloupe, 1992), 202–3. Judith Coffin and Jim Sidbury (" 'We No Longer Live in the Age That Has Just Ended': Martiniquans and Their Histories in Dessalles's Diary") also argue that after the Revolution, French colonial slave owners such as Pierre Dessalles found it more necessary to negotiate their control with slaves, while Lawrence Jennings in "Slave Resistance and the Abolition of French Colonial Slavery, 1830–1848" contends that the postrevolutionary era was marked by increased military presence and attempts to control the enslaved population (unpublished papers presented at the French Colonial Historical Society meeting, May 2000).

63 Cottias, "Marriage et citoyennité."

64 Josette Fallope, "Les affranchissements d'esclaves à la Guadeloupe entre 1815 et 1848," *Annales de l'Université d'Abidjan*, ser. 1, Histoire 1, no. 6 (1978): 10–11.

65 Gautier, *Soeurs de solitude*, 132–34; Elisabeth, "French Antilles," 146. See also Fallope, "Affranchissements d'esclaves," 31; and Debien, "Affranchissements aux Antilles," 1189–97.

66 Gabriel Moyal, "Transmitting the Sense of Property: Reporting on a Slave Massacre in 1847," in *Slavery in the Caribbean Francophone World: Distant Voices, Forgotten Acts, Forged Identities*, ed. Doris Y. Kadish (Athens: University of Georgia Press, 2000), 56.

67 Lawrence C. Jennings, *French Anti-slavery: The Movement for the Abolition of Slavery in France, 1802–1848* (Cambridge: Cambridge University Press, 2000).

68 Gilbert Pago, *Les femmes et la liquidation du système esclavagiste à la Martinique, 1848–1852* (Petit-Bourg, Guadeloupe: Ibis Rouge, 1998), 142–47, 169–87.

69 In Nippes, Saint-Domingue, 4% of female slaves were manumitted, and many of these were elderly women. Fewer than 10% of slave mistresses were manumitted in Saint-Domingue in 1780 and fewer than 3% in Guadeloupe in 1776 (Gautier, *Soeurs de Solitude*, 175).

70 John Garrigus, "Race, Gender, and Virtue in Haiti's Failed Foundational

Fiction: *La mulâtae comme il ya peu de blanches* (1803)," in Peabody and Stovall, *Color of Liberty*.

71   See esp. Sarah Hanley, "The Monarchic State in Early Modern France: Martial Regime Government and Male Right," in *Politics, Ideology, and the Law in Early Modern Europe*, ed. Adrianna E. Bakos (Rochester, N.Y.: University of Rochester Press, 1994); Hanley, "The Social Sites of Political Practice in France: Lawsuits, Civil Rights, and the Separations of Powers in Domestic and State Government, 1500–1800," *American Historical Review* 102, no. 1 (1997): 27–52; and Carolyn C. Lougee, *Le Paradis des Femmes: Women, Salons, and Social Stratification in Seventeenth-Century France* (Princeton, N.J.: Princeton University Press, 1977).

🌼 MIMI SHELLER

Acting as Free Men: Subaltern Masculinities and Citizenship in Postslavery Jamaica

Feminist theorists have recognized for some time that particular social constructions of masculinity have been the unspoken central tenet of European and American models of democratic citizenship, rights, and freedoms.[1] Yet in discussions of slave emancipation and postslavery citizenship in the Atlantic world, the formation of free subjects as specifically *masculine* has attracted little attention until recently. Over the last decade new approaches to British colonialism in particular have begun to demonstrate how shifting ideological articulations of gender and race structured white elite understandings of freedom and individual subjectivity.[2] Debates over the abolition of slavery, for example, consolidated emerging British conceptions of the sovereign free individual as male and white. As Eileen Suárez Findlay notes, however, there is not yet sufficient attention paid to working-class or "plebeian" conceptions of masculinity, freedom, and citizenship in the colonial world.[3] Moral norms surrounding gender and racial distinctions were in fact central to the construction and practice of "freedom" in all postslavery societies, for both elite and plebeian political subjects.

This chapter explores the relation between gender, "racial formations," and ethnic and national identities in popular political contention surrounding freedom, citizenship, and manhood in postslavery Jamaica. Insofar as racial meanings emerge out of political struggle, "racial formation" is "the process by which social, economic and political forces determine the content and importance of racial categories, and by which they are in turn shaped by racial meanings."[4] As Rebecca Scott argues in relation to the very different forms of racial "marking" in postslavery Louisiana and Cuba, racial boundaries and meanings cannot be assumed; they only come out of "on-the-ground" relations that are always contingent.[5] I extend her argument by showing how on-the-ground relations of gender and ethnicity also contributed to the contingent marking of racial boundaries of citizenship in postslavery Jamaica. I ground my claims in evidence detailing public conflicts over wages and labor conditions. My aim is to demonstrate not only how competing elite and sub-altern masculinities informed efforts to define and enact freedom in Jamaica, but also to go beyond existing debates by showing how working-class black masculinity came to be enacted as Christian and British through exclusion of the indentured foreigner, the "Coolie."

By "masculinities" I refer to practices and ideas that differentiate "men" from women (and boys), linked to what Robert Connell calls "gender proj-ects."[6] Recently in the Caribbean there has been a growing interest in contem-porary modes of "marginalized (black) masculinities,"[7] yet few historians have explored their nineteenth-century antecedents.[8] In Haiti, for example, highly exclusive discourses of nationalized masculinity were deployed in the construction of republican citizenship and civic militarism throughout the nineteenth century.[9] Beneath the universalizing veneer of liberal citizenship, free men in Jamaica also acted out their particular understanding of freedom in a context of gender, ethnic, and class conflict, which produced diverse experiences of freedom for differently positioned subjects. How did specifi-cally "black" claims to citizenship mobilize various kinds of nonhegemonic masculinity? My research suggests that freedmen in Jamaica strategically artic-ulated their rights of citizenship in relation not only to white men, but also to other subaltern groups such as black women and indentured foreigners. They asserted free citizenship in part by marking differences between men and women, native and foreign, free and indentured, Christian and Heathen, Negro and Coolie.

The relation between black and white masculinity is not bipolar, then, but is produced through the exclusion of more marginal others. As Gayatri Spivak reminds those who would engage in subaltern studies, one must keep asking "what subaltern is strategically excluded from organized resistance."[10] This has significant implications for our understanding of freedom and citizenship in postslavery societies. Whereas many studies of gender and race in the Atlantic world focus on the intersection of the black/white and male/female axes of power, they have not attended to the particularity of "other others" who enter the scene of embodied politics.[11] "Free black" Jamaican masculinity was measured not only as a kind of distance from white men or a difference from black women, but also marked as a relation to indentured Asian and African others. My analysis of these distinctions between *particular others* will show that freedom is not an absolute condition which is generic in its effects but is rather experienced and lived in specifically "ordered" ways, governed by intersecting gender orders, racial orders, moral orders, and political orders. An individual's freedom is relationally defined and provisionally practiced within a constellation of other individuals who are more or less free, each freedom always circumscribed by relations of gender, class, ethnicity, and racialization.

As with other areas of subaltern studies, it proves very difficult to investigate subaltern perspectives on gender and freedom. Insofar as the "native informant" is foreclosed by the rhetorical structures of dominant narratives, as Spivak argues, one cannot simply assert the ability to "speak for" or "represent" the subaltern. To speak for subordinate individuals is to reproduce the structure that already enables some but not others to speak. My method, therefore, is to seek out instances of popular political contention in which modes of direct address are recorded. These include newspaper accounts of speeches made at public meetings, and government or missionary papers enclosing petitions signed by plebeian actors.[12] However, rather than reading these rare moments of "the hidden transcript"[13] as unsullied exemplars of "subaltern resistance" against colonizing elites, I instead seek out the tensions, fault lines, and absences that structure these counternarratives as thoroughly as they structure the discourses of colonial policymakers. In these documents we find interlocking struggles over gender, racial, moral and political orders that speak to the powerful effects of multiple subaltern positions whose complex interrelations have structured (and continue to effect) the practice of freedom in the Atlantic world.

Becoming Good Christian Subjects: "Send back the Coolies"

Recent research on the "gendered worlds" of Latin American and Caribbean workers suggests that relations of power within households and communities cannot be understood apart from the wider "material and cultural factors [that] position men and women unequally within society."[14] Catherine Hall and Diane Austin-Broos, among others, have examined some of the local effects of dominant articulations of white patriarchal masculinity on Jamaican society.[15] Such work recovers the subaltern family as a site of resistance yet sometimes overlooks its own internal power relations. Struggles over working-class masculinity have often reinforced male obligations "to protect women and children, and to be the stable breadwinner and public protector of the home."[16] If becoming free required men to assert gender difference and reconstitute patriarchal families, what were the costs for black women? Maggie Sale argues that in using liberal theory African American men "were caught in recognizing the struggle for liberty as paradigmatically masculine and largely individual. This position led them rhetorically to marginalize black women . . . by basing their arguments for inclusion on their rights 'as men'— which included the possession of female family members." Thus they may have "radically contested white supremacy, but also reproduced masculine individualism."[17]

In Jamaica, too, the ideology of liberal citizenship brought with it the baggage of the patriarchal family and masculine possessive individualism. Austin-Broos, in her rich analysis of "moral orders" in Jamaica, suggests that as men moved into positions of freedom, they began to exercise male prerogatives of patriarchal household control. The missionary concern with "reordering black lower-class sexual relations . . . [became] a central characteristic not only of Pentecostalism but also of Marcus Garvey's black separatism and of the Rastafarian movement. All have sought a subordination and privatization of women as an integral part of redemption."[18] Freedom, therefore, was experienced differently by men and by women, insofar as the patriarchal conjugal family with a male head supported by the invisible, nonwaged labor of female kin and children became the basis on which freedom could most effectively be secured. Afro-Jamaican men resorted to a Christian discourse of "manhood" in order to insert themselves into British political discourses that emphasized a kind of active masculine citizenship.

It has been less noted, however, that in laying claim to Christian citizenship, black masculine freedom also came to be constituted through an exclusion of "foreigners" and "heathens"—crucial categories in political discourse from the 1840s to 1860s. When the Jamaican government responded to successful collective bargaining and strikes by freed plantation laborers in the immediate aftermath of the 1838 emancipation of slaves by sponsoring the immigration of indentured laborers into the island at taxpayers' expense, conflicts arose between the formerly enslaved and the new arrivals.[19] The immigration schemes subsidized the planters while undercutting the autonomy of the freed laborers. This fundamental conflict of class interests was deflected into tensions between indentured workers and emancipated slaves, which I argue were articulated through discourses of gender, morality, and ethnic difference. Popular understandings of gender roles and the family were not simply reworked in relation to European Christian values, they were also set in a context in which new indentured communities offered an "other other" against which native black Jamaican virtue could be measured.

The planters' first initiative was to employ liberated Africans who had been captured from foreign slaving ships and could be signed up for contracts of indenture.[20] Freedpeople from the start linked a critique of indenture to the question of familial autonomy and self-determination. At a meeting held at Rev. Knibb's Baptist Chapel in Falmouth in February 1840, for example, there were general complaints about the planters' "system of oppression" and specific concerns about the regulation of "captured Africans," in particular that families should not be broken up.[21] It is not clear in what specific ways the indenturing of these Africans threatens family autonomy. Family sanctity and autonomy were crucial to the popular idea of freedom, and Jamaicans initially seem to have recognized a kinship between themselves and the Africans.

Planters next turned to the importation of indentured laborers from the other parts of the British Empire and beyond, including Ireland, the German regions, and Portugal; the most reliable source, though, was India. Between 1840 and 1852, 14,132 East Indians entered Jamaica, with a significant impact on the labor market.[22] In a context of intense labor competition, Jamaican workers began to draw unfavorable contrasts between hard-working native Jamaican Christians and the "heathen Coolies."

The Baptists played a crucial part in the emerging discourse of the "free man" as Christian. The *Baptist Herald and Friend of Africa*, launched in 1839, described itself as a "cheap publication" aimed at the "labouring population" in order to advance the "Christian public." It used a highly gendered and racial language of Christian manhood in addressing the newly emancipated as British subjects and electors. A letter to the electors of Jamaica observed that what would "give the man of true English spirit the highest gratification, is the circumstance of being permitted to address a body of men—holding the high position of electors, in a free country, as fellow citizens, who only a few years since, were enduring all the ignominy, and wrongs of slavery." The writer marks his fellow citizens as men and as English, and therefore deserving. He then continues:

Electors of Jamaica, act a part worthy of freemen. The cause of liberty demands it of you. The cause of humanity throughout the world demands it of you. . . . If you act as Christian citizens, you have it in your power to seal the doom of slavery. You have the opportunity of demonstrating to the world, that the sons of Africa are capable of exercising the rights of citizens, even in a free, civilized community; . . . and you shall see your brethren, who are yet in bondage, before long, emerge from the degradation of slavery, and taking their position by your side in the rank of men, shall be animated by your example to aspire to a noble elevation among the nations of the earth.[23]

Such public discourses presented a model of Christian manhood that required action on the part of the recently freed in order both to demonstrate their manliness and to further the liberty of their African "brethren." Only those capable of exercising their rights could join the "rank of men," and only those belonging to that rank were capable of forming a "free, civilized community." Written on 4 July, the letter was also an implicit critique of the United States, where slavery still marred the ideal of liberty for all. Freedom required men of "English spirit" to act out their citizenship on an international stage in a way that marked both gender and national distinctions. The article also called for "the improvement of native agriculture, the encouragement of native institutions, and the development of the native resources of the Island," thus weighing local interests against foreign immigration schemes. As much as freedom was about being and acting manly, it was also about laying claim to being English and Christian, in opposition to African or "Coolie" migrants.

The arrival of indentured workers in Jamaica, living in communities with distinctive patterns of gender relations, seemingly threatened the new gender order on which a respectable free society was being built. As early as 1847 a riot was reported "among Coolies on Bogue Estate," in which they reportedly attacked "any and all blacks," who in turn attacked them. There were fifteen "broken skulls and bones," and the indentured workers involved were fined or imprisoned for a month with hard labor.[24] By this time the British market had been opened to foreign sugar (produced by slaves) by the controversial Sugar Duties Act of 1846, sugar prices had fallen, and Jamaican plantations were beginning to fail.[25] Many laborers were without work. Although native workers mainly directed their anger at the planters and the white-dominated colonial government, they also at times vented it on the indentured workers themselves.

At a public meeting held in 1847 at the Brownsville Presbyterian Chapel, planters gathered their workers to explain the crisis. Some workers objected to calls to work harder, including Ronald McArthur, a laborer from Retrieve Estate, who stated:

Jamaica ruined for true, and who to blame? . . . Attorney bring Coolies to take their work and their bread—they make good house for Coolies, but anything good enough for we black nega.—Now Coolie is the ruination of Jamaica— Coolie never can work with we; black people can work round about them; them is the most worthlessest set a people we ever saw,—them can't work, and yet attorney give them fine house and a shilling a day for doing nothing . . . Send back the Coolies, them robbers that are brought to this country and leave the country to us, and give us fair play and regular wages, and Jamaica will stand good again.[26]

McArthur's words indicate a competition for labor, which also hinged on access to good housing and "fair play." The planter's call for "regular labor" is met here with the worker's demand for "regular wages," yet it is played out in a contest of worthiness between Creole and Coolie labor.

The identity of "we black nega" is defined against the foreign Coolies through the question of who can perform better work, but also in relation to who can legitimately exercise political rights. McArthur called on the others to sign a petition, stating, "I am not afraid to sign this petition, because nobody can take our free from us." Naming themselves as the "emancipated labourers of this district of Jamaica," the act of petitioning became a way of asserting "our free." It called on Britain not to equalize the duties on sugar, which was "conferring a boon to the [foreign] slave-holder" at the expense of those "elevated to the rank of free-born British subjects."[27] This British identity is in marked contrast to the Coolies and allowed the emancipated Jamaicans to make a political claim that set them apart from both indentured laborers and foreign slaves, neither of whom had the rights of freeborn British subjects.

Such debates simmered over the next decade and led the Afro-Creole and Indian populations to distrust each other. When there was an "apprehended outbreak" detected in the Western parishes in the tumultuous year of 1848, some planters indicated that falling wages were a major grievance, but also that work was being given to Coolies and to Portuguese immigrants. In response, Governor Charles Edward Grey issued a public proclamation calling on the "good Subjects of Her Majesty" to "abhor and prevent the employment of violence or Threatening Language to others . . . [and to] endeavour, by soberness and steadiness of Demeanour, and by Prudence of Conduct and of Language to shew that they are worthy to sustain the character of Freemen, and to be the Fathers of Free Families."[28] He closely linked civic participation in a civil society to men's private character, based on their role in the patriarchal family. From the white elite's point of view, it remained open to debate whether black men could claim such a character, and on this hinged their claim to the rights of British citizenship. By setting themselves apart from the Coolies, native Jamaican men tried to assert their Christian character and claim on British rights. They increasingly framed freedom less as a universal right of man and more as a special privilege and exclusive prerogative of British men.

Economic conditions were poor enough that thousands of men left Jamaica between 1850 and 1855, recruited to work on the Panama Railroad that was being built across the isthmus by a U.S. joint-stock company.[29] The diminishing number of well-paid jobs for men exacerbated ethnic conflicts in the late 1850s. When a new immigration bill was proposed in 1858, many Jamaicans mobilized in opposition to it. Rev. J. E. Henderson prepared two memorials to the Queen from his congregations in St. James against the Immigration Bill, writing: "That the Immigrants it is proposed to bring are Heathens and Savages who will of course attend to their idolatrous customs in our very midst and set an example before our young people and children that must be most injurious."[30] The memorial also noted that "the proposed Immigrants will not be free men," thus implying that they would undermine the freedom that had been won by the native Jamaican working class. In response, the emancipated laborers of Jamaica had to actively assert the rights and privileges of freedom through notions of masculine citizenship that entailed earning a living, supporting a family, and taking an active part in politics.

Three Representations of the Family:
Emancipated, Coolie, and African Petitions

Distancing themselves from savagery and underlining their civility became crucial means for freedmen to "act a part worthy of freemen," and the family played a central part in this framework. An 1859 petition to Governor Charles Henry Darling from the "Mechanics and Peasantries" refers to the governor as "a husband, a father, a philanthropist, consequently a good man." The petitioners indicate a distinctive view of manhood as a foundation of a good society. They speak as "loyal British Subjects" of the injustice under which "every oppressive means must be employed to trample and reduce [their] aspiring to manhood." The same group also petitioned the queen in a document with over one thousand signatures.[31] Opening with an elaborate profession of loyalty to the queen and gratitude to the British nation, the petitioners assure their readers, "We shall endeavour to use our positions as British subjects and strive to evince by our loyal conduct how much we prize and value our privileges as free people." A local official informed the governor that the people involved were "more a class of yeomanry than in the ordinary sense of the word a peasantry. Possessing freeholds ranging from 1, 2, 5, to 15 and 20 acres some of them, many can read and write, whose names have been used."[32]

Crucially, in speaking of their political liberty, their privileges, and their rights, these petitioners frame themselves not only as free men, but also as heads of households. They refer to the joy of "sit[ting] with all that are dear and near to [them] around [their] family hearth without fear of molestation, notwithstanding all that have been done to prevent it." They describe their familial aspirations in these terms: "To us it is a great deal to have something which we can call our own; something which can keep us employed and from which we may, in consequence derive our honest lively-hood for ourselves and family . . . the Mechanic, or the peasant, who owns a hut and a few acres of land, feels himself contented being certain of a home and food." These petitioners emphasize that a man's ability to work and to support his family are crucial to their understanding of what freedom means and of how best it is to be lived.

This ideal was under threat from low wages, heavy taxation, and labor competition, all of which were associated with the importation of indentured workers and the employment of women and children rather than adult men.[33] As a stipendiary magistrate reported in 1859, the "rate of wages still averages at one shilling per diem for a Male Adult and from nine pence to six pence per day for a Female." He also noted that "on many Estates they employ women to carry canes and trash, etc., work that even in the time of Slavery was usually performed by Mules and light carts" driven by men.[34] Impervious to these realities, Governor Darling refused to see the deputation and asked the Colonial Office to ignore the petitions because their "genuineness and authenticity" were questionable and he blamed them on "a few Agitators." The government stepped up its immigration schemes and increasingly excluded "Negro" subjects from the rights and privileges of British citizenship. This reinforced the need for black Jamaicans to assert their British (masculine) subjectivity by distancing themselves from non-Christian heathens and savages.

What speaking positions were available to other subalterns, in Spivak's formulation, those "strategically excluded from organized resistance," and what moral orders informed them? One striking, if forgotten, petition from this period was written to the Wesleyan Methodist Missionary Society in 1864 by Muni Sarni Thomas Lawrence. This "Petition of Coolies" gives us a partial view of Indian indentured workers recently arrived in Jamaica.[35] Muni Sarni describes how he left Madras in 1846 to work in Jamaica, read the New Testament on the ship's passage, and was converted to Christianity by a Wesleyan Methodist. In 1859 the Jamaican government made him an emigration agent and sent him first to London and then to Calcutta, where he signed up indentured laborers on the promise of a shilling a day in Jamaica. On his return to

Jamaica, however, he found the laborers living in appalling conditions of illness and poverty; the men were being paid four pence a day and women and boys two pence. Many had their feet infested by chiggers and had to have amputations. They were starving and begging in the streets, and several men had committed suicide, including one who first cut his wife's throat.

These indentured workers blamed Lawrence for enticing them to come to Jamaica, and when he returned in 1861, he reported, "they assembled in a mob and with their hoes and knives and cutlasses and sticks they fell upon me." When he tried to represent their grievances he was blackballed from work on any estates. He also reported that his wife was living with her parents and "complained to the Ministers that I provide for her neither food, nor clothing, nor habitation. The Ministers say to me, Lawrence you are a bad man, you make no provision for your family."[36] This petition shows a man cast out from his family and community; unable to seek redress from the government, he turns to his church. The response of the ministers is not recorded, however Muni Sarni's own account suggests that they encouraged the formation of Christian patriarchal families as the solution to the community's problems, deflecting a challenge to the political order onto the terrain of moral order. Yet the low wages and lack of paid labor for men suggests that the ideal of a "family wage" was untenable. It is at this traumatic "intersection between structural relations and household dynamics" within changing political-economic orders that such intra-communal violence often erupts.[37]

A few white sympathizers spoke out for the "voiceless" Coolies, many of whom did not speak English. A newspaper editor, Sidney Levien, reported that "one must see—as those who live in Montego Bay cannot close their eyes to—these wretched, hungry, houseless and outcast spectres picking up in the street a chance bone, or any putrid offal they may fall in with, to realise the suffering they hourly undergo from want of sustenance." He was unsuccessfully prosecuted for libel, as was Rev. Henry Clarke in 1862, who wrote in a newspaper that the Coolies were "cheated, starved, flogged, and murdered."[38] Indentured workers did not enjoy the same political voice and wage-bargaining power as natives, and they had few means of redress. The unusual autobiographical form of Muni Sarni's "Petition of Coolies" suggests that he did not feel entitled to claim the rights of citizenship and that he was unfamiliar with the protocols of petitioning the government.

Turning to a third example, we can see how African migrants also remained foreign and marginal within the political arena. An 1865 petition to the governor from indentured African laborers in Vere refers to their being on the island for seventeen years, but as "Foreigners" they can only beg the governor's "pity." The petitioners refer to "great distress and poverty on account of not getting sufficient work to do so as to enable [them] to maintain [their] famil[ies]." "Our Wages on some Estate this crop is from three to four shillings per week," they explain, "which cannot maintain a man and his family for the week." And they point out that the "large quantity of Coolies located on the several Estates had caused us to go about wandering for work." The petition was submitted "on account of ourselves and family" and signed by thirty-eight men who indicated next to their names (all standard English, probably indicating Christian conversion) whether they had wives or housekeepers, and their number of children. Interestingly, the ten men with wives are listed first (with a total of thirty-four children between them), followed by sixteen men with housekeepers (with a total of thirty-three children) and a few listed as alone. This would seem to indicate either that marriage conveyed a certain amount of status, or, more probably, that those of higher status could afford church weddings to mark their standing in the community and consolidate their patriarchal position.

Like other Jamaican workers these men also deployed a family discourse of the male provider in making claims on the government. Yet the fact that they listed their unwed housekeepers and illegitimate children in a public document reflects a failure to recognize the bourgeois Christian forms of the British petition. The governor once again treated this subaltern petition as an "untrustworthy" document, "purporting to be a spontaneous emanation from the Peasantry, but in reality got up by designing persons to serve their purposes."[39]

In each of these cases of subaltern petitions we see men attempting to represent the needs of their families and communities, negotiating the repertoires of British modes of public address, which are Christian, bourgeois, and masculine in design. Each petition lays claim to a male and Christian identity, but in each case it is refused recognition. Even this meager speaking position was not available to the wives, "housekeepers," and families for whom these men claim to speak: from them we have no petitions and very little direct evidence in the historical archive. Yet the place of women within families became crucial to claims of political belonging.

"To speak like honorable and free men"

Contrary to government aspersions on the character of the free population, popular documents indicate a strong commitment to family and kin, and a moral discourse founded on distinctive views of the working man's responsibilities to his family, whether or not he was married to his partner. In a famous placard posted just prior to the Morant Bay Rebellion and printed in a radical newspaper, the people of St. Thomas in the East were called on "to speak like honorable and free men at your meeting. . . . Remember the destitution in the midst of your families, and your forlorn condition. . . . You are no longer Slaves, but Free men. Then, as Free men, act your part at the meeting."[40] Here, reminiscent of the political discourse of the 1840s, freedmen's masculinity is appealed to as a personal and political identity that must be performed actively.

For these men, such public acts included speaking at public meetings and signing petitions, often representing the interests of their families. The words attributed to James McLaren at a public meeting held near Morant Bay in September 1865, for example, indicate his kin-based understanding of freedom. He was reported to have said, "myself was born free, but my mother and father was slave; but now I am still a slave by working from days to days. . . . I cannot get money to feed my family, and I am working at Coley estate for 35 chains for 1s., and after five days working I get 2s.6d for my family. Is that able to sustain a house full of family? And the people said, 'No.' "[41] This indicates how a man's wages were understood as something on which the entire family was dependent, and how freedom was understood precisely as a man's capacity to support his family. Other petitions from this period made similar complaints about low wages and the inability of freedmen to support their families.

However, these documents also attest to a complex mapping not only of male and female roles, but also of evaluative comparisons of differing types of gender performances made across classes, colors, and ethnic groups. As we have seen, the character of working-class masculinity was closely linked in a number of petitions to claims to citizenship and to enfranchisement. This vision of independent free manhood was often contrasted to the state of slavery, still burning in popular memory, and to the dependent condition of indentured labor. A further example, however, indicates another contrast drawn with the *nonworking* masculinity of the white upper class and the "brown" middle class. Rev. Samuel Holt, a preacher in St. Elizabeth, addressed a meeting held in the courthouse at Montego Bay in May 1865:

> I who have worked half my life as a slave, make now 50 barrels of sugar on my own property. . . . we black people are always told to go and plant yams. Why don't the Planters go and plant yams? Because it can't pay them; because they like sugar better. We are told, the blacks are told, to dig yams. All right. But if the poor white and brown men would pull off their coat as I am obliged to do—

I worked half of my life, as a slave, for another man, never tasting my own sweat and labour. When I want a dinner I take up my hoe and I go and dig it. If the white and colored gentlemen would set an example by going to the wharves to work, the poor blackies would follow.—("Hear, hear") But instead of that these fine people have their gentility, and go and breakfast with this friend and dine with another, and walk about with a fine suit of clothes rather than work. It is not my color alone that is idle. All such men as these tend to ruin the country.—(Loud and continued cheering).[42]

Turning on its head the common elite stereotypes of idle freedmen, Holt reveals that it is the well-dressed, upper-class "gentlemen" who will not work. He expresses here not only a sense of pride in his own labor, both as a slave and as a free small sugar producer, but also a pointed critique of the suspect masculinity of the nonlaboring classes. This is an explicitly working-class consciousness insofar as he links together the labor of many kinds of workers—those who grow sugar, those who dig yams, those who work on the wharves—and sets them against those who live in idle gentility. Thus freedmen appear to have developed a valuation of independent, laboring masculinity that was contrasted against both parasitical white upper-class masculinity and dependent indentured masculinity.

This speech was just one of many made in the spring and summer of 1865 in a series of public gatherings known as the Underhill Meetings, which were called in response to a January 1865 letter by the Baptist Rev. Edward Bean Underhill to Edward Cardwell, secretary of state for the colonies, concerning starvation and poverty in Jamaica.[43] While Baptist and Methodist missionaries gathered dozens of pages of evidence of the people's grievances, especially concerning low wages and lack of justice, Governor Edward Eyre blamed the peasantry for its own impoverishment. He claimed that the deprivation "owe[d] its origin in a great measure to the habits and character of the people," including "their natural disposition to indolence and inactivity, and to remain satisfied with what barely supplies absolute wants."[44] Referring to "social disorganization and open profligacy," he also implied that black men were unable to provide the kind of moral foundation necessary for stable Christian families. At the Colonial Office, Henry Taylor added his own view that the "Negroe Race is . . . by temperament volatile and sanguine more than others and he will not exert himself to provide against rare contingencies."[45] The poverty of black Jamaicans was blamed on their attitudes toward work and their disorganized family life. As Thomas Holt points out, this view of "the Afro-Jamaicans' 'unfitness' was coupled with—indeed, was seen to be rooted in—the failure of their households and conjugal arrangements."[46] Freedom was contested in and through debates over the character of freedmen. If unable to govern their personal lives, went the argument, they surely were unable to govern their own country.

Especially in the aftermath of the Morant Bay Rebellion of 1865, white Jamaicans echoed this charge that the people of Jamaica were not like "civilized" British people. The custos of Kingston argued that if Jamaica were to remain "the white man's home," then the government must "endeavour to build up a constitution suited to the wants of the people, introducing into it much more of the paternal, and less of the free, and give up the mischievous practice of introducing British statutes unsuited to a community not possessing British feelings or sentiments."[47] Here we see an explicit argument for rolling back freedom and introducing a more paternalistic mode of governance in order to protect white sovereignty, an argument that rests on excluding the Jamaican working classes from Britishness. This whitening, in effect, of Jamaican government was finally achieved by the abolition of representative institutions, replacing the three-hundred-year-old House of Assembly with the nonelectoral system of Crown Colony rule in 1866. Jamaicans would not take their place as "honorable and free men" until the decolonization movement of the 1940s, whose own discourses of masculine citizenship and exclusive nationalism in many ways pick up the mantle of those considered here.

Conclusion

The debate about political rights and citizenship in Jamaica from the late 1830s through the 1860s was continually framed as a debate about the character of freedmen. On one side stood the white elite's charges of idleness and unwillingness of "the Negro" to work and hence his failure as a free citizen and as a member of the British community (with little mention of women, their waged work, or their rights). On the other side was a popular discourse expressing pride in working manhood, demanding a reasonable family wage, and reinforcing the rights of the formerly enslaved to "act as free men" and claim British citizenship. Both of these discourses drew on Christian family values and patriarchal notions of masculine citizenship, embedding the free male subject in particular kinds of familial relations. The plebeian masculine discourses examined here are somewhat at odds with a historical record that indicates extensive female participation in political protest in Jamaica and the equally powerful discourses of the mother and queen.[48] This reinforces the point that subaltern men tended to produce a particular version of "family values," contingent on "on-the-ground" relations of gender, class, race, and ethnicity.

I have argued that there was a special relation between conceptions of work and conceptions of masculine freedom in postslavery public discourse. What emerges in popular speeches, petitions, and protests in this era is a close association between conceptions of free labor and an ideal of masculine provision for the family, which are understood as the basis for British citizenship. Freedmen describe their work in terms of a pride in their own labor and a desire to support their families. As a positive ideal that was most often unachievable, the family wage became the focus of debates over free labor and fair wages. Insofar as men spoke of freedom, they spoke of it not as solitary individuals but in connection with earning a living that would support a family and allow for familial (not personal) autonomy. A man's ability to nurture, protect, and provide for his family became key to the popular definition of freedom, drawn in sharp contrast to the inability to do these things under slavery and under indenture. My reading of these texts highlights subaltern men's struggles not only over being or becoming free in a generic sense, but more specifically over how to act as free men in the specific context of postslavery Jamaica.

This analysis of masculinities-in-practice can complement more general analyses of Anglo-American liberalism with a fuller account of how Jamaican freedmen drew on an identity as British subjects to gain political leverage out of a certain kind of masculine identity. This examination of popular discourses of masculinity and familial duty in postslavery Jamaica demonstrates that freedom varied depending on one's position in a racial and gender order through which the rights of citizenship were refracted. Black subaltern masculinity drew on both the liberal ideology of individualism and the Christian conception of familial duty, but it also incorporated currents of working-class radicalism. Working-class familial solidarity was a powerful mode of political claim-making, even if it remained patriarchal. Nevertheless, the masculine discourse of citizenship put at risk women's right to the privileges of freedom. Jamaican working-class women were paid less than men and were excluded from many types of work. No woman of any color could vote or serve on juries, vestries, or in any other public office (including police, militias, and other armed forces); and women were excluded from most positions in the churches and other civil institutions. Indentured women were perhaps in the weakest position of all, contracted to perform the most menial work at the lowest wages while subjected to patriarchal families, racist employers, and Afro-Jamaican resentment.

Their silence in the archives speaks volumes about the unequal structural parameters for political participation.

Alongside these gender distinctions, as I have shown, ethnic divisions and conflicts were used in political discourse to reinforce masculine claims to citizenship and the rights of Jamaican natives as against immigrants and foreigners. To act as free men required black men to participate not only in a gender order that perpetuated sexual inequality under the guise of the sanctity of the family (which is not to say that such familial solidarity is not important or even necessary to subaltern politics), but also in a racial order that pitted one ethnic group against another. Their claim to rights rested on being unlike the Coolie, and more like the free Englishman. Thus in trying to empower themselves, black men were paradoxically placed in the position of alienating others with whom they might have shared either racial solidarity (their female kin) or class solidarity (other workers). In order to foreclose working-class claims to power, the white colonial government had to redefine the Jamaican as unlike the Englishman and more like the savage African, which was done in part through casting aspersions on the moral order of their families. The Jamaican experience is indicative of wider shifts in the British Atlantic world, where forms of colonial governance were being consolidated as distinct from the traditions of democracy "at home."

Part and parcel of this retreat from representative forms of democracy was a more systematic demarcation of ethnic and racial groups as more or less civilized, underwriting the move toward a more paternalistic colonial system in which colonial subjects were treated as children, rather than as free men. In this sense the limits of nineteenth-century Anglo-American liberal political orders can be found at the intersection of contested and contingent gender orders, racial orders, and moral orders whereby masculinity became a privileged subject position only allowed to white men. In becoming "black," "British," and "manly" citizens, Jamaican freedmen claimed proximity to the white elite, but to do so they had to mark their distance from heathen foreigners, from male indentured migrants, and from women in general. Even as they struggled against the dominant racial and gender order, they were inescapably positioned by it. While subaltern black masculinity has often been examined solely in relation to dominant white masculinity, it is crucial to recognize that there are multiple orderings of gender in relation to "other others." It is the complex intersection of these multiple dimensions of race and gender in located political struggles that have had a crucial effect on the practice of freedom, citizenship, and political inclusion and exclusion in the Atlantic world.

Notes

1 Carole Pateman, *The Sexual Contract* (Cambridge, U.K.: Polity, 1988); Joan Landes, *Women and the Public Sphere in the Age of the French Revolution* (Ithaca, N.Y. : Cornell University Press, 1988); Anne Phillips, *Engendering Democracy* (University Park: Penn State University Press, 1991); Mary P. Ryan, "Gender and Public Access: Women's Politics in Nineteenth-Century America," in *Habermas and the Public Sphere*, ed. Craig Calhoun (Cambridge: MIT Press, 1992), 259–88; Nancy Fraser, "Rethinking the Public Sphere: A Contribution to the Critique of Actually Existing Democracy," in Calhoun, *Habermas and the Public Sphere*, 109–42.

2 Catherine Hall, *White, Male and Middle Class: Explorations in Feminism and History* (Cambridge, U.K.: Polity, 1992); Thomas C. Holt, *The Problem of Freedom: Race, Labor, and Politics in Jamaica and Britain, 1832–1938* (Baltimore: Johns Hopkins University Press, 1992); Anne McClintock, *Imperial Leather: Race, Gender and Sexuality in the Colonial Contest* (New York: Routledge, 1995).

3 Eileen J. Suárez Findlay, *Imposing Decency: The Politics of Sexuality and Race in Puerto Rico, 1870–1920* (Durham, N.C.: Duke University Press, 1999), 5.

4 Howard Omi and Michael Winant, *Racial Formation in the United States: From the 1960s to the 1980s* (London: Routledge, 1986), 61.

5 Rebecca J. Scott, "Fault Lines, Color Lines, and Party Lines: Race, Labor, and Collective Action in Louisiana and Cuba, 1862–1912," in Frederick Cooper, Thomas C. Holt, and Rebecca J. Scott, *Beyond Slavery: Explorations of Race, Labor, and Citizenship in Postemancipation Societies* (Chapel Hill: University of North Carolina Press, 2000), 61–106.

6 Robert Connell, *Masculinities* (London: Polity, 1995), 71; cf. Kobena Mercer, "Black Masculinity and the Sexual Politics of Race," in *Welcome to the Jungle* (London: Routledge, 1994), 131–70.

7 Errol Miller, *Marginalization of the Black Male* (Mona, Jamaica: University of the West Indies Press, 1987); Miller, *Men at Risk* (Mona, Jamaica: University of the West Indies Press, 1992); Marcus Collins, "Pride and Prejudice: West Indian Men in Mid-Twentieth-Century Britain," *Journal of British Studies* 40 (July 2001): 391–418.

8 Richard D. E. Burton, *Afro-Creole: Power, Opposition, and Play in the Caribbean* (Ithaca, N.Y.: Cornell University Press, 1997), 11. And see Hilary McD. Beckles, *Centering Woman: Gender Discourses in Caribbean Slave Society* (Kingston: Ian Randle, 1999), 157; Patricia Mohammed, "Engendering Masculinity: Cross Cultural Caribbean Research Initiatives," paper presented at the Latin American Studies Association Congress, March 2000, Miami.

9 Mimi Sheller, "Sword-Bearing Citizens: Militarism and Manhood in Nineteenth-Century Haiti," *Plantation Society in the Americas* 4, no. 2–3 (1997): 233–78.

10 Gayatri Chakravorty Spivak, *A Critique of Postcolonial Reason: Toward a History of the Vanishing Present* (Cambridge: Harvard University Press, 1999), xi. For discussions

on this point, thanks to Sara Ahmed, Claudia Castaneda, Anne Cronin, Anne-Marie Fortier, Jules Pidduck, and Imogen Tyler.

11   Sara Ahmed, *Strange Encounters: Embodied Others in Postcoloniality* (London: Routledge, 2000), 44.

12   These records were consulted in London, England, and Kingston, Jamaica, for Mimi Sheller, *Democracy after Slavery: Black Publics and Peasant Radicalism in Haiti and Jamaica* (London: Macmillan, 2000).

13   James Scott, *Domination and the Arts of Resistance: Hidden Transcripts* (New Haven, Conn.: Yale University Press, 1990).

14   Heidi Tinsman, "Household Patrones: Wife-Beating and Sexual Control in Rural Chile, 1964–1988," in *The Gendered Worlds of Latin American Women Workers*, ed. John D. French and Daniel James (Durham, N.C.: Duke University Press, 1997), 288.

15   Diane J. Austin-Broos, *Jamaica Genesis: Religion and the Politics of Moral Orders* (Chicago: University of Chicago Press, 1997); Richard D. E. Burton, "In the Shadow of the Whip: Religion and Opposition in Jamaica, 1834–1992," in *Afro-Creole*, 90–155; Catherine Hall, "Missionary Stories: Gender and Ethnicity in England in the 1830s and 1840s," in *White, Male and Middle Class*, 205–54.

16   Deborah Levenson-Estrada, "The Loneliness of Working Class Feminism: Women in the 'Male World' of Labor Unions, Guatemala City, 1970s," in French and James, *Gendered Worlds*, 210.

17   Maggie Montesinos Sale, *The Slumbering Volcano: American Slave Ship Revolts and the Production of Rebellious Masculinity* (Durham, N.C.: Duke University Press, 1997), 201; cf. Evelyn Brooks Higginbotham, *Righteous Discontent: The Women's Movement in the Black Baptist Church, 1880–1920* (Cambridge: Harvard University Press, 1993).

18   Austin-Broos, *Jamaica Genesis*, 192.

19   Swithin Wilmot, "Emancipation in Action: Workers and Wage Conflict in Jamaica, 1838–1840," *Jamaica Journal* 19 (1986): 55–62; Sheller, *Democracy after Slavery*, 147–54.

20   Monica Schuler, *"Alas, Alas Kongo": A Social History of Indentured African Immigration into Jamaica, 1841–1865* (Baltimore: Johns Hopkins University Press, 1980).

21   Resolutions of a Public Meeting at the Baptist Chapel, Falmouth, 21 Feb. 1840, in *Baptist Herald and Friend of Africa*, 26 Feb. 1840; and see 3 June 1840; 1.36, 8 July 1840.

22   Hugh Tinker, *A New System of Slavery: The Export of Indian Labour Overseas, 1830–1920* (London: Hansib, 1993 [1974]), 81; Verene Shepherd, *Transients to Settlers: The Experience of Indians in Jamaica, 1845–1950* (Leeds, U.K.: Peepal Tree, 1994); Walter Rodney, *A History of the Guyanese Working People, 1881–1905* (Baltimore: Johns Hopkins University Press, 1981); David Northrup, *Indentured Labor in the Age of Imperialism, 1834–1922* (Cambridge: Cambridge University Press, 1995); Walton Look Lai, *Indentured Labor, Caribbean Sugar: Chinese and Indian Migrants to the British West Indies, 1838–1918* (Baltimore: Johns Hopkins University Press, 1993).

23   *Baptist Herald and Friend of Africa*, 9 July 1844, 220, letter signed by T. H. P. M., 4 July 1844.

24 *Morning Journal*, 16 Aug. 1847.

25 Holt, *Problem of Freedom*, 117.

26 *Morning Journal*, 6 Dec. 1847, Report of a Meeting of the Labourers, Hanover.

27 Ibid.

28 Colonial Office 137/299 Apprehended Outbreak in the Western Parishes, 1848, enclosing Report of T. F. Pilgrim, 6 July 1848, and Proclamation of Governor Charles Edward Grey, 14 July 1848.

29 Elizabeth Petras, *Jamaican Labor Migration: White Capital and Black Labor, 1850–1930* (Boulder, Colo.: Westview, 1988), 49, 52.

30 Enclosed in CO 137/343, Governor's Despatches, Darling to CO, 4 Jan. 1859.

31 CO 137/345, Governor's Despatches, Darling to CO, 9 June 1859, enclosing petitions to the queen and to the governor, 8 March 1859, signed by Rev. Charles M. Fletcher and residents in St. Thomas in the Vale, Saint Ann, Saint Mary, Saint Andrew, and Metcalfe.

32 Ibid., encl. Samuel Rennales, Custos of St. Thomas in the Vale, 7 April 1859.

33 As Walter Rodney argued, "one of the backward characteristics of indentured labor was the employment of a significant proportion of low-paid women and juveniles—all constrained to undertake arduous and often undignified tasks in order to try and build the subsistence earnings of the family" (*Guyanese Working People*, 42).

34 CO 137/346, Governor's Despatches, 8 Sept. 1859, Gov. Darling to the duke of Newcastle, enclosing Henry Walsh to Darling, 1 July 1859.

35 Wesleyan Methodist Missionary Society, West Indies Correspondence, Jamaica, box 204, Various Reports, Petitions, etc., "Petition of Coolies," 8 Oct. 1864.

36 Ibid.

37 Tinsman, "Household Patrones," 267.

38 *County Union*, 1 April 1864, "Report on Special Sessions of the Peace Held at Court House, Montego Bay, to Inquire into Alleged Ill-Treatment of Coolies"; *Jamaica Papers*, no. 1, Rev. H. Clarke to Mr. Chamerovzow, 6 Jan. 1866.

39 CO 137/392, Governor's Despatches, Eyre to Cardwell, 5 July 1865, enclosing Petition from African Laborers in the Parish of Vere, 29 May 1865.

40 *Jamaica Watchman and People's Free Press*, 21 Aug 1865.

41 *Report of the Jamaica Royal Commission* (London: Eyre and Spottiswoode, 1866), part 2, evidence of William Anderson, 165.

42 Report from S. Levien's *County Union* enclosed in CO 137/391, Eyre to Cardwell, no. 137, May 1865.

43 National Library of Jamaica, MS 106, Underhill Letter, copy of CO 137/3.98, Underhill to Cardwell, 5 Jan. 1865. See Sheller, *Democracy after Slavery*, chap. 7.

44 CO 137/391, Eyre to Cardwell, no. 128, 6 May 1865.

45 CO 137/391, Henry Taylor, 8 June 1865, attached to Eyre to Cardwell, no. 128, 6 May 1865.

46 Thomas C. Holt, "The Essence of the Contract: The Articulation of Race, Gender, and Political Economy in British Emancipation Policy, 1838–1866" in Fred-

erick Cooper, Thomas C. Holt, and Rebecca J. Scott, *Beyond Slavery: Explorations of Race, Labor and Citizenship in Postemancipation Societies* (Chapel Hill: University of North Carolina Press), 33–59.

47   PRO 30/48/44, Cardwell Papers, Original Evidence Collected by the Jamaica Royal Commission, 1866, Evidence of Lewis Q. Bowerbank, Custos of Kingston, 9.

48   Mimi Sheller, "Quasheba, Mother, Queen: Black Women's Public Leadership and Political Protest in Post-emancipation Jamaica, 1834–65," *Slavery and Abolition* 19, no. 3 (1998): 90–117.

 ROGER A. KITTLESON

Women and Notions of Womanhood
in Brazilian Abolitionism

The abolitionist movements that sprang up across Brazil during the 1870s and 1880s were gendered, "feminized" phenomena. One of the great novelties of abolitionism in nineteenth-century Brazilian history, in fact, was the high degree of visibility that women achieved in antislavery campaigns. As both contemporary propagandists and early historians of abolition often noted, women participated in most of the activities that gave the country's emancipationism its distinctive quality—from the massive underground railroad to the street-by-street liberation of cities.[1] What very few observers have recognized, however, is that women were as much symbolically as physically present in Brazilian abolitionism.[2] Both women abolitionists and the movement's male leadership made great use of constructions of elite womanhood, as well as of the campaigning by actual women, in their efforts to build an antislavery consensus. Linking their cause to qualities deemed natural to "decent" women in nineteenth-century Brazil—particularly morality, sentimentality, and charity—abolitionists in effect heeded the great activist José do Patrocínio's admonition "to make the weakness of woman into the strongest of forces" and thus achieve "liberation through the magic of her grace."[3]

These efforts to turn Brazilian abolitionism into a feminized "crusade of Justice, Love, and Truth"[4] paralleled developments in other mass antislavery movements in the Atlantic world. In Britain, as Clare Midgley has written, "abolition . . . had unusual power in impelling women to take public action."[5] Thousands of English women signed petitions, attacked bondage in the press and occasionally in public speeches, subscribed to antislavery organizations, formed their own ladies' associations, and pursued other strategies. Contemplating this range of female activity, the emancipationist George Thompson felt moved to declare women "the cement of the whole Antislavery building."[6] In the United States, women abolitionists pursued their goal with even greater vehemence than their English counterparts. Although few were as radical as Angelina and Sarah Grimké, sisters who lectured to "promiscuous" crowds of men and women, U.S. women were major protagonists in their country's struggles against slavery. In both the United States and Britain, moreover, abolitionists played off of notions of women's roles in society as they defined their campaigns. In Anglo-American propaganda, slavery became a moral concern, a "domestic evil," that women could appropriately address.[7] Indeed, for many, women's special authority in the private sphere made their participation in the public fight for emancipation a necessity; as the Ladies' New York City Anti-slavery Society put it, abolitionists "were not calling upon [women] for anything that would interfere with the sacredness of the feminine character, but rather for what is essential to prove its existence."[8] Despite the caution apparent in such assurances, many abolitionist women in the United States and Britain eagerly transformed ideas about their benevolent and charitable nature into justifications for political mobilization in abolitionism and beyond.

U.S. and British female activists thus built on their antislavery experience to create feminist organizations.[9] In Brazil, by contrast, the inclusion of women and "womanly" traits in abolitionism did not fuel a movement for women's rights.[10] By incorporating women as nonpolitical, moral agents, antislavery campaigns brought them into public political realms from which they had previously been banned and at least theoretically recognized their authority to speak and act on the gravest question of the day. Still, though abolitionism was certainly the apex of women's public political action in nineteenth-century Brazil,[11] very few of its female agents openly challenged prevailing limits on women's lives. Calls for greater rights for women simply did not gain traction in a society still deeply patriarchal. The dowry and other institutions of formal patriarchy had faded in importance, but social, economic, and political independence remained extraordinarily difficult for women to achieve, or perhaps to conceive of as a goal. Access to higher education and "respectable" occupations was highly limited even for women of the urban elite, and (outside the royal family) no women held formal political power. Women of all classes struggled to improve their lives, of course, but they generally did so on the terms of their patriarchal society.[12]

If the feminization of abolitionism did not lead to widespread challenges of male domination, as it did in the U.S. and British cases, it was, however, a vital part of antislavery coalition-building across Brazil. The transition from slavery to free labor was, as everyone agreed, the most contentious and dangerous question facing the country after the Paraguayan War (1864–70). By the 1880s, crises of various sorts seemed ready to explode—and most of them were linked to slavery and its demise. Partisan battles over emancipationist reforms produced new levels of factionalism in Parliament (although not along existing party lines). When the army refused to track down fugitive slaves in 1886, slavery also seemed to imperil relations between civilian politicians and the military. Outside the government, meanwhile, massive slave flight from coffee plantations and growing abolitionist agitation by elites and non-elites alike left slavocrats anxious about the loss of capital and shortages of laborers. Most elites worried that emancipation could lead to a breakdown of their society's basic hierarchies.[13] To quell such fears, abolitionists reformulated their cause, tying it to women and their presumably apolitical and safe nature. The feminization of abolition was, in a sense, an implicit argument that the end of slavery would be as unthreatening to the social and political peace as the genteel *senhoras* who were helping to bring it about.

Similar dynamics of feminization characterized abolitionist movements in the North, Northeast, Center-South, and South of Brazil during the early 1880s; the success of gendered antislavery campaigns, however, differed greatly from region to region. To get at these patterns, the rest of this chapter will examine the case of the city of Porto Alegre in a comparative national perspective. The political hub of Rio Grande do Sul, a southern province with a largely pastoral economy, Porto Alegre was not as directly dependent on slavery as the plantation zones of the Center-South or the Northeast. Still, only five of the country's twenty-one provinces held more slaves than Rio Grande do Sul at the start of 1884.[14] Debates over emancipation were tense in the *Gaúcho* (Rio-Grandense) capital, as elsewhere in Brazil. Porto Alegre was not only the seat of a famously contentious regional political culture, but, by the mid-1880s, also a setting where slaves attempted to define liberty in their own fashion.[15] More to the point here, the city's emancipationist movement strengthened until it was able to proclaim the city free of slavery on 7 September 1884, nearly four years before abolition came to the Empire as a whole. What this case suggests is that feminization was integral to the creation of moderate antislavery coalitions. Where slavocrats proved intransigent, feminizing and moralizing tendencies became relatively marginal to abolitionism; especially in the coffee regions of the Center-South, more radical projects sometimes confronted slavocrats violently. In contrast, in areas and periods in which gradualist projects predominated—in cities like Porto Alegre or Fortaleza and during the years 1880 to 1884—a novel politics emerged. By introducing what had generally been considered feminine, nonpolitical, and private into the masculinized realm of public politics, abolitionists reformulated the struggle to end slavery in Brazil. At the same time, while careful to present women's contributions as an extension of, rather than a break from, the accepted roles and aptitudes of women in society,[16] abolitionists also changed, if only temporarily, the nature of public political space in Brazil—privatizing and feminizing it.

Abolitionism and Women

The abolitionists of the 1880s represented their campaigns as, in part, amplifications of the traditional concerns and activities of "decent" women. By doing so, they justified women's public activism at a magnitude never before seen in Brazilian society. At no time, however, did antislavery leaders seek to introduce women as full-fledged citizens in the formal political system. Rather, they incorporated women as subordinates—albeit subordinates with some particularly useful, inherent traits—in a wide movement that would try to persuade the men who wielded official power in Brazil.

One mark of the abolitionist movements of the 1880s was precisely their removal of the emancipation issue from the normal mechanisms and conflicts of partisan politics. Private, nonpartisan organizations dominated abolitionism in Porto Alegre and across Brazil in the 1880s, enlisting increasing numbers of women in the struggle. With a smattering of female members, charitable and social groups had for decades carried out emancipations on a small scale in the Gaúcho capital; along with newer organizations formed specifically to manumit slaves, these entities redoubled their efforts in the 1880s.[17]

As in Fortaleza, Rio de Janeiro, and other cities that developed major antislavery movements, an umbrella association emerged in Porto Alegre that coordinated the activities of the many smaller abolitionist societies (and, to some extent, subsumed them into its own). Through the Abolitionist Center of Porto Alegre (Centro Abolicionista de Porto Alegre) women gained prominence in the city's campaign against slavery. From its founding in a public meeting on 29 September 1883, most of the Center's activities took place outside the spaces of institutionalized political power, although its top leaders maintained strong links to the highest political authorities in the province, always presenting to the Provincial Assembly and Municipal Council (Câmara Municipal) the "memorials" and "Golden Book" which glowingly recorded the Center's achievements.[18] Female as well as male members of the association carried its activities into the streets of Porto Alegre. Indeed, the Center created a series of seven liberating commissions, one for each district of the capital's município (municipality). Women occupied critical places in this "system of geographical emancipation"; twenty of the forty-three agents that the

Abolitionist Center charged with the city's emancipation were women.[19] No account of the commissions' proceedings survives, but these female liberators seem to have been of tremendous importance in the efforts to persuade slave owners to accept abolition. The *Jornal do commercio*, for instance, singled out for praise dona Maria Jesuína Gay, member of the commission for the city's first district: "True angel of charity, she has been directing herself personally and tirelessly to various families, asking for their cooperation in the humanitarian work of rescuing the slaves."[20]

District-by-district liberations by abolitionist confederations proceeded even more energetically in other regions, and with women in influential positions. The pioneering abolitionists of Fortaleza, in Ceará state, finalized the liberation of their city in May 1883 after adopting a strategy of block-by-block emancipation. Senhoras were at the forefront of this movement; indeed, Maria Tomásia and five other women abolitionists issued a manifesto specifically calling for such a "general liberation" of Fortaleza.[21] Within a year other cities would follow that example. Led by the Commission of Female Liberators (Comissão de Libertadoras), "composed of ladies and girls of the best society," activists managed to free the Northeastern city of Mossoró, Rio Grande do Norte, of all slaves except those held by the "slavocratic" wife of an English resident.[22] Somewhat more modest in their aims—or perhaps, given the stronger resistance they faced, more realistic—abolitionists in the imperial capital of Rio de Janeiro set their sights on the "redemption" of particular blocks of the city center, near the offices of the leading abolitionist newspaper; not finding many slaves, they still managed to convince the residents of Rua do Ouvidor and Rua da Uruguayana both to free their captives and to sign a pledge never to use slaves in their homes or businesses.[23]

In many areas, finally, women formed their own abolitionist groups. The first of these associations appeared in São Paulo and Rio during national debates over projects for a free womb law in 1870–71;[24] many more were established during the height of abolitionist fervor in the 1880s. Not Porto Alegre, but Fortaleza, Recife, Mossoró, and Messejana (Ceará) in the Northeast; Curitiba (Paraná) and São Sepé (Rio Grande do Sul) in the South; and Campos (Rio de Janeiro) and Rio de Janeiro in the Center witnessed the formation of such organizations between 1882 and 1885. Recife's club, Avé Libertas, had sixty-six female members.[25]

This manifest dedication did not, however, earn senhoras official leadership roles in Brazilian antislavery. Indeed, women were generally relegated to complementary positions. Dona Maria Jesuína and her colleagues acted bravely on their beliefs but under the supervision of male superiors in the Abolitionist

Center of Porto Alegre. The same can be said, in fact, for the members of women's abolitionist associations. Indeed, some of these groups were initially set up as female auxiliaries, while others formed in response to pleas by male abolitionists. José do Patrocínio was particularly influential in this regard, inspiring and at times impelling women in Fortaleza and Campos to coordinate their efforts in new associations.[26] As June Hahner has argued, even the more relatively autonomous of the women's groups stopped short of assuming "policy-making" power in abolitionism as a whole.[27]

The secondary status of women was especially visible in the more common forms of female antislavery activism, which often came at events "of a purely social character."[28] Although they helped organize dances, auctions, and bazaars, women seemed mostly to provide a note of normal festivity; their presence underlined the nonpartisan style of antislavery militancy by turning meetings into pleasant, nonthreatening occasions not unlike the dances or cultural gatherings that filled the calendar of "society" members. These social touches appeared in abolitionist events across Brazil, making the early conferences in Rio "gay and exuberant affairs," as Robert Conrad has written.[29] Actresses and singers of some note—such as Chiquinha Gonzaga in Rio—participated, but so, too, did unknown daughters of decent families. The principal abolitionist association of Mossoró reported in 1883, for example, that nine-year-old Joana Emília da Costa Mendes "showed the sweetest ideal of a daughter, of a strong woman" in the "innocent and naïve discourse" she offered at a decisive gathering in September 1883.[30]

Beyond lending a sheen of entertainment and sociality to public considerations of the grave and often brutal subject of slavery, these contributions by women helped associate abolitionism with the familiar and noble practice of elite charity. Many of the occasions at which women were most visible, in fact, were explicitly charitable functions. The climax of Porto Alegre's abolitionist movement, the declaration of the city's "redemption" on 7 September 1884, was built around a *kermesse* (kermis, or charity bazaar) at which abolitionists raised money to purchase the freedom of the remaining slaves.[31] Although we know somewhat less about them, similar charity events were part of abolitionist practice across Brazil. Activists in São Paulo and Bahia had raised money in the early 1870s through auctions (*leilões de prendas*) and abolitionist fairs (usually called *kermesses*). Beginning in 1881, the larger wave of antislavery organization likewise used charity bazaars in the northern provinces of Ceará, Paraíba, and Alagoas, as well as in Rio de Janeiro in the Center-South.[32] Throughout the 1870s and 80s, moreover, women partook in less grandiose acts of charity, holding parties in Paraíba and Fortaleza at which guests would be encouraged to donate to emancipation funds or stationing themselves in front of Rio's cemeteries and churches to ask for contributions.[33]

The Old and the New: Antislavery Projects

To be sure, none of the organizational or discursive processes that comprised the gendered politics of moderate abolitionism were entirely original. The innovation of the antislavery campaigns of the 1880s lay rather in how they combined old political and cultural elements and built something strikingly new. Appeals to sentiment and morality, for example, appeared in debates on other political and social questions throughout the nineteenth century. More specifically, ethical arguments had been minor themes in formal opposition to the slave trade and to slavery itself since the late eighteenth century.[34] In the 1880s, however, activists put moralized, feminized visions of abolitionism at the service of an emerging social movement.

This development represented a shift in not only the rhetoric but also the practice of abolitionism. The inevitability of slavery's demise had been obvious to all since the Brazilian government, under heavy diplomatic and naval pressure from Great Britain, terminated the slave trade to the country in the early 1850s. Brazil had always depended on the influx of enslaved Africans to maintain its population of unfree laborers; with the main source of new slaves staunched, even the most ardent supporters of slavery conceded that the institution faced demographic doom. Despite this certainty, formal antislavery initiatives were rare and restricted to discussions among powerful men. Whether in published texts or on the floor of Parliament, those emancipationist projects generally shared a top-down, secular, and pragmatic orientation. Elite arguments for and against slavery, that is, displayed several telling features: first, a strong desire to preserve elite control of both slavery and its dissolution; second, a noticeable lack of religious inspiration (in direct contrast to antislavery rhetoric in the United States); third, an absence of overt defenses of slavery as a long-term good for Brazil; and, fourth and finally, a dogged insistence on the practical effects of any emancipationist projects.[35] Elites thus tried to effect abolition in their own manner and on their own schedule.

Although legislative actions did slowly eradicate slavery in Brazil—beginning with the end of the slave trade with Africa, continuing on to the reforms that conditionally freed children of slave mothers in 1871 and sexagenarian slaves in 1885, and culminating in the 13 May 1888 "Golden Law" of final abolition—elite foot-dragging frustrated many Brazilians. Indeed, by the late 1870s, dissident elites, members of the rising urban middle sectors, and artisans and other free workers were ready to take new steps toward abolition.[36] Given the increasingly exclusionary character of the political system, these antislavery interests had to wage their struggle outside the halls of official power; in Seymour Drescher's phrase, they developed strategies of "decentralized direct action."[37] As they organized across the Empire, abolitionists carried the gravest issue of the day to people and spaces traditionally denied roles in formal political decision making. Women were just one of the disenfranchised groups mobilized. Participating in activities in theaters, on the streets, and even on slavocrats' plantations, they helped create what literary critic José Verissimo hailed as "the most remarkable social movement that Brazil ha[d] ever had."[38]

The Old and the New: Women and Womanhood

For those now eager to effect abolition—whether elite men or those politically excluded by virtue of their gender, income, or other characteristics—this new strain of abolitionism promised finally to bring Brazil more definitively into the ranks of civilized nations and to do so through peaceful and highly civilized means. Those means would, once again, make novel use of existing features of Brazilian culture. Specifically, women's emancipationism of the 1880s expanded on a well-established female political culture and the assumptions about "decent"—that is, elite—femininity that underlay it.[39] Through charitable and voluntary associations women had long been active on matters of public concern, if in constricted ways.[40] In Porto Alegre, for instance, elite women helped administer shelters and schools for orphans (especially abandoned girls), aided the education of poor workingmen, and collected money and supplies to bolster war efforts in the Farroupilha Revolution (1835–45) and the Paraguayan War.[41] These activities connected women to vital affairs in the day-to-day life of their city and, at critical moments, to the fate of the nation. What made this participation acceptable in the preabolitionism era was the discreet nature of female roles: women remained in the background, appearing simply as helpers to men on moral and social, but not partisan political, issues.

Abolitionism moved women's activities toward the center of public politics. While doing so, however, it embraced dominant notions about women's roles in society. The overriding ideal for women in nineteenth-century Brazil—and the one that factored in the remaking of abolitionism—remained the ideal of domesticity; women were to be moral guardians of the home. In part this meant, of course, that women were generally excluded from matters of the "street"—of the public world and the issues, political and otherwise, discussed in it.[42] In the classic formulation of Gilberto Freyre, women's opportunities were restricted "to domestic service and crafts, to contact with their children, their relatives, their maids, older women, slaves. And, once in a while, . . . , to contact with their confessor."[43] Men glorified the activities that women pursued in that limited sphere and the purportedly inherent qualities that women brought to their tasks in the home. Since "the morality of the family is the morality of the human species,"[44] women's place in the home made them "the center of society."[45] As the first legislation on public education in Brazil stated in 1827, "It is [women] who make men good and bad; they are the sources of great disorder, as well as of great benefits [bens]; men mold their conduct to women's sentiments."[46] Women's strong emotions could, in these constructions of femininity, make them less rational or weaker than men; passion could overpower the intelligence of a woman.[47] On the other hand, the "feminine" capacity for emotion also gave women a special sensitivity. Women were seen as more empathetic and caring than men; by their very nature, then, women had distinctive moral and charitable propensities.

Such long-standing ideas about the character and proper social place of women continued into the age of abolitionism, appearing, for instance, in prescriptive discourse that flourished during the 1870s and 1880s. In Porto Alegre, men of all political stripes reasserted women's role as helpmate to their husbands; one wit offered a fanciful metaphor in this regard, proclaiming, "Woman is an *adjective*, who needs to agree with the *substantive man*, to exist grammatically in society."[48] Men in this period also warned of the potential dangers of autonomous action by women. Women who dared to offer inconvenient opinions in public appeared in elite male accounts as a "terrible scourge." In late 1879, for example, editors of *O conservador* felt it necessary to condemn the speeches that U.S. feminist Victoria Woodhull had recently made in England. Appalled by her promulgation of "the equality and absolute leveling of duties and rights between women and men," the paper denounced Woodhull's ideas as "imprudent, illogical, fatal to institutions." To counter the image of an independent woman proclaiming a "revolutionary doctrine" in public, they suggested a markedly different model of women's behavior: "Ensconced in her modest and placid interior, mother of a brood of children, blond and adorable, for whom she is Providence and assistance, the supreme joy, wife of a strong and honest man, . . . , the action of this woman might be much more restricted, but [will be] unquestionably more useful and wholesome."[49] In a similar vein, the enigmatic Porto Alegre playwright Qorpo Santo ventured that "women have nothing to do with governmental policy." Rather, "the political party of a woman, married, widowed, or single, is the domestic arrangement of her house, the proper moral and religious and intellectual education of those persons subordinate to her, sewing, embroidery, needle-work [os picados], music, drawing & . . ."[50]

Although "the 'woman of the hearth place' [was still] the social rule," by the 1880s opinions were softening somewhat on women's activities outside the home.[51] This change, which provided an ideological undergirding for femi-nized abolitionism, was especially evident in attitudes toward women and education. Laments about the inadequacies of the country's educational sys-tem were commonplace in the second half of the nineteenth century. Often Brazilian as well as foreign observers complained with particular bitterness about the lack of education for women; the state of women's ignorance was seen as hampering the fulfillment of their "sacred mission" of educating their children. "A woman without education," one writer explained in 1881, "will not be able to give one to her children."[52] In this sense a more complete education was to reinforce women's role in the family, influential but subordi-nate to their husbands, by refining their moral "nature." At the same time, however, men increasingly—if not universally—envisioned a greater public role for women's educative and moral aptitudes.[53] Characterized as having strong ethical, religious, and sentimental capacities, women appeared to be well suited for the role of educators, beyond as well as within the home. One provincial president of Rio Grande do Sul in 1881 called woman "the educator par excellence."[54] With the proper training, such as that provided in the Em-pire's growing number of normal schools, women could be critical instru-ments for the modernization and civilization of Brazil. In fact, to a great degree the instruction of both boys and girls came to be defined as "women's work" in the last decades of the century.[55] Although it allowed women often of rather humble origins to achieve unprecedented financial autonomy, this expanded public role was not seen as revolutionary; instead, like the charita-ble initiatives of Carmelite nuns in Porto Alegre, it reflected something like "motherhood on a larger scale."[56]

Abolitionism and Womanhoods

Whether in the public worlds of the street and central plaza or in the more private confines of a salon or drawing room, women lent considerable force to the antislavery cause in Porto Alegre and the other cities of Brazil. Of even greater consequence for abolitionism than the organizational service of female activists, however, was the association their presence made possible between abolition and key "feminine" qualities. It was not, after all, simply the existence or exertions of "virgins and ladies" in antislavery ranks but the air of morality and charity they provided that allowed abolitionism to become in large part a noble, social concern, an "act [jornada] of philanthropy," as an early historian of the movement waxed in 1925.[57] This construction of the issue and the movement broadened abolition beyond the partisan battles in— and beyond the strict control of—Parliament. The implicit aim in this appeal to the "thoughts and conscience of the nation"[58] was not, however, to risk anarchy but, on the contrary, to promote a more peaceful abolition process; according to Júlio César da Fonseca Filho, a leading figure in the Abolitionist Center of Fortaleza, antislavery activists "wanted liberation to be a festival of harmony, a symphony of love, and not a product of discord."[59] Because "feminine" concerns and characteristics were critical to this vision of abolition, we can say—without denigrating women's active contributions to the movement—that in this sense womanhood was more important to Brazil's antislavery campaigns than were the women present in the meetings and marches of the 1880s.

What connected abolition to prevailing notions of womanhood were two overlapping phenomena. First, as we have already seen, abolitionism mobilized "decent" women throughout the Empire, very explicitly bringing them out into public to assist in a cause universally deemed to be the most urgent facing the nation. Abolitionist propagandists across Brazil at times gave special attention to this development; the participation of women was taken as a sign of the morality and orderliness of antislavery efforts. Just as important, though, was a discursive transformation of the abolition question in the 1880s; although they by no means abandoned discussions of the economic, political, and cultural effects of slavery on Brazil, antislavery movements increasingly framed abolition as a moral and sentimental question.

In Porto Alegre this was never clearer than in descriptions of the grand kermesse, which gave women's activities a place of honor in the antislavery campaign. The city's press applauded the "zeal, ardor, and abnegation" of the "virgins and ladies" involved, who acted as "priestesses of Humanity."[60] By linking abolition with what was best in womanhood, abolitionists rhetorically shifted abolition out of the profane world of partisan politics—and the threats to order it might pose—and raised it to a safer and more sanctified realm.

To keep their cause in such a sphere, abolitionists launched intensified new appeals to charity and morality in the last decade before abolition. In 1883, for example, the Liberal Porto Alegre paper *A reforma* carried the horrible story of "poor Laura," whose mistress "constantly inflicted barbarous punishments on those unprotected by destiny, [those] who had the misfortune of having been born under the despotic pressures of the traffickers in human flesh." Laura's life ended in "martyrdom," when her years of suffering drove her to suicide.[61] Established practices of slaveholders also became the object of abolitionists' moral disapproval in the 1880s; the imprisonment of disobedient slaves in the city jail—without any formal charges issued against them by their owners or anyone else—led to criticism from both *senhores* and government authorities in 1884. Frustrated at the lack of official response to two earlier denunciations of this practice, the editors of *O século* cried out, "Enough already of barbarism!"[62]

While local groups registered similar complaints in other cities, Joaquim Nabuco, André Rebouças, Rui Barbosa, Silva Jardim and other prominent abolitionists launched more general criticisms against the injustice of slavery, focusing on the inhuman degradations inflicted on slaves and the denial of the most basic rights to a large proportion of the national population.[63] In a characteristic passage, Nabuco wrote of the enslaved:

> No one competes in suffering with this orphan of Fate, the waif of humankind who before his birth trembles under the whip which lashes his mother's back, who has only the remains of milk which a mother employed in suckling other children can spare for her own child, who grows up in the midst of the abjectness of his own class—corrupted, demoralized, brutalized by life in the slave hut. . . . Finally, he dies without any expression of gratitude from those who worked him so hard, leaving behind his wife, his children, and his friends, if these he had, in the same endless agony.[64]

For propagandists like Nabuco, then, the immorality of slavery permeated even the intimate relationships and emotions of Brazilians.

In fact, the theme of damage to family relations ran through much of antislavery rhetoric not only in the imperial capital but also in the provinces. Some of the most touching of the moral tales that abolitionists put forward in Porto Alegre sought to expose slavery's perversion of slave families. Damasceno Vieira's poem, "A doida (scena da escravidão)" (The madwoman [scene from slavery]), is one colorful example, describing the desperate choice that captivity led an enslaved mother to make. Stripped naked and bloodied by abuse, she fled from her master's house, hoping to save her infant son from the tortures she had known. Along the way, she fantasized about the boy, grown up, protecting her:

If you saw me innocent,
Beaten brutally,
Mistreated like the dogs,
You, in a sublime impetus,
Would kill! There's no crime
In children's avenging their mothers.

Refusing to submit to capture, she plunged from the rock on which she had been standing, preferring to carry her child with her to death than to allow him to grow up a slave.[65] Cândida Fortes, meanwhile, embedded a criticism of slavery's effects on the family in her nonetheless optimistic poem "Fructo da liberdade" (Fruits of liberty). Precisely at the triumphant moment of Porto Alegre's emancipation, Fortes told of a family of female slaves, presumably like many others, dragged into misery and robbed of a male breadwinner by their captivity. In her hopeful scenario, abolition remedied the ills that slavery had caused; one of the young daughters found honest employment as a domestic servant and with her salary provided a decent living for her mother and little sisters.[66] Fortes's tale also represented a happy ending for elites, insofar as it predicted that libertos would eagerly seek out wage labor and assume appropriately dependent places in society.

Other antislavery figures voiced anxiety about the perversions that slavery had introduced into the slaveholder's family. Although they implied that emancipation would undo the damage (thus redeeming the free as well as the enslaved), these dark warnings were a powerful part of abolitionist appeals to morality. The best-known examples come from Nabuco's Abolitionism, which outlined not only the backwardness to which slavery had reduced the economy and the political system, but also the "despotism, superstition, and ignorance" that the institution had fostered among all social classes over some three hundred years.[67] Giving the slave owner virtually unlimited power, slavery led to barbarity on the part of both masters and mistresses. Moreover, although he refrains from providing details, Nabuco also argued that the masters' sexual access to female slaves had weakened the family.[68] One of the most searing exposés of racism in nineteenth-century Brazil, Aluísio de Azevedo's 1881 novel O mulato (The mulatto) similarly exposed both the cruelty and the moral degradation of the family that slavery—and the prejudices and the promiscuity that accompanied it—had created.[69] Local abolitionists picked up on these strengthened moral critiques in Porto Alegre, where newspapers of the period carried both editorials and reports depicting slavery as perverting the natural attributes of wives and husbands, mothers and fathers.[70]

As they argued that slavery had brought ruin to all sectors of Brazilian society, abolitionists called on a sense of justice and moral outrage, depicting their movement as a moral crusade that would "redeem" Brazil and usher it at long last into the ranks of civilized nations. More than simply adding another rhetorical weapon to the arsenal of antislavery groups, this moralization of abolition feminized the issue and the campaigns that were pressing it in the 1880s. Given the paucity of ethical justifications of slavery at the time, the best that slavocrats could do in response to this abolitionist strategy was to denounce it as "exaggerated and sentimental."[71] They could not, that is, retake the moral high ground that the feminized abolitionism of the 1880s had conquered.

Conclusions: Abolitionism and Womanhood

That moral high ground, and the public prominence of feminized activism and female activists that came with it, could have been a platform from which to launch attacks on the restrictions that women faced in nineteenth-century Brazilian society. When Brazilian abolitionists endorsed the inclusion of women and women's characteristics in their campaigns, after all, they demonstrated how formulations of a moral female nature could promote the participation of women in public life.[72] In the space that the new "notion of women's social utility"[73] created for them, women in antislavery movements might pry open new social and political possibilities for themselves.

In fact, individual women active in the antislavery cause were questioning the limits on female activity in society and even in politics. Two of the most famous of these women appeared in Porto Alegre; like many of their counterparts in the Center and Northeast regions, these gaúchas began as schoolteachers but came to voice their ideas in other public forums. Luciana de Abreu, who began life as a foundling, worked her way through Porto Alegre's normal school, became director of her own school, and finally became a member of the Partenon Literário before dying in 1880 at the age of thirty-two. She used her local prestige to promote wider possibilities for women's action in society. Attacking the "egoistic and improvident legislators" and other men who had left women "condemned to ignorance, denied the rights of citizens, and reduced to slaves," she pressed for an education that did not teach "servilism" to women.[74] Unlike Abreu, Ana Aurora do Amaral Lisboa lived through the entire process of abolitionism, making public comments on each stage of that final battle through the antislavery poems she published in her hometown of Rio Pardo and the provincial capital of Porto Alegre. More unconventionally still, she contributed as a political writer to a number of major newspapers, most notably in opposition to the Republican Party government that took over Rio Grande do Sul after the fall of the Empire in late 1889. Questioned late in her life about her reputation as the "first feminist" in the region, she explained that she had merely "demanded for woman the revocation of certain prejudices that limited all of her influence to the ambit of the home."[75] Even more than Abreu and Amaral Lisboa, women such as newspaper editor Francisca Diniz in Minas Gerais and Rio de Janeiro and writer and lecturer Maria Amélia de Queiroz in Pernambuco began to claim new spaces and even new forms of economic independence for women.[76]

Such projects found little or no support, however, among leading antislavery groups. Without the support of broader discourses favoring effective equality, women who tried to turn abolitionist rhetoric about the public value of feminine morality and charity into a more radical initiative—perhaps a "feminist" one—found themselves isolated. Ultimately, efforts to claim political subjectivity for women—or for ex-slaves—remained marginalized in Brazilian abolitionism. Although it did not become an antipatriarchal movement, the emergence of a gendered abolitionism in the last decade of slavery was, however, a critical step in the consolidation of antislavery campaigns across Brazil. By associating abolition with the noble qualities and concerns of women, the feminization of abolition produced an emancipationism that was not just palatable but inspirational to wider segments of society.

The success of the feminized movements therefore lay in their articulation of an antislavery consensus in much of the country; as Nabuco noted, by 1883 the abolition struggle was "morally won" in Brazil.[77] In 1883–84 that victory translated into the consolidation of broad public organizations pressing moderate abolitionist goals in important regions. In first Ceará, then Amazonas, and months later Rio Grande do Sul, these coalitions announced the liberation of their provinces; if at times they embraced only conditional schemes of emancipation, these activists and their counterparts in other cities of the Northeast, North, and South nevertheless effected abolition within a few years of the issue's reemergence in national debates. More important, the conquests made by the moralized, feminized abolitionism set the stage for the final battle over slavery.

After all, as Nabuco also admitted, abolition was not yet won "before Parliament and government."[78] Even as their moral campaign rolled triumphantly across major regions of the country, abolitionists came up against "discouraging limits" in the centers of formal power.[79] Where slave labor was of diminishing significance to regional economies (or where, as in the extractive economy of Amazonas, it had never been central), the new abolitionism flourished. The pastoral economy of Rio Grande do Sul and the decadent sugar zones of the Northeast had for decades been exporting slaves to the coffee plantations of the central region, particularly in western São Paulo state. With weaker immediate commitments to the institution, elites in the South and Northeast could more easily turn to the question of ending slavery in an orderly manner; in those regions there was space for the urban-based feminized abolitionism to attain impressive influence. Along the booming coffee frontier of São Paulo and even more so in the older plantation zones of São Paulo, Rio de Janeiro, and Minas Gerais, by contrast, slavocrats held out ferociously against the rising antislavery tide in the cities of their own region and in other provinces. Because of the dominance of such interests in the imperial state, moreover, these planters were able to withstand much of the new abolitionism's assault and delay final emancipation past the "eclipse" of moderate abolitionism after 1885.[80] By cutting away at the support of these hardcore proslavery factions, however, feminized abolitionism left them with little but assertions of their property rights and their importance to the national economy—and the use of force. In so doing, then, the moderate movements prepared the way for radical abolitionists and the enslaved themselves to end slavery by any means necessary.

If by itself the new abolitionism did not accomplish the definitive end of slavery in Brazil, it certainly moved the country toward that event. Even more significant, perhaps, it did so through the gendered construction of a "popular movement of civic resistance."[81] In an age marked by increasingly exclusive political structures, this appearance of women and non-elite men in public spaces, mobilized around a contentious economic, social, and political question, was, to say the least, an innovation. Feminization, the gendering of the antislavery movement as a moral and feminine crusade rather than a political and male program, was key to this spread of abolition from the salon to the streets.

Notes

1 Evaristo de Moraes, A campanha abolicionista (1879–1888), 2nd ed. (Brasília: Editora Universidade de Brasília, 1986), 23–24, 37, 42; Coriolano de Medeiros, "O movimento da abolição no Nordeste" (1925), rpt. in A abolição em Pernambuco, ed. Leonardo Dantas Silva (Recife: Fundação Joaquim Nabuco, 1988), 37–55; cf. David Brion Davis, Slavery and Human Progress (New York: Oxford University Press, 1984), 297.

2 On women's symbolic presence in political events in the nineteenth-century United States, see Mary Ryan, *Women in Public: Between Banners and Ballots, 1825–1880* (Baltimore: Johns Hopkins University Press, 1990); and on the often contradictory histories of women's identities in modern public politics, see, e.g., Joan B. Landes, ed., *Feminism, the Public, and the Private* (Oxford: Oxford University Press, 1998); Sonia E. Alvarez, Evelina Dagnino, and Arturo Escobar, eds., *Cultures of Politics, Politics of Cultures: Re-visioning Latin American Social Movements* (Boulder, Colo.: Westview, 1998); and Karin Alejandra Rosemblatt, *Gendered Compromises: Political Cultures and the State in Chile, 1920–1950* (Chapel Hill: University of North Carolina Press, 2000).

3 Quoted in Raimundo Girão, *A abolição no Ceará*, 2nd ed. (Fortaleza: Secretaria de Cultura do Ceará, 1969), 136.

4 Achylles Porto Alegre, "Às porto-alegrenses," *Jornal do commercio na kermesse*, 7 Sept. 1884, 1.

5 Clare Midgley, *Women against Slavery: The British Campaigns, 1780–1870* (London: Routledge, 1992), 25.

6 Quoted in ibid., 44.

7 Quoted in Amy Swerdlow, "Abolition's Conservative Sisters: The Ladies' New York City Anti-slavery Societies, 1834–1840," in *The Abolitionist Sisterhood: Women's Political Culture in Antebellum America*, ed. Jean Fagan Yellin and John C. Van Horne (Ithaca, N.Y.: Cornell University Press, 1994), 37. In addition to the other essays in that volume, see Ellen Carol DuBois, *Feminism and Suffrage: The Emergence of an Independent Women's Movement in America, 1848–1869* (Ithaca, N.Y.: Cornell University Press, 1978); Julie Roy Jeffrey, *The Great Silent Army of Abolitionism: Ordinary Women in the Antislavery Movement* (Chapel Hill: University of North Carolina Press, 1998).

8 Swerdlow, "Abolition's Conservative Sisters," 37–38.

9 See the bibliographic essay in this volume for discussion of this literature.

10 June E. Hahner, *Emancipating the Female Sex: The Struggle for Women's Rights in Brazil, 1850–1940* (Durham, N.C.: Duke University Press, 1990), 36–41; Emília Viotti da Costa, *The Brazilian Empire: Myths and Histories*, 2nd ed. (Durham, N.C.: Duke University Press, 2000), 247–65.

11 Hahner, *Emancipating the Female Sex*, 36–41; Maria Lucia de Barros Mott, *Submissão e resistência: A mulher na luta contra a escravidão*, 2nd ed. (São Paulo: Contexto, 1991).

12 Muriel Nazzari, *The Disappearance of the Dowry: Women, Families, and Social Change in São Paulo, Brazil, 1600–1900* (Stanford, Calif.: Stanford University Press, 1991); Costa, *Brazilian Empire*, 247–65; Maria Odila Silva Dias, *Power and Everyday Life: The Lives of Working Women in Nineteenth-Century Brazil* (New Brunswick, N.J.: Rutgers University Press, 1995); Martha de Abreu Esteves, *Meninas perdidas: Os populares e o cotidiano do amor no Rio de Janeiro da belle époque* (Rio de Janeiro: Paz e Terra, 1989); Eni de Mesquita Samara, *As mulheres, o poder e a família: São Paulo, século XIX* (São Paulo: Marco Zero, 1989).

13 Cf. Maria Helena Machado, *O plano e o pânico: Os movimentos sociais na década da abolição* (Rio de Janeiro: Editora UFRJ, EDUSP, 1994).

14 Robert Conrad, *The Destruction of Brazilian Slavery, 1850–1888* (Berkeley: University of California Press, 1972), 291.

15 Joseph L. Love, *Rio Grande do Sul and Brazilian Regionalism, 1882–1930* (Stanford, Calif.: Stanford University Press, 1971); Paulo Roberto Staudt Moreira, "Os contratados: Uma forma disfarçada da escravidão," *Estudos ibero-americanos* (Porto Alegre) 16, nos. 1–2 (1990): 211–24; Roger Alan Kittleson, "The Problem of the People: Popular Classes and the Social Construction of Ideas in Porto Alegre, Brazil, 1846–1893" (PhD diss., University of Wisconsin–Madison, 1997), chaps. 6–7.

16 Cf. Hahner, *Emancipating the Female Sex*, 38.

17 Most groups were elite or middle-class associations, though a few included slave or *liberto* members. See, e.g, *Actas dos trabalhos do Centro abolicionista, aos 7 de setembro de 1884*, rpt. in "O Centro abolicionista," *Anais do III congresso sul-riograndense de história e geografia* (Porto Alegre: Instituto Histórico e Geográfico do Rio Grande do Sul, 1940), 2:187–201; Margaret Marchiori Bakos, *RS: Escravismo e abolição* (Porto Alegre: Mercado Aberto, 1985), 41; processo 1556, réus Theodoro de Oliveira Ramos et al., maço 61, Arquivo Público do Estado do Rio Grande do Sul.

18 "Centro abolicionista," 187, 189.

19 Conrad, *Destruction of Brazilian Slavery*, 191; "Centro abolicionista," 189, 191–92.

20 *Jornal do commercio*, 14 Aug. 1884; cited in Verônica A. Monti, *O abolicionismo: Sua hora decisiva no Rio Grande do Sul—1884* (Porto Alegre: Martins, 1985), 91.

21 Girão, *Abolição no Ceará*, 158–60; Conrad, *Destruction of Brazilian Slavery*, 202.

22 Raimundo Nonato, *História social da abolição em Mossoró* (n.p., 1983), 126.

23 Conrad, *Destruction of Brazilian Slavery*, 196, 202–3; Moraes, *Campanha abolicionista*, 50. Across Brazil, furthermore, women abolitionists took part even in campaigns that adopted illegal means of freeing slaves; see "Catalogo da Exposição realizada no Teatro Santa Izabel de 13 a 31 de maio de 1938" (1938), in Silva, *Abolição em Pernambuco*, 67; Medeiros, "Movimento da abolição no Nordeste," 44; Moraes, *Campanha abolicionista*, 48, 191–92; Carneiro Vilela, "O club do cupim" (1905), in Silva, *Abolição em Pernambuco*, 33; Hahner, *Emancipating the Female Sex*, 39; Girão, *Abolição no Ceará*, 121.

24 Charles Pradez, quoted in *A condição feminina no Rio de Janeiro, século XIX: Antologia de textos de viajantes estrangeiros*, ed. Míriam Moreira Leite (São Paulo: Hucitec, 1984), 140; Emília Viotti da Costa, *Da senzala à colônia*, 3rd ed. (São Paulo: Brasiliense, 1989), 417–18; Mott, *Submissão e resistência*, 77.

25 "Catalogo da Exposição," in Silva, *Abolição em Pernambuco*, 69–70. See also Girão, *Abolição no Ceará*, 65, 119, 136; Nonato, *História social*, 125–26; Octavio Ianni, *As metamorfoses do escravo*, 2nd ed. (São Paulo: Hucitec, 1988), 197; Monti, *Abolicionismo*, 111; Moraes, *Campanha abolicionista*, 51–52; Mott, *Submissão e resistência*, 78–79; Hahner, *Emancipating the Female Sex*, 39.

26 Mott, *Submissão e resistência*, 78; Girão, *Abolição no Ceará*, 65, 136.

27 Hahner, *Emancipating the Female Sex*, 38, 40.

28 *Jornal do commercio*, 1 Aug. 1884; cited in Monti, *Abolicionismo*, 85–86.

29 Conrad, *Destruction of Brazilian Slavery*, 148–49. Cf. also Hahner, *Emancipating the Female Sex*, 38–39.

30 Edinha Diniz, *Chiquinha Gonzaga: Uma história de vida* (Rio de Janeiro: Codecri, 1984), 144; "Ata da sessão da 'Libertadora Mossoroense,' em 30 de setembro de 1883," in Nonato, *História social*, 255–56. Cf. also *O século*, 23 March 1884, 2; Moraes, *Campanha abolicionista*, 39, 52–53; Osório Duque-Estrada, *A abolição (esboço historico)* (Rio de Janeiro: Leite Ribeiro & Maurillo, 1918), 108–9.

31 The uncertain fate of the collected funds became a source of scandal in Porto Alegre; e.g., "O dinheiro das kermesses," *O conservador*, 15 Oct. 1884.

32 Moraes, *Campanha abolicionista*, 192–93; Viotti da Costa, *Da senzala à colônia*, 417; Girão, *Abolição no Ceará*, 87; Medeiros, "Movimento da abolição no Nordeste," 50; Conrad, *Destruction of Brazilian Slavery*, 184, 194–95; Duque-Estrada, *A abolição*, 114–17; and cf. Jeffrey, *Great Silent Army*.

33 Medeiros, "Movimento da abolição no Nordeste," 50; Girão, *Abolição no Ceará*, 64–65; Hahner, *Emancipating the Female Sex*, 39.

34 Viotti da Costa, *Da senzala à colônia*, 353–54; Conrad, *Destruction of Brazilian Slavery*, 83, 100–103; Girão, *Abolição no Ceará*, 21; Leslie Bethell, *The Abolition of the Brazilian Slave Trade* (Cambridge: Cambridge University Press, 1970), 313.

35 See esp. Celia M. Azevedo, *Abolitionism in the United States and Brazil: A Comparative Perspective* (New York: Garland, 1995).

36 Rebecca Baird Bergstresser, "The Movement for the Abolition of Slavery in Rio de Janeiro, 1880–1888" (PhD diss., Stanford University), 1973.

37 Seymour Drescher, "Brazilian Abolition in Comparative Perspective," *Hispanic American Historical Review* 68, no. 3 (1988): 451.

38 Quoted in Carolina Nabuco, *The Life of Joaquim Nabuco*, trans. and ed. Ronald Hilton (New York: Greenwood, 1968), 117.

39 Cf. Lori D.Ginzburg, *Women and the Work of Benevolence: Morality, Politics, and Class in the Nineteenth-Century United States* (New Haven, Conn.: Yale University Press, 1990); Paula Baker, "The Domestication of Politics: Women and American Political Society, 1780–1920," *American Historical Review* 89, no. 3 (1984): 620–47.

40 Hahner, *Emancipating the Female Sex*, 36; Viotti da Costa, *Brazilian Empire*, 252; Dias, *Power and Everyday Life*, 64–65; Dain Borges, *The Family in Bahia, Brazil, 1870–1945* (Stanford, Calif.: Stanford University Press, 1992), 156.

41 "Instituto de artifices," *Jornal do commercio*, 1 Jan. 1882; "A caridade," *Colibri*, 8 May 1887; *Relatorio do Vice-Presidente da Provincia de S. Pedro do Rio Grande do Sul* (Porto Alegre: Typographia do Mercantil, 1857), appendix; "As irmãs de charidade," *O século*, 16 Jan. 1881, 1; "Associação das mães cristãs," *O conservador*, 20 Oct. 1888; Pedro Maria Soares, "Feminismo no Rio Grande do Sul: Primeiros apontamentos (1835–1945)," in *Vivência: História, sexualidade e imagens femininas*, ed. Maria Cris-

tina A. Bruschini and Fúlvia Rosemberg (São Paulo: Brasiliense, 1980); Aldira Correa Retamozo et al., *O papel da mulher da Revolução Farroupilha* (Porto Alegre: tchê!/Casa Masson, n.d.); Walter Spalding, *Pequena história de Porto Alegre* (Porto Alegre: Sulina, 1967), 223–25.

42 "The house" and "the street" are common analytical shorthand in Brazilian studies; Roberto Da Matta, *A casa e a rua: Espaço, cidadania, mulher e morte no Brasil* (Rio de Janeiro: Guanabara, 1987).

43 Gilberto Freyre, *Sobrados e mucambos: Decadência do patriarcado rural e desenvolvimento do urbano*, 3rd ed., 2 vols. (Rio de Janeiro: José Olympio, 1961), 2:93; on Porto Alegre, cf. "ãs maes de familia (fragmentos)," *O século*, 9 Dec. 1880; "Pensamentos matrimoniaes (Offerecido às leitoras do Seculo)," *O século*, 24 April 1881; "A mulher," *O século*, 3 May 1882; Moacyr Flores, "A educação da mulher na propaganda republicana positivista," *Estudos ibero-americanos* (Porto Alegre) 20, no. 2 (1990): 127; Soares, "Feminismo no Rio Grande do Sul," 133.

44 "Vicios d'educação," *O século*, 12 Oct. 1884.

45 *Annaes da Assembléa Legislativa da Provincia de S. Pedro do Rio Grande do Sul: 20a. legislatura, segunda sessão, 1882* (Porto Alegre: Typ. da Reforma, n.d.), appendix, 24 April 1882, 6.

46 Guacira Lopes Louro, "Mulheres na sala de aula," *História das mulheres no Brasil*, org. Mary del Priore, 2nd ed. (São Paulo: Contexto, 1997), 447.

47 Carlos de Iracema, "A mulher ante o fanaticismo religioso," *O século*, 14 Oct. 1883, 21 Oct. 1883; Flores, "Educação da mulher," 121–22.

48 "Grammatica das mulheres," *O século*, 3 Oct. 1886.

49 "Victoria Woodhull: Uma oradora americana," *O conservador*, 29 Nov. 1879.

50 [José Joaquim de Campos Leão] Qorpo Santo, *Enciclopédia ou seis mezes de uma enfermidade* (Porto Alegre: Typografia Qorpo Santo, 1877), 66; cf. "A mulher," *A reforma*, 21 Nov. 1875; "Ainda a mulher," *A reforma*, 23 Dec. 1875; and Flores, "Educação da mulher," 127.

51 "Dois suicidios," *O mercantil*, 5 May 1888. On changes in patriarchy in this period, see Freyre, *Sobrados e mucambos*; Maria ãngela d'Incao, "Mulher e família burguesa," in del Priore, *História das mulheres*; Viotti da Costa, *Brazilian Empire*, 247–65; Hahner, *Emancipating the Female Sex*, chaps. 1–2.

52 "Ãs maes de familia (fragmentos)," *O século*, 9 Dec. 1880; "Economia domestica: Breves considerações offerecidas às mãis de familia a proposito das amas," *O século*, 18 Sept. 1881; "Vicios d'educação," *O século*, 12 Oct. 1884; Louro, "Mulheres na sala de aula," 447; Hahner, *Emancipating the Female Sex*, 13–14; Leite, *Condição feminina*, 68–73, 74–78.

53 Hahner, *Emancipating the Female Sex*, 20–26; Lopes Louro, "Mulheres na sala de aula," 443–54.

54 *Falla com que o Exm. Sr. Dr. Joaquim Pedro Soares Presidente da Provincia abrio a 1a. sessão da 19a. legislatura da Assembléa Legislativa Provincial no dia 7 de março de 1881* (Porto Alegre: Typ. da Reforma, 1881), 4.

55 Lopes Louro, "Mulheres na sala de aula," 448.

56 Hahner, *Emancipating the Female Sex*, 24–25. Viotti da Costa reports, though, that in 1869 directors of a Rio school felt it necessary to reassure parents that a more balanced education would not "promote women's emancipation"; *Brazilian Empire*, 253.

57 Medeiros, "Movimento da abolição," 45.

58 *Gazeta de notícias* (Rio de Janeiro), 21 Feb. 1881, in José do Patrocínio, *Campanha abolicionista: Coletânea de artigos* (Rio de Janeiro: Fundação Biblioteca Nacional, Dep. Nacional do Livro, 1996), 37.

59 Quoted in Girão, *Abolição no Ceará*, 135.

60 *Jornal do commercio na kermesse*, 7 Sept. 1884; "Centro abolicionista," 199.

61 "Scenas da escravidão," *O mercantil*, 8 June 1883.

62 "Encarcerados," *O século*, 24 Aug. 1884; "Presos sem culpa," *O século*, 5 Oct. 1884.

63 Robert Brent Toplin, *The Abolition of Slavery in Brazil* (New York: Atheneum, 1972), 115–16.

64 Joaquim Nabuco, *Abolitionism: The Brazilian Antislavery Struggle*, trans. Robert Conrad (Urbana: University of Illinois Press, 1977), 34–35.

65 Damasceno Vieira, *A musa moderna* (Porto Alegre: Typ. do Jornal do commercio, 1885), 75–79; cf. "Infeliz escravo," *O mercantil*, 20 April 1883.

66 *Jornal do commercio na kermesse*, 7 Sept. 1884; see also Cândida Fortes, her "Canto da liberdade" on the same page.

67 Nabuco, *Abolitionism*, 10, 19–20; and see Viotti da Costa, *Brazilian Empire*, 164.

68 Nabuco, *Abolitionism*, 32, 101; Azevedo, *Abolitionism*, 42–43.

69 Aluísio Azevedo, *Mulatto* (1881), trans. Murray Graeme MacNicoll (Austin: University of Texas Press, 1993).

70 "A mulher brasileira é esclavocrata?," *O mercantil*, 17 March 1884; "Um pai no tempo da escravidão," *O mercantil*, 28 Aug. 1883.

71 This was Antonio Prado's charge against the proposed Sexagenarian Law in 1885, quoted in Moraes, *Campanha abolicionista*, 95.

72 Cf. Ginzburg, *Women and the Work of Benevolence*, 18 and passim.

73 Silvia Marina Arrom, *The Women of Mexico City, 1790–1857* (Stanford, Calif.: Stanford University Press, 1985), 49.

74 Luciana de Abreu, "Prelecção," *Revista mensal da Sociedade Parthenon Litterario*, 2nd. ser., 20th year, no. 12 (Dec. 1873) (Porto Alegre: Typ. do Constitucional, 1873), 535–39; "Revista semanal," *O colibri*, 15 April 1877, 4; Soares, "Feminismo no Rio Grande do Sul," 137–38; Hahner, *Emancipating the Female Sex*, 54; Mott, *Submissão e resistência*, 75–76; Andradina de Oliveira, *A mulher riograndense*, 1st ser., *Escriptoras mortas* (Porto Alegre: Oficinas Graphicas da Livraria Americana, 1907), 43–49.

75 Walter Spalding, *A Grande Mestra: Ana Aurora do Amaral Lisboa eo castilhismo—A vide e a obra da Grande Mestra* (Porto Alegre: Sulina, 1953), esp. 147–50, 164–67; Soares, "Feminismo no Rio Grande do Sul," 140–41.

76   Hahner, *Emancipating the Female Sex*, 31–39.

77   Nabuco, *Abolitionism*, 35.

78   Ibid.

79   Davis, *Slavery and Human Progress*, 294–95.

80   This usage comes from Joaquim Nabuco, *O eclypse do abolicionismo* (Rio de Janeiro: n.p., 1886).

81   Cf. Borges, *Family in Bahia*, 20.

 CAROL FAULKNER

A Nation's Sin: White Women and U.S. Policy toward Freedpeople

As politicians, planters, and former slaves struggled with the material reality of freedom in the aftermath of the American Civil War, white antislavery women joined the fight to shape the outcome of emancipation, applying abolitionist and feminist ideals to Reconstruction policy. Though antislavery activism contributed to the growth of the women's rights movement around the Atlantic world, historians describe a trajectory away from racial equality in the United States, where suffragists adopted racist rhetoric following the 1868 extension of the vote to black men only.[1] Yet many abolitionist feminists continued to link the rights of women to those of former slaves, organizing a broad social movement to feed, clothe, and educate freedpeople despite public fears of black dependency. Abolitionist feminists not only fought for white women's suffrage, but also for a broad reconstruction of the relationship between the state and its citizens, including expanded federal aid for former slaves, women's participation in public policy, and universal political rights.

White women's involvement in government and in aid to former slaves provoked a national debate and exposed a gender divide over Reconstruction policy. Building on studies of the intersection of gender and race in the Reconstruction South, this examination of Northern white women's activism further illuminates the gendered political conflicts that followed emancipation.[2] Employing middle-class gender ideology, women in the freedmen's aid movement asserted control over the welfare of former slaves by noting women's traditional role as agents of benevolence. They also sought recognition for their work in the form of paid government commissions and a more active role in the political life of the nation. As white abolitionist feminists embraced the transformative possibilities of an activist federal government, however, their opponents invoked racial and sexual stereotypes to limit both women's role in Reconstruction and the radical changes to the social and political order that these women demanded.[3]

Julia A. Wilbur and Josephine S. Griffing exemplify the white abolitionist women who pushed the federal government to offer greater material assistance to destitute freedpeople. Both entered the freedmen's aid movement as experienced antislavery and feminist activists. They believed that white women should advise and advocate for former slaves, particularly freedwomen. But even as they established their political authority as caretakers of former slaves, Wilbur and Griffing urged the nation to focus on its obligation to freedpeople rather than on the preoccupation with dependency. Like many policy makers throughout the Atlantic world, American politicians and Freedmen's Bureau agents worried that former slaves might give up plantation labor and become idle paupers, existing solely on government largesse.[4] Consequently, these men singled out Wilbur and Griffing for criticism, drawing on the cultural link between race, gender, and dependency to limit women's participation in Reconstruction. Their individual histories thus offer important insight into the larger political conflict over aid to former slaves.

Networks of abolitionist women supported the relief efforts of Wilbur and Griffing. Wilbur (1815–95), an unmarried Quaker schoolteacher from Rochester, New York, became involved in the antislavery movement in the 1850s, when she joined the Rochester Ladies' Anti-slavery Society (RLASS).[5] British abolitionist Julia Griffiths, a friend and ally of Frederick Douglass, established the RLASS in 1851 to support Douglass's newspaper, aid fugitive slaves en route to Canada, and mend factionalism in the antislavery movement.[6] Griffiths and other British women corresponded with the women of the Rochester Society, asking for information on fugitive slaves and the sectional conflict; they also contributed money to the RLASS and exchanged items to sell at antislavery fairs.[7] Their support continued after the abolition of slavery in the United States, as women seized on the new opportunities provided by war and emancipation.

The American Civil War transformed abolitionist politics, bringing former radicals into the mainstream of American life. Prior to the outbreak of violent conflict in 1861, Josephine Griffing (1814–72) combined her career as an agent for the Western Anti-slavery Society with participation in the burgeoning feminist movement.[8] As a follower of William Lloyd Garrison, Griffing advocated the immediate abolition of slavery, but she rejected political or violent means in favor of moral suasion. Garrisonian abolitionists had vowed to separate themselves from a government that condoned slavery. But, during the war,

Griffing and other abolitionist feminists lobbied for a constitutional amendment abolishing slavery.[9] The Thirteenth Amendment, passed in 1865, confirmed abolitionist feminists' investment in the federal government, and this victory shaped their approach to women's rights and freedmen's aid after the war. In 1864, Griffing petitioned Congress to commission women as freedmen's agents "to look after, and secure the general welfare of these women and children of the freedmen."[10] Griffing proposed a new partnership between women and the state, expressing particular interest in two populations already ceded to the realm of the feminine: freed women and children. That same year, she left her husband and moved to Washington, D.C., to work with the government and former slaves.

When Griffing moved to the nation's capital the freedmen's aid movement was already well underway. The process of reconstruction began as soon as the Union Army occupied parts of the Confederacy and found itself in control of abandoned land and slaves. Teachers, missionaries, investors, and superintendents headed south to aid the military in managing plantations and former slaves. The Rochester Ladies' Anti-slavery Society sent Wilbur to Alexandria, Virginia, in October 1862. They believed that emancipation opened a new field of labor for female abolitionists in "comforting, cheering, advising, educating, the *freed* men, women and children."[11] In Alexandria, Wilbur worked with the military and other reformers to feed, clothe, and shelter slave refugees.[12] In 1865, she also moved to Washington, D.C., where she acted as a visitor for the newly established Bureau of Refugees, Freedmen, and Abandoned Lands (the Freedmen's Bureau).[13]

Abolitionist women embraced the Freedmen's Bureau as a way to bring women's reform into national politics. Staffed by the military, the agency oversaw the transition from slave labor to a free plantation system in the South, and directed the efforts of male and female reformers. But as Josephine Griffing wrote in a letter to William Lloyd Garrison, she hoped the bureau would be the basis for a "new & purer system of Politics," which would include women's moral influence. She wanted a man to head the Freedmen's Bureau who was "fully committed to give us *women* what we do so much need in the *Gov.*—in *Commissions* to carry forward the work of Relief to the Freedmen which he sees to be *our* work *legitimately.*"[14] Though Griffing used the all-encompassing term "women," as a Garrisonian abolitionist she did not confine her meaning to white women, and she worked closely with Sojourner Truth in the freedmen's aid movement.[15] In a remarkable fulfillment of Griffing's vision, General Oliver Otis Howard, the commissioner of the Freedmen's Bureau, appointed her assistant to the assistant commissioner for the District of Columbia. By the end of the decade, many abolitionist women worked directly for the Bureau.

Abolitionist women also believed that the Freedmen's Bureau could help the nation atone for its complicity in the national sin of slavery. As Julia Wilbur wrote, "The Government of the U.S. having sanctioned the robbing of these people, not only of their earnings, but of themselves through the long years that are past, it now owes them a debt it can never repay nor can it ever repair the wrongs it has done the colored race." Wilbur told the Rochester Society that, "in this hour of trial the liberated slave is well entitled to assistance from the Government; and I believe the Government means to deal fairly by them."[16] Rather than criticizing former slaves for their dependence on government benevolence, as many white Americans did, Wilbur emphasized the nation's dependence on slave labor. She and other abolitionist women lobbied the Freedmen's Bureau to extend greater relief to freedpeople as payment for this debt, and they insisted that women act as public advocates for former slaves.

Women's perspective on Reconstruction grew from their own position in American society. In the mid-nineteenth century, Americans believed that some members of society, including women, children, and slaves, were inherently dependent.[17] Abolitionist feminists in the freedmen's aid movement viewed the struggles of former slaves as reminiscent of their struggle for economic independence and political equality. They rejected free labor policies that stipulated a stark dichotomy between independence and dependence, thus continuing the exclusion of women and former slaves from equal citizenship. Instead, abolitionist feminists saw dependence as a temporary condition, produced by years of oppression and inequality. These women urged the federal government to repay freedpeople for their labor and protect those irreparably injured by slavery.

Abolitionist women's efforts for freedpeople belonged to a larger women's political culture, which posited a specific set of women's values based in motherhood, religion, and domesticity.[18] Both Griffing and Wilbur used the gendered language of women's reform to raise national awareness of freedpeople's plight. Pointing out that not all former slaves were able-bodied men, Griffing wrote, "There is a great distress, and alarm felt among the old and infirm, that after giving their labor and strength to slavery, they are at last to die of hunger." She highlighted the situation of the wives, children, and elderly relatives of black soldiers, believing them "worthy objects of charity." Griffing emphasized the inevitability of dependency for these groups and argued that aiding them would be "assisting those only who were unable by their own efforts to procure the necessaries of life, and were not otherwise provided for."[19]

By focusing on the needs of freed women and children, abolitionist women also reinforced their vision of gender solidarity. Building on antislavery images of sisterhood between white and enslaved women, Griffing argued that Northern women understood the "wants and necessities" of freed women and children.[20] And, as a self-supporting woman, Griffing identified with freedwomen's struggle to support their families. She noted that "women who go out to service put their little ones in bed or cover them with rags on the floor, and go in search of five or ten cents' worth of work to buy a stick of wood and a loaf of bread."[21] Though she believed in finding work for freedwomen and promoting women's economic independence, Griffing used domestic images to stress the necessity of immediate relief for women and children. She argued that freedwomen could not support their families by working for minimal wages because they needed childcare, food, and housing.[22]

Abolitionist women cited both gender and morality as justification for their participation in aid to freedmen. In Alexandria, Wilbur immediately noticed the importance of a woman's presence, especially for freedwomen: "there are women here that need woman's care & counsel & kind words." Aside from Wilbur and military officials, the male reformers with whom Wilbur boarded and worked were the only individuals aiding freedpeople in Alexandria. This situation horrified Wilbur. She emphasized her opposition to white men working closely with freedwomen: "there are none but white men to care for them & minister to their most delicate necessities. I was sick. I was disgusted." Wilbur told the Rochester Society that the white men treated freedwomen with "coarse familiarity."[23] She and other members of the RLASS concluded that women could care for freedwomen in ways that male reformers could not.

Griffing and Wilbur also pushed the bounds of appropriate women's charity by criticizing government policy, especially the latter's pressure on freed people to immediately transform into self-supporting wage laborers. In Alexandria, Wilbur argued for government aid to slave refugees who needed temporary assistance before they found work and shelter. She suggested that "the new comers, and such as are disabled for a time, and the sick who are not fit subjects for the hospital, should receive rations until they have a chance to keep themselves." When the "Government" planned to withhold rations, Wilbur angrily proclaimed that if this "is done to make it appear they are not needed it is a gross deception."[24] Both Wilbur and Griffing questioned government policy that neglected the real needs of former slaves. Rather than stigmatizing these groups as "dependent," they focused on the specific circumstances of widows, children, and refugees, among others, arguing that their situation derived not from racial or sexual inadequacies but from war and the unraveling of the institution of slavery.

But women confronted opposition to both their public participation and their demand for material aid to freedpeople. Reconstruction policy makers, including Republican politicians, bureau agents, and male reformers, sought to establish former slaves as self-supporting wage laborers, preferably on Southern plantations, as quickly as possible. Policy makers believed that with equal political and civil rights freedmen would be able to defend their families and their freedom of contract.[25] To facilitate the independence of freedmen, the Freedmen's Bureau resisted offering freedpeople direct assistance. Believing in African Americans' propensity for dependency, General Howard, commissioner of the Freedmen's Bureau, vowed not to support former slaves "in idleness."[26] Similarly, the male abolitionists who headed the freedmen's aid movement emphasized "laissez-faire equalitarianism," and doubted the wisdom of charity to former slaves.[27] Though they shared with antislavery women a commitment to racial justice, male abolitionists gained new ties to the political establishment as the vanguard of antislavery sentiment. Comfortable in their new social position, they allied themselves with more conservative reformers. The American Freedmen's Union Commission, run by abolitionist J. Miller McKim, reflected this new conservatism. Following the Freedmen's Bureau and political reality, the commission and its affiliated societies turned their focus away from relief to educational endeavors.[28] White men throughout the North put their faith in political rights as the basis for equality, a solution that disenfranchised women viewed with skepticism.

Northerners' suspicions regarding female reformers confirmed their objections to direct material aid for former slaves. Despite women's extensive involvement in the war effort, as nurses and in voluntary organizations, many white Americans remained contemptuous of women who stepped out of the domestic sphere.[29] As the only Northern white woman among the male reformers and military personnel in Alexandria, Julia Wilbur experienced hostility in the first few months following her arrival in 1862. Wilbur met opposition not only because of her sex, but also because of her perspective on aid to former slaves. As she informed the Rochester Society, "it has been said that my only object is to see that the contrabands have an easy time, and in this light I have been misrepresented to the War Department."[30] Wilbur pursued this conflict, as she initially reported Provost Marshal Henry H. Wells and Rev. Albert Gladwin to the War Department. Wilbur disapproved of Wells's policy of renting inadequate barracks to slave refugees, and she believed Gladwin was a racist and "unfit" for the position of superintendent of freedmen. With these men in charge, she asserted, former slaves were in danger of becoming "the prey of selfish and designing men."[31] Instead, she proposed that the military grant humane abolitionists control over former slaves, and she asked Secretary of War Edwin Stanton for "a little more authority": "There is much that I do that does not come within a man's province, & perhaps it is quite as necessary & important as any work that is done. . . . Although a *woman* I would like an appointment with a fair salary attached to it."[32] Wilbur's desire for a salaried position tested the boundaries between women's voluntary and paid labor, laying new claims to recognition and pay for women's work.[33]

Provost Marshal Wells responded to Wilbur's charges by noting both the sexual and racial dangers in her proposals for the care of former slaves. Wells objected to being "directed by" a woman regarding the contrabands. He criticized Wilbur's sympathetic approach to freedmen's aid, distinguishing his actions as calculated "to benefit the colored people. and not render them more dependent and indolent than they now are." Wells believed former slaves were predisposed to dependency and that Wilbur's policies only encouraged pauperism. In addition, Wells denigrated Wilbur's desire to have the "control" and "management" of former slaves in Alexandria, a reaction based on both her policies and her sex.[34] Wells viewed the presence of a female agent, advocating policies promoting "indolence," as indicative of the pitfalls of women's involvement in military issues. Gladwin concurred. Wilbur reported that Gladwin had told her, " 'I am out of my sphere, & he does not like to see a woman wear men's clothes.' "[35]

To counter her opponents, Wilbur expressed her commitment to "teaching the liberated slaves to rely upon themselves." But she also stressed her continued dedication to freedmen's relief: "I would not turn a deaf ear to their necessities and ignore their rights entirely. The situation of the Freedmen is so peculiar that many difficulties must be encountered in their struggle to live as becomes a free people. I hope I shall never be found adding one iota to their burden, and I mean never to cease speaking in their behalf until they are in a situation to speak for themselves."[36] Wilbur saw freedpeople as her subjects, who relied on her to speak for them and provide them with necessities. To a certain extent, Wilbur's own position depended on freedpeople's continued need for assistance. But while she valued her position as benefactor, and relied on her work as a freedmen's agent to support herself, Wilbur did everything in her power to vindicate freedpeople from accusations of "idleness."

Wilbur contended that government policies actively discouraged dependence. Freedmen and women worked two months before receiving any wages, from which the government deducted five dollars per month for the "Contraband Fund" to pay the expenses of the sick and destitute. Wilbur emphasized that many freedpeople were independent of the state: "Many of the Freed people have never received any assistance from Government. They have sustained themselves wholly and are justly proud of doing so."[37] Howard's numbers substantiated Wilbur's statements. He reported that in 1865 the total amount the Freedmen's Bureau received from the Contraband Fund was more than $466,000.[38] Wilbur filled her reports with evidence of freedpeople's self-support. The freedpeople expected "to help themselves, and they do so," she wrote. "It is slander upon these people to say that they are dependent upon Associations for clothing, and upon Government for food."[39] Former slaves also asserted their independence from government support; like Wilbur, they noted whites' dependence on the labor of African Americans. A delegation of Richmond freedmen asserted that "none of our people are in the poor-house, and when we were slaves, the aged and infirm who were turned away from the homes of hard masters, who had been enriched by their toil, our benevolent societies supported while they lived, and buried when they died; and comparatively few of us have found it necessary to ask for government rations, which have been so bountifully bestowed upon the unrepentant rebels of Richmond."[40] Despite these protests against charges of indolence and dependency, the military and the government continued to combine gender and racial arguments to distance themselves from direct relief of former slaves.

Griffing's appeals on behalf of freedpeople also antagonized the male leaders of the freedmen's aid movement. Reformers and bureau agents expressed outrage at Griffing's influential position and sought to limit her various responsibilities as a distributor of relief, employment agent, and industrial-school teacher. But Griffing's efforts to obtain material aid for freedpeople aroused the most opposition. By appealing for aid to the old, the sick, and those desperately requiring help, she hurt her career as a commissioner of the Freedmen's Bureau. Howard revoked her appointment as assistant to the assistant commissioner for Washington, D.C., on 7 November 1865, only five months after she accepted the position.[41]

Griffing concentrated on raising Northern awareness of freedpeople's "woful" condition in the District, undermining the efforts of male Freedmen's Bureau agents who claimed that the crisis was over, their efforts had been successful, and the freedpeople were self-supporting. In a controversial appeal, published in antislavery and Republican newspapers, Griffing described the condition of "twenty thousand" freedpeople who had migrated to the city during the war. "A host of miserable women, with large families of children, besides old, crippled, blind and sick persons" sought refuge in the District, according to Griffing, many of whom lived in "shanties, garrets, cellars, and stables" and were without wood, beds, blankets, food, or clothing. Griffing stated, "mothers and sons and wives and children, of soldiers still in Government service as Regular U.S. troops, are suffering for the necessaries of life."[42] In "A Plea for Humanity," Griffing again outlined her concern for "old men, invalids, and babes" and "wives and mothers of men in Government service." After giving examples of specific cases, Griffing pointed out that "these cases might be multiplied. Their name is legion." She called on the "friends of humanity" "to aid now" and that "in succoring these victims of a nation's sin ye are succoring Christ."[43] Though Griffing hoped that her appeals would highlight the inevitability of dependency and the necessity of charity, her appeals prompted criticism from male reformers and bureau agents.

In October 1865, Jacob R. Shipherd of the American Freedmen's Aid Commission, an abolitionist organization, explained the danger of Griffing's appeal to Howard: "Mrs. Griffing is simply irrepressible: & yet she must be repressed, so far as you and I have to do with her, or else we must bear the odium of her folly. She still represents the '20,000 utterly destitute' as needing *outright support* from Northern charity." Shipherd informed Howard that Griffing's strategy was politically unsound, arguing that she provided fuel for those who wanted a quick reconciliation with the South at the expense of former slaves: "Located as she is, & endorsed by the head of the Bureau, she sends her appeal everywhere to the glee of the copperheads, who want no better reading to confirm their 'I told you so!' but to the sore annoyance of all sensible men." He urged Howard to fire Griffing: "Mrs. Griffing is hopelessly unfit for the responsible position she fills, & cannot be too permanently separated from it."[44] Griffing not only challenged the efficacy of Shipherd's policies, but her position as a woman, "endorsed by the head of the Bureau," undermined Shipherd's authority. Shipherd and other male abolitionists proposed that the Bureau "help a man become more manly," and Griffing's opinions and gender obstructed that vision.[45]

Shortly thereafter, the Freedmen's Bureau issued a press release dissociating itself from Griffing and her appeals: "This Bureau has not received any funds from Mrs. Griffing and does not assume responsibility of the collections she is making. The number of actual dependents upon the Gov't for support, through this Bureau in Washington, varies between three and four hundred."[46] Agent S. N. Clark explained to a concerned citizen that Griffing was no longer connected to the bureau: "That connection has ceased. She has no authority to solicit funds for the Freedmen's Bureau and no official information to sustain her statements of the suffering among the Freedmen."[47] Clark's strong disavowal of Griffing resulted from her accounts of Washington freedpeople; and he hurried to reassure the public that the bureau did not support a large number of dependent freedpeople. His denial that Griffing had "official information" assuaged the fears of those who worried that a woman dictated Freedmen's Bureau policy.

Even though she was no longer a commissioned official of the Freedmen's Bureau, Griffing still challenged male agents. After her dismissal, she continued to be associated with the Freedmen's Bureau, working as an agent for the National Freedmen's Relief Association of Washington. She also acted as a visitor for the bureau, which gave financial support to her employment agency and industrial school. Bureau agents criticized Griffing because her activities violated free labor ideals of independence and self-reliance, but their complaints were also thinly veiled criticisms of women stepping beyond their sphere. For example, William F. Spurgin, local superintendent of the Freedmen's Bureau in the District, blamed Griffing and other reformers who shared her views for encouraging freedpeople's dependence on the government. He believed Griffing was one of those individuals who "seemingly actuated by the best of motives visit among the colored people with a view of ascertaining cases of distress." But in Spurgin's view, these visitors did not distinguish between the deserving and undeserving poor: "They bend ear to their complaints, make no discrimination between those able to work and those unable and advise them to apply to the Freedmen's Bureau for assistance. Some of these should be assisted, others should not." In other words, he believed Griffing advised freedpeople to apply for aid when they did not really need it. This gendered criticism of Griffing's methods labeled her overly sympathetic, indiscriminate, and generous to a fault.

Spurgin felt that freedpeople should be encouraged and even forced to work. He also believed that freedpeople themselves would willingly be supported by the bureau if not told otherwise:

> I am deeply impressed with the opinion that persons able to work, white and colored, should be forced to do so and as this Bureau is held responsible for the colored people, I have the honor to recommend that all charitable associations and individuals working for their good be made to understand this point. This would lessen the dissatisfaction among the freedmen and do away with the idea prevalent among them that the Government is always to be responsible for their support.[48]

Spurgin's philosophy emphasized the virtues of wage labor for all freedpeople. Like Shipherd, Spurgin disapproved of Griffing's appeals, which "made an exhibit of the great destitution and starvation of the freedmen of the District." He described her reports as "basic fabrications." Spurgin concurred with Clark that these reports reflected badly on the freedpeople and the government: "These reports are a libel upon the freedmen themselves, upon the citizens of the District, and upon the Government which has provided and still continues to provide all the assistance necessary for the relief of the destitute colored poor of the district."[49] Griffing's appeals for aid to destitute freedpeople provoked hostility and backlash. While male reformers and bureau agents promoted independence and free labor as the basis for freedom, Griffing rejected this approach and advocated government protection and aid.

Tensions over gender, race, and dependency grew as many politicians and bureau agents called for an end to government assistance. At every opportunity, Howard cut the supply of rations and turned the bureau's efforts in other directions. By 1867, Howard wanted education, in his view, the best kind of aid, to be the primary focus of the agency. As he recalled in his *Autobiography*, "While we were laboring hard to reduce the number of freedmen's courts, hospitals, asylums, and eleemosynary features generally, we extended the school operations."[50] By the end of 1868, Howard claimed that he felt comfortable ending the operations of the bureau: "Matters in all respects touching Bureau operations during the year gave assurance that at the end of the term fixed by law, 16 July 1868, I could lay down my heavy burden of responsibility with good hope of the future."[51] Howard maintained that the Freedmen's Bureau had largely met its goals. Despite the protests of abolitionist women, most Americans agreed.

As the staff of the Freedmen's Bureau moved to close its operations, Wilbur and Griffing argued that the nation had not yet met its obligations to former slaves. Both women emphasized the needs of the aged and sick who could not survive without government aid. To promote a home for dependent freedpeople, Wilbur wrote, "Many of these persons became helpless and dependent through the hardships and abuses of slavery; and it seems quite right that they should continue to receive, as they have done since the first of their being free, the special care of the Government which so long upheld a system calculated to make its victims helpless and dependent." Wilbur stressed that the nation owed former slaves for their forced labor. An asylum for dependent freedpeople would be "a perpetual rebuke to the atrocities of the past."[52]

Griffing resisted the end of the Freedmen's Bureau's relief work by personally appealing to Howard's famous Christian sympathies. In 1869, Griffing wrote Howard that "there still remains a duty to be performed in feeding and clothing the worn-out Slaves not properly belonging to the Hospital or Poorhouse, and who are in this District Wards of the Gov't."[53] On 22 November 1870, Griffing informed Howard that forty-nine elderly people had visited her and "applied for 'just a little,' as they had no fire and I could only supply a few of those absolutely sick in their shanties & homes. For this purpose alone the Sec. let me have two cords for this week now all gone and thinks he may let me have a small amount next week for the aged who are sick." Griffing felt strongly that their care was her responsibility, General Howard's, and the government's: "At this moment a dozen old women and men, standing waiting at my door—some of them actually shaking with ague—asking for clothes, wood and shoes & stockings. I am in distress on their account, as from years of working among them their wants have become my wants. How shall we provide for them?"[54] Griffing's use of "we" suggested her desire to reestablish a unified freedmen's aid movement dedicated to the amelioration of poverty caused by the slavery, even as many Freedmen's Bureau agents saw the government's work at an end.

In addition to their concern over the fate of former slaves, abolitionist feminists viewed the Freedmen's Bureau as a source of political and economic power for women. The dismantling of the Freedmen's Bureau signaled the closing of political doors opened by emancipation. Yet abolitionist feminists also depended in a very real sense on the continuation of the Freedmen's Bureau. Wilbur supported herself through her work as a freedmen's agent, and she constantly renegotiated her salary with the RLASS and demanded remuneration from the government. Although Wilbur wanted to continue her work in aiding destitute freedpeople after 1868, the funds of the Rochester Society were "exhausted."[55] Forced to find other means of support, Wilbur took a job as a clerk in the U.S. Patent Office, where she worked until her death in 1895.

The scramble for financial support only increased abolitionist feminists' identification with former slaves. After the bureau discharged Griffing along with most of its other agents in August 1868, Griffing asked to be reinstated to her duties under the Educational Division, one of the only remaining divisions of the bureau. She asked for reinstatement both because she believed freedpeople still needed her services and out of personal need. Griffing described her financial situation to Howard in a letter written in September 1868: "I have no home whatever outside of this city—having put my house and village lot into Freedmen's work in 1865–66 as I deemed it my duty to do." Griffing added that she had difficulty supporting herself and her daughters: "I am now greatly embarrassed to pay the board and necessary expenses of three without remunerative employment."[56] Several months later she appealed to Howard to buy the house in which she had lived for the past four years, offering to repay him. She wrote, "I need not say to you that with my three daughters I need a home." But Griffing also wanted to continue her work in Washington: "I feel that I am called to work in this District—and shall be greatly strengthened by your encouragement in this matter."[57] Although Howard did not lend her money, she remained in the District and continued to work with freedpeople until her death in 1872. In Griffing's mind, her needs and the needs of freedpeople were interrelated: their wants had become her wants.

However condescending or unrealistic this identification was, freedpeople accepted their assistance and actively worked with Wilbur and Griffing. Wilbur and her partner Harriet Jacobs, the famous author of *Incidents in the Life of a Slave Girl*, hired a freedwoman to care for children in the barracks at Alexandria. Lucinda proved a crucial ally in the struggle against Gladwin, foiling one attempt to move destitute freedpeople out of the barracks by stating, "I don't want the rations if they will let me alone."[58] Former slaves were not passive recipients of charity, as their willingness to bring their grievances to the Freedmen's Bureau indicates. Freedpeople clearly accepted aid when they needed it, while rejecting assistance that was coercive or manipulative.[59]

But, by drawing national attention to the poverty of freedpeople, abolitionist women portrayed former slaves as needy supplicants. As Wilbur and Griffing steadfastly defended freedpeople against charges of dependency, they created a hierarchical relationship between themselves and former slaves. Indeed, Wilbur's and Griffing's male critics charged them with denigrating freedpeople. Frederick Douglass also pointed out the paternalism and racial repercussions of freedmen's aid efforts, stating that "they will serve to keep up the very prejudices, which it is so desirable to banish from the country."[60] Ignoring these criticisms, abolitionist women justified their employment as freedmen's agents by noting the services they could provide former slaves. Though Wilbur and Griffing never expressed anything less than their full support for African American political equality, their construction of freedpeople as needy and dependent may have fed the racist arguments of feminists who believed that white women deserved the vote before African American men.[61] Nevertheless, in the political climate of Reconstruction, they were radicals, arguing that women and the state should jointly aid former slaves.

Feminists connected the freedmen's aid movement to their fight for suffrage, but universal male suffrage tested their commitment to racial equality. After black men received the vote in Washington, D.C., Wilbur "rejoiced that I had lived to see so much progress," but she also felt "a little jealous—the least bit humiliated" when the men voting demonstrated that they did not know how to read. But while other feminists, including Elizabeth Cady Stanton and Susan B. Anthony, indulged in racially divisive attacks on the Fourteenth and Fifteenth Amendments, Wilbur's comments expressed her desire for universal suffrage.[62] She continued, "No earthquake followed these proceedings, and I presume no convulsion of nature would have occurred, had white *women* and black *women* increased that line of voters."[63] Wilbur's experiences in Reconstruction Alexandria and Washington only increased her commitment to women's rights. In 1869, she and six other white and black women petitioned the judges of election for the right to vote in Washington, D.C., "because we believe ourselves entitled to the franchise." The women concluded: "we hereby solemnly protest against an exclusion from the highest privilege of American citizenship, to which our consent has never been asked."[64]

Griffing also continued to fight for women's right to vote. She joined the National Woman Suffrage Association, founded by Stanton and Anthony, and hosted suffrage conventions in Washington, D.C. In one suffrage speech, Griffing combined her critique of Reconstruction policy with a demand for the franchise, arguing that the solution to "the corrupt, inconsistent, one-sided, and inadequate legislation of the country" was the "admission of the counter-poising moral element of the woman nature."[65] Griffing viewed both freedmen's aid and suffrage as a way to exert the moral influence of women in government policy.

In the face of political opposition, Griffing and Wilbur struggled to make the welfare of former slaves a national concern and bring the real economic problems of emancipation to the attention of the country. When the Freedmen's Bureau ended its work, Griffing saw herself as the bureau's inadequate replacement: "So far as a humble individual can be, I am substituting to these a freedman's (relief) bureau; sanitary commission; church sewing society, to aid the poor; orphan asylum; old people's home; hospital and alms-house for the sick and the blind; minister-at-large, to visit the sick, console the dying and bury the dead."[66] But Griffing also believed that private charity alone could not help freedpeople. In 1871, she appealed to the city of Washington for money: "the want of food is so great among at least a thousand of these, not one of whom is able to labor for support, that it is impossible to provide the absolute relief they must have, by further contributions from the charitable and the humane."[67] In Griffing's view, government assistance was the only solution to the poverty of freedpeople in Washington.

Women in the freedmen's aid movement shared a gendered approach to emancipation and government responsibility, and a commitment to women's involvement in Reconstruction. Wilbur and Griffing accepted dependency as a normal relation in American society—brought about by marriage, childbirth, illness, and old age. In their view, the Freedmen's Bureau was a positive response to the poverty, displacement, and new social relations that followed the Civil War. Griffing, Wilbur, and other women struggled to secure assistance for freedpeople and sought to demonstrate to the nation its responsibility toward former slaves. But their vision for Reconstruction was undermined by the sexual and racial politics of Reconstruction. Male reformers and military officials resisted women's involvement in national policy and rejected their proposals for freedmen's aid as violating the tenets of independence and free labor. Despite this resistance, abolitionist women believed that only with the moral influence of women in politics would the nation make amends for the sin of slavery.

Notes

1 For references to the extensive literature on women's rights and abolitionism, see the section on abolitionism in the bibliographic essay in this volume. In addition to the works cited there, see Bonnie S. Anderson, *Joyous Greetings: The First International Women's Movement, 1830–1860* (New York: Oxford University Press, 2000); Ellen Carol DuBois, *Feminism and Suffrage: The Emergence of an Independent Women's Movement in America, 1848–1869* (Ithaca, N.Y.: Cornell University Press, 1978); and Louise Michele Newman, *White Women's Rights: The Racial Origins of Feminism in the United States* (New York: Oxford University Press, 1999).

2 I am thinking in particular of work by Elsa Barkley Brown, Laura Edwards, Martha Hodes, Tera Hunter, Leslie Schwalm, and LeeAnn Whites. For full references to these and other works, see the bibliographic essay's section on North America.

3 Elizabeth Leonard, *Yankee Women: Gender Battles in the Civil War* (New York: W. W. Norton, 1994); Jeanie Attie, *Patriotic Toil: Northern Women and the American Civil War* (Ithaca, N.Y.: Cornell University Press, 1998); Eric Foner, *Reconstruction: America's Unfinished Revolution, 1863–1877* (New York: Harper and Row, 1988), 68–69, 151–53. Most histories of the freedmen's aid movement focus on education, see Robert C. Morris, *Reading, 'Riting, and Reconstruction: The Education of Freedmen in the South, 1861–1870* (Chicago: University of Chicago Press, 1981); Jacqueline Jones, *Soldiers of Light and Love: Northern Teachers and Georgia Blacks, 1865–1873* (Athens: University of Georgia Press, 1980, 1992); and Julie Roy Jeffrey, *The Great Silent Army of Abolitionism: Ordinary Women in the Antislavery Movement* (Chapel Hill: University of North Carolina Press, 1998), chap. 6.

4 Newman, *White Women's Rights*, 7–8; Peggy Pascoe, *Relations of Rescue: The Search*

for *Female Moral Authority in the American West, 1874–1939* (New York: Oxford University Press, 1990). Thomas C. Holt, " 'An Empire over the Mind': Emancipation, Race, and Ideology in the British West Indies and the American South," in *Region, Race, and Reconstruction: Essays in Honor of C. Vann Woodward*, ed. J. Morgan Kousser and James M. McPherson (New York: Oxford University Press, 1982); Joanne Pope Melish, *Disowning Slavery: Gradual Emancipation and "Race" in New England, 1780–1860* (Ithaca, N.Y.: Cornell University Press, 1998), 63–64; Saidiya Hartman, *Scenes of Subjection: Terror, Slavery, and Self-Making in Nineteenth Century America* (New York: Oxford University Press, 1997); Foner, *Reconstruction*, 152.

5 Wilbur folder, Livingston County Historical Society, Geneseo, N.Y.; Julia A. Wilbur Papers, Collection #1158, Quaker Collection, Haverford College.

6 "Circular: The First Report of the Rochester Ladies' Anti-slavery Sewing Society," box 2, Rochester Ladies' Anti-slavery Society Papers, William L. Clements Library, University of Michigan, Ann Arbor (hereafter RLASS); Nancy Hewitt, *Women's Activism and Social Change: Rochester, New York, 1822–1872* (Ithaca, N.Y.: Cornell University Press, 1984), 152, 150–51, 185, 193–94, 198–99, 207; William S. McFeely, *Frederick Douglass* (New York: W. W. Norton, 1991), 145, 163–66.

7 Maria Webb of Dublin to RLASS, 24 Oct. 1855; Sarah Plummer of Dalkeith (Scotland) Anti-slavery Soc. to RLASS, 24 Jan. 1859; Julia Griffiths Crofts to Anna M. C. Barnes, 5 Aug. 1859; Maria Webb to A. M. C. Barnes, 10 Oct. 1859, box 1, RLASS.

8 Dorothy Sterling, *Ahead of Her Time: Abby Kelley and the Politics of Antislavery* (New York: W. W. Norton, 1991), 261; Keith Melder, "Angel of Mercy in Washington: Josephine Griffing and the Freedmen, 1864–1872," *Records of the Columbia Historical Society of Washington, D.C., 1963–1965*: 243–72; James M. McPherson, *The Struggle for Equality: Abolitionists and the Negro in the Civil War and Reconstruction* (Princeton, N.J.: Princeton University Press, 1992 [1964]), 389–92.

9 Bertram Wyatt Brown, *Lewis Tappan and the Evangelical War against Slavery* (Cleveland: Press of Case Western University, 1967); Lewis Perry, *Radical Abolitionism: Anarchy and the Government of God in Antislavery Thought* (Knoxville: University of Tennessee Press, 1995 [1973]); Wendy Hamand Venet, *Neither Ballots nor Bullets: Women Abolitionists and the Civil War* (Charlottesville: University of Virginia Press, 1991).

10 Petition presented 9 May 1864, HR38A–G10.5, Records of the House of Representatives, Record Group 233, National Archives and Records Administration, Washington, D.C. Griffing and her husband probably divorced. See Records of the U.S. District Court in the District of Columbia, RG 21, entry 115, box 118, no. 7679, National Archives.

11 *Twelfth Annual Report of the Rochester Ladies' Anti-slavery Society* (Rochester, N.Y.: A. Strong, 1863), 3–4; Willie Lee Rose, *Rehearsal for Reconstruction: The Port Royal Experiment* (New York: Oxford University Press, 1964); Foner, *Reconstruction*, chap. 2.

12 *Fourteenth Annual Report of the Rochester Ladies Anti-slavery Society* (Rochester, N.Y.: William S. Falls, 1865), 26.

13 The federal government created the Freedmen's Bureau in 1865 as part of the Department of War. The bureau supervised employment contracts between planters and freedpeople, oversaw the establishment of a public education system in the South, ran hospitals and refugee camps, distributed rations and clothing, and protected the legal rights of former slaves. The bureau also encouraged freedpeople to marry, and many of their policies favored the male-headed, two-parent household. As part of its initial mission, the bureau controlled confiscated and abandoned lands, which it was charged with renting and selling to former slaves. This aspect of the bureau's mission waned when President Andrew Johnson returned most of the land to former confederates. The bureau ended all but its educational and pension work in 1868, finally closing in 1872. Paul A. Cimbala and Randall M. Miller, eds., *The Freedmen's Bureau and Reconstruction: Reconsiderations* (New York: Fordham University Press, 1999).

14 Josephine Griffing to William Lloyd Garrison, 24 March 1864, Ms.A.1.2.v.33 p. 32b, Boston Public Library.

15 Nell Irvin Painter, *Sojourner Truth: A Life, A Symbol* (New York: W. W. Norton, 1996), 213–19; Carol Faulkner, *Women's Radical Reconstruction: The Freedmen's Aid Movement, 1862–1876* (University of Pennsylvania Press, forthcoming), chaps. 6, 7.

16 *Thirteenth Annual Report of the Rochester Ladies' Anti-slavery Society* (Rochester, N.Y.: Democrat Steam Printing House, 1864), 22.

17 Nancy Fraser and Linda Gordon, "A Genealogy of *Dependency*: Tracing a Keyword of the U.S. Welfare State," *Signs* 19, no. 2 (1992): 309–36.

18 Kathryn Kish Sklar, "The Historical Foundations of Women's Power in the Creation of the American Welfare State, 1830–1930," in *Mothers of a New World: Maternalist Politics and the Origins of Welfare States*, ed. Seth Koven and Sonya Michel (New York: Routledge, 1993), 51–53.

19 *Fourth Annual Report of the National Freedmen's Relief Association of the District of Columbia* (Washington, D.C.: McGill and Witherow, 1866), 14–16.

20 HR38A–G10.5, Records of the House of Representatives, NARA; Jean Fagan Yellin, *Women and Sisters: The Antislavery Feminists in American Culture* (New Haven, Conn.: Yale University Press, 1989); Kathryn Kish Sklar, *Women's Rights Emerges within the Anti-slavery Movement, 1830–1870* (New York: Bedford, 2000); Nancy Cott, *The Bonds of Womanhood: Women's Sphere in New England, 1780–1835* (New Haven, Conn.: Yale University Press, 1977).

21 "A Plea for Humanity," in the *Third Annual Report of the National Freedmen's Relief Association of the District of Columbia* (Washington, D.C.: McGill and Witherow, 1865), 4–5.

22 *Fourth Annual Report of the National Freedmen's Relief Association of the District of Columbia*, 11.

23 Wilbur to Anna M. C. Barnes, 12 Nov. 1862, 13 Nov. 1862. See also 26 Nov. 1862, RLASS.

24 *Thirteenth Annual Report of the Rochester Ladies' Anti-slavery Society*, 23.

25 David Montgomery, *Beyond Equality: Labor and the Radical Republicans, 1862–1872* (New York: Knopf, 1967), chap. 1; Amy Dru Stanley, *From Bondage to Contract: Wage Labor, Marriage, and the Market in the Age of Slave Emancipation* (New York: Cambridge University Press, 1998), chaps. 2, 3; Laura F. Edwards, *Gendered Strife and Confusion: The Political Culture of Reconstruction* (Urbana: University of Illinois Press, 1997), 68–80, 92–106; Leslie A. Schwalm, *A Hard Fight for We: Women's Transition from Slavery to Freedom in South Carolina* (Urbana: University of Illinois Press, 1997), chaps. 6, 7; Hartman, *Scenes of Subjection*, 126–30.

26 O. O. Howard, *Autobiography of Oliver Otis Howard* (New York: Baker and Taylor, 1908), 2 vols., 2:220–21. Foner, *Reconstruction*, 152; Mary J. Farmer, " 'Because They Are Women': Gender and the Virginia Freedmen's Bureau's 'War on Dependency,' " in Paul A. Cimbala and Randall Miller, eds., *The Freedmen's Bureau and Reconstruction: Reconsiderations* (New York: Fordham University Press, 1999); Melish, *Disowning Slavery*, 5.

27 McPherson, *Struggle for Equality*, 187. Jonathan A. Glickstein, " 'Poverty Is Not Slavery': American Abolitionists and the Competitive Labor Market," in *Antislavery Reconsidered: New Perspectives on the Abolitionists*, ed. Lewis Perry and Michael Fellman (Baton Rouge: Louisiana State University Press, 1979); *The Antislavery Debate: Capitalism and Abolitionism as a Problem in Historical Interpretation*, ed. Thomas Bender (Berkeley: University of California Press, 1992).

28 Carol Faulkner, "The Hard Heart of the Nation: Gender, Race, and Dependency in the Freedmen's Aid Movement" (PhD diss., SUNY Binghamton, 1998).

29 Leonard, *Yankee Women*; Attie, *Patriotic Toil*; Mary Poovey, *Uneven Developments: The Ideological Work of Gender in Mid-Victorian England* (Chicago: University of Chicago Press, 1988), chap. 6.

30 *Thirteenth Annual Report of the Rochester Ladies' Anti-slavery Society*, 23.

31 Quoted in Ira Berlin, Steven F. Miller, Joseph P. Reidy, and Leslie S. Rowland, eds., *Freedom: A Documentary History of Emancipation, 1861–1867*, ser. 1, vol. 2, *The Wartime Genesis of Free Labor: The Upper South* (New York: Cambridge University Press, 1993), 282.

32 Ibid., 281–82.

33 Leonard, *Yankee Women*, chap. 2; Leonard, "Civil War Nurse, Civil War Nursing: Rebecca Usher of Maine," *Civil War History* 41 (1995): 190–207.

34 Berlin et al., *Wartime Genesis*, 285–86, 251.

35 Wilbur to Barnes, 27 Feb. 1863, RLASS.

36 *Thirteenth Annual Report of the Rochester Ladies' Anti-slavery Society*, 23.

37 *Thirteenth Annual Report of the Rochester Ladies' Anti-slavery Society*, 23–24. See also *Twelfth Annual Report of the Rochester Ladies' Anti-slavery Society*, 12.

38 *Fourteenth Annual Report of the Rochester Ladies' Anti-slavery Society* (Rochester, N.Y.: William S. Falls Book and Job Printer, 1865), 12; Howard, *Autobiography*, 2:264; *Fifteenth Annual Report of the Rochester Ladies' Anti-slavery Society* (Rochester, N.Y.: Wm. S.

Falls, 1866), 9. For more information on the Contraband Fund, see Berlin et al., *Wartime Genesis, 1861–1867*, 251–55.

39 *Fourteenth Annual Report of the Rochester Ladies' Anti-slavery Society*, 11.

40 Quoted in *Delegation of Richmond Freedmen, Statement of Grievances*, Fourteenth Annual Report of the Rochester Ladies' Anti-slavery Society, 19; Peter Rachleff, *Black Labor in Richmond, 1865–1890* (Urbana: University of Illinois Press, 1989 [1984]), 24–25; Elsa Barkley Brown, "Negotiating and Transforming the Public Sphere: African American Political Life in the Transition from Slavery to Freedom," *Public Culture* 7 (1994): 107–46; Frederick Douglass, *Narrative of the Life of Frederick Douglass* (New York: Bedford, 1993), 65–66.

41 John Murray Forbes to Edward Atkinson, 15 Feb. 1865, Edward Atkinson Papers, Massachusetts Historical Society; Horace Greeley to Josephine Griffing, 7 Sept. 1870, Griffing Collection, Columbia University.

42 "Appeal in Behalf of the Freedmen of Washington, D.C.," *Liberator*, 3 Nov. 1865. The black population of Washington increased from 10,983 to 35,455 between 1860 and 1870. Allan Johnston, *Surviving Freedom: The Black Community of Washington, D.C., 1860–1880* (New York: Garland, 1993), 107–8; Laura S. Haviland, *A Woman's Life Work: Labors and Experiences of Laura S. Haviland* (Chicago: C. V. Waite, 1887), 457–62.

43 *Third Annual Report of the National Freedmen's Relief Association of the District of Columbia*, 4–5.

44 Jacob R. Shipherd to O. O. Howard, 30 Oct. 1865. Letters Received, Office of the Commissioner, M752, RG 105, Bureau of Refugees, Freedmen, and Abandoned Lands (BRFAL), National Archives and Records Administration.

45 Jacob R. Shipherd to C. H. Howard, 13 July 1866, Letters Received, M1055, Records of the Assistant Commissioner for the District of Columbia (ACDC), BRFAL. See also J. Miller McKim to Jacob R. Shipherd, 10 Jan. 1866, McKim Letterbooks, Samuel J. May Anti-slavery Collection, Kroch Library, Cornell University.

46 S. N. Clark to Associated Press, 19 Dec. 1865. Letters Sent, Assistant Commissioner for the District of Columbia (ACDC), M1055, BRFAL.

47 S. N. Clark to Mr. E. Carpenter, 5 Dec. 1865. Letters Sent, ACDC, BRFAL.

48 W. F. Spurgin to S. N. Clark, 1 Nov. 1865. Letters Received, ACDC, BRFAL. Wilbur had a more favorable impression of Spurgin, *Fifteenth Annual Report of the Rochester Ladies' Anti-slavery Society*, 10.

49 W. F. Spurgin to S. N. Clark, 1 Jan. 1866. Letters Received, ACDC, BRFAL.

50 Howard, *Autobiography*, 2:226; George R. Bentley, *A History of the Freedman's Bureau* (New York: Octagon, 1970), 76; John William De Forest, *A Union Officer in the Reconstruction* (New Haven, Conn.: Yale University Press, 1948), 58–60.

51 Howard, *Autobiography*, 2:346.

52 *Seventeenth Annual Report of the Rochester Ladies' Anti-slavery and Freedmen's Aid Society* (Rochester, N.Y.: Wm. S. Falls, 1868), 16–17.

53 Josephine Griffing to O. O. Howard, 20 April 1869. Letters Received by the Commissioner, BRFAL.

54 Josephine Griffing to O. O. Howard, 23 Nov. 1870. Letters Received by the Commissioner, BRFAL.

55 *Seventeenth Annual Report of the Rochester Ladies' Anti-slavery Society*, 27.

56 Josephine Griffing to O. O. Howard, 15 Sept. 1868. Letters Received by the Commissioner, BRFAL.

57 Josephine Griffing to O. O. Howard, 22 Nov. 1869. Letters Received by the Commissioner, BRFAL.

58 Quoted in Wilbur to A. M. C. Barnes, 8 Aug. 1863, RLASS; Faulkner, *Women's Radical Reconstruction*, chap. 1.

59 The only complaints about Griffing in the Freedmen's Bureau records involve her work as an employment agent. See Faulkner, *Women's Radical Reconstruction*, chap. 7. Barbara Jeanne Fields, *Slavery and Freedom on the Middle Ground: Maryland during the Nineteenth Century* (New Haven, Conn.: Yale University Press, 1985), 148–49.

60 Frederick Douglass to J. Miller McKim, 2 May 1865, Samuel J. May Anti-slavery Collection, Kroch Library, Cornell University.

61 DuBois, *Feminism and Suffrage*, chaps. 3, 6.

62 *Sixteenth Annual Report of the Rochester Ladies' Anti-slavery and Freedmen's Aid Society* (Rochester, N.Y.: Wm. S. Falls, 1867), 22; DuBois, *Feminism and Suffrage*, chap. 6.

63 *Sixteenth Annual Report of the Rochester Ladies' Anti-slavery Society*, 22; Newman, *White Women's Rights*, 65.

64 *National Anti-slavery Standard*, 1 May 1869; Ann D. Gordon, ed., *The Selected Papers of Elizabeth Cady Stanton and Susan B. Anthony*, vol. 2, *Against an Aristocracy of Sex, 1866–1873* (New Brunswick, N.J.: Rutgers University Press, 2000), 647, 649.

65 *Revolution*, 24 March 1870; Josephine Griffing to Elizabeth Cady Stanton, 27 Dec. 1870, in Gordon, *Selected Papers of Stanton and Anthony*, 2:390–91.

66 Griffing to Horace Greeley, 2 Sept. 1870, rpt. in *History of Woman Suffrage*, ed. Elizabeth Cady Stanton, Susan B. Anthony, and Matilda Joslyn Gage (New York: Source, 1970 [1881]), 6 vols., 2:36.

67 Griffing to the mayor of Washington, 8 April 1871, Stanton, Anthony, and Gage, *History of Woman Suffrage*, 2:35. Griffing's appeals for aid to freedpeople continued to arouse hostility after the Freedmen's Bureau closed. See Horace Greeley to Griffing, 7 Sept. 1870, Griffing Collection, Columbia University; *History of Woman Suffrage*, 2:36–37.

PART II

Families, Land, and Labor

BRIDGET BRERETON

Family Strategies, Gender, and the Shift to Wage Labor in the British Caribbean

The women (who in croptime on sugar estates . . . formed two-thirds of the Field Gangs) have now withdrawn themselves, to a very great extent, from field labour, to pursue those avocations to which females usually devote themselves in other countries.—Special Magistrates' Report for St. George's Parish, Jamaica, 20 March 1839

From Brazil to the Caribbean to the United States, one "meaning of freedom," R. T. Smith has proposed, was "the withdrawal of female labour from plantation work." Contemporary observers—planters and estate managers, officials, missionaries, and others—certainly devoted a great deal of comment to this development in the months and years after the final end of slavery in the British Caribbean (August 1838). But a review of the literature suggests that historians have not systematically analyzed the withdrawal of female labor. Both the extent and the significance of the movement seem uncertain. Was it in fact the case, as the American journalist W. G. Sewell commented some twenty years after 1838, that "the effect of freedom was to abolish almost entirely the labour of women in the cane-fields"? And what lay behind the withdrawal of women, whatever its actual extent? As Smith asks, was it "an attempt by freedmen to establish their control over women, women's own declaration of their primary interest in domesticity, or what?" It may well have been the case, as Frederick Cooper has recently written, that "divisions of labor among men and women, as much as between planter and worker, were thrown into question throughout the West Indies" after emancipation.[1] In this chapter, I will marshal evidence about the extent and timing of the withdrawal of women from estate labor in the British Caribbean in order to examine how ex-slaves used "family strategies" to secure a degree of autonomy and economic security. This evidence will also help us consider the role of gender ideologies in women's removal from the estate labor force.

There is now a scholarly consensus that enslaved women played a key role in the field labor force of British Caribbean sugar plantations, outnumbering men in the crucial "first gangs" during the last two decades of slavery. On the semi-industrial sugar estate, there was relatively little gender differentiation in field work. But as sex ratios among Caribbean slave populations began to even out with the abolition of the slave trade (1806–7), as more and more men were absorbed in nonfield occupations, and as sugar consolidated its hold on most of the British colonies, women came to be *more* fully exploited in the field labor force than men, outnumbering men as field workers nearly everywhere by around 1815, if not earlier (much earlier in the case of Barbados).[2] Women's labor was absolutely essential to British Caribbean sugar plantations, especially in the last twenty years of slavery.

During the four-year transitional "apprenticeship" (1834–38), many of the "indulgences" to pregnant and nursing women, and to mothers of several children—which had become customary in the last years of slavery as planters attempted to raise birth rates on their estates—were abruptly withdrawn. This move was deeply resented throughout the British Caribbean colonies during the apprenticeship years, as the testimony of the special magistrates, appointed under the Emancipation Act to implement its provisions, makes clear. A Grenadian magistrate reported in 1837 that "the aged—pregnant women— and those who had borne a certain number of children, had advantages and indulgences in slavery, which they either do not now possess, or by not being expressed in the abolition act, give rise to dissention and to frequent collisions between the Special Magistrates and the Employers." In Jamaica, too, apprentices in the late stages of pregnancy were sometimes forced to work in the fields, mothers of many children were sent back into the cane pieces, the services of infant nurses might be withdrawn, and nursing mothers were denied special breaks during the working day.[3]

But the arbitrary reversal of the customary concessions to mothers was not the only grievance that affected women during the apprenticeship and which no doubt helped to alienate them further from plantation labor. The situation of the "free children"—those under six on 1 August 1834, who were not automatically apprenticed to their mothers' masters—became a significant issue contested between apprentices (especially mothers) and planters. In most colonies, planters generally refused to continue "allowances" (food rations, clothing, free medical care) to the free children, unless they were *earned*, either by letting them work on the estate, or by the mothers giving additional, unpaid labor in return for these allowances. In Grenada, one magistrate reported, "the majority of Estates withhold, even Medical aid, unless the Mother will give four days of her own time every year." Clause 12 of the Imperial Emancipation Act gave mothers the option of apprenticing their free children to their masters, which would have secured them the contested allowances. But, throughout the four Windward Islands, parents rejected this option, despite planters' inducements and the magistrates' advice; only six such children were apprenticed in the four years after August 1834. In Grenada, for instance, some mothers refused offers of medical care for their free children "lest they should compromise them" or lest the children be "trapped" in some way; when a magistrate advised them to apprentice their sons and daughters, the mothers complained that "the Special Magistrate wanted them to sell their children for Slaves!" Jamaican women responded similarly. "A greater insult could not be offered to a mother," reported a magistrate in 1835, "than by asking her free child to work." The Select Committee of the House of Commons on the apprenticeship was told by a Jamaican witness: "Negro mothers have been known to say, pressing their child to their bosoms, 'We would rather see them die, than become apprentices.' " In Barbados, where provision grounds were inadequate or nonexistent and apprentices lived mainly on rations from their masters, the situation of the free children was especially difficult. Planters refused to supply the customary allowances to the island's fourteen thousand free children, despite the governor's appeals. And the mothers refused to apprentice their children; "magnificently adamant," as W. A. Green puts it, they said they would prefer to see them starve than to bind them to the estates. Despite evidence of rising infant and child mortality, it was not until 1837 that the Barbadian free children were guaranteed customary allowances by a local act.[4]

These grievances and issues surrounding the apprenticeship, affecting primarily women who were mothers and their young children, must have further worsened relations between planters and freedpeople. They must have brought home to the ex-slaves, men and women, the precariousness of family life for people who were fully dependent on the estates for survival, and the fragility of "customary" privileges extended to them. Certainly, these contests during the apprenticeship must have made many women—and, no doubt, many of their male relatives—determined to withdraw from regular estate labor once "full free" came in August 1838.

It seems accepted in the literature that most ex-slave women who were married, or had small children, withdrew from the full-time labor force of the British Caribbean sugar estates after 1838. For many contemporary commentators—such as the Jamaican special magistrate quoted in this chapter's epigraph—this was "natural"; it was to be expected that women would take up maternal and domestic duties, their proper "avocation," once they were no longer coerced by law into field labor. And this also seems to have been the view of those few historians who have considered this development; generally, they have accepted uncritically the observations and interpretations about the female withdrawal from wage labor made by contemporary writers, mostly British officials and clergymen. A good example is Douglas Hall, writing about postemancipation Jamaica.[5] There can be no doubt that European gender ideologies that promoted this view were powerfully operative in the Caribbean colonies after the end of slavery, and I shall consider their influence later on. Nevertheless, it is important to "problematize" the women's withdrawal from estate labor, granted that they had been the backbone of the field gangs during slavery and apprenticeship; and granted also that it is by no means clear that European gender norms were significantly entrenched among the ex-slaves (or, at least, most of them) during the immediate postemancipation period. To problematize the withdrawal is to seek to explain it, one of the objectives of this chapter. It will also encourage us to examine carefully the *extent* of the withdrawal; and we are likely to find that Sewell's sweeping statement that freedom virtually eliminated women's labor on the sugar estates, is wildly exaggerated.

The evidence suggests that many women, including mothers of young children, remained in the estate workforce in the months and years after August 1838. Whether this was the result of coercion by managers, the lack of alternative modes of survival, or the women's own wishes, female labor in the field continued to be important to plantation production in most places.

Probably this was particularly true in Barbados and the Leeward Islands, small, intensively cultivated sugar colonies where the "provision grounds complex" was relatively underdeveloped by 1838. A witness to the 1842 Parliamentary Select Committee on the West India Colonies stated that Barbadian women engaged in field labor as willingly as men; "generally speaking, at the ordinary work of the estate, I think they do as much, and quite as willingly" (as the men). In the middle of 1839, the eleven police magistrates responded to various queries on the working of free labor in Barbados; the replies certainly do not suggest that the ex-slave women had withdrawn from field labor to any significant extent. A large proportion of Barbadian women continued to work full-time on the sugar estates into the 1850s and 1860s, including mothers of small children.[6] Antigua, another densely populated sugar island, opted to proceed straight to complete freedom in August 1834; and four years later, it was reported that women were fully engaged in field labor. A witness to the 1842 Committee stated that Antiguan women were "considered equally efficient with the male labourers." Throughout the 1840s, many women were still employed on the sugar plantations, and this remained the case in the second half of the century. St. Kitts planters, too, considered the female laborers "as effective as the men," even for demanding tasks such as "holeing."[7]

There is no doubt that many women left plantation labor in the Windward Islands, which were less intensively cultivated and had well developed provision ground/marketing complexes. Nevertheless, significant numbers stayed. A St. Lucian special magistrate reported early in 1842 that "females claim no exemption from the usual work of an estate, and, indeed, are in many instances the foremost in setting the example of industry." In Tobago, many women were still on the estate payrolls by 1847; in Grenada, over half of the estate laborers were women, according to the 1851 census.[8]

Evidence from British Guiana also suggests that many women remained on the estates after August 1838. A magistrate reporting on his "tour" of Berbice toward the end of 1840 quoted a manager's remark that "the number of women at work is not so large as during the apprenticeship, but those who do go to the field labour well and steadily and frequently earn at their favorite employment, cane cutting, a dollar per day each." Another told him that "the women upon this property (Lochaben) work steadily and industriously," though many had withdrawn from field labor since August 1838. Special magistrate J. A. Allen of Berbice stated that, in his district, about two-thirds of the adult women on the estates during the apprenticeship were still at work by the end of 1840. Allen and his colleagues in Berbice reported that the women worked the same hours as the men, received exactly the same wages for the same type and quantity of work, and performed the same tasks in the fields, except that trenching ("shovel work") was done only by men; women cut canes "better than men."[9]

In Trinidad, planters do not seem to have complained of a female exodus from the fields, at least not during the first years after 1838. In a newspaper exchange in August 1839, a correspondent claimed that women were the best workers, that much of the labor previously lost "in hospitals, nursings and pregnancies" had now been restored to the estates, that females and boys provided the "most continuous" services to the plantations, and that many women performed two tasks in a day while men rarely did. "This may arise," he speculated, "from a deep-rooted African idea of female inferiority." The anonymous correspondent received some support for his views from experienced Trinidad managers who gave evidence to a local inquiry conducted in

1841. The Philippine manager (himself an ex-slave) testified that many women on the estate performed exceptionally well: "I have two women on the estate who do three tasks per day with ease," though he admitted that this was a rare feat. Richard Darling, "planting attorney" for seven estates, was asked: "Are you supposing that the women are to work as steadily as in a period of slavery, and would you calculate upon this as a probable result?" He replied, "I find in general that the women work much more steadily now than I expected, and I am not disposed to make any material deduction on that account."[10]

Sufficient evidence has been presented here, I hope, to show that many ex-slave women remained in the estate labor force of the British Caribbean in the decade after August 1838, for whatever reason or combination of reasons. But there is also abundant documentation to show that the female "withdrawal" was a reality, though far from universal, and naturally more pronounced in some colonies than in others. I now turn to review some of it.

W. K. Marshall believes that perhaps one-third of the workforce in Grenada, St. Lucia, Tobago, and St. Vincent had withdrawn from the plantations by 1846, and that "women were probably the largest group" among the "permanent defectors from estate labour." A St. Vincent estate manager suggested to the 1842 Committee that "many women who used to work, refuse to labour now on the plea of being married," and that "fully two-thirds" of St. Vincent females had given up working in the field, though Marshall comments that he probably meant two-thirds no longer worked regularly rather than rejecting all estate employment. In Tobago, the magistrates' returns suggest that while there were 4,305 female apprentices on 31 July 1838, only 2,037 women were on the estate payrolls by July 1842, and Susan Craig agrees that most of the *permanent* withdrawal from estate labor on that island was by women. The withdrawal from estate labor in Tobago was accelerated by the reduction of wages in 1846–48, and by a disastrous hurricane in 1847, but the figures suggest that far more women than men left the workforce in these years.[11] In British Guiana, significant numbers of women left the estate labor force. A Berbice special magistrate wrote in December 1840 that "we find the number of women and children occupied in agricultural employment to be considerably, I may add, alarmingly, diminished." One Berbice manager thought that "one-half at least" of his women had withdrawn from field labor since August 1838; a magistrate believed that only one-third of the female apprentices turned out on an average day on the sugar estates and about two-thirds on the coffee properties, and even they seldom stayed in the fields for more than four hours.[12]

Labor relations in Jamaica, relatively large and ecologically diverse, were especially volatile during the apprenticeship and after its end. Swithin Wilmot has shown how Jamaican ex-slave women and their families fought to secure the freedom of wives and mothers not to work for the estates on pain of eviction from houses and grounds. All over Jamaica, ex-slaves insisted that mothers of young children and large families should be exempted from regular field labor without facing eviction; and managers were often forced to concede the point. On Golden Grove, St. Thomas, it was reported, "the females generally have declared they are not again to work in the field, although determined, as they say, to continue on, and be supported by the estate"; management had to agree (in the case of mothers). On Hopewell estate, Hanover, "it is agreed that married women are . . . not required to labour unless they are so disposed to labour. Children also are not to be [required to work] unless it is the wish of their parents and guardians." In the first few months after 1 August, significant numbers of women withdrew from full-time labor on the Jamaican sugar estates, especially in those districts where provision grounds were available and profitable.[13]

The planters complained bitterly of the loss of so much female labor, a loss they may well have overstated to make their point. In Hanover, they claimed that before 1 August 1838, there were 4,253 "persons" resident on the estates, by January 1839, there were 2,143; "of the former number, about one-half were females, while of the latter, the proportion is between one-fifth and one-sixth." Similar claims were put forward by planter-dominated committees in other parishes. Though magistrates and clergymen felt that these claims were exaggerated, at least with respect to the numbers abandoning estate labor completely, there was wide agreement that a significant withdrawal by married women and mothers had occurred by the middle of 1839. And it was not only the sugar estates which experienced a loss of female labor; coffee properties reported the same trend, though it seems to a lesser degree. On the cattle estates ("pens"), Verene Shepherd shows that the proportion of female laborers steadily declined after August 1838. Pen labor forces became increasingly male by the midcentury, the result both of voluntary withdrawal by females and the gradual elimination of "women's tasks" by managers.[14]

During slavery and apprenticeship, women had been the backbone of the field gangs on the sugar estates. It is not surprising, therefore, that managers attempted to coerce them into continued labor after 1 August, especially by tenancy at will and other arrangements involving the huts and grounds. These efforts reflect the importance of female labor to sugar production. When women, and men, resisted them, they were demonstrating that they were not prepared to subordinate their own and their families' welfare to the needs of the plantation. As Mimi Sheller has argued, women's withdrawal from full-time labor on the estates was part of a political struggle fought out on the plantations: "To claim the rights of wife and mother was to assert political autonomy and community solidarity under highly disadvantageous economic conditions."[15]

In the Windward Islands, planters tried to compel the labor of women (and children) by insisting, as a condition of "free" occupancy of a house and grounds, that every family member of working age should do regular estate work at stipulated wages; wives and children could not enjoy a right of residence in their husbands' and fathers' houses unless they complied. A St. Vincent magistrate thought that the system forced women to labor continuously to avoid eviction, but it was the general "desire of the peasantry" to release wives and mothers from regular estate work. Tenancy arrangements were also exploited in St. Lucia and Grenada to compel women (and children) to work for the estates.[16]

It was, however, particularly in Jamaica that planters tried to compel the labor of women (and children), especially during crop time, by manipulating payments for huts and grounds in 1838–39, charging per capita rents for every member of a resident family judged capable of estate work. Wilmot has described the intense struggles that ensued between ex-slaves and managers in the island's sugar parishes, which often resulted in concessions by which wives and mothers were relieved of the obligation to turn out in the fields every day on pain of eviction. The Jamaican special magistrates fully documented these struggles over the coercive manipulation of rents in the months after 1 August 1838. In September 1838, a Trelawney magistrate reported,

> I have this week been visited by several married, and some aged and decrepit females, from Gibraltar Estate, who have exhibited notices . . . served on them by the overseer, because they had devoted their attention to their husbands and families who are working on the same estate, evidently with the design of compelling them, under the fear of a separation, to relinquish their attention to their domestic duties, and apply themselves unremittingly to the labours of the field.

The magistrates recognized that the main object of these strategies was to compel women back into the fields, and one warned "*the binding down of married women should be studiously avoided, the people never will be induced to consent to this.*" The magistrates saw that the rent exactions were driving people away from the estates, especially the "respectable, confidential men," who were anxious to get their wives and children out of the planters' control.[17]

The coercive tactics to compel the women and children to give regular labor to the estates generally failed in those colonies and districts where ex-slave families could maintain themselves without the wages of wives, mothers, and young children. The "withdrawal" by women was a reality, and on a fairly large scale except in Barbados and the Leewards, though naturally its extent and timing varied considerably. I now turn to an investigation of the ex-slaves' motives and strategies.

The survival and welfare of the family group were probably paramount for most freedpeople in the unsettled aftermath of 1 August 1838. Women and children had been especially vulnerable to abuse of all kinds during slavery and apprenticeship, and it is reasonable to assume that the ex-slaves wanted to assure them a degree of protection and security. One way of doing so was to remove them, wherever possible, from the direct control of estate management, and to locate their lives and productive labor in the household and on the family farm rather than on the plantation. As R. T. Smith puts it, freedom might mean the opportunity for women to work on behalf of their families "within the protected spheres of household and community." Family welfare, moreover, might dictate that the mothers of young children should devote much of their time to child care. As M. P. Johnson has written about U.S. freed women who had withdrawn from wage labor, "they, not their masters, decided what household chores to do, when, and how. They and their family members—not their masters—were the beneficiaries of their labors."[18]

It is clear, in fact, that one of the primary motives behind the withdrawal of women from estate labor was to allow them to give more time and attention to child rearing. Clergymen, antislavery activists, magistrates, and planters all made the same point, though with varying degrees of approval. "Those who are mothers and have families," John Scoble asserted, "or who have young infants, are mostly found at home, taking care of their children." William Knibb of Jamaica said the women were spending more time on their "domestic duties, and the care of their families." A St. Vincent planter noted that the ex-slaves were "constantly looking out for land where they can go and live, and allow their wives to sit down, as we call it, and take charge of the children." In 1848 a British Guiana planter told a Parliamentary enquiry that since 1838, the better-off ex-slaves "keep their wives at home to take care of their houses, or look after the children, who used all to be reared in the nursery of the estate; and for that reason at least half the female laborers have been taken from the field and from the estate." In Jamaica, a magistrate rejoiced that pregnant and nursing women, and mothers of large families, were no longer forced into the fields each day; they were now free to choose "those pursuits best suited to their condition and necessities." And a colleague suggested that one of the greatest "blessings of freedom to the labouring people" was the fact that "no women, suffering from pregnancy or from having numerous children, are now brought before magistrates to be punished for not turning out to work in the fields."[19]

There is a great deal of evidence to show that children under the age of sixteen or seventeen were not generally allowed by their parents to do field work on the estates in the post-1838 years, especially not on the plantations on which they resided. (In Barbados, it was noted that when "juveniles" worked on sugar estates, "their engagements are not generally assumed on the same properties where their parents are located.") Planters complained loudly that the young people were idle, that they were being kept away from agriculture; but it is clear that they were routinely employed on their parents' grounds or family farms, or were taught a trade in the case of the boys. In Berbice, a magistrate thought that "dire necessity alone would induce parents to allow them to perform field labour." In Trinidad, R. H. Church stated that virtually no children under the age of twelve were put to field labor; many of them were sent away from their parents' estates to live with godparents or relatives in other places. A Barbadian planter agreed: "they will not put their children in any respect to learn the labour of the fields"; a magistrate from the same island asserted in 1839, "I know of no case where the parents will permit their children to be brought up to agricultural pursuits," despite offers of "liberal" wages and kind treatment.[20] Moreover, parents showed extreme eagerness to send their young children to school, especially immediately after 1838. Church stated that Trinidad parents "exult very much in the idea of sending them to school; and it gratifies them very much when one of their children can read"; "whenever they can get to school they will go." In Barbados, a deputation of (male) laborers from St. George Parish told the governor's secretary in 1839 that getting their children to school was very important to them, because they had "to learn to read the Bible."[21] Keeping young children, as well as their mothers, out of field labor on the estates, sending children to school if possible, and using the older boys and girls in domestic production, marketing, and housework, as part of a family work unit, were important aspects of the ex-slaves' strategies.

As many historians have argued, and as contemporary observers were well aware, one of the most important objectives of ex-slaves in 1838 was to become independent cultivators. The ability to grow crops, for family subsistence and for sale, was crucial in securing a degree of independence from the plantation. The "provision grounds complex," already well developed in most colonies long before 1838, was central to the freedpeople's family strategies. The goal was to combine wage labor (mainly by men, but perhaps also by young, single women) with independent farming carried out by all family members, but especially by women and children. Where suitable land could be procured—by purchase, renting, or squatting—or estate-owned grounds farmed by resident laborers, this was the preferred family strategy. The labor of female and youthful members of the family would, for the most part, be absorbed in domestic agriculture and marketing, while the men worked for wages on the estates, or practiced artisan skills, as well as helping out on the farm. Certainly, the care of children and domesticity provided important motivations for wives and mothers to withdraw from estate labor; but farming and marketing on lands controlled by the family were equally crucial to most of these women.

Similar strategies were followed by ex-slave families nearly everywhere in the British Caribbean after 1838. I will illustrate the point by using the Windward Islands as my example. In St. Vincent, H. M. Grant of Calder estate believed that "every industrious family" could earn a hundred dollars per annum from its provision ground, "besides keeping the family"; the men were always "looking out for land on which they can go and live, and allow their wives to sit down." He had been obliged to give his female workers every second Friday off, so that they could have extra time for provision cultivation and marketing. Most ex-slaves wanted to establish themselves on lands wholly independent of the plantation. On such lands, family farms were established, "abounding with poultry and livestock raised by the industry of the Cottager's family," while the men often gave labor to nearby sugar estates. In Tobago, the cottager's wife "acts the part of Domestic, Gardener, and Marketer, whilst he readily earns one shilling a day on an Estate when he likes to work, or he may cultivate Canes on the Metairie [cropping] system." Everywhere, parents used their children's labor to help on the provision grounds and family farms. "So long as a family by sending one member of it, in routine to the cane field daily, can retain acres of fruitful soil," lamented a Grenadian newspaper in 1839, sugar estates would always be short of hands.[22]

Many ex-slave families after 1838 adopted a gendered strategy of employing women and children in domestic production and marketing, while men sought wage jobs as estate laborers or artisans. In general, in the Caribbean as elsewhere, the ex-slaves expected men to work at skilled trades and in occupations requiring long absences from home (fishing, seafaring, and forestry, for instance), while women were mostly involved in child care, domestic work, and independent farming. The most important exceptions to this generalization are probably those of the women known variously as hucksters, higglers (Jamaica), or *marchandes* (Trinidad, St. Lucia, Dominica). Highly mobile, they routinely traveled relatively long distances to markets and rural villages. These women dominated the markets and the street life of postemancipation towns, and they were usually highly visible in urban "mobs" and collective political action throughout the region. But except for seamstresses and laundresses, people employed in skilled, mechanical, and artisanal trades were nearly always men. Everywhere, parents tried to have their sons learn a trade: the ideal family strategy after 1838 included at least one member who was a skilled worker. Work on the sea and the rivers, and in the forests, was also a male preserve. In St. Lucia, men cut timber, made charcoal, fished, and made boats. In British Honduras, virtually all adult men worked in the timber industry, and the women were nearly all domestic servants in Belize Town. In remote ex-slave settlements up the rivers and creeks of British Guiana, the men fished and transported goods by boat, cut timber, made charcoal, and tapped ("bled") balata; women did some subsistence farming.[23]

In the small nonplantation colonies—the Bahamas group, the Grenadines, Anguilla, the British Virgin Islands, Barbuda, and probably Montserrat and Nevis after 1850—the ex-slaves engaged chiefly in subsistence agriculture, with little possibility of wage work for men or women. Peasant farming was combined with exploitation of the sea (fishing and whaling, sponging and wrecking in the Bahamas, boat building and seafaring) and of the forests (timber cutting, charcoal production, hunting, and foraging). The men monopolized these occupations while the women farmed. Moreover, in many of these small islands, male out-migration became the norm after 1838. By this "emigration adaptation," young men left their impoverished home islands for long spells working abroad, although the intention was always to return and family ties were usually maintained. Postemancipation migration was chiefly, though not entirely, male; the women left behind with the children survived by farming and by remittances.[24]

These gendered occupational strategies, followed by ex-slaves in the decades after emancipation, were no doubt the result of negotiations within individual family groups. There must have been divisions between men and women, between parents and children, as these strategies were developed and implemented by ex-slave families. While the current state of my research does not allow me to expand on this theme, I do not wish to suggest that assertions of control (men over women, parents over adolescent children), and resistance to them, were absent in the development of ex-slave strategies in this period.

Nevertheless, it was, I believe, concern for the welfare of the family unit, the eagerness to secure a degree of independence from the planter and his demands, and a desire to protect vulnerable women and children, which lay behind the withdrawal of women from the estate labor force after 1838. But there can be no doubt that imported gender ideologies played a part, too, reinforcing the family strategies that were pursued by many ex-slaves.

Antislavery activists, clergymen, officials, and British policy makers all shared a basic assumption: the ex-slaves should model their domestic lives on the middle-class Western family. Husbands should be the head of the family, the main breadwinner, responsible for family support, and endowed with authority over wives and children; wives should be dependent and domestic. Of course, life-long monogamy based on Christian marriage should be the norm. Men must both control and protect their wives (and daughters), something that slavery had made impossible; the sexual abuse of female slaves had been an attack on the "rights" of their menfolk as well as on the chastity of the women. Wives and mothers must rear their children and provide a decent, comfortable, Christian home. Missionaries like J. M. Phillippo and William Knibb thought that "the wife's proper release from toil"—plantation labor—was an important, wholly positive result of freedom, allowing her time and energy to create a model home for her family and to secure the comfort of her breadwinner. This was a consensus shared by antislavery opinion and by most officials in the islands.[25]

It was generally assumed that male ex-slaves would assume the responsibilities of heads of families once the apprenticeship ended. Governors addressed gendered appeals to the ex-apprentices based on this premise (or promise). Henry Light of British Guiana told them "if you did not work for the Estate you could not remain on it—you must take away yourselves, children, wives, and old people dependent on you." And Sir Lionel Smith exhorted the "Praedial Apprentices" of Jamaica in July 1838:

> Remember that in freedom you will have to depend on your own exertions for your livelihood, and to maintain and bring up your families. You will work for such wages as you can agree upon with your employers. . . . Be honest towards all men—be kind to your wives and children—spare your wives from heavy field work, as much as you can—make them attend to their duties at home, in bringing up your children, and in taking care of your stock—above all, make your children attend divine service and school.[26]

Husbands and fathers were to exercise authority over wives and children; females were to be primarily dependent housewives; independent wage labor away from the home was unsuitable for married women and mothers.

Estate labor was also seen as generally dangerous to female morality, unless women and adolescents worked for the planter as a family unit under the immediate control of a male relative. Though the end of slavery meant an end to the flagrant, routine sexual abuse of women and girls by plantation staff, there can be little doubt that free estate laborers were still vulnerable; and men and women (including teenagers) worked together in gangs and might be housed together in barracks. This situation helps to explain why antislavery activists and clergymen were anxious to remove women from field labor. E. B. Underhill, the prominent British Baptist cleric, wrote that the "careful, respectable men" of the Jamaican sugar parishes did not let "their women" (or children) work on the estates, complaining of the handouts of rum, the night work during crop time, and the "promiscuous mixing" of males and females in the barracks.[27]

Certainly, women must have wanted to remove themselves and their daughters from the risks of sexual abuse (whether at the hands of estate staff or fellow workers) in the labor gangs even after 1838; and men must have wanted the same for the female members of their families. An important "meaning of freedom" for women and men—but above all for women—must have been the right to control one's own body, the right to be free of violation and abuse. Ex-slaves hardly needed European gender ideology to persuade them of that.

But the testimony quoted above does suggest that many ex-slaves, men and women, had come to accept European ideas about female morality and femininity, or at least many ex-slaves who were under missionary influence. It seems reasonable to think that European gender norms did exert influence on some of the freedpeople, especially men and women who were upwardly mobile and who were strongly influenced by the churches. It was especially (though not exclusively) in the church-dominated villages that the wives and mothers withdrew from estate labor and concentrated on domesticity and household production. No doubt the ability to let their wives "sit down" and devote their time to home and children became an index of status for many ex-slave men, as well as part of a family strategy to seek the welfare of all its members.[28]

The "respectable" and "confidential" men, former slaves seeking a better life for their families and strongly influenced by missionaries, were most likely to adopt British gender ideology. Of course the ex-slaves had their own concepts of status hierarchies that owed little to European ideologies. Respectability, which involved a cluster of qualities and credentials (economic stability, active church membership, legal marriage, a nuclear family, etc.), may have depended to an extent on imported norms and values, but it was clearly highly valued by many ex-slaves. And respectability inevitably had a gender dimension. The respectable woman did not work for wages on the plantation; once married, she concentrated on home duties and domestic production. The respectable man provided for his family and protected his wife and children from external threats. In this context, having a wife who could "sit down" at home was probably an important element in one's claim to respectability and was positively valued by men, and women, in upwardly mobile families.

That some Caribbean freedpeople adopted all or part of the British gender ideology of the mid-nineteenth century seems highly likely. But, on the whole, the ex-slaves, men and women, declined to buy the package. They did not enthusiastically embrace monogamous Christian marriage, except during the immediate aftermath of August 1838 (and even then probably only a minority did so); they rejected the notion that confinement to domesticity and economic dependence on a husband were necessary to female respectability. Such ideas were too contrary to African Caribbean family forms and gender roles, not to mention those derived from West Africa. In postslavery Caribbean societies, as Sidney Mintz has pointed out, women's right to economic independence was generally acknowledged among the people, who did not see such a right as implying any corresponding loss of status for the women's husbands. The idea of male economic dominance within the family and household was not imbedded nearly so deeply as in the West, except among the (small) middle and upper strata. Few Caribbean women outside those strata became wholly dependent housewives confined to strictly domestic roles, even if many—most, in some places—had withdrawn from estate labor. Women—and men—negotiated between European, Christian, African, and African Caribbean concepts of marriage, motherhood, and femininity.

Caribbean freedwomen did not withdraw from estate labor because they, or their men, aspired to European bourgeois gender norms. They did so in order to exchange hard, dangerous, and degrading gang labor for child care, for work in the household, on the family farm, and in the market. One reason for the withdrawal was certainly to escape the risk of sexual and other abuse which was still inseparable from gang labor on the sugar estates, even after slavery had ended; another was to allow mothers to devote more attention to rearing their children. But ex-slave men and women were not blindly obeying imported gender ideologies or seeking to transform freedwomen into dependent housewives confined to the home. They were pursuing rational family strategies aimed at securing the survival and welfare of their kin groups, in the face of appalling odds, and at carving out lives which would not be wholly dependent on the plantation.[29]

Notes

This chapter is a condensed, and revised, version of my essay published under the same title in *The Colonial Caribbean in Transition: Essays on Post-emancipation Social and Cultural History*, ed. Bridget Brereton and Kevin Yelvington (Mona, Jamaica: University of the West Indies Press, 1999), 77–107.

1 Raymond T. Smith, "Race, Class, and Gender in the Transition to Freedom," in *The Meaning of Freedom: Economics, Politics, and Culture after Slavery*, ed. Frank McGlynn and Seymour Drescher (Pittsburgh, Penn.: University of Pittsburgh Press, 1992), 267–68, 278; William G. Sewell, *The Ordeal of Free Labor in the British West Indies* (New York: Harper and Brothers, 1861), 79; Frederick Cooper, "Africa in a Capitalist World," in *Crossing Boundaries: Comparative History of Black People in Diaspora*, ed. Darlene Clark Hine and Jacqueline McLeod (Bloomington: Indiana University Press, 1999), 399.

2 Marietta Morrissey, *Slave Women in the New World: Gender Stratification in the Caribbean* (Lawrence: University Press of Kansas, 1990), esp. chap. 2 and 74–79, 140–43; Barbara Bush, *Slave Women in Caribbean Society, 1660–1838* (London: James Currey, 1990), chap. 4; Hilary McD. Beckles, *Natural Rebels: A Social History of Enslaved Black Women in Barbados* (London: Zed, 1989), chap. 2; Beckles, *Centering Women: Gender Discourses in Caribbean Slave Society* (Kingston: Ian Randle, 1999); L. Mathurin Mair, *Women Field Workers in Jamaica during Slavery* (Mona, Jamaica: Department of History, University of the West Indies, 1987).

3 W. K. Marshall, "Apprenticeship and Labour Relations in Four Windward Islands," in *Abolition and Its Aftermath: The Historical Context*, ed. David Richardson (London: Cass, 1985), 203–23; Edward Cox, "From Slavery to Freedom: Emancipation and Apprenticeship in Grenada and St. Vincent, 1834–1838," in Hine and McLeod, *Crossing Boundaries*, 379–83; Mathurin Mair, *Women Field Workers*.

4 Marshall, "Apprenticeship and Labour Relations," 211–12; Colonial Office (hereafter CO) 101/87, Grenada Special Magistrates' (hereafter SMS') Monthly Reports for 1838, ff. 218, 250; Roderick A. McDonald, ed., *Between Slavery and Freedom: Special Magistrate John Anderson's Journal of St. Vincent during the Apprenticeship* (Kingston: University of West Indies Press, 2001), 130–31; Cox, "From Slavery to Freedom," 380–83; Mathurin Mair, *Women Field Workers*; William A. Green, *British Slave Emancipation: The Sugar Colonies and the Great Experiment* (Oxford: Clarendon, 1976), 134–35; Hilary Beckles, *A History of Barbados: From Amerindian Settlement to Nation-State* (Cambridge: Cambridge University Press, 1990), 97.

5 Douglas Hall, *Free Jamaica, 1838–65* (New Haven, Conn.: Yale University Press, 1969), 19. An excellent discussion of the U.S. situation is Amy Dru Stanley, *From Bondage to Contract: Wage Labor, Marriage, and the Market in the Age of Slave Emancipation* (Cambridge: Cambridge University Press, 1998), esp. chap. 5.

6 Parliamentary Papers (hereafter PP) 1842 XIII (479), Select Committee on West India Colonies (PP 1842), evidence of W. Sharpe; CO 28/130, no. 56, Replies from

Barbados Police Magistrates (April 1839); Claude Levy, *Emancipation, Sugar and Federalism: Barbados and the West Indies, 1833–1876* (Gainesville: University Presses of Florida, 1980), 113.

7   *Port of Spain Gazette* (hereafter *POSG*), 28 Aug. 1838: Extract from the *Gazette* (St. Kitts), 27 July 1838; PP 1842, evidence of N. Nugent (Antigua) and G. Estridge (St. Kitts); F. Lanagan, *Antigua and the Antiguans* (London: Saunders and Otley, 1844), 2 vols., 2:142–47.

8   PP 1842, appendix: Report of J. V. Drysdale, St. Lucia SM, Jan. 1842, 732; CO 290/4, Tobago SMs' Half-Yearly Report for 1847, f. 159; George Brizan, *Grenada, Island of Conflict: From Amerindians to People's Revolution, 1498–1979* (London: Zed, 1984), 180.

9   CO 111/182, no. 10, Reports by SMs in Berbice (British Guiana), Dec. 1840.

10   *POSG*, 27 Aug. 1839, Letter from Candidus, n.d., and editorial; W. H. Burnley, *Observations on the Present Condition of the Island of Trinidad* (Port of Spain, 1842), 51–52, 77.

11   W. K. Marshall, "The Ex-slaves as Wage Labourers on the Sugar Estates in the British Windward Islands, 1838–1846," paper presented at the Eleventh Conference of Caribbean Historians, Curaçao, 1979; PP 1842, Evidence of H. M. Grant (St. Vincent); S. E. Craig, "The Popular Struggle to Possess the Land in Tobago, 1838–1855," paper presented at the Twenty-second Conference of Caribbean Historians, Trinidad, 1990; CO 290/4, Tobago SMs' Half-Yearly Tabular Returns, f. 205 (1847), f. 281 (1848), f. 614 (1852).

12   CO 111/182, no. 10, Reports of Berbice SMs, Dec. 1840.

13   Swithin Wilmot, " 'Females of Abandoned Character?' Women and Protest in Jamaica, 1838–1865," in *Engendering History: Caribbean Women in Historical Perspective*, ed. Verene Shepherd, Bridget Brereton, and Barbara Bailey (Kingston: Ian Randle, 1995), 279–95; CO 137/232, no. 189, SMs' Reports, Jamaica, Oct. 1838; CO 137/242, no. 53, SMs' Reports, Hanover, Jan. 1839.

14   CO 137/242, no. 47, Report upon the State of the Labouring Population of Hanover, Jan. 1839; no. 74, Report of SMs, St. George's Parish, 20/3/1839; Verene Shepherd, "Alternative Husbandry: Slaves and Free Labourers on Livestock Farms in Jamaica in the Eighteenth and Nineteenth Centuries," *Slavery and Abolition* 14, no. 1 (1993): 57–60.

15   Mimi Sheller, "Quasheba, Mother, Queen: Black Women's Public Leadership and Political Protest in Post-emancipation Jamaica, 1834–65," *Slavery and Abolition* 19, no. 3 (1998): 98.

16   Marshall, "Ex-slaves as Wage Labourers"; W. K. Marshall, ed., *The Colthurst Journal* (Millwood, N.Y.: KTO, 1977), 228–30; PP 1842, appendix: Report of R. Sutherland, SM of St. Vincent, 1 Jan. 1842; *POSG*, 18 Jan. 1839: Extract from St. Lucia *Royal Gazette and Times*, 1 Dec. 1838; *POSG*, 13 Aug. 1839: Notice, Grand Bras estate, Grenada, d. 30 July 1839.

17   Wilmot, " 'Females of Abandoned Character?' "; CO 137/232, no. 182, Report

of SM, Trelawney, 15 Sept. 1838, and Report of SM, St. Catherine, 20 Sept. 1838; and no. 216, Report of SM, Hanover, 3 Dec. 1838 (italics in original); CO 137/242, no. 41, SMS' Reports, Jan. 1839; CO 137/243, no. 113, SMS' Reports, April–May 1839. See also PP 1839 35:602–3; and Sheller, "Quasheba," 94–98.

18 Smith, "Race, Class, and Gender," 267–68; M. P. Johnson, "Out of Egypt: The Migration of Former Slaves to the Midwest during the 1860s in Comparative Perspective," in Hine and McLeod, Crossing Boundaries, 234.

19 PP 1842, evidence of J. Scoble, W. Knibb, H. M. Grant; evidence to 1848 Select Committee quoted in Alan H. Adamson, Sugar without Slaves (New Haven, Conn.: Yale University Press, 1972), 40; CO 101/92, no. 3, Grenada SMS' Reports for 1841, f. 18; CO 260/57, St. Vincent SMS' Replies, Aug. 1838, f. 44; CO 137/242, no. 53, R. Hill to Governor of Jamaica, 20 Feb. 1839, and no. 74, Report of SM, St. Mary's, 1 April 1839.

20 PP 1842, evidence of J. Bascom, R. H. Church, W. H. Burnley, G. Carrington; CO 111/182, no. 10, Berbice SM's Report, Dec. 1840; POSG, 23 Oct. 1838, Letter from a Planter, 19 Nov. 1838; CO 28/130, no. 56, Return of Police Magistrate, St. Thomas, Barbados, April 1839.

21 PP 1842, evidence of R. H. Church; CO 28/130, no. 50, Meeting with Deputation of Labourers of St. George, Barbados, 23 April 1839.

22 PP 1842, evidence of H. M. Grant and appendix, Report of St. Vincent SM, R. Sutherland, 1 Jan. 1842, 748; CO 253/78 St. Lucia, no. 22, SMS' Reports for 1842; CO 290/4, Tobago SMS' Reports for 1850, ff. 457–58; Trinidad Standard, 15 March 1839, Extract from Grenada Free Press, 27 Feb. 1839.

23 M. Louis, " 'An Equal Right to the Soil': The Rise of a Peasantry in St. Lucia, 1838–1900" (PhD diss., Johns Hopkins University, 1981), 186–93; O. Nigel Bolland, Struggles for Freedom (Belize City: Angelus, 1997), 59–60; Adamson, Sugar without Slaves, chap. 3.

24 Bonham C. Richardson, Caribbean Migrants (Knoxville: University of Tennessee Press, 1983), chap. 4; Richardson, "Freedom and Migration in the Leeward Caribbean, 1838–1848," Journal of Historical Geography 6, no. 4 (1980): 391–408; K. Fog Olwig, "The Migration Experience: Nevisian Women at Home and Abroad," in Women and Change in the Caribbean, ed. Janet Momsen (London: J. Currey, 1993), 150–66.

25 Diane Austin-Broos, "Redefining the Moral Order: Interpretations of Christianity in Post-emancipation Jamaica," in McGlynn and Drescher, Meaning of Freedom, 221–43; Smith, "Race, Class, and Gender," 277–79; Claire Robertson, "Africa into the Americas? Slavery and Women, the Family and the Gender Division of Labor," in More Than Chattel: Black Women and Slavery in the Americas, ed. David Barry Gaspar and Darlene Clark Hine (Bloomington: Indiana University Press, 1996), 18–24; Catherine Hall, "Gender Politics and Imperial Politics: Rethinking the Histories of Empire," in Engendering History, 48–59; Hall, "William Knibb and the Constitution of the New Black Subject," Small Axe 8 (2000): 31–55; Thomas Holt, "The Essence of

the Contract," in Frederick Cooper, Thomas Holt, and Rebecca J. Scott, *Beyond Slavery: Explorations of Race, Labor, and Citizenship in Postemancipation Societies* (Chapel Hill: University of North Carolina Press, 2000), 45–46; Diana Paton, "Decency, Dependence and the Lash: Gender and British Debate over Slave Emancipation, 1830–34," *Slavery and Abolition* 17, no. 3 (1996): 173–80; Sheller, "Quasheba," 90–98; Clare Midgely, "Anti-slavery and Feminism in Nineteenth-Century Britain," *Gender and History* 5, no. 3 (1993): 343–62.

26 CO 111/158, no. 30, Governor's Address to Free Labourers of 1 Aug., 13 Aug. 1838; CO 137/231, Proclamation of Sir Lionel Smith, 9 July 1838.

27 CO 137/244, no. 124, J. Kingdom, Manchioneal, to Governor's Private Secretary, 27 June 1839; E. B. Underhill, *The West Indies* (London: Jackson, Wolford and Hodder, 1930 [1862]), chap. 3.

28 Hall, "Gender Politics," 54–57; Sidney Mintz, "Black Women, Economic Roles and Cultural Traditions," in *Caribbean Freedom*, ed. Hilary Beckles and Verene Shepherd (Kingston: Ian Randle, 1993).

29 On these issues, see the important essay by Diana Paton, "The Flight from the Fields Reconsidered: Gender Ideologies and Women's Labor after Slavery in Jamaica," in *Reclaiming the Political in Latin American History: Perspectives from the North*, ed. Gilbert M. Joseph (Durham, N.C.: Duke University Press, 2001). On the United States, see Amy D. Stanley, " 'We Did Not Separate Man and Wife, but All Had to Work': Freedom and Dependence in the Aftermath of Slave Emancipation," in *Terms of Labor: Slavery, Serfdom and Free Labor*, ed. Stanley L. Engerman (Stanford, Calif.: Stanford University Press, 1999).

✿ MARTIN KLEIN AND RICHARD ROBERTS

Gender and Emancipation in French West Africa

This article explores patterns of female emancipation and freedwomen's strategies in French West Africa from the mid-nineteenth century to end of the Great Exodus of slaves around 1914. During this period, female emancipation was shaped by the increase in domestic slave use, the halting efforts of the French to abolish slavery, the expansion of colonial conquest into the interior, and the establishment of native courts. Both before and after the end of slavery, women's strategies to seek control over their lives were constrained by prevailing conceptions of gender and marriage shared by French and African men. While most freedwomen operated within the constraints of a patriarchal family, a few sought to use the new courts to claim a greater degree of choice. Female former slaves had little room for maneuver. A single, unattached female was a social anomaly. In French West Africa, a woman might have a large degree of commercial autonomy, but she was always a daughter, a wife, a widow, and/or a mother. Marriage in most of the region's patrilineal, virilocal societies transferred rights to a woman's labor and reproductive power from her father's kin group to her husband's. Brides were rarely consulted. Like their free counterparts, slave women lived in domestic units headed by men who were either their masters, their mistress's husbands, or their husbands (sometimes also slaves).

In 1905 began the Great Exodus, the colonial prohibition on transactions in persons, and the establishment of native courts. These events empowered women and female slaves, at least briefly, to challenge the authority of husbands and former masters. Not all women were willing to do this, but strategies used by female slaves hint at a reshuffling of gender categories and new avenues for female agency. Both free and former slave women came before the newly created native courts and requested the end of marriages they did not want.

Many were granted divorces. By the end of the decade, however, the French began to worry about "unstable" African families and loose women. While some divorces continued to be granted, they were rarer after 1910 than in the five years before. Even administrators who had supported women's choice in marriage never seriously questioned their assumptions that women should be affiliated with male-centered households; they assumed that divorced women would speedily remarry husbands of their own choosing. After 1910, native courts increasingly forced runaway wives to return to their husbands.[1]

Patterns of Female Slavery and Emancipation in French West Africa Prior to 1905

The condition and treatment of slaves in West Africa varied over time and place.[2] Slaves in centralized states fared differently from those in lineage-based decentralized societies. It is virtually impossible to reconstruct the condition and practices of slavery before the mid-nineteenth century. With few written sources, historians are wary of descriptions of custom since they define norms rather than practices.[3] Treatment of slaves was influenced by the power of states to support the extraction of labor and services from slaves; the strength of market forces, which provided masters with incentives to exploit their slaves; prevailing religious ideologies of slavery; and, of course, the abilities of slaves to resist their masters.[4] Beginning with the mid-nineteenth century, historians have more data.

In West Africa, women were in all periods a majority of the newly enslaved, both because they were easier to enslave and because Africans were willing to pay higher prices for women.[5] There were a number of reasons for women's value on the market. Once enslaved, they were easier to control and less likely to flee, particularly after they had children, and they could be forced to do a greater range of tasks.[6] In a sense, female slaves were the cement of society. The young and pretty became concubines for the rich and powerful. Most became wives and farmed. Finally, offering a male slave a slave wife was important in keeping male slaves productive and obedient. Different roles of women in slavery and different kinds of slavery meant that the situation of female slaves throughout West Africa varied radically. Under Islamic law, the slave concubine who bore her master a child was freed on his death. Her offspring were free and had equal rights to inherit. Thus, a female slave could be well off if she was the favorite of a wealthy man or the mother of a favored son. When they lost a master's favor or economic conditions changed, concubines and slave wives could find themselves back in the field.[7] The master's favor was often transient and the slave powerless. In spite of this, many women sought freedom, often at great personal risk. They struggled for control of their personal lives, for control of their children, for the right to recreate family life, and for their own personal property. One heritage of the slave trade was the reduction of women to objects of conflict, commodities fought over by diverse male actors.

The French did not initially impose radically different values. Colonial administrators and missionaries, even those hostile to slavery, shared with African male elites a belief in the importance of marital and paternal authority. Emancipation took place over a long period, but during the half-century after French abolition in 1848, many more people were being enslaved than were being freed. For most of this period, the only possible strategy for most female slaves was to seek a male protector. In most cases, they had little choice, but many nonetheless strove to make a choice.[8] With the creation and then extension of colonial rule, their room to maneuver was increased by the presence of missions, colonial courts, and by greater security of movement, but they still operated within narrowly defined boundaries.

Emancipation was always a selective process that reinforced the power of the masters. Deathbed manumissions were pious acts for Muslims. Some slaves were allowed to ransom themselves and some were assimilated over several generations. Most second and third generation slaves found themselves in continuing dependent relationships with their masters. Masters did not have to marry their slave concubines, but female slaves were attractive wives because they were powerless.[9] For most, however, life was harsh, particularly as they aged. Female slaves were given to slave warriors, and they farmed and fed their masters. Some accompanied their masters on military campaigns, serving as porters, making camp, and cooking. Spouses of agricultural slaves had an even more difficult life. They owed their masters certain kinds of seasonal labor and a large part of their crops. Given the low productivity of hoe agriculture, they had little surplus. The slave ménage thus could not afford the luxury of unproductive persons, either young or old. Female slaves, like their male counterparts, had customary rights to leisure time and could, in principle, produce commodities on their own account, but the limited time available to them made accumulation very difficult.

Female slaves had two defining characteristics. First, they had no kin. Meillassoux argues that slaves did not marry.[10] By that he means that they had none of the rights in each other or in their offspring that married couples normally exercised. They did form stable long-term relationships, but bridewealth was rarely paid for slaves, and when paid, it was a derisory sum. Low bridewealth reflected low status and made slave marriages susceptible to easy breakdown. When free couples divorced, bridewealth was returned to the husband or his kin. High bridewealth was thus a barrier to divorce.[11] Slaves also could not count on their offspring during old age, since their children belonged to their master. Second, the female slave had no honor. She was owned and thus sexually available. Her obligations to her master included both sex and lascivious entertainments.

Until the last quarter of the nineteenth century, the French presence was limited to two island towns created to service the slave trade, Saint-Louis and Gorée. These towns included a small number of European and African merchants, some free Africans, and a slave majority.[12] Women were very important among both the free and slave populations. The most successful were the *signares*, women united to French men in temporary marriages called *mariage à la mode du pays*.[13] Because employees of French slaving companies could not trade on their own, they often did so through their African wives. When a European died, as many did, his African wife inherited, although the archives contain records of metropolitan wives seeking to recover their husband's wealth.[14] The *signares* thus came to control both urban property and shipping on the Senegal River and were the foundation of a métis community. The largest group of slaves were *pileuses*, women who pounded millet and prepared meals on riverboats and in housing compounds of Saint-Louis and Gorée. *Pileuses* who worked the riverboats also traded and could accumulate wealth. Compared to farm slaves, they were generally well off.

In Senegal, the French abolition of slavery after the revolution of 1848 applied only to small areas under French sovereignty, but it threatened relations with slave-owning neighbors.[15] The local administration soon found ways to limit its application to slaves resident in the towns in 1848. First, to protect nearby kingdoms from slave flight, a local ordinance provided that runaway slaves claimed by their masters were to be expelled from the city as vagabonds. Their masters were usually told when they would be expelled. Runaway slaves were freed only if they spent three months in town without being claimed.[16] Second, to provide domestic labor, local people were authorized to purchase slave children and bring them to town, where they would be freed and assigned to the person declaring them as wards.[17]

As France extended its control into the interior, it used the distinction between citizens and subjects to avoid freeing slaves in areas under its control. In the 1870s, pressure from the Protestant mission and an energetic West Indian–born prosecuting attorney forced changes in French policy.[18] The Protestant mission was small and poorly funded, but it occasionally hid runaway slaves and, once the slaves were freed, helped them establish themselves.[19]

The Protestants also provided information about slavery in Senegal for a press campaign in France, which led to a reduction in the waiting period for liberty papers.[20] In 1883, Governor René Servatius held that a freed slave had only to report to judicial authorities to get liberty papers. From this time forth, any slave reaching areas under direct administration was freed, but the administration limited the scope of this law by disannexing large parts of Senegal and placing them under protectorate. Under a protectorate, the French agreed to respect prevailing customs, including the right to own slaves.[21] A case in 1886 shows how the French limited slave claims in areas of direct administration. Two female slaves took refuge with a trader in a railway station town in the kingdom of Kajoor. When the trader asked the judicial service for liberty papers, he was told the women had to come to Saint-Louis to get them. The stations were under French authority, but the colonial regime refused to deliver liberty papers there because that would deprive Kajoor peanut farmers of needed labor. The trader could not smuggle the women out, and they were eventually reenslaved by Kajoor warriors.[22]

In spite of the administration's reluctance, the number freed rose steadily over the years. Between 1857 and 1862, it was under a hundred a year, then it rose to 350 in 1875 and 674 in 1881. During the 1880s, the number fluctuated from a thousand to over two thousand a year. From 1868 to 1888, most of the liberations in Saint-Louis were listed in the *Moniteur du Sénégal*. While there are gaps in these lists, they provide us a statistical picture of slave flight. Seventy-two percent of those listed were adults, and of these almost 60 percent were women. Some may have been women freed by soldiers, traders, or riverboat workers who were attracted to them, but most were fleeing slavery. Many fled with children. Of the slave children who were "freed" and then adopted, about four-fifths were girls, mostly between ages seven and ten, and were sold as servants. They were always assigned to a woman, probably the wife of the man who paid the purchase price. Writing in 1904, the year the system was abolished, Georges Deherme suggested that about two hundred slave children were being brought into Saint-Louis every year between 1898 and 1904.[23] Boats which went up the Senegal River often returned with a child or two, bought for a friend or a client. Adoptions took place in all kinds of families, European, métis, and African Muslim, including some people of modest standing. We have little data on what happened to these girls as they became women. Deherme suggests that many were pushed into early marriage and some into prostitution.[24] Most, however, were purchased very young by owners who clearly intended them to be servants. Our hypothesis is that for some, the guardian collected bride-price, and that in general, either they were married off to a relative or client or they remained servants.

French Conquest and Complicity with Slavery and the Slave Trade in the Soudan

The Soudan (now Mali) was dominated by large states, though with large areas inhabited by decentralized societies. Slaves were the most important item of trade and the basis of economic and military life. Large slave-worked estates surrounded commercial towns, where slaves were over two-thirds of the population. French commanders learned that with limited financial support from Paris, they could wage war only if they adapted to local ways of fighting.[25] Their armies were made up largely of slaves freed in exchange for military service. When the French made alliances, they were careful not to threaten the slaveholdings of their allies. Slaves were also the most important reward for those allies and for African soldiers. When an inexperienced lieutenant asked for his men to be paid before beginning a campaign, he was told "that *captifs* should not be paid since they were going to war and would surely take *captives*, which would be their reward."[26] The French army traveled with what one missionary called its "battalion of women."[27] Every *tirailleur* had at least one woman, who carried his personal effects, cooked, and prepared camp. Many had other women back at their base, though they also sold their human booty for spare cash.[28] This behavior did not begin with the conquest. During the nineteenth century, slave women were constantly being given away. When Amadou Tal, the ruler of Ségou, detained French explorers Eugene Mage and Louis Quintin in 1866, he gave them two slave women so that their confinement would be more tolerable. And when French soldiers left, they either gave away or deserted the women who had served them.

French officers threw themselves into this society with great gusto. Some had concubines, but many were quite promiscuous. Thus, the White Fathers at Ségou received complaints about a French sergeant who had an African family but sent men out every day to find him two pretty young girls. When the missionaries complained, the local commandant told them they were not likely to get far with the regional commandant, who kept six women, five of them between ten and fifteen years of age.[29] After most victories, the captives, mostly female, were distributed. When Sikasso fell in 1898, an estimated three thousand slaves were brought to the French camp, including hundreds of nude women from the harem. Some found relatives in the French forces; others were divided up. African allies and agents received as many as twenty each. The literature on the French army often stresses the desire for military action and promotion. Letters from missionaries and an occasional dissident make clear that freedom from the repressive sexual morality of Catholic France was also an attraction for the soldiers. The most important cause of death was not wounds or malaria but venereal disease.[30]

In 1887, the military began creating "liberty villages" to supply labor near French posts and along major supply routes, to provide a home for runaways and to encourage slaves to escape from France's enemies.[31] Slave owners could reclaim slaves for up to three months, but only within one month for slaves enlisting in the French army. In the liberty village, the French also placed slaves collected as taxes—there was a 10 percent tax on all caravans. Labor demands were so heavy that few stayed long in the villages. Within the villages, women could flee, they could accept their lot, or they could find male protectors. Unattached persons, both men and women, were attached to the head of a household. Land was given only to family heads. With women more than twice as numerous as men in many of the villages, there was competition for protection. A woman was probably better off in a chief's household, but many formed other liaisons. A man needed a wife and, if possible, other dependents in order to farm. The White Fathers, who controlled Catholic mission activities in the Soudan, were critical of the government's liberty villages. Augustin Hacquard suggested that female ex-slaves simply became concubines.[32] The White Fathers were also unhappy with the dissolute atmosphere around French posts and thus founded their own network of villages, where possible, far from government posts.[33]

The Great Exodus

In 1898, Samori Touré, the most resolute enemy the French faced, was captured. The same year, the fortress at Sikasso fell to the French. A year later, a civilian governor, William Ponty, was appointed in the Soudan. Ponty and from 1902, Governor-General Ernest Roume in Dakar began to create a new colonial order. Slave raiding and trading were banned. In 1903, Roume decreed a new, federation-wide legal system.[34] When Ponty in the Soudan gave instructions setting up this new system, he insisted that the status of slavery could not be invoked in the new tribunals.[35] The French did not actually abolish slavery; but by denying it legal recognition, they effectively withdrew state support for slavery and thus gave slaves the "right" to leave their masters. In December 1905, Roume issued a decree that prohibited enslavement and any transactions in persons. Together, these two decrees led huge numbers of slaves to leave their masters between 1905 and 1914. Slave flight had long been a major problem, but the French often returned runaways to their masters, and in some areas they continued to do so even after 1905. At Banamba, the most important market in western Soudan and a major center of slave agriculture, slaves tried to leave their masters in the spring of 1905. In 1906, they tried again, and Ponty told the local administrator to let them go if they had paid their taxes and had passes.[36]

The Banamba slaves began a massive movement that swept French West Africa. Over two-thirds of a million left masters in Senegal, Mali, and Guinea, and perhaps over a million in French West Africa as a whole.[37] Most of those who left returned to earlier homes. The exodus involved groups, often family groups, sometimes much larger. Massive as the exodus was, most of those born into slavery remained where they were but renegotiated the conditions of their servitude. Fearing even more massive departures, masters were forced to concede slaves increasing control over their work life and their family life. Some slaves simply moved out of the master's household, often forming new villages nearby.[38] Former slaves sought to reestablish families and rebuild communities, particularly in Wasulu, a once populous area in southern Soudan literally stripped clean of people by Samori. There they tried to recreate communities that no longer existed. They brought news of those who had not left slavery because they were old, sick, or simply cautious. As refugees reestablished themselves, they sent kinsmen out to find and bring back lost family members. The lack of resources—guns to hunt, tools to work the land, or money to pay taxes—meant that these areas became major sources of labor migration. Freed slaves, mostly male, went to the peanut fields of Senegal, to the gold fields of upper Guinea, worked as porters, or hired themselves out to build the railways. The desire to reestablish families and rebuild communities was an important motif of the exodus. Others did not make it home or left home to settle in new communities where there was work.

There were, however, tensions in the process. Reconstructed communities received help from neither the administration nor the missions. Sometimes spouses did not want to go to the same place. Many were men and women whose families had long dispersed. And while new labor was always needed, returning slaves were initially a drain on the resources of communities that had suffered dramatically from decades of warfare and enslavement. Often, freedmen and freedwomen arrived without clear ties of kinship. In some cases, they did not remember their clan names and had to be assigned to clans. Some returnees were clearly dissatisfied. "The freed slave," wrote Deherme in 1906, "is a dissolvent, a fomenter of trouble in the village when he returns."[39] Deherme probably exaggerated, but a preliminary reading of 101 entry-level civil disputes heard before the native court in Bouguni in Wasulu indicates that 16 percent of the cases heard from 1905 to 1911 had either plaintiffs or defendants clearly identified as former slaves. Many of these cases involved disputes over child custody, marriage, and bridewealth transfers.[40] Recreating communities and families after slavery occurred against a backdrop of conflicts between men and women, many of whom had been in slave marriages.

Strategies of Female Slaves

Efforts of male slaves to reestablish their autonomy have been described elsewhere. Many choices available to freedmen were not available to freedwomen. One strategy of slaves heading home was to put the women and children into a liberty village until the men could establish contact with kin, find land, and make sure that there was enough food to feed the family. Needing money to pay taxes and buy tools and weapons, men migrated. They worked as porters, built railroads, and grew peanuts in Senegal. They also hunted and panned gold. In Senegal, many men found economic independence in agricultural settlements founded in frontier areas by the Mouride religious community. A young man would work for about eight years as part of a collective, clearing the land and establishing a new village. Only then was he freed to marry. Marriage was a reward for hard work and loyalty. The women remained home, raising crops and taking care of children, or, in the case of the Mourides, they entered the scene only after the men had done the heroic work.[41] This, in fact, was what the men wanted. They migrated in order to have a family life, but that depended on having a woman to return home to.

The French also did not want women taking part in migrations. They had an obsessive fear of vagrancy, crime, and disorder. The French position was deeply contradictory. On the one hand, they wanted to extend to African women some of the rights recently granted to French women, including the right to sue for divorce. On the other hand, they wanted to respect African customs, especially those regarding marital authority. The 1905 decree abolishing the slave trade coincided with a lively debate among colonial administrators regarding marriage. Many administrators argued that in the work they did, their lack of choice in marriage partners, and the transactional nature of bridewealth, wives were like slaves.[42] Barbara Cooper has termed the lack of distinction between marriage and enslavement a "conceptual fuzziness" that allowed aristocratic men and women of Maradi to maintain control over women. The colonial state, Cooper argues, turned a blind eye to de facto domestic slavery.[43] By excluding marriage from its antislavery policies, the French reinforced the patriarchal family.

Some women sought out missions. "A day does not pass," a missionary in Ségou wrote in 1897, "without some unfortunate coming to the mission."[44] Both male and female slaves took refuge in mission villages and then often sought to free their spouses.[45] Before 1905, the mission often had to pressure the local commandant to arrange purchase of a slave's freedom.[46] Some came to missions because they had been beaten or because they were not being fed.[47] Others came because they were about to be sold. The missions were eager to accept female runaways so that the boys who were a majority in their schools and orphanages could have Christian wives. Thus, even when hard-pressed financially, the missions tried to come up with money for bridewealth or for purchase of a slave woman who wanted to marry one of their Christians.[48] For the missionaries, Christian households were the building blocks of the Christian communities they sought to create. The slaves were more interested in being able to choose their own partners.[49] For many female slaves, Christian marriage within a Christian community afforded a measure of control of their own lives. Some of these women found security in Christianity and became the most deeply committed Christians.

Freed slaves, male and female, also made great efforts to find and free their children. Much of the struggle during the exodus took place over children. Masters in Banamba seized women and children in 1905, and, when the exodus restarted in 1906, seized the children again.[50] In Issa-Ber, three women who came looking for their children were killed and a fourth was sequestered. The administrator began sending guards along on such missions.[51] During famines, people often pawned their children to the missions.[52]

Freedwomen and the Native Courts

The legal system created in 1903 was important not only because it contributed to the exodus, but because it created an arena for Africans to seek resolution of their conflicts. The first courts for African subjects in the Soudan were up and running in the spring of 1905. Not surprisingly, disputes dealing with slavery appeared in court records, even though the courts were not legally permitted to recognize slave status in adjudicating cases.[53] For some disputes, however, we are able to identify the litigants as former slaves and the grievances as emanating from slavery. These cases cluster around three categories of dispute: marriage, child custody, and property.[54]

Even before the new courts opened, tensions emerged in the harems of many French allies. One of these was Aguibou Tal, who sided with the French and received as a reward Bandiagara in central Mali. Aguibou used his first years to increase the number of his slaves. When the French stopped his raids, he preyed on his own villages, asking each one to present him with a woman. In May 1903, twelve women fled to the French commandant claiming that they were poorly fed. Aguibou sent his men to bring them back, but the next day, three more came, and finally a group of thirty-eight.[55] Mademba Sy, the French-appointed king of Sinsani (also in Mali), not only built a kingdom, but peopled his palace with over one hundred "wives." Many of Mademba's wives fled the palace when Mademba was charged with malfeasance and interned in Kayes in 1900. After he was acquitted, Mademba asked the governor-general for help in recovering his runaway wives.[56]

The newly opened courts had to deal from the first with women seeking divorce or refusing to return to their husbands. Some administrators identified the problem as poor treatment and physical abuse; others suggested that husbands were abandoning their wives. With the departure of their slaves, household heads may well have turned to wives and children to make up for lost labor in the fields. Most abandonment cases were also rooted in the departure of slaves as males left their families, either to return to their homelands or to seek new ways of earning a living. Free men as well as freed slaves left during this period. The numerous cases of women seeking divorce or refusing to return to their husbands convinced many administrators that African women were beasts of burden and exploited workers. The high incidence of divorce, wrote the Koutiala administrator in 1909, was due to the "conception that the woman is a captive, an instrument of work and of exchange, who can be sold, given away, and repossessed according to the [husband's] whims and means without ever consulting her." The next year, the Koutiala administrator pressed his attack on African marriages by calling them "disguised sales," thus making them subject to the criminal provisions of the 1905 legislation abolishing the slave trade.[57]

Many slaves wanted to reconstruct their families as soon as possible, but some women used the opportunity to leave both free and slave husbands. This trend is especially marked in the Bouguni data, where fully 69 percent of the cases identifying slaves as litigants were about female ex-slaves refusing to return to their husbands. Fanta Kone and Mamadou Fofana were both slaves. They established a household and had one child. When slavery ended, Fanta Kone went home to her parents with their child and without telling Mamadou Fofana where she was going. When Fofana located her and asked that she return, she refused. Fofana even offered to regularize the marriage by paying bridewealth. Kone continued to refuse. Fofana eventually brought the dispute before the Bouguni native court, which rejected his claim.[58]

A slightly different strategy is indicated in the case Birama Kone brought against Tene Taraore. Kone actually bought Tene Taraore from her original master for three hundred francs in order to make her his wife. They had one child together. Kone had promised to bring Taraore back to her family, which he did. Taraore's parents thanked Kone and gave him two cows to compensate him for "ransoming" their daughter. Kone, however, wanted to keep Taraore as his wife. When she refused, he asked the court to force Taraore to return to him. The court ruled that the Taraore family's offer of two cows effectively reimbursed him for his original cost and that Tene Taraore was free to do as she wished. Moreover, the court ruled that since there was no bridewealth, Taraore had custody over her child.[59] The women in these cases remembered their original homes and found kin there. Not all women were so fortunate. Signiyoro Konare found herself in an unhappy marriage to Halla Diakite. Diakite had paid bridewealth to Konare's master. Rather than travel with him to Kati, Konare fled back to her former master. The court did not accept Konare's grounds for refusing to follow her husband, and, because he had formally married her, the court ruled that Konare had to return to her husband.[60] Even when a female slave was integrated into her master's household, the end of slavery could rupture that relationship. This was the issue when Karounga Samake asked the court to force Fili Diabite to return to him. Samake argued that he was married to Diabite. Diabite, however, convinced the court that they were not formally married because no bridewealth was paid, that she was actually his slave and lived as his concubine. The court agreed and ruled that Diabite was free to leave.[61]

Many marriage and divorce cases were also about child custody. If bridewealth was paid, even if only partially, the courts generally ruled in favor of the male claimant.[62] Breastfeeding infants remained with their mothers until they were four or five.[63] Female slaves often benefited from the fact that few slave marriages involved formal transfer of bridewealth: female slaves usually gained custody of children. The Koutiala administrator noted that many child custody cases had their origins in "the former state of slavery, where a couple is married without other formalities. From this union issue one or more children. Upon emancipation, each person has freedom of action. The women often refused to deliver the children and kept them. This gave rise to numerous disputes."[64] Kelebana Koulibaly and Kouma Diallo had two children while they were slaves. They were not formally married. When slavery ended, Kouma Diallo took the children and left her slave husband. In 1911, Koulibaly sought custody of the children, but the court ruled in favor of their mother.[65] Sometimes slave women left without their children only to try to recover them later. This was the case in 1912, when Guine Toukoula brought a case against Lahi Diara, her slave "husband." Toukoula argued in court that while she was a slave, her master had forced her to live with Lahi Diara, another slave. They had children. In his defense, Diara claimed that they were regularly married, but he had no proof to offer. Nor could he recall whether any bridewealth had actually been paid. In absence of proof, the court ruled for Guine Toukoula and gave her custody of the children.[66]

Court records indicate a third area where the end of slavery provided a reshuffling of gender roles. Before 1905, slave ownership and polygyny were the most significant forms of capital investment. The end of slavery and the commercial boom associated with colonial conquest ushered in a period during which men and women, masters and slaves, and elders and youth redefined their relationships to each other and to wealth. Men and women sought new opportunities for accumulation and new forms of investment. Money once invested in slaves went into livestock.[67] Slaves always had the right to time of their own, and if they worked hard, both male and female slaves were able to accumulate some wealth. According to custom, a slave's possessions were granted as usufruct by the master who could claim them as his own. This right was often litigated in places like Gumbu, when former masters seized slave property.[68] Soukoma Taraore argued in court that she was Karfala Diara's "domestic" for thirteen years and was given one day free each week. Taraore had invested her earnings in a cow, which had since produced two calves. When she left her master, she wanted her property, but he refused. The court ruled in favor of Taraore's claim.[69] Taraore's success points to the fact that even as slaves, women had the right to accumulate wealth. Controlling wealth empowered women, particularly in their marriage decisions. Even in marriage, women were able to maintain their own property separate from their husbands'. This was crucial when marriages broke up. Women who controlled their own wealth were better able to secure divorces because they could repay bridewealth that their kin had received. Since the bride's kin wanted to use their wealth to secure brides for their sons, unhappily married women could not count on kin to return their bridewealth. Thus, access to their own wealth provided women with greater independence and choice in marriage partners.

Conclusion

It is easy to see marriage as a new form of slavery, the father selling his daughter to a husband. The freedom of slave women was deeply constrained by concepts of gender and marriage held by African males and by male colonial officials. For a brief moment, African women were quick to use these opportunities to end marriages they did not want. This window of opportunity closed after 1910, however, as French colonial officials became more concerned with preserving male family authority.

Unions formed by women in slavery did not always last. Sometimes partners were chosen by masters. Freedwomen had little choice but to seek attachments with men, whether as protectors or partners. The life of freed slaves was harsh. The French gave little help except for assistance available in the liberty villages—and the colonial state insisted from the beginning on the payment of taxes in specie. The Catholic Church had few resources in what for it was a difficult period. Slaves were generally returning to poor areas. In some they had to protect themselves against predators, clear land, find seed, and buy tools. Freedom for the former slaves amounted to working for themselves and controlling their own family life.[70] The former slave had to be able to feed herself and guarantee her security, neither of which were completely assured under slavery. All of these objectives could only be achieved within a family unit, though efforts to form family units often involved other conflicts. The primary goal of the freed slaves was to re-create the network of ties that the slave trade had destroyed.

Notes

1 See Richard Roberts, "Representation, Structure, and Agency: Divorce in the French Soudan in the Early Twentieth Century," *Journal of African History* 40, no. 3 (1999): 389–410; Barbara M. Cooper, *Marriage in Maradi: Gender and Culture in a Hausa Society, 1900–1989* (Portsmouth, N.H.: Heinemann, 1997); Alice Conklin, *A Mission to Civilize: The Republican Idea of Empire in France and West Africa, 1895–1930* (Stanford, Calif.: Stanford University Press, 1997), chap. 3; Ghislaine Lydon, "The Unraveling

of a Neglected Source: A Report on Women in Francophone West Africa in the 1930s," *Cahiers d'études africaines* 147 (1997): 555–84; Maurice Delafosse, *Haut-Sénégal-Niger* (Paris: Maisonneuve and Larose, rpt. Paris, 1972), 3 vols., 3:2–3, 61–62. See also Richard Roberts, *Litigants and Households: African Disputes and Colonial Courts in the French Soudan, 1895–1912* (Portsmouth, N.H.: Heinemann, 2005), chaps. 5 and 6.

2 On slavery in Africa, see Walter Rodney, "African Slavery and Other Forms of Social Oppression on the Upper Guinea Coast in the Context of the Atlantic Slave Trade," *Journal of African History* 7 (1966): 431–43; John Fage, "Slavery and the Slave Trade in the Context of West African History," *Journal of African History* 10 (1969): 393–404; Suzanne Miers and Igor Kopytoff, eds., *Slavery in Africa: Historical and Anthropological Perspectives* (Madison: University of Wisconsin Press, 1977); Paul E. Lovejoy, *Transformations in Slavery: A History of Slavery in Africa*, 2nd ed. (Cambridge: Cambridge University Press, 2001).

3 Terence Ranger, "The Invention of Tradition in Africa," in *The Invention of Tradition*, ed. Eric Hobsbawm and Terence Ranger (Cambridge: Cambridge University Press, 1983); Martin Chanock, *Law, Custom and Social Order: The Colonial Experience in Malawi and Zambia* (Cambridge: Cambridge University Press, 1985); Kristin Mann and Richard Roberts, eds., *Law in Colonial Africa* (Portsmouth, N.H.: Heinemann, 1991).

4 See, among others, Frederick Cooper, "The Problem of Slavery in African Studies," *Journal of African History* 20, no. 1 (1979), 103–25; Martin Klein, ed., *Breaking the Chains: Slavery, Bondage, and Emancipation in Modern Africa and Asia* (Madison: University of Wisconsin Press, 1993); Lovejoy, *Transformations in Slavery*; Jonathon Glassman, *Feasts and Riots: Revelry, Rebellion, and Popular Consciousness on the Swahili Coast* (Portsmouth, N.H.: Heinemann, 1995).

5 Claire Robertson and Martin Klein, eds., *Women and Slavery in Africa* (Madison: University of Wisconsin Press, 1983). See also Claude Meillassoux, ed., *L'esclavage en Afrique pré-coloniale* (Paris: Maspero, 1975); Richard Roberts, *Warriors, Merchants and Slaves: The State and the Economy in the Middle Niger Valley, 1700–1914* (Stanford, Calif.: Stanford University Press, 1987); Lovejoy, *Transformations in Slavery*; Martin Klein, *Slavery and French Colonial Rule* (Cambridge: Cambridge University Press, 1998).

6 See Claude Meillassoux, "Female Slavery," and the response by Martin Klein, "Women and Slavery in the Western Soudan," both in Robertson and Klein, *Women and Slavery*.

7 Paul Lovejoy, "Concubinage and the Status of Women Slaves in Early Colonial Northern Nigeria," *Journal of African History* 29 (1988): 245–66; Paul Lovejoy, "Concubinage in the Sokoto Caliphate (1804–1903)," *Slavery and Abolition* 11 (1990): 159–89; Paul Lovejoy and Jan Hogendorn, *Slow Death for Slavery: The Course of Abolition in Northern Nigeria, 1897–1906* (Cambridge: Cambridge University Press, 1993), chaps. 4, 8.

8 For a similar argument, see Marcia Wright, *Strategies of Slaves and Women: Life Stories from East Central Africa* (New York: Lilian Barber, 1993).

9 The high rate of female retention and the death of men in slave raids meant that there was always a surplus of women in slaving societies. See John Thornton, "Sexual Demography: The Impact of the Slave Trade on Family Structure," in Robertson and Klein, *Women and Slavery*.

10 Claude Meillassoux, *Anthropologie de 1'esclavage: le ventre de fer et d'argent* (Paris: Presses Universitaires de France, 1986); Meillassoux, "Female Slavery."

11 Camilla Toulmin, *Cattle, Women, and Wells: Managing Household Survival in the Sahel* (Oxford: Clarendon, 1992); Roberts, "Representation, Structure, and Agency."

12 James Searing, *West African Slavery and Atlantic Commerce: The Senegal River Valley, 1700–1860* (Cambridge: Cambridge University Press, 1988); Bernard Moitt, "Slavery and Emancipation in Senegal's Peanut Basin: The Nineteenth and Twentieth Centuries," *International Journal of African Historical Studies* 22 (1989): 27–50.

13 George Brooks, "The Signares of St. Louis and Gorée: Women Entrepreneurs in Eighteenth Century Senegal," in *Women in Africa*, ed. E. Bay and N. Hafkin (Stanford, Calif.: Stanford University Press, 1976). On their role in the nineteenth century, see Mohammed Mbodj, "The Abolition of Slavery in Senegal, 1820–1890: Crisis or the Rise of a New Entrepreneurial Class," in Klein, *Breaking the Chains*, 197–211. On female entrepreneurs elsewhere on the West African coast, see George Brooks, "A Nhara of the Guinea-Bissau Region: Mae Aurelia Correia," in Robertson and Klein, *Women and Slavery*, 295–319; Bruce Mouser, "Women Slavers of Guinea-Conakry," in Robertson and Klein, *Women and Slavery*; Carole MacCormack, "Slaves, Slave Owners, and Slave Dealers: Sherbro Coast and Hinterland," in Robertson and Klein, *Women and Slavery*, 271–94.

14 Archives Nationales, République du Sénégal (hereafter ARS), Section L'Afrique occidentale française (hereafter AOF), series M, subsection "Réclamations."

15 Martin A. Klein, *Slavery and Colonial Rule in French West Africa* (New York: Cambridge University Press, 1998), chap. 2; Mbaye Guèye, "La fin de l'esclavage à St. Louis et à Gorée en 1848," *Bulletin de 1'Institut Fondamentale d'Afrique Noire* 28 (1966): 637–67; Roger Pasquier, "A propos de l'émancipation des esclaves au Sénégal au milieu du XIXe siècle en 1848," *Revue française d'histoire d'outre-mer* 54 (1967): 188–208; François Renault, *L'abolition de l'esclavage au Sénégal: L'attitude de l'administration française, 1848–1905* (Paris: Société française d'histoire d'outre-mer, P. Geuthner, 1972).

16 Decree of 11 Nov. 1857, ARS K 11.

17 Minutes Conseil d'Administration, 5 Dec. 1857, Archives Nationales, Section Outre-Mer (ANSOM), Paris, Senegal 14 15b. See also Mbaye Guèye, "L'esclavage au Sénégal du XVIIe au XIXe siècle" (PhD diss., Université de Nantes, 1969); Georges Deherme, "L'esclavage en Afrique Occidentale Française: Etude historique, critique et positive (1904)," in *Slavery and Its Abolition in French West Africa*, ed. Paul Lovejoy and Sydney Kanya-Forstner (Madison: University of Wisconsin Press, 1994), 125.

18 Klein, *Slavery and Colonial Rule*, 60–64.

19 Correspondence of Société des Missions Evangéliques de Paris, Sénégal (SMEP).

20 Victor Schoelcher, L'esclavage au Sénégal (Paris: Librairie centrale des publications populaires, 1880).

21 H. O. Idowu, "The Establishment of Protectorate Administration in Senegal, 1890–1914," Journal of the Historical Society of Nigeria 4 (1968): 247–65; Klein, Slavery and Colonial Rule, 66–67.

22 Governor of Senegal to Minister, 14 Nov. 1886, and Chief, Judicial Service, to Minister, 19 July 1887, Archives Nationales de la France, Section d'Outre Mer (hereinafter ANSOM), Sénégal 14 15 d.

23 Deherme, "Esclavage," 145. We have also profited from unpublished research of Bernard Moitt on this question.

24 Deherme, "Esclavage," 145.

25 A. S. Kanya-Forstner, Conquest of the Western Sudan (Cambridge: Cambridge University Press, 1969); Klein, Slavery and Colonial Rule, chaps. 5, 7.

26 Charles Monteil, "Journal d'un jeune administrateur stagiaire, 1896–98," unpublished manuscript, 138.

27 Chroniques, no. 68, Oct. 1895, Archives of the White Fathers (hereafter AWF).

28 Henri Frey, Campagne dans le Haut Niger (1885–1886) (Paris: Plon, 1888), 77–85; Jacques Méniaud, Les pionniers du Soudan, avant, avec et après Archinard (Paris: Société des publications modernes, 1931), 2 vols., 1:66–68. See also Myron Echenberg, Colonial Conscripts: The Tirailleurs Sénégalais in French West Africa, 1857–1960 (Portsmouth, N.H.: Heinemann, 1991). For a case from Senegal of a soldier's selling his "wife," see Martin A. Klein, Islam and Imperialism in Senegal; Sine-Saloum, 1847–1914 (Stanford: Stanford University Press, 1968).

29 Diaire, Ségou, April 1896, AWF, Rome.

30 Commandant Louis Baron, a retired military officer who was researching the history of the colonial army, personal communication with Klein. Cf. Ronald Hyam, Empire and Sexuality: The British Experience (New York: Manchester University Press, 1990).

31 Denise Bouche, Les villages de liberté en Afrique noire française, 1887–1910 (Paris: Mouton & Co et École Pratique des Hautes Études, 1968); Andrew Clark, "Freedom Villages in the Upper Senegal Valley, 1890–1910: A Reassessment," Slavery and Abolition 16 (1995): 311–30.

32 Quoted in R. P. Cros, "Mission de Kita (Soudan français)," Annales 9 (1894): 41–57.

33 Bouche, Villages de liberté, part 2.

34 Roberts, "Representation, Structure, and Agency."

35 This quote is Ponty's, but it was borrowed virtually word for word by Secretary-General Martial Merlin and then by Roume. No title, dealing with instructions regarding implementing the 10 Nov. 1903 decree, n.d. [Feb. 1904], Archives Nationales de Mali (hereafter ANM), 2 M 34.

36 Martin Klein and Richard Roberts, "The Banamba Slave Exodus of 1905 and the Decline of Slavery in the Western Sudan," Journal of African History 21 (1980): 375–

94. For a review of this period, see Klein, *Slavery and Colonial Rule*, chaps. 8 and 10; Richard Roberts, "The End of Slavery in French Soudan, 1905–1914," in *The End of Slavery in Africa*, ed. Suzanne Miers and Richard Roberts (Madison: University of Wisconsin Press, 1988), 282–307.

37 On the problems of calculating numbers, see Klein, *Slavery and Colonial Rule*, 170–73.

38 Roberts, "End of Slavery," describes the movement of slaves who remained in the Sahel but moved to better-watered districts. See also Klein, *Slavery and Colonial Rule*, chaps. 11–13.

39 Georges Deherme, *L'Afrique occidentale française: action politique, action économique, action sociale* (Paris: Librairie Bloud, 1908).

40 Bouguni data are derived from ANM 2 M 109.

41 Donal Cruise O'Brien, *The Mourides of Senegal* (Oxford: Clarendon Press, 1971), chap. 8; Jean Copans, *Les marabouts de l'arachide* (Paris: L'Harmattan, 1988).

42 Roberts, "Representation, Structure, and Agency."

43 Cooper, *Marriage in Maradi*, xlv, 9.

44 *Diaire*, Ségou, Jan. 1897, AWF; Mgr. Toulotte, "Compte-rendu du voyage d'un missionnaire d'Alger à travers le Sénégal, le Soudan et la Guinée," AWF, no. 953.

45 *Chroniques*, Patyana, Nov. and Dec. 1909, AWF.

46 *Diaire*, Ségou, 13–24 Jan. 1897, AWF.

47 On cases from Ouagadougou during a famine in 1906 and 1907, see AWF, *Diaires*.

48 *Diaire*, Ségou, 1897, AWF. At Banankorou, the nuns wanted to provide two hundred francs to buy the freedom of a female slave who caught the eye of a freed slave named Bilali. *Diaires*, Banankorou, 3 Jan. 1907, AWF. See also *Diaires*, Kita, 1903, AWF.

49 See, e.g., *Diaires*, Ouagadougou, 1906 and 1907.

50 Telegram, Lt. Gov. Fawtier, 29 May 1905, ANM, 15 G 170; Commandant Vidal to Lt. Gov. Fawtier, 25 June 1907, ANM, 1 N 27; Political Report, Bamako, 1 April 1906, ANM, 1 E 19. For a similar case in Kita, see *Chroniques*, Feb. 1908, AWF.

51 Annual Report, Issa-Ber, 1910, 1911, ANM, 1 E 43.

52 *Chroniques*, Baninkorou, no. 89, Jan. 1901, AWF; Report of Mgr. Bazin, n.d., AWF, i/074/015. In 1904, there is a report of children being pawned because parents cannot pay taxes. *Chroniques*, Baninkorou, no. 103, Jan. 1904, AWF.

53 Roberts has argued that in Gumbu masters tried to entangle former slaves in disputes over property and loans to keep them from leaving; Roberts, "The End of Slavery, Colonial Courts, and Social Conflict in Gumbu, 1908–1911," *Canadian Journal of African Studies* 34 (2000): 684–713.

54 Based on a very preliminary survey, we have thirty-four cases from Bamako, sixteen cases from Bouguni, and fourteen cases from Ségou. Roberts is coding the complete run of six thousand civil disputes heard before the *tribunaux de province* in the French Soudan from 1905 to 1912.

55   Monthly reports, May–Dec. 1903, ANM 1E 23.

56   Mademba, letter to governor-general, 5 March 1900, Medine, ARS-AOF 15 G 176. See also the case of Moussa Molo. Gov. Gen. AOF to Gov. Gambia, 11 June 1903, enclosure to Conf., 3 July 1903, Public Record Office, London, CO 87/168; Gov. Gambia to Colonial Office, 5 Oct. 1903, PRO, CO 87/170.

57   Rapport sur le fonctionnement de la justice indigène, Koutiala, 2nd quarter 1909, ANM 2 M 75.

58   The court ruled in favor of Fofana's claim for custody, but only after he paid one hundred francs. This ruling is not consistent with "custom" or with rulings in other child custody cases, but it suggests that the court felt that Fofana's willingness to pay bridewealth established his claim to the children. Mamadou Fofana v. Fanta Kone, 16 July 1910, Bouguni, ANM 2 M 109.

59   Birama Kone v. Tene Taraore, 18 Aug. 1910, Bouguni, ANM 2 M 109.

60   Halla Diakite v. Signiyoro Konare, 11 Nov. 1912, Bamako, ANM 2 M 105.

61   Karounga Samake v. Fili Diabite, 28 June 1907, Bamako, ANM 2 M 104.

62   See John Comaroff, ed., The Meaning of Marriage Payments (London: Academic, 1980); and Roberts, "Representation, Structure, and Agency."

63   E.g., Rapport sur le fonctionnement des tribunaux indigènes pendant le 2ème trimestre 1906, Bamako, ANM 2 M 54.

64   Rapport sur le fonctionnement de la justice indigène pendant le 4ième trimestre, Koutiala, 1908, ANM 2 M 75.

65   Kelebana Koulibaly v. Kouma Diallo, 29 Sept. 1911, Bamako, ANM 2 M 105.

66   Guine Toukoula v. Lahi Diara, 14 Oct. 1912, Bamako, ANM 2 M 105.

67   Roberts, chap. 7 in "Colonial Courts and Social Conflict in the French Soudan," in progress.

68   Roberts, Litigants and Households: African Disputes and Colonial Courts in the French Soudan, 1895–1912 (Portsmouth, N.H.: Heinemann, 2005), chaps. 5 and 6.

69   Soumoma Taraore v. Karfala Diara, 30 April 1912, Bamako, ANM 2 M 104.

70   Cf. Eric Foner, Nothing but Freedom: Emancipation and Its Legacy (Baton Rouge: Louisiana State University Press), 1982.

MICHAEL ZEUSKE

Two Stories of Gender and Slave Emancipation in Cienfuegos and Santa Clara, Central Cuba: A Microhistorical Approach to the Atlantic World

One of the peculiarities of the debate on Cuban slave emancipation is precisely its focus on *los negros esclavos*, the black male slaves of Fernando Ortiz's famous book title.[1] In this historiography, male slaves appear as the primary objects of slave emancipation in Cuba, with female slaves appearing only occasionally. Furthermore, these debates do not focus on all male slaves, but only on the *clase negra*, or rural, sugar-plantation slaves, and on what Dale W. Tomich has called "the second slavery."[2] This gap in the scholarship persists despite the early demand by Francisco de Arango y Parreño, a veritable Adam Smith of Atlantic slavery, that the Spanish Crown regulate the slave trade to ensure the arrival of more enslaved African women in Cuba.[3] Moreover, Arango promoted women's work in sugar production.[4] Thus while the historiography centers on men and on plantation society, the plantations (and the slaves' economies of the *conucos*)[5] often relied also on women for arduous agricultural work. Meanwhile, women frequently predominated among urban slaves, above all in domestic slavery.

The analytic categories of class and race dominate social histories of slave emancipation in Cuba. As Rebecca J. Scott's work demonstrates, it is not that these histories lack the concept of gender. Rather, they lack an analysis that asks what new perspectives we gain by using the concept of gender to analyze the process of emancipation. A few exceptions deal with female slaves in Cuban history but none with female former slaves shortly after emancipation.[6] But replacing the concept of class with that of gender does not resolve the problem. The process of slave emancipation (1869–86) overlapped the wars of independence from Spain (1868–98). "As Spain's major remaining New World colony," Scott writes, "and at the same time an island with an increasingly vigorous anticolonial movement, Cuba posed a political problem for its mother country that often overshadowed the issue of slavery itself."[7] To the extent that men dominated the anticolonial movement and the armed struggle, the gendering of emancipation remains overshadowed in political history and generally underexplored.[8]

Working for many years on the history of former slaves in Cuba, I formed part of the mainstream, using the analytical concepts of class or race rather than gender. More recently, I have moved from a focus on structural-regional history toward a more anthropological and microhistorical approach. Women play very important roles in the sources that one uses at this level of analysis, particularly in the notarial records available in almost every Cuban local or provincial archive. Nevertheless, my categories of analysis remained those of class and race until I began, with Scott, to use the Cienfuegos and Santa Clara notarial records (comparing them with material from other local Cuban archives) for research on naming patterns and access to property among ex-slaves.[9]

In the course of this work I read Alejandro de la Fuente's research[10] and was invited to contribute to this book. I realized that de la Fuente's claim that Cuban slaves required only fifteen years (1886–1901) to become citizens with full electoral rights is only half true. True, the 1901 constitution gave "universal suffrage" to men over twenty-one. But women only received the vote at thirty, and in 1934, a generation later.

This point should be considered in conjunction with the well-known fact that Cuban manumission rates were significantly higher among women (and particularly among young women) than among men. There is almost no research on this topic.[11] No one has undertaken in-depth research on Manuel Moreno Fraginals's 1986 observation, based on a sample of 1,320 eighteenth-century manumission deeds, that many more women than men obtained freedom. For Moreno this sample "shows an interesting interrelation among the legal institutions offering juridical routes to freedom."[12] One might generalize from Moreno's remarks using Stuart B. Schwartz's observation that the ease by which a person could move from slavery to legal freedom was indeed "an essential measure of a slave regime."[13] But how does one measure this "ease"? According to comparative criteria, one might argue that, on the one hand, Cuban slavery proved more permeable for women than for men and that, on the other, the discourse of the republican system relied quite heavily on the visibility of male ex-slaves. Perhaps female slaves preferred to emancipate themselves through legal routes while men, according to mainstream historiography, preferred to fight? Or were there rules and possibilities in this system that allowed women to liberate themselves more easily through legal means, such as manumission and *coartación*?[14]

And, finally, another set of problems: the stories of women buying land and constructing new spaces for their families are obtained from very local and individualized sources—but are these "small" processes only local ones? Are these stories only local or regional parts of macrohistorical, Atlantic, processes of American fights against European colonial powers? Or are the stories of fighting men, including black soldiers, taken from national narratives, so strong because they have to drown out the independent and very creative struggle of ex-slave women for emancipation within the juridical rules of Spanish empire? Or were the young sons of ex-slave mothers and land buyers also fighting against the new racism that had to be overcome through this attempt at integration? Were there also conflicts between mothers and sons (and other men) over participation in the war?

Gender in the First Stage of Emancipation in Cuba: Women, Notarial Records, and Subsistence in Microhistorical Perspective

Women ex-slaves become visible as social agents and purchasers of land primarily when we look at local archives such as the provincial and municipal archives of Cienfuegos, Santa Clara, Santiago de Cuba, and Remedios. A gendered approach to social history therefore requires the use of such archives. To understand what I found I had briefly to turn away from a focus on structure and attend instead to life histories. Combining the oral and the written, I attempted microhistory in the Italian style, tracing ex-slaves' property rights and access to land. Through this method women not only appear as important actors, but they even constitute a majority. As a result I asked whether female slaves and ex-slaves might have played a special role in the process of Cuban slave emancipation. At least two indicators suggest that the answer is yes.

1. The absolute majority of notarial records in which the actors are men and women labeled with the marker *s.o.a.* (*sin otro apellido*, "without another surname," often used as shorthand for "former slave")[15] deal with the purchase of land for urban houses (*fincas urbanas*) as well as houses (*casas de tabla y tejas*, that is, places of the "household") and land (*fincas rústicas, terrenos, sitios de labor*). Fewer records deal with wills (*testamentos*), loans (*créditos*), the recognition of *hijos naturales* (natural children), or the granting of *poder* (power of attorney) to lawyers or other citizens. Women are very well represented in notarized purchases of property.

2. Women were already prominent as property owners in the official documentation from the first census of rural property (1888) sent to the central authorities. Of eighteen *pardo* (mulatto) and *moreno* (black) landowners listed in one table of landholdings—very much an official source—covering the rural town of Lajas in the sugar hinterland of Cienfuegos, six were women of color (one *parda* and five *negras*).[16] Unfortunately, while these sources differentiate by color, they do not distinguish between former slaves and those who had been free prior to emancipation.

Only the local notarial records demonstrate the significance of female slaves and ex-slaves in relation to property, although even they do not allow precise quantification. They record women's involvement in many transactions related to property, finance, and wills. Here I give some representative examples from the most developed late-nineteenth-century sugar-producing zone, the hinterland of Cienfuegos and Sagua la Grande, a port city on the north coast with strong connections to the countryside in the central Cuban province of Santa Clara.[17]

One of the first purchases of land by a *morena* occurred in 1870 in Santo Domingo, an important rural center in northeast Santa Clara. We do not know if she had been a slave or was from the free black population. A white *vecino* (resident) sold "to the free morena María García . . . half a *caballería* [one *caballería* equals 13.4 hectares] of the land of the hacienda San Bartolomé . . . for the price of six hundred pesos or one thousand two hundred escudos which she received from the buyer."[18] Another example appears in the Lajas land transaction records. The free morenos León and Natalia Fortún, "without second surnames, from Africa," paid fifty pesos for a 698-square-meter plot of empty land in the La Guinea barrio on the outskirts of Lajas.[19] The purchase took place six years after former slaves in Lajas began frequently to buy small houses.[20] I found records of many similar sales in Sagua la Grande, Cienfuegos, Santiago de Cuba, and Remedios.

Purchases by morenas were most evident in Sagua la Grande. The majority acquired houses with their *solares* (portions of cultivable land of up to one thousand square meters). For instance, the forty-four-year-old María Jacinta Fernández, described as a morena "without second surname," paid two hundred gold pesos to don Felipe Obeso y Robles, described as "employed in business," for a *casa de alto y bajo de tabla y tejas*, situated on a 1,380-square-meter solar.[21] In the same city, the unmarried Bibiana Varela, like Fernández described as a morena without second surname, purchased one caballería of land for 170 pesos from a white woman, Petrona Ando.[22] Neither party could sign the deed. The witnesses required in such cases were always men, meaning that women always had to make alliances with men.

Women with the surname Ribalta appear in the Sagua la Grande deeds. Since Tomás Ribalta was one of the region's largest slaveholders, this strongly suggests former slave status.[23] For instance, forty-nine-year-old Ana María Ribalta, described as a morena "without second surname," sold a rural property of three caballerías, ten hectares to don Victor Gómez y Mollinedo for 119 pesos.[24] This example is contrary to the usual pattern of ex-slave women buying land.

In the phase of emancipation from 1878 to the 1890s, the primary goal of this group of women—whose size we do not know—was to secure their families' subsistence through mass purchase of urban solares and rural sitios (farms). They maintained a precarious subsistence by using personal alliances and existing rights. They made alliances with men who were lovers, husbands, notaries, and witnesses, men who took them to the notary's office. And sometimes they allied with other women. While these alliances were also unstable, the evidence gleaned from the registries suggests that the women who made them at least gained written titles and property rights.[25] According to certain sources from the period of political emancipation (1895–98), these women did not turn to violence, as did their sons and male ex-slaves.

In the following example, two morenas allied with a chino in order to save an urban house, six months after the final abolition of slavery. In February 1887, Dominga Lima, "without second surname," sold a very small finca urbana (low wood-and-tile house) to don Cárlos Rafael Valdés y López for 186 pesos and 20 centavos as a pacto de retracto.[26] About six weeks later, Valdés y López sold it back to Lima for the same price.[27] That same day Dominga, whose financial problems apparently persisted, sold the same land to another morena, Martina Aroes, also "without second surname." This time, however, she sold it for 250 pesos.[28] Two days later Martina Aroes divided her new property in two and sold one half to the asiático Manuel Núñez for 125 pesos.[29] The much higher price paid by Aroes, and the subsequent division of the land into two suggests that hers was an act of solidarity. Such alliances between Asian men and morenas also took place in other cities, such as Remedios.[30] These details demonstrate that women used almost everything they had to obtain a small house and plot of land. Despite having little money, they used some of it to pay the notary for a written deed.

Most notarial records in which Afro-Cuban women appear as actors deal with the buying and selling of property. Because these sources describe the location of the property, they allow us to trace the formation of "barrios negros," as men, women, and children emerged from slavery. One can closely follow the emergence of black residential areas in Sagua. In one record a white man, don Pedro Espinoza y Pérez, sold a solar for 250 pesos to "the morena Bernarda Reinoso, without second surname." His testimony explains the development of the nucleus of a new neighborhood. It records that he owns a ten-hectare *finca rústica* in the eastern part of town, which is crossed from southeast to northeast by a railroad. He has divided the land into small solares, composing blocks that are mostly six solares each. The solar he sold to Reinoso is one of these.[31]

The following notarial record from Sagua la Grande in 1888 likewise gives clues to the shaping of new neighborhoods. A physician and his brothers owned an old *sitio rústico* named "La Veguita," in the extreme south of Sagua la Grande. When former slaves began their search for land, La Veguita's owners divided the two caballerías (about sixty-seven acres) into 247 solares of one thousand square meters each. They sold part of a solar to don Manuel López y Fernández in *dominio directo*. This solar was bordered to the north by the solar of the moreno Eusebio Pérez, while to the west was the land of "the morenos Elías Ribalta y Felipa Larrondo."[32] The mention of the neighbors demonstrates the shaping of new black quarters with many black or colored residents.

A parallel process seems to have occurred in the rural village of Santo Domingo;[33] in the barrio El Seborucal of Abreus; and in the barrio Pueblo Nuevo of Cienfuegos, which was established in the late 1840s as a neighborhood of white and colored poor, but which after 1878 became a black and mulatto quarter. The new barrios were often formed near railroad lines. The division of land into small plots for sale to former slaves was big business for owners of marginal land in the years immediately before and during slave emancipation.

The best-known barrio of these times is undoubtedly La Guinea in Lajas. Local collective memory attributes the acquisition of a few hectares of land to a donation by a powerful landowning family, the Terrys, during the emancipation period. The donated land was on the far side of the railroad track on the edge of the town center, almost forming a ghetto, and was also almost adjacent to the land of the Caracas sugar *central*. Collective memory, published by historians, linguists, and ethnologists,[34] also states that in 1885–86 the Terrys partitioned small lots of this land into market gardens, and built plankwood huts with *guano* (palm-thatch) roofs. There, ex-slaves with the surnames Terry and Moré settled, among them the ancestors of the famous musician Benny Moré. The new settlement became known as La Guinea. With this transaction, which might be called reformist, the Terrys have long been thought to have killed two birds with one stone, assuring themselves of a nucleus of workers for their nearby *central* and avoiding uncontrolled settlement on their land. However, interviews conducted in Lajas in March 2000, as well as archival research, suggest a more complex picture. The residents of La Guinea have legal title to their solares, which were purchased by their ancestors, often by ex-slave mothers. The Terrys did not grant the land to its new owners, as the myth claims, but rather they and others sold it to them, at fifty pesos per plot. Many of the buyers were recognizably ex-slaves.[35] There is no documentary trace of the Terrys giving a single plot of land to an ex-slave, although they may have given some money, probably for the *Casino* (Club) *Congo San Antonio de Lajas*, which has been the cultural heart of the barrio since its foundation.

In addition to land transactions, the notarial records also include wills. These were important not only in registering living people's ownership of small amounts of land but also in transforming this ownership into a durable written form for future generations of kin.

The first case involves a morena and ex-slave, Juana Beronda, who explains in her will how she acquired the slave name "according to custom": "The morena Juana Beronda, without second surname, native of Gangá, in Africa, spinster, eighty years old. . . . Declares herself to be a native of Africa, and to have lost her parents, whom she did not know and whose names she does not remember, for this reason she took the name of her owners, according to custom."[36] Juana could not sign her name. The same day the "moreno Juan Bautista Bernal y Soto, known as Juan Ajuria, native of Puerto Príncipe," made a will naming Juana Beronda as his only heir.[37] The two were not officially married, but may have been common-law partners.

The will of a parda, Francisca Bulí, signed in the year after the abolition of slavery, shows that she owned a house and a very modest plot of land. Bulí used her will to ask the man with whom she had lived without marriage for many years to recognize their children as his, so that they did not grow up "without another surname." Naming the moreno Pedro Núñez Torres as her executor, shareholder (*tenedor*), administrator of her goods, and guardian and tutor of her young children, she also noted that she would like him to "recognize them as she desires."[38] Like most Afro-Cubans in these records, Francisca Bulí could not sign her name.

The will of a seventy-year-old morena from Remedios demonstrates the poverty of her small house and solar, but like similar wills it also mentions her limited means of subsistence. Josefa Broche, who described herself as a childless widow, listed her goods as "a solar, thirty by fifty *varas*, containing two small mud and guano-tiled rooms and many fruit trees."[39] She could not sign her name.

Did women maintain the conucos with their fruit trees under slavery? The maroon Esteban Montejo, of Miguel Barnet's *Cimarrón*, recalled that after 1886, "the conucos continued to exist, but only in a few places. With emancipation, black men stopped worrying about the conucos. Those who kept theirs tended them during the dead time. I didn't have conucos, because I didn't have a family."[40] If one accepts Montejo's voice as authentic, then what we might call the problem of conucos and gender results from a combination of factors. While most women with children had to create a more or less stable home (a precarious, but recognizable, stability), male ex-slaves, who made up the core of sugar-cutting workers, were frequently much more mobile. This mobility resulted as much from their work as it did from the fact that they had multiple family relationships (often very unstable, of course). Montejo describes this instability: "I always went around unattached. I didn't get married until I was old; I was a bachelor in many places. I met women of all colors. Arrogant ones and kind ones."[41]

Gender in the Second Stage of Emancipation: Men, Revolution, State Formation, and Citizenship

In researching the early postemancipation period I found records of individual slaves and ex-slaves only in very local archival material. From a structural perspective one might say that we were dealing only with isolated pieces of information within territories and sources defined by elites: plantation lists, lists of local boards of *patronato*, notarial records dealing with the buying and selling of male and female slaves, individual tickets of freedom, and so on. Slaves remained symbolically interred in the local texts that mentioned their names (e.g., lists of hacienda staff, records of the purchase of slaves). Metaphorically speaking, most male slaves had no home region—and female slaves even less so. Nor, in the early postemancipation period, did they become visible as actors in most of the spaces defined by elites. From the point of view of my sources, slaves initially had nothing to do with territorial structures, such as regions, the state, the political imaginary, or the nation, the most important space of the political imagination of that period.

Of course, in reality slaves and ex-slaves defined their own spaces. But these spaces hardly appear in the written sources. Instead, these spaces were the former slaves's conucos, houses (made of wood and tile, or sometimes built with the lumber of royal palms and roofed with leaves), families, casinos (clubs), solares, sitios, and complex trading networks around the plantation and between the sugarcane field and the mountain (monte). All had their own names within the slave community. Reyita (María de los Reyes Castillo Bueno, a black woman born in eastern Cuba in 1902) explains that the revolutionary war of 1895–98 in some cases produced the social right to choose a surname of one's own, that is, to define oneself as a family with a proper name.[42] Alain Yacou correctly affirms that in these places the ex-slaves were forced to develop very rapidly a sense of this other spatiality. This sense clearly forms part of cubanía (in the sense of the core Cuban identity), or perhaps it formed the basis of cubanía from below, since many white Cubans had come to the island as immigrants.[43]

The conceptual tool of the historical region, a territorial structure, developed by Germán Cardozo Galué, enabled me to analyze the most important zone of Cuban sugar production in the late-nineteenth and early twentieth centuries.[44] To understand male and female slaves as actors within elite-defined regions I had to reduce greatly the level of focus and enlarge my microhistorical lenses. I had to focus on "life histories" and move from the structural to the anthropological. As a result, I also began to use the concept of gender. This concept has transformed my understanding of periodization, sources, and institutions.

In terms of periodization, what is most important is men's and women's different roles at different stages of emancipation. I should underline that I am discussing the visibility of certain groups of women and men in specific types of sources. I should therefore emphasize that I do not know the size of these groups. If we consider the two essential moments of emancipation to be, first, manumission itself (and the thousands of individual manumission acts that appear up to 1886 in the notarial records under the title "freedom")—that is, individual and social freedom—and, second, full citizenship with suffrage in a Cuban state—that is, political freedom—gender is an extremely useful analytic category. My material demonstrates that women slaves and ex-slaves played an important role (possibly more important than did men) in all facets of the fullest process of manumission, the emancipation of families between 1878 and 1886. The life histories of Bárbara Pérez and Gregoria Quesada, both of whom lived near Cienfuegos, exemplify such women.[45]

Cuban ex-slave men needed three wars (or four, if one counts the so-called Spanish-American War as a separate war) to appear en masse as military and political actors in official sources (1895 recruitment lists from the final war against Spain, 1898 autonomist electoral lists as republicans). The same is true of their ability to define their own identity and own land. The men who returned from the war against Spain had at least gained the status of *mambí*, veteran, and liberator. Some of the most important biographies of such men are those of Ciriaco and Cayetano Quesada and Esteban Montejo. [46]

On the other hand, freedmen waited only fifteen years—half a generation—after the abolition of slavery in 1886 before they achieved enfranchised citizenship through the 1901 Constitution, which embodied Martí's ideal that "to be Cuban is more than to be black, more than to be mulatto, more than to be white."[47] Female ex-slaves, and all Cuban women, only gained the right to vote in 1934, from the new independent state that emerged out of the 1933 revolution.

In terms of sources, the concept of gender has sharpened my attention to the fact that some male and a few female ex-slaves are identified as such only in a few of the lists that relate *mambises* to territorial entities determined by elites. Later on, electoral lists, as sources for the construction of the Cuban republican state, render women both invisible and mute. In the old sources such as plantation lists, notarial records including manumission records, conucos, solares, loans of money, alliances, small houses, and workplaces, women ex-slaves had been the most important actors. The later sources, by contrast, erase women, ceding these new spaces—such as regions, provinces, and sometimes even the central state—to men. Black men appear here primarily as clients of the old and new white elites, although during the war there had been black and mulatto leaders as well as strong interracial alliances.[48] We may establish a general rule: the higher the level of the state, the whiter the leadership, although there were exceptions, such as the writer Martín Morúa Delgado or the journalist Juan Gualberto Gómez. The definition and construction of the new Cuban nation on the political foundations of the centralized state relied on a large majority of white men and a few black men. Yet because of masculine "universal suffrage," the national reputation of some black men, and the interracial alliances of the mambises in the wars of independence, the new nation never had an explicitly white supremacist ideology. There were many complicated negotiations in these processes.[49] From 1897 (separatist Constitution of Yaya), 1898 on (with autonomist legislation), and particularly after 1901, the Constitution's criteria for universal male suffrage greatly reinforced this basis of possible definition of political structures, including by Afro-Cuban men.

In terms of institutions, the concept of gender and the notarial materials allow us to rethink the institution of coartación[50] (which Scott notes was largely financed through the sale of conucos and pigs).[51] This was a key feature of urban slave life, linking self-purchase with the means of family substance. In addition, the concept of gender shows that we need to consider how the conuco–family subsistence complex emerged into the world of written rights.

Coartación had long nourished the growth of a free population of color. In the countryside, however, self-purchase was generally far beyond the reach of ordinary field slaves. Self-purchase rates in the plantation zones were very low through the 1860s. As the process of legally supervised gradual emancipation began in the 1870s with the freeing of newborns and the elderly, however, the rate of self-purchase and the purchase of children accelerated, even in the countryside. Perhaps we should imagine the small plots of land (first the co-nuco,[52] then the solar, the casa de tablas y tejas, and the sitio rural) as institutional cornerstones for the rural regions dominated by slavery. Perhaps we should imagine the women who managed to purchase their own freedom and the basic means of subsistence as the front line in the struggle for the final dissolution of slavery through legal methods. Thus the conuco and solar were Archimedean points for some female slaves or ex-slaves. Women may well have played a more important role than men in the process of gaining access to land at or immediately after the abolition of slavery. In that case, these institutions should be added to the urban *cabildo*,[53] which has until now been considered the most important institution of solidarity between free black people and their still-enslaved kin.

Preliminary Conclusions

The first conclusion is methodological. From the notarial records themselves we cannot draw comparative conclusions about the "ease" of access to freedom. We cannot make large-scale comparisons before collecting more material and before we have some sense of the size of the group of women whose transactions figure in notarial records, relative to the group of female slaves and ex-slaves who did not own property or who did not have access to notaries.

The second preliminary conclusion is that a gendered social history reveals two stories about access to land, the most important means of subsistence. The first relates to women. Before the final war for independence (1870s–1890s), women frequently controlled the conucos during slavery and the solar afterward, acquiring them according to the legal rules of the colonial state.[54]

The other story is that of the veteran mambises. The men returned to the rural villages after the war with the reputation of "liberators" and with new access to institutions created under new political conditions (the rural guard, political clientalism, wages from the state, the electoral system, the vote). This, along with the construction of the Cuban republican state, gave this group of ex-slaves, now liberators, new ways to obtain land. Thus the heroic role of the mambí overcame the more modest, but more stable, female role of small property owner in the years before the war.

We lack a narrative for one of these two stories. Perhaps in the Cuban case the story of conflict over children, the story of the family, may unify the contents of these two narratives. Scott mentions this conflict over children during the period of *patronato* (apprenticeship; 1880–86) and in the process of self-purchase. It was the most serious conflict of the era, and it bitterly marked the experience of emancipation.[55] Such conflicts were frequently reflected in the notarial records. To give only one example: the archives include the deed of sale of Mercedes, a twenty-one-year-old parda with a free four- or five-year-old daughter, Sabina. The six hundred pesos paid for Mercedes also included Sabina's patronato.[56] Perhaps the sons of these enslaved mothers, who had experienced their mothers' struggles for access to land under conditions of colonial state control, experienced this struggle as humiliating and very difficult for their mothers. Perhaps, as I have argued elsewhere, these sons, the *muchachones*, as a result became an important group in the Cuban Army of Liberation.

How do we explain men's and women's different attitudes to land? Perhaps the words of Esteban Montejo provide a clue, along with an explanation that directs or channels the actors more within structures and institutions. Thus my third preliminary conclusion is that in the process of emancipation in Cuba there were, as in all slave societies, many actors with very different interests. Male and female slaves were both subjects and objects of this process. Slave emancipation characteristically emerged from an explosive interplay between transformations in structures of production and politics, insistent demands from slaves themselves, and grudging efforts by the state to control an accelerating transition. Throughout the Americas, war was often the catalyst that triggered the crisis of slavery, or made the direction of change irreversible. The Spanish state, seeking to end the Ten Years' War, initiated deep structural and political transformations. A resettlement program started in the late 1870s (*reconstrucción*), distributing small plots of land in closely supervised settlements, the majority on land near the railroads, to Cubans to reinforce (or buy) their loyalty to Spain.[57] In addition, the Spanish constitution of 1876, which was applied to Cuba, defined towns with at least eight thousand inhabitants as *términos municipales* (municipalities), the lowest level of a new state structure. The new términos municipales had the right to manage some of their tax incomes. This linked the Spanish Empire's state interests with the interests of the Cuban vecino elite of small rural towns.

When, in 1884, the imperial government declared its intention to withdraw término municipal status from all towns with fewer than eight thousand inhabitants, the *ayuntamiento* (local government) of Lajas, where La Guinea is located, felt "threatened with death." The secretary of the ayuntamiento, Agustín Cruz y Cruz, wrote on 31 December 1883 that Lajas had 7,548 inhabitants. During the following year there was a large increase in the number of inhabitants. Lajas acquired 828 new residents through birth and, even more interesting, immigration. There were only 191 deaths and emigrations, leaving a net increase of 637 inhabitants. Thus Lajas had by 1884 a population of 8,185.[58] Among the individuals who made up this net increase were 107 persons listed with race markers such as *moreno, morena, pardo,* or *parda.* Thirty-six of these were female heads of households, and 99 percent of them had only one surname.[59] The town's power-holders, in effect, benefited from an influx of former slaves that pushed the population over eight thousand. Some of these new inhabitants, so desired by the taxpaying vecino elite, appear in notarial records as buyers of land, as in the cases referred to in this essay. Despite the fact that women were a minority of the immigrants to Lajas, they were a majority of the purchasers of land in the notarial records.

Finally, if the concepts of gender and agency are to have explanatory power, more research is needed that examines the relationship between the macro, the "big picture" of the Atlantic world (e.g., the pressure of the competition between sugar cane and sugar beet) and the micro. Then we will see that the postemancipation world was filled with women (and men) trying to exercise agency, even within a very small field of activity. Not all of these actors are visible, but some are. Analyzing new types of narratives and sources, we can detect that these "small fields of activity" seem to have been quite general on the ground. Microhistory enables us to see them in the big picture of slave emancipation in the Atlantic world.

Notes

I wish to thank Rebecca J. Scott, Lara Putnam, and Diana Paton for their close readings and valuable criticism.

1 Fernando Ortiz, *Hampa afro-cubana: Los negros esclavos—Estudio sociológico y de derecho público* (Havana: Revista Bimestre Cubana, 1916); new ed., *Los negros esclavos* (Havana: Ciencias Sociales, 1976).

2 Dale W. Tomich, "The 'Second Slavery': Bonded Labor and the Transformations of the Nineteenth-Century World Economy," in *Rethinking the Nineteenth Century: Contradictions and Movement*, ed. F. O. Ramírez (New York: Greenwood, 1988), 103–17.

3 Francisco de Arango y Parreño, "Certificación de la Secretaría del Consulado de La Habana y Real Orden reservada de 22 de abril de 1804, sobre escasez de hembras esclavas y medios de propagar la especie negra," in *Obras de D. Francisco de Arango y Parreño*, 2 vols. (Havana: Publicaciones de la Dirección de Cultura del Ministerio de Educación, 1952), 2:196–98; Arango y Parreño, "Discurso sobre la agricultura de La Habana y medios de fomentarla," in *Documentos para la historia de Cuba*, 5 vols. (published in 4 books), ed. Hortensia Pichardo (Havana: Ciencias Sociales, 1973), 1:162–97; Michael Zeuske, *Sklavereien, Emanzipationen und atlantische Weltgeschichte: Essays über Mikrogeschichten, Sklaven, Globalisierungen und Rassismus*, Arbeitsberichte des Instituts für Kultur und Universalgeschichte Leipzig e.V., vol. 6 (Leipzig: Leipziger Universitätsverlag, 2002).

4 Manuel Moreno Fraginals, "Sexo y producción," in *El ingenio: Complejo económico social cubano del azúcar*, 3 vols. (Havana: Ciencias Sociales, 1978), 2:38–57.

5 See the romantic but quite authentic description in Anselmo Suárez y Romero, "El domingo en los ingenios" (1840), in *Costumbristas cubanos del siglo XIX*, ed. Salvador Bueno (Caracas: Ayacucho, 1985).

6 Digna Castañeda, "The Female Slave in Cuba during the First Half of the Nineteenth Century," in *Engendering History: Caribbean Women in Historical Perspective*, ed. Verene Shepherd, Bridget Brereton, and Barbara Bailey (London: James Currey, 1995), 141–54.

7 Rebecca J. Scott, *Slave Emancipation in Cuba: The Transition to Free Labor, 1860–1899* (Princeton, N.J.: Princeton University Press, 1985), 283.

8 Exceptions include María Eugenia Chaves, "La mujer esclava y sus estrategías de libertad en el mundo hispánico colonial de fines del siglo XVII," *Anales* (Göteborg), new ser., no. 1 (1998): 91–117; and Barbara Bush, "From Slavery to Freedom: Black Women, Cultural Resistance and Identity in Caribbean Plantation Society," in *History and Histories in the Caribbean*, ed. Thomas Bremer and Ulrich Fleischmann (Madrid: Iberoamericana, 2001).

9 I had previously used these records in work on client relationships. Michael Zeuske, " 'Los negros hicimos la independencia': Aspectos de la movilización afrocubana en un *hinterland* cubano—Cienfuegos entre colonia y república," in *Espacios, silencios y los sentidos de la libertad: Cuba entre 1898 y 1912*, ed. Fernando Martínez Heredia, Rebecca J. Scott, and Orlando García Martínez (Havana: Unión, 2001).

10 Alejandro de la Fuente, *"A Nation for All": Race, Inequality, and Politics in Twentieth-Century Cuba* (Chapel Hill: University of North Carolina Press, 2001); Alejandro de la Fuente, "Slavery, Claims-Making and Citizenship in Cuba: The Tannenbaum Debate Revisited," *Law and History Review* 22, no. 2 (2004): 339–69 (I thank the author for sharing with me an earlier version of this essay).

11 With a few important exceptions, such as María Elena Díaz, *The Virgin, the*

King, and the Royal Slaves of El Cobre: Negotiating Freedom in Colonial Cuba, 1670–1780 (Stanford, Calif.: Stanford University Press, 2000). Díaz demonstrates that among the king's slaves of El Cobre "males . . . were not only more likely to be free than females but also more likely to manumit themselves," contrary to the more general tendency on the island (256–57).

12 Manuel Moreno Fraginals, "Peculiaridades de la esclavitud en Cuba," Islas: Revista de la Universidad de Las Villas (Santa Clara), no. 85 (1986): 3–12.

13 Stuart B. Schwartz, Sugar Plantations in the Formation of Brazilian Society: Bahia, 1550–1835 (Cambridge: Cambridge University Press, 1985), 253.

14 Stuart B. Schwartz, "The Manumission of Slaves in Colonial Brazil: Bahia, 1684–1745," Hispanic American Historical Review (hereafter HAHR) 54, no. 4 (1974): 603–35; Lyman L. Johnson, "Manumission in Colonial Buenos Aires, 1776–1810," HAHR 59, no. 2 (1979): 258–79; Manuel Lucena Salmoral, "El derecho de coartación del esclavo en la América española," Revista de Indias 59, no. 216 (1999): 357–74; Rebecca J. Scott and Michael Zeuske, "Property in Writing, Property on the Ground: Pigs, Horses, Land, and Citizenship in the Aftermath of Slavery, Cuba, 1880–1909," Comparative Studies in Society and History 44 (2002): 669–99; Zeuske, "Hidden Markers, Open Secrets: Race Marking and Race Making in Cuba," New West Indian Guide/Nieuwe West-Indische Gids 76, nos. 3–4 (2002): 235–66.

15 Zeuske, "Hidden Markers." To understand the implications of being sin otro apellido (without another surname) or sin segundo apellido (without second surname, abbreviated s.o.a.), one must understand naming patterns in Castilian-Cuban culture. In this culture every person with legally married parents has two apellidos (surnames). For example, Juan Martínez García is the son of the couple Pedro Martínez Mena and María García Jiménez. Juan's first surname (apellido) is the first surname of his father Pedro (Martínez); his second surname (segundo apellido) is the first surname of his mother María (García). For daily use he would be called only Juan Martínez. During abolition slaves received the first surname of one of their last owners as a civil surname, written down in their new cédula personal. See Rebecca J. Scott and Michael Zeuske, "Le droit d'avoir des droits: Les revendications des ex-esclaves à Cuba (1872–1909)." Annales, Histoire, Sciences sociales 59, no. 3 (2004): 521–45.

16 Padrón de la riqueza rústica of 1887–88. See the circular of the governor of Santa Clara province, 26 Sept. 1885, fol. 2r–3r, "Expediente relativo al amillaramiento de fincas urbanas y rústicas según el reglamento," inv. 1, exp. 135, leg. 2, Archivo Provincial de Cienfuegos, Fondo Ayuntamiento de Lajas (hereafter APC, FAL); and "Expediente que contiene documentos sobre amillaramiento o padrón de la riqueza rústica" (25 Oct. 1887–17 Dec. 1888), exp. 136, leg. 2, APC, FAL.

17 Michael Zeuske, "Estructuras, mobilización afrocubana y clientelas en un hinterland cubano: Cienfuegos, 1895–1906," Tiempos de América: Revista de historia, cultura y territorio (Castellón), no. 2 (1998): 93–116.

18 Archivo Histórico Provincial de Villa Clara (hereafter AHPVC), Protocolos

Antonio Palma, Sagua la Grande, 1870, vol. 1 (Jan.–July), fols. 143v., 145r., escritura no. 138, "Venta de terreno," Sagua, 22 Feb. 1870.

19 APC Protocolos D. José Rafael Villafuerte y Castellanos, 1883 (Jan.–Dec.), fols. 418r–21r, escritura no. 98, "Venta de solares yermos," 14 June 1883.

20 Ibid., 1878 (Jan.–Dec.), fols. 387r–88v, escritura no. 149, "Venta de solares." This document refers to the earliest record of a sale to persons with slave surnames, in 1877; I could not find the original record to which it refers.

21 AHPVC, Protocolos Calixto María Casals y Valdés, Sagua la Grande 1886, vol. 1, fols. 631r–32v, escritura no. 187 "Venta de finca urbana," Sagua, 15 June 1886.

22 Ibid., 1886, vol. 2 (fols. 651–1279), fols. 1015r–17r, escritura no. 262, "Venta de terreno," Sagua, 27 Sept. 1886.

23 On Ribalta, see the list made by Carlos Rebello (*Estados relativos a la producción azucarera de la Isla de Cuba, formados competentemente y con autorización de la Intendencia de Ejército y Hacienda, s/i* (Havana: 1860). For Pablo Rivalta as owner of the Santa Marta sugar estate, see Enrique Edo y Llop, *Memoria histórica de la Villa de Cienfuegos y su jurisdicción* (Cienfuegos: El Telégrafo, 1861), appendix, 54–60; while Tomás Ribalta is listed as the owner of Santa Teresa.

24 AHPVC, Protocolos Calixto María Casals y Valdés, Sagua la Grande, 1886, vol. 2 (fols. 651–1279), fols. 1019r–20v, escritura no. 263 "Venta de terreno," Sagua, 29 Sept. 1886.

25 Scott and Zeuske, "Property in Writing."

26 AHPVC, Protocolos Calixto María Casals y Valdés, Sagua la Grande, 1887, vol. 1 (Jan.–June), fols., 159r–60v, escritura no. 45, "Venta en pacto de retracto," Sagua, 7 Feb. 1887. The *pacto de retracto* (and *retroventa*) was a form of short-term loan. The seller remained in the house and had first right to repurchase it.

27 Ibid., fols. 341r–43r, escritura no. 90, "Retroventa," Sagua, 24 March 1887.

28 Ibid., fols. 345r–46v, escritura no. 92. "Venta de finca urbana," Sagua, 24 March 1887.

29 Ibid., fols. 353r–54v, escritura no. 94, "Venta de la mitad de finca urbana," Sagua, 26 March 1887.

30 Archivo Histórico Municipal de Remedios (hereafter AHMR), Escribanías y Notarías, partido judicial de Remedios, protocolos José Miguel Jiménez, fondo no. 67, 1884, vol. 1 (Jan.–March), fols. 285r–88r, escritura no. 62, "Venta de un pedazo de solar," Remedios, 22 Feb. 1884.

31 AHPVC, Protocolos Calixto María Casals y Valdés, Sagua la Grande, 1887, vol. 1 (Jan.–June), fols. 347r–50r, escritura no. 92, "Venta de terreno," Sagua, 25 March 1887.

32 Ibid., 1888, vol. 2 (July–Dec.), fols. 1047r–50r, escritura no. 244, "Venta de dominio directo," Sagua la Grande, 2 July 1888.

33 Ibid., 1889 (Jan.–Dec.), fols. 1142r–43v, escritura "Venta de solar," Sagua, 10 Dec. 1889.

34 John Dumoulin, "El primer desarrollo del movimiento obrero y la formación del proletariado en el sector azucarero: Cruces, 1886–1902," *Islas: Revista de la Univer-*

sidad de Las Villas, no. 48 (1973): 3–66, esp. 19; Gema Valdes Acosta, "Descripción de remanentes de las lenguas bantues en Santa Isabel de las Lajas," *Islas: Revista de la Universidad de Las Villas*, no. 48 (1973): 67–85; Román García Herrera: "Observaciones etnológicas de dos sectas religiosas afrocubanas en una comunidad lajera: La Guinea," *Islas: Revista de la Universidad de Las Villas*, no. 43 (1972): 145–81.

35 Most of the notarial records appear in the records of José Rafael Villafuerte y Castellanos, e.g.: A P C, Protocolos D. José Rafael Villafuerte y Castellanos, no. 12 (1883), fols. 412r–15v, escritura no. 97; and ibid., no. 12 (1883), fols. 418r–21r.

36 A H P V C, Protocolos Calixto María Casals y Valdés, Sagua la Grande, 1889 (Jan.–Dec.), fols. 1076r–77v, escritura no. 300, "Testamento," Sagua, 22 Nov. 1889.

37 Ibid., fols. 1074r–75v, escritura no. 299, "Testamento," Sagua, 22 Nov. 1889.

38 Ibid., 1887, vol. 1 (Jan.–June), fols. 299r–302r, escritura no. 75, "Testamento," Sagua, 4 March 1887.

39 A H M R, Escribanías y Notarías, partido judicial de Remedios, protocolos José Miguel Jiménez, fondo no. 67, 1884, vol. 2 (21 March–16 Aug.), fols. 983r–85r, escritura no. 212, "Testamento nuncupativo" (Remedios, 12 July 1884).

40 Miguel Barnet, *Cimarrón* (Havana: Gente Nueva, 1967), 75; translations from this book are my own. See also Barnet, *Biography of a Runaway Slave*, trans. Nick Hill (Willimantic, Conn.: Curbstone, 1994).

41 All from Barnet, *Cimarrón*, 78–79. Michael Zeuske, "Más novedades de Esteban Montejo," *Del Caribe* (Santiago de Cuba), no. 38 (2002): 95–101.

42 Reyita recalls that her surnames "should be Castillo Hechavarría, because my mother had the surname of my grandmother's owner, who was also her father. But all of us children felt such hatred toward that family—whom we didn't even know—that my brother Pepe decided that we should change it to Bueno." María de los Reyes Castillo Bueno, *Reyita, sencillamente testimonio de una negra cubana nonagenaria*, ed. Daisy Rubiera Castillo (Havana: Prolibros, 1997), 18. The note says that the source of the right to choose a surname was the rural insurrection: "According to Reyita, her brother Pepe heard that in the insurrectionary countryside the black mambises, who had been slaves, said that at the end of the war they would stop using the surname of their owners. Due to the hatred that he felt toward the former owners of his mother and grandmother, at the beginning of the Republic and helped by a cousin who was a lawyer, the son of a great aunt, he changed the Hechavarría to Bueno, which from that moment on his children used as a first or second surname, depending on whether they were natural or recognized children. The name Bueno may have been that of the lawyer cousin" (173).

43 Alain Yacou, "Altérité radicale et *convivencia*: Le marronnage dans l'île de Cuba dans la première moitié du XIXe siècle," in *Structures et cultures des sociétés ibéro-américaines au-delà du modèle socio-économique: Colloque international en hommage au professeur François Chevalier, 29–30 avril 1988* (Paris: CNRS, 1990).

44 Germán Cardozo Galué, *Maracaibo y su región histórica: El circuito agroexportador, 1830–1860* (Maracaibo: Editorial de la Universidad del Zulia, 1991).

45 Rebecca J. Scott, "Reclaiming Gregoria's Mule: The Meaning of Freedom in the Arimao and Caunao Valleys, Cienfuegos, Cuba, 1880–1899," *Past and Present*, no. 170 (2001): 181–216; Scott, "Tres vidas, una guerra. Rafael Iznaga, Bárbara Pérez y Gregoria Quesada entre la emancipación y la ciudadanía," in *Historia y memoria: sociedad, cultura y vida cotidiana en Cuba, 1878–1917* (Havana: Centro de Investigación y Desarrollo de la Cultura Cubana Juan Marinello/Latin American and Caribbean Studies Program of the University of Michigan, 2003), 83–99.

46 Scott and Zeuske, "Droit d'avoir des droits."

47 José Martí, "Mi raza" (*Patria*, 16 April 1893), in *Obras completas*, 28 vols. (Havana: Editorial Nacional de Cuba, 1963–1973), 2:298–300; Martí, "Los cubanos de Jamaica y los revolucionarios de Haití" (1894), in ibid., 3:103–6; de la Fuente, "A Nation for All," 26–44; de la Fuente, "Slavery, Claims-Making and Citizenship in Cuba."

48 The families—and particularly the mothers, wives, and sisters—reappear in the sources produced by the problem of "back pay" for the combatants of the Cuban Liberation Army after the war; that is, after the conflict women again formed the majority in sources that deal with money for subsistence. See Zeuske, " 'Los negros hicimos la independencia.' "

49 Ada Ferrer, *Insurgent Cuba: Race, Nation, and Revolution, 1868–1898* (Chapel Hill: University of North Carolina Press, 1999).

50 Salmoral, "Derecho de coartación del esclavo."

51 Scott, *Slave Emancipation*, 149–55.

52 David Sartorius, "Conucos y subsistencia: El caso del ingenio Santa Rosalía," in Martínez Heredia, Scott, and García Martínez, *Espacios*.

53 Philip A. Howard, *Changing History: Afro-Cuban Cabildos and Societies of Color in the Nineteenth Century* (Baton Rouge: Louisiana State University Press, 1998).

54 This is one of the arguments in Rebecca J. Scott and Michael Zeuske, "Demandas de propiedad y ciudadanía: Los exesclavos y sus descendientes en la región central de Cuba," in *Illes e imperis* 5 (Barcelona): 109–34; see also Scott and Zeuske, "Property in Writing."

55 Scott, *Slave Emancipation*, 166–67.

56 APC, Protocolos José Rafael de Villafuerte y Castellanos, 1877 (Jan.–Dec.), fols. 49r–50v, escritura no. 18, "Venta de esclava," Cienfuegos, 8 Feb. 1877.

57 Ferrer, *Insurgent Cuba*, 73, 100–104; Scott and Zeuske, "Property in Writing," 10; Imilcy Balboa Navarro, *Los brazos necesarios: Inmigración, colonización y trabajo libre en Cuba, 1878–1898*, prologue by José A. Piqueras (Valencia: Centro Francisco Tomás y Valiente U N E D Alzira-Valencia, 2000), 49–54.

58 APC FAL leg. 2, exp. 108, no. 111, inv. 1, fols. 7r–8r. In 1846 Lajas had only 147 inhabitants, nearly all of them of Galician or Canarian ancestry.

59 Ibid., leg. 2, exp. 132, inv. 1 (14 Dec. 1884–2 Jan. 1885): "Rectificación del padrón vecinal del año 1884"; ibid., no. 111, leg. 2, exp. 133, inv. 1: Expediente que contiene documentos relativos a la rectificación del padrón vecinal del año 1885 (31 Dec. 1885–20 Jan. 1886), ibid., fols. 6r–21r.

 ILEANA RODRÍGUEZ-SILVA

Libertos and Libertas in the Construction of the Free Worker in Postemancipation Puerto Rico

Through the three-year apprenticeship period and a forced contract system (1873–76), colonial authorities and conservative elites (Spanish loyalists) in Puerto Rico intended to maintain their hold and control over former slaves, an important sector of the laboring class.[1] To Liberal, abolitionist elites, apprenticeship regulations were a means to incorporate the liberto class into the modern society the Liberals envisioned.[2] Former slaves, however, subverted the apprenticeship system by appropriating elites' language of labor and assuming an identity as workers. As free laborers, libertos and libertas pressed for their rights and demanded improvement in working and living conditions. Consequently, former slaves became workers conscious of their rights and responsibilities, constituting themselves into a critical political force, one vital in the struggle for the island's political autonomy from Spain during the last two decades of the nineteenth century.

The interplay between the apprenticeship legislation, its legal practice, and former slaves' actions forged a gendered political identity of the worker in the postemancipation period. The contract system was meant to create a compliant labor force out of the new free workers. Through contracts, island elites, especially the Liberal class, also attempted to impose a gendered division of labor and a moral code on the lower classes in an effort to ignite a social regeneration they viewed as crucial for the industrial and intellectual advancement of the island. In this endeavor, Liberal elites envisioned the free worker of the future as a reliable masculine force engaged in the primary economic activities of the island, such as the cultivation and processing of sugar and coffee, the highly skilled occupations, and heavy physical work in urban construction and transportation.[3] In the Liberal ideal, free workers were the backbone of society because of their productive roles. In response, the Liberal state had a responsibility toward producers; therefore, in this view, the free worker was a political entity (though with very limited rights). To Liberals, only men were producers, while women's primary obligation was to the patriarchal family. Nevertheless, freedwomen on the island, unlike their upper-class counterparts, were expected to labor, preferably in occupations considered appropriate to their sex (such as domestic-related work) or, if in agriculture, only during short periods (during harvest) and in selected tasks (e.g., picking coffee).

The more conservative sugar elite did not seek the total withdrawal of women from the agricultural world. To a certain extent, they agreed with Liberals that the primary role of a woman, even a woman of color, was reproductive.[4] Even these conservative elites regarded men's work as productive and female labor as supplementary.[5] The economic reality many sugar planters faced often betrayed these gender designs and led sugar planters to seek out freedwomen's labor. Many freedwomen responded by taking advantage of higher remuneration in the fields. In general, the elites' project sought the moral uplift of former slaves: moral men were compliant, dependable, and hardworking, while decency and domesticity defined respectable womanhood, especially for those females who would come into close contact with the elites' households.

However, freedpeople creatively appropriated this language of labor to their benefit. Male former slaves pressed for demands as reliable, hardworking men not only in regard to improvements in working and living conditions but also to assert their new authority at home. Most important, freedwomen also manipulated the language of labor and became workers as an unintended result of a labor system that applied to all former slaves, regardless of their gender, and the economic constraints that led to their recruitment in crucial tasks like fieldwork. In fact, women made contracts more often than their male counterparts did.[6] Through their contract bargaining and appeals to the authorities in order to achieve more freedom from employers and sometimes from their domestic partners, libertas often challenged the gendered characterization of the free worker and the prevalent understanding of female labor as supplementary, especially through their centrality in the sugar fields and domestic work. Despite few alternatives, freedwomen negotiated with employers and officials, contradicting the Liberal ideal of female subordination to the male head of household. At other times, libertas manipulated dominant interpretations of femininity—which underscored the centrality of motherhood, family, and domesticity in women's lives—to defy regulations and gain freedom to reconstitute their families and communities. In so doing, female former slaves subverted the system of control while contradictorily legitimizing dominant mores of femininity.

In order to understand the gendering of the postemancipation free worker, we should look closely at how female and male former slaves challenged the norms established by the process of emancipation. How did the everyday practices of men and women influence how they became contractual workers? How did slave gender roles open up alternatives or limit their ability to carry out full emancipation? How did the process of abolition redefine or reproduce gender roles among libertos? To answer these questions, I will narrow my analysis to a group of labor contracts agreed upon by former slaves and their employers. Through their contract negotiations with employers and state regulators, libertos and libertas found an effective language to present their demands and claims.

The Moment of Emancipation in Puerto Rico

The study of emancipation in Puerto Rico requires a broader historical framework that uncovers the tension between the rise of Liberal bourgeois politics and the more restrictive politics of Spanish rule in the Caribbean islands. Events such as the Haitian Revolution, the independence wars in the Spanish continental colonies, and the economic competition from France and England led Spain to hold on to its Caribbean possessions and the system of slavery as a way to maintain economic viability.[7] To many Creole elites in the colonies, Spanish resistance to abolition, even after emancipation in the French, British, and Dutch islands, and in the United States, was one more example of Spain's unwillingness to negotiate reforms in the governance of its Caribbean possessions.

Local conflicts also determined the processes of emancipation. The island's sugar industry had been struggling since the 1840s due to the low international price of sugar. Planters resorted to increased cultivation and production, which in turn led to greater exploitation of the slave population and the free peasantry.[8] At the same time, coffee production in the central mountain areas was becoming highly profitable and by the late 1870s took a leading role in the island's economy. The expansion of the two export-oriented industries limited free peasants' access to land and pushed them into plantation and hacienda labor.

By the mid-1860s, colonial authorities in Puerto Rico witnessed a rising tide of dissatisfaction from various fronts: overexploited slaves, the dispossessed free peasantry, and underrepresented Creole elites who wanted more political control and better opportunities for economic development. Spain's failure to address these conflicts prompted Creole elites, peasants, and slaves to revolt against Spain in 1868.[9] The revolt was short-lived; colonial authorities reestablished control over the population and imprisoned or exiled key participants. Consequently, colonial authorities temporarily neutralized the most radical wing of Liberalism. In contrast, the 1868 revolt in Cuba sparked a tenyear, bloody war, which over time became increasingly radicalized. During the war, for example, numerous slaves achieved emancipation and fiercely fought for the Cuban separatist, antislavery, anti-Spanish cause.[10]

In the context of a threatening war in Cuba, Spanish authorities understood that some changes were necessary in order to retain the Caribbean colonies, especially the more passive Puerto Rico. The Cuban conflict and the need to reinforce the metropole's ties with Puerto Rico forced the Spanish administration, albeit gradually, to revise the terms of its colonial slave systems. Authorities enacted the Moret Law in 1870 for both islands and, finally, issued the Abolition Act for Puerto Rico on 22 March 1873.[11] Though crucial, the Puerto Rican enslaved population was significantly smaller than that of Cuba and the economic and social consequences of emancipation were far less dangerous.[12] Furthermore, Spain needed to diffuse radicalism by demonstrating to the opposition forces in Puerto Rico that it was prepared for change.

Contract Legislation in the Apprenticeship System

The Abolition Act and the subsequent regulations for the apprenticeship period in Puerto Rico embodied Spain's urge to balance the struggle between two forces (those proponents of newer forms of governance and economy versus conservatives interested in maintaining the old rule) within its crumbling empire.[13] While abolition legislation intended to prolong forced labor, the liberal language of the law betrayed that purpose and opened a window of opportunity for former slaves to modify the apprenticeship system to their advantage.

The 1873 Abolition Act forced freedpeople to establish three-year contracts with their former masters, some other party, or the state, with full emancipation coming in 1876. It only granted them political rights in 1878. According to subsequent regulations, the island was divided into three main departments, each supervised by a libertos' advocate (*protector de libertos*) and several assistants who oversaw contract negotiations, filed and registered documents, and updated information on each contract.[14] These officials were required to keep track of every liberto and liberta within their geographic area. Both parties to the new contracts were supposed to sign the document in the presence of a *protector* or an assistant. In practice, planters frequently used labor recruiters to negotiate contracts with workers and later passed on the information to the protectores, thus circumventing state regulations.[15] However, this practice also allowed former slaves to negotiate contracts to their advantage, such as short-term contracts or exchanging wages for other sorts of benefits. At times, these short-term contracts led to intense competition for labor among planters.

Though contradictory, some of the provisions in the emancipation laws, designed to perpetuate exploitation of former slaves, echoed Liberal ideals then fashionable in much of the Atlantic world. The language of the contract law in Puerto Rico regarded former slaves not as commodities, whose contracts could be sold or exchanged among "employers," but as individuals with rights and responsibilities.[16] For instance, the thirteenth article stated that contracts had to be agreed on freely by employer and employee, and it defined clear boundaries between regulated work-time and individuals' free time.[17] The fourteenth article went even further, recognizing the right of the employer and the employee to rescind the contract if either side did not comply with contract stipulations. No doubt, contract provisions such as the fourteenth article were meant to protect employers should they no longer require liberto labor and to provide planters with tools to bargain for cheaper labor. However, former slaves soon learned to use the legal system to increase their physical mobility, abandon former masters, and to improve living conditions. The 1873 regulations, for example, only exempted former slaves from contracting in the case of physical or mental incapacity. Former slaves often reinterpreted the law and used their family obligations, alternative sources of income (self-employment), or contracting with relatives as reasons to justify an exemption to the contracting law or to be taken into consideration during the negotiating process.

For example, the *Register of Local Matters* of police authorities in the southern city of Ponce states that on 17 July 1873 authorities granted permission to the liberto Bartolo to move to the town of Humacao in order to "get a contract with whoever suited him."[18] Bartolo's legal request forced authorities to recognize his right as a former slave to change employers. In another case, the liberta Catalina Rivera explained to authorities that before emancipation she had lived and worked on her own, though regularly paying rent to her master.[19] Under the new system, she could employ the money she usually sent to her master for her own support. In the request, the liberta portrayed herself as a self-sufficient worker and claimed her right to freedom from an employer and authorities. According to the register, authorities complied with Rivera's demand.

According to the historian Luis Díaz Soler, at least 92 percent of former slaves made contracts or were accounted for by authorities (including freed-people exempted from the law—the libertos and libertas under twelve or over sixty years of age).[20] The high number of contracts made signals that former slaves on the island had few other options for their economic support, especially because of their limited legal access to cultivable land. The relative success of the forced-contract system led many contemporary observers to define former slaves as passive or obedient and to praise the island for its ability to implement a potentially dangerous transition so efficiently. In contrast, many former masters and new employers complained that freedpeople repeatedly defied the contract system and the social project it embodied.[21]

Constituting a Free Worker

The apprenticeship system embodied much more than a compromise between the island's conservative forces and more Liberal elites with regard to labor and the future of the sugar economy. Through the regulations, policies, and surveillance practices of this system, different elites converged in an effort to reshape Puerto Rican society. The most conservative elites wanted to shape former slaves into reliable and moral workers. The Liberal class hoped to turn them into future subjects of the Spanish Crown or citizens of the Puerto Rican nation, depending on their political orientation. For these Liberals, former slaves were to become not only free workers but a particular kind of men and women; the sort who not only would reproduce the economic and social hierarchies that secured local elites' power in the colony, but that would lead to the social regeneration needed for the island's industrial development and progress.

Elites sought to inculcate a work ethic of compliance and reliability among libertos and to discipline libertas into domesticity and decent behavior. Though elites profited from libertas' compulsory labor, and indirectly recognized the centrality of their economic performance, they did not perceive freedwomen as legitimate workers. To Liberals and Conservatives, men were the main producers. For example, in the 1867 *Project for the Abolition of Slavery in Puerto Rico*, Puerto Rican abolitionists underscored to both authorities and planters that emancipation would not disturb production or the island's political stability, because they could only be affected if male slaves refused to work.[22] Abolitionists contended that the island only had ten thousand male slaves, a small number easy to discipline. These Liberals addressed the issue of male labor not only because of their own notions on women but also because planters preferred male hands. Consequently, abolitionists dismissed the crucial role of female slave labor in agriculture.

Practices in regards to female slave labor in the years prior to emancipation indicated a shift in some planters' attitude. Male slave labor became more valuable than female slave labor. This perspective was especially unusual at a time when the rapid decline of the slave force and an increased number of complaints about the unreliability of free workers coincided with expanding production. For example, a study of the southern sugar town of Guayama demonstrated that two-thirds of manumissions in 1870–73 were granted to females. Planters were attempting to hold on to male slaves. In the case of Adjuntas, an emerging coffee producing area near Ponce, only four of eighteen slaves working in agriculture in 1870 were women.[23] After emancipation, the surviving contracts indicate that libertas in Adjuntas were hired as domestic workers.

This shift in attitude toward female slave labor is also evident during the apprenticeship period. As the contract system came closer to an end, members of the conservative class introduced a new set of regulations for workers to Governor Segundo de la Portilla.[24] The project required that all jornaleros (wage workers), defined as everyone without property or capital, work for a wage. In a separate paragraph, the proponents added that single women without family should also work for a wage. The staunch conservative governor made some corrections to the original project before introducing it to his superiors in March 1876. Governor de la Portilla's redefinition of jornaleros included all single and married women over fifteen years old.[25] However, the Ministerio de Ultramar (the administrative office of the overseas possessions) rejected the project and ordered a reissue of the 1874 Vagrancy Law, with a non-gender-specific definition of jornalero. The conservatives' insistence on including women in the definition of wage worker was a response to the lack of a systematic policing of female labor in the rural area by authorities. This did not change significantly with the reissuing of the 1874 legislation. However, the different definitions of jornaleras in the two proposals points to contradictions within the conservative camp regarding the role of women in labor and family. We can argue that for an important number of conservative proponents, many of them landowners, women's wage labor should not interfere with their reproductive role in the family. In fact, colonial authorities' recognition of freedwomen's requests for exemption to regulations on the basis of family needs also suggests that many colonial administrators understood that the reproductive role of women, including former slaves, superseded their productive role.

For ruling elites before and after emancipation, the identity of the free worker was essentially masculine. Fernando Picó's study of the jornalero system (1849–73) showed that it targeted men above sixteen years of age.[26] Given the increasingly limited access to slave imports from midcentury onward, authorities and planters enacted a set of regulations geared to transform the self-sufficient, racially mixed, free peasantry into a reliable labor force for sugar plantations and coffee haciendas, a law that applied to men. After the abolition of slavery and the jornalero system, police authorities consistently prosecuted an overwhelming number of males for not complying with the contract system (in the case of libertos) or with the vagrancy laws (in the case of free male peasants). Police records for the southern sugar district of Ponce, for example, attest to authorities' concerted efforts within the city and with other municipalities in searching for former slaves who had abandoned their contract arrangements. Although I do not have a statistical breakdown of these records, I noticed that men engaged in fieldwork for sugar plantations were more often prosecuted. Once found, these libertos were required to pay a fine and return to their former place of employment. At other times, they were imprisoned and forced into manual labor in public works.

On the other hand, authorities did not systematically apply vagrancy laws to lower-class free women, but libertas had to comply with contract regulations during the apprenticeship period.[27] As historian Félix V. Matos Rodríguez demonstrates in his study of San Juan, antiabolitionists were concerned about the shortages of sugar field hands and of reliable domestic female workers, whose performance within and outside the domestic unit was crucial for the maintenance and economic viability of their masters' household.[28] Therefore, it is not surprising that a high number of women worked in domestic-related occupations in the postemancipation decades, while fieldwork increasingly became a masculine endeavor. The need for female labor led authorities to force freedwomen into contract arrangements. However, authorities did not prosecute libertas who had abandoned their contractual relationship in the rural areas as frequently as they did freedmen. Nonetheless, female former slaves were systematically policed, mostly in the urban setting, and especially when authorities thought they had transgressed the boundaries of accepted female behavior. Ponce police records show a large number of women, among them female former slaves, arrested for scandalous behavior (gambling, drinking, dancing, fraternizing with men, etc.). For example, the liberta Felicita Garrats was arrested several times for her scandalous behavior and Josefa Besares was detained at least eleven times for similar reasons. Each time, both women, unlike free lower-class females, were forced into labor arrangements, which they repeatedly defied.[29] Given that most policing of women occurred in urban areas, I suggest that their contract arrangements were meant to ease the demand for domestic-related work.

Former slaves responded to the apprenticeship regulation in multiple ways. Men resorted to direct challenges such as physical confrontations with employers, violent acts against property, or running away to other towns or cities. Women tended to use more subtle strategies such as foot-dragging, disobedience, feigning illness, or missing work. At the same time, many freedpeople worked within the contract system and used the system's language creatively to legitimize their claims and gain more autonomy over their lives. Among all freedpeople, women engaged the legal system more directly. For example, women constituted 63 percent of the contracts I analyzed. Often libertas appropriated the language of womanhood to argue that legislation interfered with their female duties and they should therefore be exempted from making contracts. While women subverted the contract system, they often did so by legitimizing dominant mores of domesticity and consequently eroded their political legitimacy as workers. Men, in contrast, stressed their role as workers to increase their autonomy and benefits. A closer look at the contracts reveals these complex dynamics.

In this essay, I focus on two samples of contracts: a set of 148 contracts dated from 28 April to 9 May 1873 for the Ponce agricultural areas, and a collection of 380 contracts registered in the San Juan urban areas from 25 April to 7 May 1873.[30] To uncover how these former slaves challenged contract stipulations, I also used the fines and complaints in the *Register of Infractions to the Authorities* (April 1874–April 1876) and the authorities' recollection of daily events in the *Register of Local Matters* (24 April–31 Dec. 1873).[31] Finally, the set of San Juan contracts consists of a small sample extracted from the *Register of Former Slaves Contracts in San Juan, 1873–75.*[32]

What Do Contracts Tell Us? Emancipation in an Agricultural Setting

An analysis of the contracts shows how libertas in agricultural areas became free workers in spite of elites' gendered economic and social designs. The moment of emancipation posed great difficulties, especially to the planter class. Ponce planters, for instance, were in an unusually fragile situation because authorities had enacted the Abolition Act in the middle of harvest time, jeopardizing the planters' investments. The immediacy of the harvest gave leverage to field workers in contract negotiations. Female fieldworkers, like male laborers, bargained successfully for better contracts. Consequently, many libertas remained longer on the plantations as fieldworkers instead of migrating quickly to urban areas to work in female occupations deemed more appropriate. Economic constraints led planters to seek out freedwomen's labor, despite the planters' higher valorization of male labor. Simultaneously, the lack of alternatives led freedwomen to look for the highly remunerated work on the fields.

Compared with documents from San Juan, the Ponce archive shows a slightly higher tendency to provide benefits such as food, housing, health care, clothing, or some combination of these. For example, 85 percent of the contracts in Ponce provided for medical care and 94 percent included housing.[33] Given the circumstances of the harvest, the provision of housing may have been understood by planters as an imperative rather than a means to control workers' private lives. Many former slaves in agricultural areas negotiated for housing in their contract bargaining.

Although the San Juan data for wages is insufficient to allow for a reliable comparison with Ponce, it is noteworthy that the wages paid in Ponce seem to be higher for freedmen and freedwomen.[34] The high demand for plantation labor at this time, the tendency of many libertos and libertas to change employers, and the competition for labor among hacendados were good reasons to offer better wages. In Ponce, 76 percent of the employees in the sample received wages that ranged from two to eight pesos per month; in contrast, in San Juan only 30 percent of the contracts recorded wages within that range, while the rest of the employees received less than two pesos per month. Given that emancipation took place during the harvest, it is not surprising that former slaves engaged in fieldwork received higher wages irrespective of their gender.[35]

Contracts show that libertas, like libertos, learned quickly how to increase their bargaining power and physical mobility. For instance, the data for both San Juan and Ponce reveals that 55 percent of former slaves decided to work for another employer (64 percent were women and 35 percent men).[36] On 7 May 1873, for example, doña Bernardina Franco hired two of her former slaves and provided them with benefits but no wages. Her former slave Andrea left and signed a contract with don Santos Almiroti, who provided her with all the benefits supplied by Franco plus four pesos as a monthly wage.[37] In contrast, don Salvador Más was successful in keeping his fieldwork team of twenty-four freedpeople by providing both good benefits and better wages.

The majority of the contracts in Ponce were signed for short periods, ranging from two to eight months, instead of the stipulated three years. The common practice of establishing short-term contracts can be understood only within the contradictory dynamics of the processes of emancipation in a plantation area. First, contracting for a short period was in part a planter's strategy. Harvest time lasted from January to May. Therefore, freedpeople's labor was only needed for two or three months. In regard to women, short-term contracts could have benefited planters who believed that female family obligations compromised their labor. Nevertheless, this interpretation does not take into account planters' concern not only about that particular harvest season but also about the future of the sugar industry and their investments. How would they attract and retain enough workers for future seasons? In addition, many planters found free workers unreliable despite labor regulations. The scarcity and irregularity of labor placed planters in a weak negotiating position with freedmen and freedwomen.[38] One could argue, therefore, that former slaves sought short-term contracts so as not to compromise their recently acquired freedom. Short-term contracts provided former slaves with enough room to bargain with other parties for better benefits since the law allowed them to contract with former masters, another party, or the state. Furthermore, most former slaves in Puerto Rico did not have material investments such as provision grounds that tied them to any specific plantation.[39] This may explain the high number of former slaves who changed employers. For instance in Ponce 45 percent of freedpeople in my sample changed employers (64 percent women and 35 percent men) while 59 percent (64 percent women and 35 percent men) in San Juan did the same. Furthermore, women changed employers at a higher rate than men.

Another unintended result of the provision that allowed for a change in employer was the sharp increase in the physical mobility of libertos and libertas. That mobility was not confined to the plantation districts. Many former slaves moved to more urbanized areas in search of better opportunities, and often authorities, especially mayors, sanctioned these relocations. In the *Register for Local Matters* almost 50 percent of the entries were about former slaves who moved to Ponce from surrounding rural areas. At the time, Ponce was a center for opportunities given its economic diversity as a sugar enclave, its urban core, and its small but rising role in coffee production. Nonetheless, 22 percent of the entries registered former slave migration out of Ponce. For example, the liberta Eleuteria went to live with her mother in Aibonito. The entry stated that Eleuteria did not have an employer yet, but authorities still granted her permission.[40] Eleuteria's example highlights not only female former slaves' initiatives to look for better opportunities but also stresses the importance of family ties in their lives. More important, Eleuteria used the state's language of labor to reunite with her mother.

Freedwomen's migration had a broader impact; libertas' increased physical mobility under the pretext of finding a job (which included plantation fieldwork) contradicted elites' expectations of female domesticity. Although I do not have a complete statistical breakdown of the two Ponce registers, there was a clear tendency for women to migrate to Ponce from other towns. Rural female slaves often had the opportunity to develop easily marketable skills that they could transfer to Ponce's large urban settings. The impact of Liberal gender ideologies on the job market reinforced that transition. But females also migrated to mountainous areas, where they remained active in agricultural work. Further research may reveal that the rising coffee industry (while the sugar industry was in decline) became an attractive opportunity for libertas.[41] Notably, freedwomen in Puerto Rico, like those in most of the British Caribbean, remained crucial to agriculture in the postemancipation years.[42] By taking advantage of the rural elites' economic situation, negotiating contracts, and changing employers, libertas often resisted the pull toward urban domestic employment, consequently challenging elites' understanding of female domesticity and the definition of the free worker as male. However, one should consider that freedwomen's challenges to the gendered ideal of labor may have stemmed from their lack of economic alternatives and their need to support their families, for which many freedwomen were sole providers.

Some Urban Considerations: A Look at San Juan

Libertas in the urban areas did not directly challenge the gendered ideal of labor as they did in the rural setting. In towns and cities, lower-class men participated in heavy physical or manual work such as construction and transport, while others entered more specialized occupations as artisans (shoemaking, masonry, carpentry, etc.). Women, on the other hand, were excluded from artisanship and were expected to perform domestic-related duties in and out of elite households. These households were spaces to discipline women into acceptable female behavior while profiting from their labor. Many lower-class women worked as seamstresses, laundresses, childcare providers, and dominated the business of food preparation, distribution, and selling. Nonetheless, libertas' practices of domestic services defied elites' attempts to gain absolute control over former slaves' mobility and tested dominant notions of womanhood. Women's productive labor was essential for the functioning of the city. Freedwomen showed a similar rate of intra-city mobility as their male counterparts. They changed employers as often as freedmen. Furthermore, contracts demonstrate that libertas, more often than libertos, actively manipulated contract legislation in order to increase benefits in labor arrangements and achieve more autonomy.[43]

Like Ponce, San Juan shows an increase in physical mobility among the liberto class, men and women. The documents I examined contain several cases of former slaves who were hired out of the city for rural work. [44] At the same time, others were attracted to move into the city to better exploit their specialized skills.[45] Freedpeople's initiatives to expand their autonomy and improve their lives while using the authorities' legal framework resulted in a continuous movement of people who directly challenged the foundations of the system of control imposed on them. Furthermore, former slaves' attempts to increase their physical and social mobility blurred even further the tenuous boundaries between urban and rural areas. Unskilled former slaves in the capital were compelled to take advantage of higher wages in the agricultural settings, while skilled freedpeople on the plantations could enjoy better economic opportunities in the capital.

The capital area of San Juan was the site of multiple and complex economic activities, drawing commerce from its rural neighboring towns, distant Spain, and other foreign lands. The continuous flow of goods into San Juan provided numerous opportunities for freedpeople to make a living and to rise or advance in the social hierarchy. Nonetheless, the higher rate of migration toward urban centers during these years created a large pool of laborers, benefiting city employers. As a result, the elites' gendered design was not overtly subverted in San Juan, unlike in the sugar fields, where women remained in "productive" roles. Contracts show that most men joined specialized jobs while libertas engaged in domestic service. For instance, the contracts include examples of libertos working as *caleteros* (stevedores), as dockworkers, and as cart drivers transporting goods from the southern port area through the gates and up the city hills.[46] The need for transportation in the urban setting provided freedmen many more opportunities for physical mobility and social interaction than in agricultural areas. Many of these caleteros and *carretilleros* (cart drivers) worked for a wage; benefits were not usually provided. Although wages were not enough to live on comfortably, working only for a wage allowed these freedmen a sense of liberty that they had not experienced before.

Benefits for males in the urban settings, if they were provided, could be understood as a way to foster dependency on the employer. Moreover, the strong competition among laborers in the urban setting could also have favored employers who did not provide benefits.

Notably, the majority of these caleteros did not make contracts with their former owners. For instance, Juan Pedro Otero, an overseer at an important caletero company in San Juan, employed many former slaves as stevedores. Among them, he hired two of his sons, libertos Manuel Ríos and Benigno.[47] Otero's proximity to the liberto class probably made him a desirable manager in the eyes of his superiors, the perfect mediator to recruit workers from the recently freed population. Otero illustrates how lower-class men's interactions with slaves later facilitated the incorporation of libertos into the ranks of artisans and other occupations such as cart drivers and stevedores, workers who later in the century became politically well organized. Most important, this example demonstrates freedmen's use of the possibility of changing employers as a means to reconstitute their families. Unlike freedwomen, male former slaves did not use family obligations to legitimize a contract arrangement with their sons. As I will explain below, for libertos, the family connection appeared in the contract language as a side note (as in Juan Otero's case) while libertas justified their labor arrangements (or the lack of) by stressing family responsibilities.

The San Juan documents reveal the occupational diversity of this urban area. Nonetheless, among freedwomen, domestic service was the most common occupation. Domestic service entailed many tasks other than work within the home. The contracts refer to various services that could be understood as being performed in the intimacy of one household or labor sold to other housing units to the benefit of their employer. For example, laundresses and cooks often worked for several households and contributed their earnings to the household of their employer. The liberta Aquilina, for instance, was hired to "cook outside the house for her as well as for other people paying the standard price."[48] San Juan inhabitants held laundresses in high regard.[49] Washing clothing was made very difficult by the lack of fresh water in the city. Therefore, laundresses had to carry heavy loads of clothing to the areas where the few wells were to be found. Because many of these tasks required flexibility and physical mobility similar to men's transportation-related occupations, domestic services such as laundering also allowed for greater autonomy among libertas.

In contrast to libertos' contracts, most of the contracts for domestic service included benefits such as food, clothing, housing, and medical assistance.

This is an example of the interplay between gender and occupation. In San Juan and Ponce, women were more likely than men to receive benefits, perhaps because they were responsible for providing for their offspring. Nevertheless, there is a subtle difference between the two areas. The capital city had fewer former slaves engaged in contracts that provided benefits. Probably San Juan offered freedpeople more ways to make a living without depending on their employer and accepting restrictions. At the same time, San Juan employers were in a better negotiating position than sugar planters. However, libertas in domestic service managed to include some unusual benefits in their labor arrangements. Employers' willingness to accept some of the libertas' demands suggests San Juan's high demand for domestic workers. Freedwomen's labor was crucial in sustaining elite households. For example, the libertas María Isabel and Simplicia Velázquez, hired for domestic service but by different employers, confirmed in their contracts their right to sleep out of the employer's house whenever they needed to.[50] Both women used legislation, and manipulated notions of free labor, to reaffirm their right to a private life. In negotiations, these women probably stressed the need to attend to their own family responsibilities, which coincided with dominant mores of femininity.

In challenge to elites' expectations of domesticity, libertas in the urban areas used a language of labor in order to look for employers who paid better or were more to their liking. Women in San Juan and Ponce changed employers at a similar rate as did their male counterparts. For example, the contract of the liberta María Francisca Rivera for domestic services stated "that the employee is going to Curazao and she is forced to comply with her obligations as soon as she returns from that place." Notably, during slavery, this sort of accommodation was impossible and, after emancipation, employers must have perceived it as undesirable. But libertas manipulated the liberal notions embedded in contractual language to prevent others from intervening in the most intimate dimensions of their lives. It is not surprising, then, that according to the San Juan data, libertas were responsible for most of the 106 contract cancellations. Although few of these cases provide sufficient information to support generalizations, these cases are evidence of libertas' clear knowledge and understanding of their new situation. The nullified cases of some freedwomen were registered immediately above their contracts with different employers.[51] This strongly suggests that these women revoked their contracts in order to engage in better labor agreements with different employers.

Freedmen and freedwomen alike challenged the statutes of the apprenticeship system by appropriating the language of labor, and in the process becoming workers. Though urban freedwomen did not challenge the gendered ideal of labor organization as did their rural counterparts, through their practices they repeatedly contested the male characterization of the worker. As domestic workers, these women were the main producers in the households. But as I will explain, libertas' actions and petitions were contradictory in nature. While female former slaves openly contested the contract system in creative ways, their use of the legal framework also legitimized its patriarchal authority over them. For example, both men and women used labor legislation to reconstitute their families and communities. Nevertheless, men did not compromise their identity as workers in the reconstitution process. Authorities probably did not recognize male former slaves' claims to fatherhood and family as readily as they accepted women's claims. On the other hand, libertas' technique of stressing family needs as a means to achieve more freedom limited their legitimacy as workers and heightened dominant understandings of womanhood.

The Family and Community of the Emancipation Years

Former slaves' perceptions of gender roles had a crucial impact on their responses to postemancipation regulations. Contracts reveal that libertas' choices were dictated by the system as well as by their responsibilities as women. These responsibilities could partially explain the higher number of libertas in my sample of contracts. The need for greater material security not only for themselves but also for their families is another factor explaining the agency and initiative of women in manipulating labor legislation. According to the data from Ponce and San Juan, 93 percent of the freedpeople charged with the guardianship of children were females. Being the primary caretakers of children affected labor choices in several ways. For example, it could force women to seek plantation work, which although extremely exploitative offered higher wages. This might also explain the large number of women who were field workers. In Puerto Rico, women left plantation work for other occupations gradually. In the plantation area, according to the Ponce data, half of the fieldwork force in the months following emancipation was female.

Family obligations could also encourage freedwomen to accept contractual relationships, mostly domestic service, with lower or no wages, if these provided other material benefits for themselves and their children. This may explain why most freedmen's contracts in San Juan did not include benefits like those of libertas. In San Juan, for example, women continued their work as domestics, laundresses, and cooks. Women were attracted to domestic service not only because it was one of the very few options available to them (and because of the high demand for these services in the urban areas), but also because domestic work offered benefits to them and their offspring. It allowed women to keep their children close to them. Although illegal, these arrangements allowed children to be assigned household tasks.[52] In return for being allowed to keep young children under their immediate care and protection, women might also have accepted working without a wage. It is not surprising that freedwomen represented 66 percent of the domestic servants hired without pay.

In the few cases in which men took care of children, all of them in San Juan, the children were old enough to be trained in some sort of profitable task. For example, the liberto Celedonio was hired to work on the estate of don Pedro Gerónimo Goyco and brought with him his sixteen-year-old son, Martín, in order to teach him carpentry and to have him work on the farm.[53] Arguably, most freedmen viewed young children as an obstacle to getting better-paying jobs. Therefore, children usually proved to be another burden in women's already complex lives. Without question, child bearing and raising influenced the choices of freedpeople. Perceptions of the division of gender roles within the family provide a new dimension to our understanding of the intricacies of personal interactions and relationships within postemancipation society. These gendered family roles did not contradict elite mores; in fact, postemancipation regulation heightened the gendered division of labor within the liberto family.

Women's initiative in reconstituting familial connections after abolition also underscores their vital role in the liberto family. The sample for San Juan included 28 cases of freedpeople, the majority of them women (82 percent), who made claims for relatives, such as sons, daughters, spouses, and grandmothers. The liberta Carmen Barril also "claimed her underage son, the liberto Eusebio who was a slave of Mr. Llompars y Pons."[54] Distant and substitute relatives also participated in this process, which reveals the tendency to form alternative family arrangements during slavery. For example, the twelve-year-old liberta María Avelina went to "Barranquitas in order to join her godmother [doña Felipa Rivera] who claimed her."[55]

It seems likely that these attempts to bring families together were more frequent than the data reflects. Former masters seemed to be aware of freedpeople's attempts to reconstitute their families. Doña Ysabel, for example, was in charge of two underage children "until their relatives claim them."[56] The reconstitution of families went beyond the simple desire to reestablish family relations. It allowed freedpeople, especially female former slaves, to subtly avoid becoming subjected to an employer. Thus when the liberta Gavina's employer released her from her contract obligations, she did not search for a new employer. Instead, Gavina's mother, Josefa Besares, informed the authorities that her daughter and her two children could live and work with her. According to Besares, "they can all support the family and her daughter can take care of her during illness."[57] Authorities released Gavina and her children to the care of Besares.

Freedwomen used their obligations to the family to avoid the normal process of contracting that was imposed on them. For instance, the liberta Margarita requested to be released from her obligation to sign a contract, arguing that she had to take care of her children.[58] Similarly, the liberta Albina stated to the authorities "that it was inconvenient to sign a contract with her former employer or any other person because she is in an interesting state and for now she will live with her sister Catalina Díaz who is willing to sign a contract for domestic service."[59] By "an interesting state," Albina probably meant that she was pregnant and was demanding time to wean her newborn child. Albina not only asserted her right to have a family but she also used her female condition to manipulate the widely accepted notions of motherhood and, consequently, avoid contracting. Furthermore, cases such as those of the libertas Albina and Gavina reveal the importance of a network of women, most of them relatives, in former slaves' maneuverings for more autonomy.

Libertas' claims of family responsibilities to justify exemption from the apprenticeship regulations not only denote freedwomen's specific role within the liberto family as caretakers, but they also reveal libertas' awareness of elites' stress on domesticity in their definitions of acceptable womanhood. As free workers, libertas used their contracts to design labor arrangements that could accommodate their roles as employees and family caregivers. At other times, freedwomen appealed successfully to the authorities to recognize their family duties over their labor obligations. Nonetheless, libertas' subversion of the system was limited, given that their claims reinforced dominant notions of female domesticity. For instance, the liberta Elvira Romaní requested her release from contract obligations so she could live with her father, Alejo López, who had the economic means to support her. Officials recognized Elvira's obligations as a daughter and released her to her father's care, thus enabling her to achieve greater autonomy. However, Elvira's challenge to patriarchal rule was limited; she substituted her father's authority for that of the state. For libertos, the emancipation process provided them with an opportunity to renegotiate family roles. Men sought to reassert their authority over their family.

On the other hand, women did not comply easily. Also, freedwomen could have perceived emancipation as an opportunity for greater liberation as women. The case of Paulino Márquez can help us to understand this paradox. On 21 June 1873, Márquez filed a complaint against his wife, a liberta, with the mayor of Ponce.[60] Márquez contended that his wife refused to meet her traditional obligations as a married woman. His wife responded that she was impeded from fulfilling her traditional role as a wife because she was forced to undertake contractual labor. This could be understood as one more example of how apprenticeship perpetuated the exploitation of former slaves and its constraints on their family lives. In particular, it underscores the burden for women of serving two masters: a husband and an employer. However, it is also possible that Paulino Márquez's wife used her obligations as a contract worker to justify leaving her husband. Either way, Paulino sought out the mayor's intervention because the two men coincided in their belief that women's role as workers did not supersede their roles as wives and mothers. For Paulino, authorities provided a framework that aimed to ensure his patriarchal authority at home, although not always successfully. After emancipation, freedmen were able to assert their masculinity over women at home in ways impossible during previous slave times.

In sum, women were the heart of liberto families, a role that both limited their choices for employment and provided justification for avoiding or subverting the contract labor system to their own advantage. Often, freedwomen used family resources to claim that they could rely on the support of others for sustenance or to claim that family obligations did not allow them to comply with their contract obligations. Contradictorily, such claims reinforced elites' definitions of women's place in society. In other instances, emancipation also allowed freedwomen to look for their own benefits as women. In their individual lives, freedwomen were able to challenge the oppressive patriarchal system in both its colonial and its personal dimensions. Generally, freedwomen articulated these challenges through legal channels. While partially recognizing the legitimacy of government authorities, many freedwomen and freedmen managed to avoid the system they saw as a continuation of slavery.

Conclusion

Through the apprenticeship regulations, colonial authorities, Conservatives, and the more Liberal elites sought to mold the liberto class not only into free workers but, most important, into hardworking men and decent family women who could enable the industrial and social development of the colony. Police records reveal that elites envisioned the free worker as male. Though women's labor was crucial for the economic viability of the island, elites sought to restrict them to occupations deemed more appropriate to their sex, such as domestic-related services; if they worked in agriculture, it was only for brief periods or in tasks deemed appropriate to them. Nevertheless, freedwomen, like their male counterparts, appropriated the dominant language of labor in order to manipulate apprenticeship regulations and assert their rights as workers. The demand for female workers betrayed elite desires to confine libertas to private domains. The economic situation on Ponce plantations, for instance, led women to remain as field workers, defying elites' gender designs. In San Juan, the economic circumstances were slightly different. Freedwomen did not directly contest the gendered division of labor but, as in Ponce, they were crucial in sustaining the city's economy and persistently pushed to redefine labor regulations and achieve greater autonomy. At other times, freedwomen's family obligations pushed women to support elite understandings of the gendered division of labor and reinforced the dominant paradigm of womanhood (domesticity and decency). But family obligations also forced women to deal with employers and the colonial state as workers in order to expand benefits and recognize their rights to reconstitute families and communities. Libertas' practices as contract-bargaining agents intrinsically contested masculine definitions of workers. Freedwomen were producers and owned their labor. Many were heads of households without a male to mediate between them and their employer, as many Liberals thought ideal. But elites' rejection of women's political agency, freedmen's understandings of women's family roles, and libertas' use of family duties as a strategy to defy the contract system limited the recognition of a female political identity as "worker" in late-nineteenth-century Puerto Rico.

Notes

I would like to thank Solsirée del Moral and, especially, Eileen Suárez Findlay for her generosity and clever suggestions during the early stages of this project.
  1 Out of a total population of 617,328, Puerto Rico had about 30,000 slaves in 1872. James L. Dietz, *Historia económica de Puerto Rico* (Río Piedras, P.R.: Huracán, 1989), 48, 53.
  2 It is impossible to draw clear-cut ideological distinctions between Conservatives and Liberals given that each group encompassed a wide spectrum of political,

economic, and social interests, which often coincided with the interests of sectors in the opposite camp. For details, see Astrid Cubano Iguina, *El hilo en el laberinto: Claves de la lucha política en Puerto Rico (siglo XIX)* (Río Piedras, P.R.: Huracán, 1990). For the purposes of this essay, let us keep in mind that Conservatives comprised a sector of the sugar planter elite, merchants, and a large sector of the colonial, military, and church administration. They opposed political and social reforms that threatened the profitability of the sugar industry, especially policies regarding labor. The Liberal class included some sugar and coffee producers, the emerging urban middle class—mostly professionals—and few members of the colonial administration. Their main goal was to increase their political representation in the colony and to modernize the island.

3 Félix V. Matos Rodríguez, *Women in San Juan, 1820–1868* (Princeton, N.J.: Markus Wiener, 1999), 23–33.

4 Diana Paton argues that Jamaica's planters did not believe black women capable of the domesticity expected from middle-class white women. See Paton, "The Flight from the Fields Reconsidered: Gender Ideologies and Women's Labor after Slavery in Jamaica," in *Reclaiming the Political in Latin American History: Essays from the North*, ed. Gilbert M. Joseph (Durham, N.C.: Duke University Press, 2001). Certainly, Puerto Rican planters' racism was no less insidious. The equation of blackness with domesticity was problematic to conservative elites. But clearly, they did not see these as necessarily mutually exclusive concepts, or they would have systematically forced free peasant women (mostly mulatto) into plantation work after the 1849 legislation.

5 Recent studies about San Juan have shown that nineteenth-century Conservatives were also interested in aspects of modernity and development, as well as limited reform. See Matos Rodríguez, *Women in San Juan*; and Teresita Martínez-Vergne, *Shaping the Discourse on Space: Charity and Its Wards in Nineteenth-Century San Juan, Puerto Rico* (Austin: University of Texas Press, 1999).

6 Women constituted 63 percent of the 528 contracts in my sample.

7 Christopher Schmidt-Nowara, "National Economy and Atlantic Slavery: Protectionism and Resistance to Abolitionism in Spain and the Antilles, 1854–1874," *Hispanic American Historical Review* 78, no. 4 (1998): 603–29. See also Schmidt-Nowara, *Empire and Antislavery: Spain, Cuba, and Puerto Rico, 1833–1874* (Pittsburgh, Penn.: University of Pittsburgh Press, 1999).

8 See Fernando Picó, *Libertad y servidumbre en el Puerto Rico del siglo XIX* (Río Piedras, P.R.: Huracán, 1979).

9 Laird W. Bergad, "Toward Puerto Rico's *Grito de Lares*: Coffee, Social Stratification, and Class Conflicts, 1828–1868," *Hispanic American Historical Review* 60, no. 4 (1980): 617–42.

10 Rebecca J. Scott, *Emancipation in Cuba: The Transition to Free Labor, 1860–1899* (Princeton, N.J.: Princeton University Press, 1985); Ada Ferrer, "Social Aspects of Cuban Nationalism: Race, Slavery, and the *Guerra Chiquita*, 1879–1880," *Cuban Studies* 21 (1991): 37–56.

11 Asamblea Nacional de Puerto Rico, "Ley de abolición," in El proceso abolicionista en Puerto Rico: Documentos para su estudio, vol. 2 (San Juan: Centro de Investiga-
ciones Históricas and Instituto de Cultura Puertorriqueña, 1978), 144. Slavery was
not abolished in Cuba until 1888.

12 For centuries, Puerto Rico was at the margins of the empire and had a scant
population. It therefore lacked the highly racial and social stratification associated
with export-oriented economies, which explains the frequent racial miscegenation
of its inhabitants. The colony developed a sugar-slave complex at the beginning of
the nineteenth century and imported sixty thousand to eighty thousand slaves, a
fraction of the number of slaves shipped to Cuba (approximately 350,000). By
midcentury, the slave population had declined significantly. Consequently, planters
and authorities forced the multiracial, free peasantry into labor. By the 1860s, the
sugar industry depended on both slave and free workers. Unlike other Caribbean
islands (Jamaica, Saint-Domingue, and Cuba), free people of color and the slave
population did not comprise more than half of the inhabitants. In contrast to Cuba,
1870s planters in Puerto Rico did not fear a racial war, although they were deeply
concerned about the racial impurity of the peasantry. See Francisco A. Scarano, Sugar
and Slavery in Puerto Rico: The Plantation Economy of Ponce, 1800–1850 (Madison: University of Wisconsin Press, 1984).

13 Schmidt-Nowara's study of nineteenth-century Spanish politics demonstrates how different Liberal groups (from more conservative to radical) fought over
the limits to individual freedom and free trade. Radical Liberals took power in 1873,
a position they lost to the most conservative forces in the following year. Schmidt-
Nowara, Empire and Antislavery.

14 General Rafael Primo de Rivera, "Reglamento para la aplicación y cumpli-
miento de la Ley de 22 de Marzo de 1873 sobre abolición de la esclavitud en su parte
relativa a la contratación del servicio de los libertos," Proceso abolicionista en Puerto
Rico, 149–54.

15 André Ramos Mattei, "El liberto en el régimen de trabajo azucarero de Puerto
Rico, 1870–1880," Azúcar y esclavitud (1982): 91–124.

16 The apprenticeship legislation in the British Caribbean and Cuba was more
restrictive: it did not allow for a change in employer or legal cancellation of arrangements, and planters continued to sell, rent, or exchange their rights over former
slaves' contracts. See O. Nigel Bolland, "The Politics of Freedom in the British
Caribbean," in The Meaning of Freedom: Economics, Politics, and Culture after Slavery, ed.
Frank McGlynn and Seymour Dresher (Pittsburgh, Penn.: University of Pittsburgh
Press, 1992), 113–46; and Scott, Slave Emancipation in Cuba, 127–40.

17 Primo de Rivera, "Reglamento," 150–51.

18 Copiador de oficios a autoridades locales y particulares, 1872–1875, Archivo Municipal Histórico de Ponce (hereafter AMHP), no. 129, Ayuntamiento, Secretaría,
Copiadores.

19 *Libro de contratos de libertos de San Juan, 1873–1875*, 26 April 1873, Archivo General de Puerto Rico (AGPR).

20 Luis Díaz Soler, *Historia de la esclavitud negra en Puerto Rico* (Río Piedras, P.R.: Universitaria, 1969), 355.

21 See Ileana M. Rodríguez-Silva, "Freedmen and Freedwomen: Processes of Social Re-configuration in Post-emancipation Puerto Rico, 1873–76" (M.A. thesis, University of Wisconsin, Madison, 1997), chap. 1.

22 Segundo Ruiz Belvis, José Julián Acosta, and Francisco Mariano Quiñones, *Proyecto para la abolición de la esclavitud en Puerto Rico, presentado a la Junta de Información, reunida en Madrid, el 10 de abril de 1867* (San Juan: Instituto de Cultura Puertorriqueña, 1969), 60.

23 Carlos Buitrago, with Beatriz Riefkohl, "Transiciones: Esclavos y libertos en Adjuntas, Puerto Rico: 1870–1903," *Revista de ciencias sociales* 30, nos. 3–4 (1995): 101–46.

24 "Gobierno General de la Isla de Puerto Rico" (document no. 254), *Proceso abolicionista en Puerto Rico*, 340–55.

25 Janis Palma noticed Portilla's modification to the original proposal in her essay "Vienen tumbando caña (todavía)," in *Historia y género: Vidas y relatos de mujeres en el Caribe*, comp. Mario R. Cancel (San Juan: Asociación Puertorriqueña de Historiadores, 1997).

26 Picó, *Libertad y servidumbre*, 45. The regulations of 1849, like the 1874 Vagrancy Law, did not specify gender. In practice, they targeted males.

27 Before 1876, vagrancy laws applied to free workers while the apprenticeship regulations applied to the liberto class.

28 Matos Rodríguez, *Women in San Juan*, 94–96.

29 *Libro para anotar los correccionales por faltas gubernativas*, AHMP, Ay., Sec., Judicial, Faltas Gubernativas (1874–1880), box S146.

30 Contracts for libertos in Ponce are found in the AGPR, Fondo de Gobernadores Españoles, Municipalidades: Ponce, 1870–80, box 535. The contracts provide names, wages, duration, and benefits (housing, access to health care, and clothing).

31 *Copiador de oficios dirigidos a las autoridades locales y particulares*, AHMP, Ay., Sec., Cop. and *Libro para anotar los correccionales por faltas gubernativas (1874–1880)*, AHMP, Ay., Sec., Judicial, Faltas Gubernativas (1874–80), box S146.

32 The San Juan register includes contracts for the year 1873 with information on wages, benefits, and updates on the current status of the contract.

33 Medical care was a recurrent benefit in the contracts although it is not clear what it entailed.

34 Nonetheless, women's wages in Ponce were lower than that of men.

35 Better wages and benefits in fieldwork partially explain why 50 percent of women stayed on the plantations in the early emancipation years.

36 Men and women changed employers at a similar rate, 55 percent of each population.

37 Liberto contracts for the Municipality of Ponce, 7 May 1873, AGPR, Gob. Esp., Mun. Ponce, box 535.

38 Puerto Rican planters could not afford to import indentured labor. They were also aware of the postabolition sugar crisis in other Caribbean islands. "Letter from the British Consul in the island, H. August Cowper, 6 April 1873," *Proceso abolicionista en Puerto Rico*, 288–89.

39 Luis Antonio Figueroa, "Facing Freedom: The Transition from Slavery to Free Labor in Guayama, Puerto Rico, 1860–1898," PhD diss., University of Wisconsin, Madison, 1991.

40 *Copiador de oficios dirigidos a las autoridades locales y particulares*, 27 June 1873, AMHP, Ay, Sec., Cop.

41 On coffee production, see Fernando Picó, *Amargo café: Los pequeños y medianos caficultores de Utuado en la segunda mitad del siglo XIX* (Río Piedras, P.R.: Huracán, 1981); and Guillermo Baralt, *La Buena Vista, 1833–1904: Estancia de frutos menores, fábrica de harinas y hacienda cafetalera* (San Juan: Fideicomiso de Conservación de Puerto Rico, 1988).

42 See Bridget Brereton's essay, "Family Strategies, Gender, and the Shift to Wage Labor in the British Caribbean," in this volume.

43 Sixty-five percent of contracts in San Juan and most of contract cancellations were by women.

44 *Libro de contratos de San Juan, 1873–1875*, AGPR, 6 May, 2 May 1873.

45 Ibid., 29 April 1873.

46 Ibid., 26 April, 28 April, 30 April, 3 May, 6 May 1873.

47 Ibid., 28 April 1873.

48 Ibid., 3 May 1873.

49 Matos Rodríguez, *Women in San Juan*, 89–94.

50 *Libro de contratos de San Juan*, AGPR, 25 April, 26 April 1873.

51 Ibid., 30 April, 2 May, 5 May, 6 May 1873.

52 The law exempted children under twelve years old from contracting. Article 31, "Reglamento para la aplicación de la Ley de 22 de marzo de 1873," in *Proceso abolicionista en Puerto Rico*, 153.

53 *Libro de contratos de San Juan*, AGPR, April 1873.

54 *Libro de contratos de San Juan*, AGPR, April 1873.

55 *Copiador de oficios*, AMHP, Ay, Sec., Cop., July 1873.

56 Ibid., May 1873.

57 Ibid., April 1873.

58 *Copiador de oficios*, AMHP, Ay, Sec., Cop., July 1873.

59 *Libro de contratos de San Juan*, AGPR, April 1873.

60 *Copiador de oficios*, AMHP, Ay, Sec., Cop., June 1873.

PART III

The Public Sphere in
the Age of Emancipation

MELANIE NEWTON

Philanthropy, Gender, and the Production of
Public Life in Barbados, ca. 1790–ca. 1850

During the final decades of slavery and the early postemancipation era, between 1790 and 1850, gendered discourses of legal status, race, and class
powerfully shaped public life in the British Caribbean. In Barbados, philanthropic societies were among the principal venues in which new forms of civic
participation emerged during this period.[1] Philanthropy gave marginalized
groups, in particular free people of color, a means to challenge the sociopolitical dominance of the plantocracy; it also helped to reproduce the public sphere
as an elitist and patriarchal realm, reaffirming the elite male monopoly on
political power.

In this chapter I will argue that, between 1790 and 1850, lower- and middle-
class challenges to the aristocratic dominance of civic life transformed the
public sphere in Atlantic world societies. One manifestation of this reshaping
of public space was the middle-class and community-based civic organization,
a category that included philanthropic societies. Networks of these societies
became the basis for mass political movements, among the largest and most
politically powerful of which was transatlantic abolitionism.[2] Abolitionism
sparked rapid growth in the number of philanthropic organizations in the
British Caribbean during the early nineteenth century. In Barbados the "philanthropic boom" was intimately tied to the emergence of a local struggle by
free people of color against racial discrimination.

Charitable endeavors were the only area of civic life in which all groups,
regardless of race, could participate without restriction. Although philanthropy was merely one means through which elite white men reaffirmed their
right to rule, it became a primary basis from which the male nonwhite elite
launched claims for political equality. Philanthropy in Barbados developed as
an arena in which racialized forms of elite patriarchal political power and

feminine domesticity were displayed and contested. Through philanthropy, elite nonwhites sought to establish themselves as the leaders of a community of people of color. The combination of this local antiracist campaign and British abolitionism challenged the moral basis of white rule. White men and women of the planter class fought this challenge through philanthropic organizing, reasserting the right of male planters to govern society.

The participation of elite women of color and white women in early nineteenth-century philanthropy provided new opportunities for their civic participation. However, while elite men of color challenged planters, they shared many of the fundamental gender and class assumptions that buttressed the plantocratic order. The free black and colored struggle for political rights was patriarchal: it aimed to establish equal legal status for men. Women's philanthropic work served the patriarchal contest between white and nonwhite men over racial equality in politics. In particular, the new moral order which elite men of color envisioned rested on women of color's "domestication" and strict male control of any female involvement in public life. Ultimately, the philanthropic endeavors of both elite whites and Afro-Barbadians during this era confirm Eileen J. Suárez Findlay's observation that "dominant social orders . . . simultaneously incorporate and exclude different members of society in various ways. Projects claiming to be radically liberatory often share key assumptions with those which they oppose."[3]

Planter Philanthropy in Eighteenth-Century Barbados

Neither the planter-dominated government nor individual whites established philanthropic societies for slaves or free nonwhites during the eighteenth century. White elites rarely displayed concern for the island's large population of impoverished whites. While the principle of white racial supremacy was enshrined in public institutions, Hilary Beckles notes that "planter elitism was not offended, but confirmed, by the existence of a white working-class culture of poverty on the periphery of the plantations."[4] Men of the planter class tightly controlled all levels of government, except for the post of governor, and parish vestries provided the minimum services required to maintain the superior social status of whiteness. The government supported one free school for poor white boys but, with one short-lived exception during the 1790s, there were no charity schools or scholarships for indigent girls.[5] White women in eighteenth-century Barbados also did not establish charities to dispense relief for poor white women and girls.

Those rare planters who formed charities to improve the condition of poor whites were motivated by a fear that impoverished whites contradicted the doctrine of white supremacy. White poverty was largely caused by the entrenchment of plantation agriculture, the consolidation of the planter class and the growth of free and enslaved nonwhite laboring classes during the seventeenth and eighteenth centuries. By the eighteenth century a small white minority owned most of the island's arable land and it was difficult for any person without land, whether of European or African descent, to enter the ranks of the landed elite. These developments led to white population decline, as white immigration decreased and large numbers emigrated from Barbados. By the mid-eighteenth century, a distinctive "poor white" group was a permanent feature of the Barbadian social landscape.[6] Even so, gestures of planter philanthropy were rare and received only token support from the state.[7]

The Emergence of the Free Elite of Color

The plantocracy was also concerned about the steady growth of the free population of color. Between the mid-eighteenth century and emancipation, free people of color were the fastest growing segment of the Barbadian population, increasing from a mere 107 (0.2 percent of the population) in 1748 to 4,524 (4.6 percent of the population) in 1825. Most free people of color were fairly poor and worked in similar occupations to nonagricultural slaves, contributing to poor whites' marginalization.[8]

Planter solutions to the "problem" of the free nonwhite population were racialized and gendered. While women of all races were excluded from serving in political, judicial, and administrative positions, the Barbadian government sought to ensure that black and colored men were excluded from politics and all public institutions. The legislature, in common with other British Caribbean governments, passed laws defining citizenship as the preserve of white, property-owning, Christian men. As early as 1721, although the free population of color was still tiny, a law limited the holding of elective office, jury duty, and the right to testify in court to white, Christian, adult males who owned at least ten acres of land or a house with an annual taxable value of £10.[9]

Prior to the late eighteenth century, one cannot speak of a free nonwhite "elite" in the same way that one can identify white planter elites. Although no laws restricted the amount of property that free people of color could own, Barbados lacked an equivalent to the large and powerful "colored" planter class of Jamaica or prerevolutionary Saint-Domingue. Competition was tight between landless whites, free people of color, and slaves in most nonagricultural occupations, and free people of color rarely made large fortunes as merchants, artisans, or lodging-house keepers.

Women appear to have been the majority among free people of color until the early nineteenth century. It was rare for anyone to manage to buy their freedom, but legislative proposals in 1744 and 1801 to raise the cost of manumitting female slaves suggest that the ex-slave mistresses of white men were significant among the small free black and colored population.[10] Many such women would have been relatively economically privileged. By the turn of the century the number of independently wealthy urban free people of color appears to have increased, with clear differences between the economic advancement of women and men. Women of color owned a significant number of urban lodging-houses throughout the British Caribbean.[11] By the 1790s a small number of nonwhite hucksters and shopkeepers in Barbados, often ex-slaves, had accumulated wealth, sometimes enough to buy family members out of slavery and bequeath significant amounts of property. Many of these were women; however, by the early nineteenth century the wealthiest merchants of color were men. A male merchant elite of color, whose businesses sometimes rivaled large white-owned merchant houses, emerged in the towns in the 1790s. With the exception of only four nonwhite planter families identified for the entire period between 1780 and 1834, these men were the island's most affluent group of color.[12]

White representations of free people of color were deeply gendered. During the 1790s the symbol of nonwhite business success in Barbados was the mixed-race female hotelier, typically represented as a prostitute or owner of a brothel where free and enslaved women of color provided sexual services for white men. Such representations sexualized and delegitimized nonwhite businesswomen in particular and free people of color in general and epitomized whites' almost obsessive tendency to represent free people of color as women whose public role was sexual transgression. Such representations of women of color, both enslaved and free, as insatiable temptresses absolved white men of responsibility for their sexual involvements with and abuse of these women.[13] Moreover, as John D. Garrigus has argued for eighteenth-century Saint-Domingue, this feminization and sexualization of free people of color reflected white anxieties about the presence of free people of color, particularly those of mixed racial background, whose existence suggested that sexual acts were undermining slavery's legal and racial boundaries. Additionally, such representations reinforced arguments for excluding free people of color from public life.[14]

Patriarchy, Philanthropy, and Early Demands for Civil Rights

In the 1790s propertied men of color began to challenge their exclusion from state institutions with a series of petitions. This intervention into public life was the first collective public opposition by free blacks and coloreds in Barbados to racial discrimination. Their petitions were written "on behalf" of free people of color in general but, in reality, they demanded rights for themselves on the assumption that their property and their sex entitled them to participate in institutions which, hitherto, had been the preserve of rich white men. They objected to the racial limits of these public institutions but not to their class or gender exclusivity.[15]

Caribbean women of color, both free and slave, participated in collective struggles against racial discrimination. Working-class free women of color and slave women in Barbados took part in street riots, demonstrations, and confrontations with state authorities to protect other people of color. Non-white women often carried out their economic activities in defiance of laws designed to limit economic opportunities for slaves and free people of color.[16] Yet, there is no evidence that protests against racial segregation ever questioned women's exclusion from the institutions of the state.

Throughout much of the eighteenth century, well-to-do free people of color went to great lengths to improve the lot of their kin, but they did not establish poor relief, missionary, or educational societies until the close of the eighteenth century. During the 1790s male merchants of color began to use charitable work to carve out a niche of public prominence for themselves and assert themselves as the leaders of the free community of color. Charities and social societies expressed the desire of these men to establish themselves as the leaders of a parallel social hierarchy, rather than to be accepted into the social sphere of whites.[17] Philanthropy also supported their civil rights demands by allowing them to display their leadership capacities and organizing skills. In 1798, elite men of color formed the Samaritan Charitable Society of the Free People of Color, a poor relief organization. Although the Samaritans' mandate was allegedly nonpolitical, its establishment coincided with the first collective protest by elite men of color against the discriminatory laws excluding them from state institutions. In 1799, fifty-eight free men of color petitioned the governor for the right to testify in court.[18] The Samaritans were closely connected to the political aspirations of upper-class nonwhite men—all known members of the charity's executive committee were men of color, many of who were active in the nonwhite civil rights struggle. It is unclear if women played any role in the society's operations.[19]

As Garrigus suggests in the Saint-Domingue case, such silence on the issue of women's political rights was not accidental. He argues that the "fraternal rhetoric of the French Revolution provided Saint-Domingue's men of color with a powerful vocabulary to reject accusations of moral and physical effeminacy."[20] Elite free black and colored men in Barbados went out of their way to disavow any sympathy with the Haitian revolutionary cause, yet the French Revolution's patriarchal language of rights spurred their own demands for greater civil rights at the close of the eighteenth century. As I will show, elite men of color's rise to public prominence was predicated on masculinization of the public persona of free nonwhites and on replacing the image of the sexually and racially transgressive free woman of color with an image of patriarchal, domestic harmony. In the nineteenth century abolitionism created a political opening for Barbadian men of color to claim public patriarchal status equal to that of white men.

New Publics: Abolitionism, Antiracism, and the Philanthropic Challenge

At the end of the eighteenth century free nonwhite organizing posed no fundamental threat to the social hierarchy or the power of white planters, who ignored it as they ignored antidiscrimination petitions from nonwhite men. However, the growth of British abolitionism transformed the political significance of philanthropy in the West Indies in the second decade of the nineteenth century. For West Indian planters and the British aristocracy, abolitionism—with its giant network of extraparliamentary committees and societies, mass meetings and petitions—was part of a new political culture which attacked the institution of slavery and the foundations of aristocratic governance.[21] Abolitionism was one aspect of a widespread demand for the reform of public life unleashed in the Atlantic world after the American, French, and Haitian revolutions. Abolitionism in the British empire resembled what Mary Ryan has termed the "proliferation of publics" in the nineteenth-century United States, in which groups marginalized because of race, class, or gender sought to "constitute themselves as a public," using different forms of civic activity—such as newspapers and mass meetings—to participate in American political life.[22]

Planters and their close allies, the West Indian Anglican clergy, had always strenuously, and largely successfully, opposed the establishment of missionary societies in the Caribbean. However, in the early 1800s, support began to flow from new, often nonconformist, missionary organizations in Britain seeking allies in the Caribbean willing to conduct missionary and philanthropic work among slaves and free nonwhites. Frequently free people of color, both men and women, initiated or responded to the missionary call. Having for so long been excluded from or marginalized in public life, they were eager to use this opportunity to play an unprecedented public role.[23]

None of the philanthropic missionary societies which sprang up in Barbados was abolitionist. However the kind of work they conducted and the public prominence that they conferred on the free people of color who coordinated them were inherently unsettling to the racial hierarchy. The philanthropic challenge to the white Barbadian elite began in 1818, when, as an amelioration measure, the new governor acted as patron for the Colonial Charity School, founded and run by a committee of men of color. Established to provide education for nonwhites, both slave and free, it was the British Caribbean's first publicly supported school for children of color.[24] The school was controversial because it resulted directly from imperial slave amelioration policies, had gubernatorial sanction, and because its administrative board was composed entirely of men of color—the first time that nonwhite men held such important positions.[25]

The Charity School was not the first school where teachers of color instructed legally mixed classes of pupils. Some men and women of color taught small classes of enslaved and free nonwhite children. Numerous women of color taught music and singing.[26] However, the Charity School was a symbol of collaboration between the imperial government and local free men of color, lacking the approval of the Barbadian legislature. Although philanthropic, the project was connected to the debate over slavery. The school was also founded two years after a slave rebellion had swept the island. Although some free men of color had received the right to testify in court as a reward for helping to suppress the rebellion, whites feared that Barbadian slaves and free people of color would follow the Haitian example and massacre them, or help Haitian "emissaries" and abolitionists to infiltrate the island. As a result, many whites saw the school as imperial sanction for the suspected political designs of free men of color and were outraged by the school's plan to teach mixed classes of free children of color and slaves.[27] Neither the governor's support nor the applications of the school committee moved the legislature to give the school financial support.[28]

The school's founding added to unease among whites about amelioration and about the maintenance of legal and racial hierarchies in public life. Two years after the school opened, a white music teacher published an angry disclaimer to rumors that he had provided music for a "*Mulatto Dance*": "It is most true, I gave my services at a colored Concert, for the benefit of the Charity School, which, as a Christian, I could not refuse; and shall do the same whenever requested."[29] "Mulatto dance" was a term for private parties given by mixed-race prostitutes, usually for white men.[30] The use of references to illicit interracial sex to discredit a school fundraiser indicates the depth of public hostility and fear. At the same time, the rumor conjured up a delegitimizing picture of women of color participating in society as white men's sexual objects. Whites perhaps found this gendered image of free people of color less unsettling than that of pious free men of color working with the imperial government to provide a Christian education for the nonwhite poor.

In 1819, the Colonial Charity School was joined by the Barbados Auxiliary Bible Society of the People of Color, a colonial offshoot of the new nondenominational British and Foreign Bible Society, which distributed Bibles to the lower classes in Britain and the empire, and had strong abolitionist connections.[31] The St. Mary's Society for the Education of the Colored Poor in the Principles of the Established Church and for Other Charitable Relief was formed in the mid-1820s. The boards of the societies in Barbados were a who's who of the island's nonwhite merchant elite, many of whom were active in petitioning for civil rights for free people of color.[32]

Several of the societies formed by free men of color during the 1820s had female auxiliaries. Their committees were subordinate to the primary boards composed of men, and were responsible for female pupils or recipients of benefits. These committees consisted of prominent women of color, most of whose surnames indicate a family relationship to men on the main committees. In 1827, the president of the Ladies' Branch Association for the Education of Female Children of the Colored Poor—the auxiliary of the St. Mary's Society—was Mary Montefiore, whose husband, the leading merchant of color John Montefiore, was on the St. Mary's committee. Mrs. (Thomas) Cummins, Mrs. (Joseph) Shurland, Mrs. (Benjamin) Massiah, and Mrs. (Charles) Phipps were among the nine auxiliary members whose husbands were either on the main committee of the St. Mary's Society or were prominent in other nonwhite charities.

While such philanthropic work created a new public role for women of color, it reinforced gendered hierarchies in public and family life, and established the "respectability" of women of color with kin relationships to elite nonwhite men at the expense of unmarried and financially independent women. The first names of most female philanthropists of color are not known—their family names and marital status provide the sole guide to who they were. Their public presence served to establish the social respectability of their family name, emphasizing their husbands' role as household patriarchs. Furthermore, by emphasizing their married status and family connections, these women distinguished themselves from the nonwhite "concubines" of white men who, although often wealthy, were not "respectable" married women. These elite married women of color were also distinguishing their public role from that of working women of color, such as lodging-house keepers and hucksters, who were usually not married. In the lists of names for the Ladies' Branch Association, married members were listed before unmarried members, further elevating the status of marriage within their own socioeconomic circle. It is likely that many of the unmarried members of the Ladies' Branch Association were also the kin of politically active men of color. Miss Lynch, for example, was probably the sister-in-law of Mrs. (Hamlet) Lynch, who was also a committee member, and whose husband sat on the St. Mary's Society committee. Hamlet Lynch had signed civil rights petitions in 1799, 1811, and 1823.[33]

Free women of color did not form philanthropic organizations independently of men in their community as did black women in the United States during the Jim Crow era.[34] Elite free women of color in Barbados must have felt as deeply invested in the struggle to end racial discrimination as men. However, they used philanthropy to define and make public their social position as morally upright and privileged women while channeling their political agency through men. The women of color who established these charities may have calculated that women's charitable work under the direction of men would present a united and "respectable" impression of the free black and colored community. Such a strategy may have made it difficult for white opponents to mobilize the stereotype of the "loose" and dangerously independent free woman of color to delegitimize their efforts, thereby shielding free black and colored female philanthropists from accusations of being immoral "public" women. Thus, elite women of color may have used emerging patriarchal structures to conduct community work which would otherwise have attracted derision from whites.

Never before had nonwhite men and women assumed such prominent public roles. Furthermore, they provided services for slaves and free people of color which the government could not even competently provide for whites. During the 1820s the Colonial Charity School was the fourth largest school on the island. In the first year of its existence the St. Mary's Society and the Ladies' Branch Association already had 87 free boys, 60 free girls, 112 slave boys, and 70 slave girls attending their school, for a total of 329 students.[35]

"All the pains I have taken to make you good":
The White Elite and Philanthropy

The establishment of the Colonial Charity School and the Auxiliary Bible Society alarmed planters, who scrambled to establish their own philanthropic organizations for poor whites. In 1819, local planters and clergymen established a branch of the Anglican British Society for Promoting Christian Knowledge (SPCK). The chairman of the new Barbados affiliate, a planter, made it clear that the society's purpose was to maintain the dominance and assert the moral superiority of whites in the face of threats from uppity free people of color, even claiming that nonwhite charities were an "emulation" of white philanthropy.[36] The SPCK founded the Bridgetown Central School for indigent white boys in 1819 and established a girls' Central School, the first free school for poor white girls from all over the island, in 1826. In 1822 the local legislature assumed financial responsibility for the Central School, support which it never extended to similar organizations run by free people of color while slavery lasted.[37]

Particularly after May 1823, when the imperial parliament voted to work toward the "gradual abolition" of slavery, planters sought to wrest control of the amelioration process from the Colonial Office by establishing their own charities for slaves.[38] From mid-1823 the rhetoric of planter paternalism changed, the beginning of a shift away from the blatant language of proprietorial rights to describing slaves as the dependent vassals, almost members, of the planter's extended family. An 1824 letter to the Barbadian newspaper from "A Master of a Family," titled "Family Religion," exhorted planters to encourage "family worship" among their own kin and slave domestics, and asked: "Christian! are you a father and a master? Remember . . . that you have others to take care of . . . as well as for yourself."[39] As they publicized their philanthropic schemes, planters worked to strengthen racial segregation. In the late 1820s the island's parish vestries, which were responsible for parochial schools, restated the racial segregation policy, making it clear that no free children of color would be admitted. By the 1830s, only two of the island's parishes funded schools for free children of color, who were educated separately from whites.[40]

The explosion of philanthropic organizing during the 1820s provided wealthy white women with new opportunities to assume an influential public role. In so doing these women assisted elite white men in their efforts to reassert white authority and reinforce the endangered racial hierarchy. Wealthy white Barbadian women established their own independent charities during the 1820s, such as the Ladies' Association for the Relief of the Sick and Indigent Poor of Bridgetown and Its Environs, founded in 1825. Its members were all wealthy white women, and its charity was initially for poor whites only. The Ladies' Association became the showpiece of a reinvigorated sense of white moral leadership. In contrast to poor relief organizations run by free people of color, the Ladies' Association received generous grants from the legislature. Through philanthropy upper-class white women invented a new public image of themselves to replace the typically derogatory representations in the local press. One newspaper, which printed several satirical articles during the 1820s implying that wealthy white women were ignorant, spoiled, and a nuisance, patronizingly praised the "perseverance" of white female philanthropists in the 1830s, stating that, if men had run these societies "they should have folded long before."[41] This might indicate that most charities established and run by wealthy white men were not effective in their operations. This seems likely given that few if any of them published annual activity reports, in contrast to the Ladies' Association and the largest nonwhite charities.

Through philanthropy elite white women assumed a maternal public role which mirrored the language of male planter paternalism. The Ladies' Association first began to provide charitable services for slaves and the nonwhite poor around 1829, dispensing poor relief and distributing Bibles and religious books in order to rescue young people "from the contagion of vice."[42] In some instances, such undertakings extended the domestic role of female members of planter families as mistresses of the house. For example, the Moravian mission at Mount Tabor in St. John was opened in 1826 under the auspices of a planter's wife, Mrs. Haynes, who gave the Moravians land for the mission station. She was personally involved in teaching the children at her husband's plantation. In letters, Haynes maternally and condescendingly referred to the slave children at the mission school as "her Negro children."[43] Such philanthropy was part of a reinvention of the domestic role of wealthy white women. Images of white domestic harmony and moral rectitude were exhibited for the reading public's consumption. Displays of white maternal guidance of blacks provided ammunition during the apprenticeship period, as West Indian planters sought to reconstruct their image after abolitionists had successfully represented white West Indian men as profligate, promiscuous, and violent, and white West Indian family life as morally bankrupt.[44] One planter invited American abolitionists J. A. S. Thome and Horace Kimball to observe one of his daughters teaching a class of girls from the estate, claiming that both his daughters did this every week.[45]

Such moralizing also served as a weapon in the postemancipation struggle over the terms and conditions of labor. During and after apprenticeship, one of the justifications which planters used for harsh labor conditions and legislation was that former slaves were like children in need of moral guidance and parental discipline. Without such discipline, so the argument went, they would abuse their freedom. Philanthropy strengthened white ex-slaveowners' efforts to use this language of moral superiority to chastise apprentices for disobedience. In a particularly instructive case from 1836, a stipendiary magistrate in Barbados presided over the trial of Dutchess, a black domestic apprentice who had stolen a large sum of money from her former owner and spent it on expensive clothes. Upon learning that Dutchess had committed the theft, her employer, a middle-aged white woman who was a member of the Ladies' Association, announced: "This is a pretty return, you black wretch, for all the pains I have taken to make you good. . . . Oh vanity, vanity, vanity. . . ." During the trial, which attracted a large crowd, Dutchess was publicly humiliated for wishing to dress above her station, and then sentenced to six months in jail and hard labor.[46]

Gender and the Suppression of "Licentiousness": Reinventing the Norms of Elite Behavior

After emancipation, elite whites and people of color used philanthropy to establish new codes of conduct for the elite. Men and women of the white and nonwhite upper classes reinvented their public image in ways that benefited the political and gender interests of both white men and men of color. Forms of gendered and interracial social interaction which had previously passed with little public comment now came under unprecedented attack. However, what is being described here is a new public discourse about behavioral norms whose importance derives as much from their role as social ideals which few achieved as from their influence on the actual behavior of elite whites and people of color.

For the white elite one of abolitionism's most damaging aspects had been its condemnation of the "licentiousness" of West Indian society, with particular focus on the arbitrary violence, drunkenness, and promiscuity which were the hallmark of wealthy white masculinity.[47] During apprenticeship, planters and clergymen attempted to rehabilitate the public image of white men, and temperance societies sprang up in several British Caribbean territories. Although membership was open to all, and planters claimed to be setting an example for ex-slaves, temperance festivities served to exclude the majority from the privilege of moral grandstanding, reserving this right for upper-class men. This community leadership was also, by implication, political.[48]

While elite whites and free people of color on other islands jointly organized similar societies, the membership of the newly formed Barbados Temperance Society in 1835 was composed entirely of white planters, clergymen, and merchants. Although many prominent men of color espoused temperance views, they were not invited to join. Through the postemancipation moral assault on drunkenness, upper-class men distanced themselves, at least in the public eye, from the alcohol abuse which was associated throughout the West Indies with white men of all class backgrounds. Even planters admitted that neither people of color free before 1834 nor ex-slaves provided such regular displays of public drunken behavior. White teetotalers in the Caribbean were therefore as concerned with policing the behavior of white men as they were with moralizing to the laboring classes. Many upper-class whites now per-ceived white male "licentiousness" as a threat to the status quo, and they distanced themselves, at least publicly, from such behavior.[49]

Friendly societies, formed after 1828 throughout the West Indies, were per-haps the most widespread philanthropic means of controlling the public de-bate on morality.[50] These mutual benefit organizations were directed by clergy-men, planters, and merchants and based on a members' subscription to provide financial assistance in time of need. They were also designed to pro-mote elite notions of correct behavior for men and women by encouraging thrift, modesty, and marriage among members. Married couples were encour-aged to join, and men or women discovered having relationships out of wed-lock were expelled.[51] Friendly societies were ostensibly organized for the bene-fit of ex-slaves and attracted some interest from them. However, evidence suggests that they attracted mainly comparatively comfortable apprentices and free people of color. In 1835 the St. Mary's Society's male and female friendly societies had three hundred members, mostly apprentices, "but a considerable number also of very respectable free persons." After a severe yellow fever epidemic in 1836 and 1837 it emerged that few members of the St. Mary's Friendly Societies applied for aid, with the majority saying that they "did not absolutely require it." The Anglican bishop considered this an indica-tion that the members were "not of the poorest class."[52] Additionally, the majority of the names attached to an 1839 petition from members of the St. Mary's Male Friendly Society were those of prominent merchants and political campaigners of color free before emancipation.[53]

The expansion of philanthropic activity among elite people of color during the 1820s and 1830s coincided with and expressed a growing cult of domesticity, resembling what Barbara Welter termed the "cult of True Womanhood" in the antebellum United States, which prescribed "piety, purity, submissiveness, and domesticity" for women. In Barbados, as wealthy men of color sought political rights, both upper-class men and women of color attempted to attain "respectable" status in the eyes of the community. In the 1820s married status was already becoming a hallmark of "respectability" for women of color. After emancipation, both white men and men of color condemned common-law interracial relationships between white men and elite women of color, promoting instead "respectable" marriages between women of color and, increasingly, black and colored men. Such "illegitimate" relationships no doubt continued, but, as one North American observed in the 1850s, condemnation of "illicit intercourse" between whites and people of color "pervades the whole of Barbadian society."[54] Another author noted that "respectable" upper-class women of color were expected to marry men of color, and "concubinage" with a white man was considered a "disgrace."[55]

This reverence for marriage and family life paralleled contemporaneous shifts in Britain, especially among middle-class people who, like Caribbean merchants, were economically privileged but were not as wealthy as large landowners.[56] Nevertheless it would be simplistic to assume that Barbadian developments demonstrate a cultural diffusion from Britain to the empire, as opposed to a local manifestation of transnational sociopolitical forces at work among the societies of the northern Atlantic world. The Barbadian "cult of domesticity" was a response by local elites to social forces unleashed by abolitionism, debates about the "rights of man," race, and emancipation. These elites publicly disowned the values associated with slavery.[57] Sexual relations between white women and men of color had always been frowned upon. However, the right of white men, particularly wealthy white men, to have access to the bodies of free women of color and slave women symbolized and perpetuated white masculinity and white supremacy during slavery. After emancipation interracial relationships between white men and women of color were condemned as a symbol of social disorder.

After slavery interracial relations represented a dangerous defiance of the authority of men to define the boundaries and set the terms of "legitimate" interracial relations. In the new legal reality of the postemancipation era where, on paper at least, "race" no longer mattered, many whites probably saw such relations as a threat to white control of property and white "racial purity." Upper-class white women likely supported and benefited from attempts to reform the hard drinking and sexual promiscuity of many of their male kin. For elite women of color, marriage offered a degree of security and social standing which contrasted significantly with the marginal social status, absence of legal protection, and lack of long-term security which characterized "concubinage" relationships with white men, however wealthy.

"The charities . . . of the true Christian": Elite Women of Color in Public Life after Emancipation

After emancipation, elite black and colored men attempted to set the parameters of any appearance by elite women of color in political life, often depriving these women of an individual public identity. These men sought to make "their" women into a collective public expression of their political and social views. In 1844, a delegation of "Ladies" of color presented the first man of color elected to the House of Assembly with three hundred dollars to celebrate his victory, a rare reference to elite female involvement in politics. The gift was presented before a delegation of businessmen who had supported the campaign. While the names of the businessmen were reported in the newspaper, the names of the women were omitted, suggesting that the presentation was a statement of the political strength and wealth of the male merchant elite.[58] There are no recorded references to women of color speaking at political meetings. It may be that women were present at such meetings but were either not allowed to speak or made remarks that men did not consider important enough to be recorded.

After his visit to the West Indies in the 1850s, British medical doctor John Davy noted that he knew little about upper-class nonwhite women because they were "so little in society. From the few opportunities I had of judging, they appeared inferior in manners, and greatly inferior in information to the men, the natural consequence of a more secluded life, and a more limited and imperfect education."[59] For elite women of color, charitable work provided a modicum of space for independent community activity, interactions with other women and the poor from a position of authority and the development of organizing skills. Yet philanthropy also represented the domestication of elite women of color. "Christian" philanthropic work for ex-slaves and the poor became the sine qua non of respectability for upper-class free women of color, and women who participated in such work were held up by prominent nonwhite men as models for others to follow.

The case of Sarah Hope, the daughter of a prominent free man of color, sums up the ambivalence of the public persona which female black and colored philanthropists assumed. When she died in 1838, the *Liberal*, a newspaper edited by two prominent male civil rights activists of color, praised her for her philanthropic work and for devoting herself "to her service and the good of her fellow creatures." According to the *Liberal*, Sarah Hope organized Sunday and evening schools, "was also a strong supporter of that useful body, the Friendly Society," was the Bible Society's secretary, was one of the principal organizers of the St. Paul's Anglican church choir, and collected clothes for the poor. The *Liberal* lamented that, with her death, "the poor have lost an invaluable friend and supporter; her charities being those of the true Christian—secretly and unostentaciously [sic] bestowed."[60] Sarah's charitable activities likely gave her a platform from which she commanded authority and respect in the community. Given the importance of philanthropy to the political designs of free men of color, women like Sarah would have shaped both philanthropy and politics among people of color. At the same time, the ease with which this obituary condensed her life into a public symbol of "proper" nonwhite womanhood encapsulates the limits of the ability of female philanthropists to mold their own public image. Charities and church activities were among the few areas of public life in which "respectable" women of color could participate. Their involvement in these activities was neither "secret" nor "unostentacious"—it was a stage for parading the domesticity of the nonwhite elite, illustrated by the conformity of many privileged women of color to new standards of "respectable" femininity.

After emancipation, in contrast to the praises heaped on a "respectable" philanthropist like Sarah Hope, positive public references to wealthy unmarried businesswomen of color are rare. Upper-class men writing in the white and nonwhite press often hinted that self-employed women, particularly hucksters, were a step removed from prostitution.[61] Although many independent female lodging-house keepers continued to flourish, they were excluded from the philanthropic and political network of the male merchant elite.[62]

By contrast, philanthropic activity brought some upper-class men of color precisely the public recognition and influence that they sought. During the 1830s and 1840s male members of the old preemancipation free black and colored elite finally gained access to circles of political power. A small number were appointed or elected to positions on commissions of inquiry and in the magistracy, the legislature, and the vestry for St. Michael parish, in which Bridgetown was located. Politicians of color such as Thomas Cummins and Joseph Thorne, who had risen to public prominence as philanthropists or missionaries before the end of slavery, now used their positions to force desegregation of several vestry services. However, these changes belied a postslavery reality in which planters, with support from some wealthy non-white men, blocked efforts by progressive and frequently lower-class men of color for political enfranchisement. Until the 1840s the legislature tenaciously clung to a law which set a higher franchise qualification for men of color than white men. Although a law equalized the franchise in 1842, most men of color, including ex-slaves, had their hopes of gaining the right to vote dashed when the legislature set it at a rate too high even for many white voters.[63]

Elite observers treated the involvement of lower-class women of color in politics as a sign of the lower classes' unsuitability for political enfranchisement. This was evident in June 1834, during the final House of Assembly elections, when lower-class blacks and coloreds, both slave and free, turned out in large numbers to support a white lawyer who challenged the planter candidates for the St. Michael parish seat. One proplanter newspaper reserved its most scathing commentary for the lawyer's black female supporters. "Could any thing be more disgusting," the editor inquired, "than to see negro women, dirty trollops, swaggering up and down the aisles of the cathedral, with their bows of blue ribbon on their arms, the distinguishing badge of those, respectable as well as vulgar, who professed to be the supporters of Mr. Sharpe[?]"[64] In the late 1830s and early 1840s, when white men and men of color debated franchise reform, some elite men of color challenged the class exclusivity of the reforms, in contrast to the 1790s. However, there was never a suggestion that women of any color or social class should be enfranchised.

Conclusion

In this chapter, I have asserted that involvement in philanthropy was a political, racialized, and gendered process through which old and new elites jostled with each other for control of public life. Philanthropy both undermined and reproduced the race, class, and gender inequalities of Barbadian civic life. Free nonwhite philanthropic societies were a political challenge to the principles of slave society and helped elite men of color in their demands for political rights. However, philanthropy also helped planters to reaffirm their dominance over politics despite challenges posed by abolitionism and demands for racial equality. Although involvement in philanthropy gave elite women new opportunities for public participation, white women's charitable work tended to reinforce white supremacy, while philanthropy helped to consolidate patriarchal hierarchies among free people of color. Philanthropy was part of a cult of domesticity among elite people of color that both augmented the public role of elite women of color and undermined the independence of all women of color in public life.

Many historians have focused on the postemancipation efforts of Christian missionaries to "Europeanize" the behavior of former slaves and lower-class free nonwhites. The aim, ostensibly, was to reshape black men and women into a deferential working class, whose behavior would fit the mold prescribed by prevailing upper- and middle-class desires. However true this might have been for foreign missionaries who came to the West Indies, the evidence suggests that, for local philanthropists, actually reforming the behavior of the lower classes was rarely the main aim. For local elites, charity was primarily a means of pursuing their own political interests while simultaneously establishing themselves as the dispensers of correct morality, prescribing and expressing new behavioral norms for their own social equals.

In studying the history of the emergence of new kinds of social movements or trends, like the emancipation debate or the struggle by free people of color for greater civil rights, historians should not treat the patriarchal, racist, or elitist nature of these movements as somehow natural or self-explanatory. Challenges to existing political and social barriers frequently result in the shifting, rather than the actual destruction, of those barriers. Understanding the role of gender in the reshaping of the Anglophone Caribbean's public sphere during the transition from slavery to freedom—especially gender's relationship to struggles over racial equality—has much to tell us about the legacy of slavery and emancipation in shaping public life in the contemporary Caribbean. Recognizing this is important for conceptualizing and forging political alliances within and across boundaries of race, class, and gender which are self-reflexive, inclusive, and capable of building on the past without repeating its mistakes.

Notes

I wish to thank Jens Hanssen, Barbara Todd, Jerome Handler, and Nigel Bolland for their careful readings and helpful suggestions.

1 This chapter does not aim to provide an exhaustive list of all of the charities which sprang up in Barbados during this period; instead it focuses on those about which there is most information and which exercised the widest social and political influence.

2 David Brion Davis, *The Problem of Slavery in Western Culture* (Ithaca, N.Y.: Cornell University Press, 1966); Davis, *The Problem of Slavery in the Age of Revolution, 1770–1823*

(Ithaca, N.Y.: Cornell University Press, 1975); J. R. Oldfield, *Popular Politics and British Anti-slavery: The Mobilisation of Public Opinion against the Slave Trade* (Manchester, U.K.: Manchester University Press, 1995), 125.

3 Eileen J. Suárez Findlay, *Imposing Decency: The Politics of Sexuality and Race in Puerto Rico, 1870–1920* (Durham, N.C.: Duke University Press, 1999), 4. For discussions of philanthropy, race, gender, and emancipation in Puerto Rico, see also Félix V. Matos Rodríguez, *Women and Urban Change in San Juan, Puerto Rico, 1820–1868* (Gainesville: University Press of Florida, 1999); and Teresita Martínez-Vergne, *Shaping the Discourse on Space: Charity and Its Wards in Nineteenth-Century San Juan, Puerto Rico* (Austin: University of Texas Press, 1999).

4 Hilary McD. Beckles, *A History of Barbados: From Amerindian Settlement to Nation-State* (Cambridge: Cambridge University Press, 1990), 48–49.

5 Cecily Ford-Jones, "Mapping Racial Boundaries: Gender, Race, and Poor Relief in Barbadian Plantation Society," *Journal of Women's History* 10, no. 3 (1998): 9–31. White girls could attend parish schools.

6 Hilary Beckles, "Black over White: The 'Poor White' Problem in Barbados Slave Society," *Immigrants and Minorities* 7, no.1 (1988): 1–15; Richard S. Dunn, *Sugar and Slaves: The Rise of the Planter Class in the English West Indies, 1624–1713* (Chapel Hill: University of North Carolina Press, 1972); Jack P. Greene, "Changing Identity in the British Caribbean: Barbados as a Case Study," in *Colonial Identity in the Atlantic World*, ed. Nicholas Canny and Anthony Pagden (Princeton, N.J.: Princeton University Press, 1987), 240–42; Jill Sheppard, *The "Redlegs" of Barbados: Their Origins and History* (New York: KTO, 1977), 40, 43.

7 Colonial Office (hereafter CO) 30/16 Acts of Barbados, 1782–1796, no. 141, "An Act for Encouraging Mechanic Industry in Barbados . . ."; William Dickson, *Mitigation of Slavery*, part 1 (London, 1814), xix–xx. See also Beckles, *History of Barbados*, 48–50.

8 Jerome S. Handler, *The Unappropriated People: Freedmen in the Slave Society of Barbados* (Baltimore: Johns Hopkins University Press, 1974), 18–19.

9 Ibid., 18–21, 66–81.

10 Ibid., 33–34, 40. The 1744 bill was defeated but the 1801 bill passed.

11 F. W. N. Bayley, *Four Years' Residence in the West Indies, during the Years 1826, 7, 8 and 9* (London: William Kidd Ltd., 1833), 27–28, 149–50; Handler, *Unappropriated People*, 33–37; Paulette Kerr, "Victims or Strategists? Female Lodging-House Keepers in Jamaica," in *Engendering History: Caribbean Women in Historical Perspective*, ed. Verene Shepherd, Bridget Brereton, and Barbara Bailey (Kingston: Ian Randle, 1995), 197–212; Jerome Handler, "Joseph Rachell and Rachael Pringle-Polgreen: Petty Entrepreneurs," in *Struggle and Survival in Colonial America*, ed. D. G. Sweet and G. B. Nash (Berkeley: University of California Press, 1981), 376–91; Jerome S. Handler, Ronald Hughes, and Ernest M. Wiltshire, *Freedmen of Barbados: Names and Notes for Genealogical and Family History Research* (Charlottesville: Virginia Foundation for the Humanities and Public Policy, 1999), 43. William Lloyd, *Letter from the West Indies, during a Visit of*

1836, and the Spring of 1837 (London, 1839), 7; Pedro Welch and Richard A. Goodridge, *Red and Black over White: Free Colored Women in Pre-emancipation Barbados* (Bridgetown, Barbados: Carib, 2000), 72–78.

12 Handler, *Unappropriated People*, 84, 121.

13 Deborah Gray White, *Ar'n't I a Woman: Female Slaves in the Plantation South* (New York: Norton, 1985), 27–61.

14 See image of " 'Rachel Pringle of Barbadoes,' Print by T. Rowlandson from a drawing by an unknown artist, 1796," the Barbados Museum and Historical Society, reprinted in Handler, *Unappropriated People*, 135; John D. Garrigus, "Redrawing the Color Line: Gender and the Social Construction of Race in Pre-revolutionary Haiti," *Journal of Caribbean History* 30, nos. 1–2 (1996): 28–50.

15 Melanie Newton, "Race for Power: People of Color and the Politics of Liberation in Barbados, 1816–c1850," in *Contesting Freedom in the Postemancipation Caribbean*, ed. Gad Heuman and David Trotman (London and Basingstoke: MacMillan Caribbean, forthcoming 2005).

16 Hilary Beckles, *Afro-Caribbean Women and Resistance to Slavery in Barbados* (London: Karnak House, 1988); Beckles, "Slaves and the Internal Market Economy of Barbados: A Perspective on Non-violent Resistance," paper presented at the Twentieth Conference of the Association of Caribbean Historians (U.S. Virgin Islands: University of the Virgin Islands, St. Thomas, 1988); Lucille Mathurin-Mair, "The Rebel Woman in the British West Indies during Slavery" (Kingston: African-Caribbean Institute of Jamaica, 1975); Welch and Goodridge, *Red and Black over White*, 56–99.

17 Newton, "Race for Power"; see similar observations in Susan Lowes, " 'They Couldn't Mash Ants': The Decline of the White and Non-white Elites in Antigua, 1834–1900," in *Small Islands, Large Questions: Society, Culture and Resistance in the Postemancipation Caribbean*, ed. Karen Fog Olwig (London: Frank Cass, 1995), 31–52.

18 Handler, *Unappropriated People*, 76.

19 *Barbadian*, 25 March 1828; Handler, Hughes, and Wiltshire, *Freedmen of Barbados*.

20 Garrigus, "Redrawing the Color Line," 50.

21 See Davis, *The Problem of Slavery in the Age of Revolution* (Ithaca: Cornell University Press, 1975); Oldfield, *Popular Politics*.

22 Mary Ryan, "Gender and Public Access: Nineteenth-Century America," in *Habermas and the Public Sphere*, ed. Craig Calhoun (Cambridge: MIT Press, 1992), 267–68. See also Mimi Sheller, *Democracy after Slavery: Black Publics and Peasant Radicalism in Haiti and Jamaica* (London: Macmillan, 2000), 41–68.

23 Moira Ferguson, *The Hart Sisters: Early African Caribbean Writers, Evangelicals, and Radicals* (Lincoln: University of Nebraska Press, 1993); Mary Turner, *Slaves and Missionaries: The Disintegration of Jamaican Slave Society, 1787–1834* (Urbana: University of Illinois Press, 1982), 105, 198.

24 Handler, *Unappropriated People*, 173–76.

25 *Barbados Mercury and Bridgetown Gazette* (hereafter *Mercury*), 6 Feb. 1819.

26   Nathaniel Hawthorne, ed., *The Yarn of a Yankee Privateer* (New York: Funk and Wagnalls, 1926), 12.

27   *Mercury*, 1, 8 Dec. 1818.

28   CO 31/47, 30 May 1820.

29   *Mercury*, 16 May 1820.

30   Hawthorne, *Yarn of a Yankee Privateer*, 104.

31   *Barbadian*, 16 May 1826; Midgley, *Women against Slavery: The British Campaigns, 1780–1870* (London: Routledge, 1992), 46.

32   See, e.g., *Barbadian*, "First Annual Report of the Society for the Education of the Colored Poor," 14 Sept. 1827.

33   *Barbadian*, 18 Sept. 1827; Handler, Hughes, and Wiltshire, *Freedmen of Barbados*.

34   See Deborah Gray White, *Too Heavy a Load: Black Women in Defense of Themselves, 1894–1994* (New York: W. W. Norton, 1999).

35   *Barbadian*, 14 Sept. 1827.

36   *Mercury*, 2 March 1819.

37   CO 31/49, 20 March 1821; CO 30/20, "An Act for the Better Management and Support of the Central School Established . . . by the Barbados Society for Promoting Christian Knowledge," 18 Jan. 1822.

38   *Mercury*, 8 Aug. 1823; CO 31/51, 17 March 1829, petition from the Barbados Society for the Encouragement of Arts and Promoting Mechanical Trades and General Industry; *Barbadian*, 29 Nov., 8 Dec. 1829.

39   *Barbadian*, 24 Sept. 1824.

40   St. George vestry minutes, 7 Aug. 1826; St. Philip vestry minutes, 25 March 1830; *Barbadian*, 8 June 1830, Christ Church vestry minutes, 30 Aug. 1832.

41   See *Barbadian*, letter from "Amelia Sobersides," 9 Aug. 1825, letter from "Patty Lackbrain," 20 Jan. 1829 and editorial on the Ladies' Association and the St. Michael Clothing Society, 7 Jan. 1835.

42   *Barbadian*, 12 Oct. 1829.

43   Diary of the Moravian Mission at Mount Tabor, St. John, Barbados, microfilm BS59, Barbados Public Library, see, e.g., entry for 5 Aug. 1827.

44   Barbara Bush, "White Ladies, Colored Favourites and Black Wenches," *Slavery and Abolition* 1, no. 3 (1981): 245–62; Midgley, *Women against Slavery*, 182–83.

45   J. A. S. Thome and Horace Kimball, *Emancipation in the West Indies: A Six Months' Tour of Antigua, Barbados and Jamaica in the Year 1837* (New York: American Anti-slavery Society, 1838), 56.

46   Woodville Marshall, ed., *The Colthurst Journal* (New York: KTO Press, 1977), 121–22.

47   Bush, "White Ladies."

48   Thome and Kimball, *Emancipation in the West Indies*, 21–22; Mrs. Flannigan, *Antigua and the Antiguans; A Full Account of the Colony and Its Inhabitants . . .* (London: Spottiswoode, Ballantyne, 1967 [1844]), 171–74.

49   Thome and Kimball, *Emancipation in the West Indies*, 26–27; *Barbadian*, 3 Jan.

1835. Men of color who were abolitionists and supporters of temperance, like Samuel Jackman Prescod, probably became involved in the international Temperance Movement, which had strong abolitionist connections; see Richard Blackett, *Building an Anti-slavery Wall: Black Americans in the Atlantic Abolitionist Movement, 1830–1860* (Baton Rouge: Louisiana State University Press, 1983), 32–33.

50   A. F. Wells and D. Wells, *Friendly Societies in the West Indies: Report on a Survey by A. F. and D. Wells* (London: HMSO, 1953); *Barbadian*, 6, 10 June 1835.

51   *Barbadian*, 18 June 1836.

52   Ibid., 13 May 1837.

53   CO 28/129, vol. 3, no. 127 MacGregor to Russell, 17 Dec. 1839, enclosing "An Address from Certain Inhabitants of This Colony, to the Reverend W. M. Harte," dated 26 Nov. 1839.

54   For similar observations on the declining respectability of extralegal interracial relations after emancipation in other Caribbean contexts, see Gad Heuman, *Between Black and White: Race, Politics and the Free Coloreds of Jamaica, 1792–1865* (Oxford: Greenwood, 1981), 75; and Lowes, " 'They Couldn't Mash Ants,' " 42; Thome and Kimball, *Emancipation in the West Indies*, 79; *Liberal*, 27 June 1838; William G. Sewell, *The Ordeal of Free Labour in the British West Indies* (London: Harper and Brothers, 1861), 67–68; and Barbara Welter, "The Cult of True Womanhood, 1820–1860," *American Quarterly* 18, no. 2 (1966): 151–74.

55   John Davy, *The West Indies before and since Emancipation, Comprising the Windward and Leeward Islands' Military Command* (London: W. F. and G. Cash, 1854), 79.

56   Leonore Davidoff and Catherine Hall, *Family Fortunes: Men and Women of the English Middle Class, 1780–1850* (Chicago: University of Chicago Press, 1987); Dror Wahrman, " 'Middle Class' Domesticity Goes Public: Gender, Class and Politics from Queen Caroline to Queen Victoria," *Journal of British Studies* 32 (1993): 396–432.

57   Cf. Joanne Pope Melish, *Disowning Slavery: Gradual Emancipation and "Race" in New England, 1780–1860* (Ithaca, N.Y.: Cornell University Press, 1998).

58   *Liberal*, 12 June 1844.

59   Davy, *West Indies*, 81.

60   Ibid., 12 May 1838.

61   See, e.g., the *Barbadian*, 4 June 1836, 12 Jan. 1839; *Liberal*, 10 March 1838.

62   See, e.g., *Liberal*, 16 July 1842.

63   Melanie Newton, " 'The Children of Africa in the Colonies': Free People of Color in Barbados during the Emancipation Era, 1816–1854" (PhD diss., University of Oxford, 2001), 301–7.

64   *Barbadian*, 4 June 1834.

SHEENA BOA

Young Ladies and Dissolute Women: Conflicting Views of Culture and Gender in Public Entertainment, Kingstown, St. Vincent, 1838–1888

The historiography of emancipation in the British Caribbean has tended to concentrate on rural societies, and on the discrete experiences of freedpeople. A focus on urban popular culture demonstrates the importance of the urban setting to the character of life after emancipation, and points to significant interconnections between different groups as they sought to reframe society. Urban women played a central role in shaping the cultural landscape of freedom. This chapter explores how women used a variety of types of entertainment to define themselves. Within elite society, the changing expectations of public behavior resulted in a new emphasis on politeness and respectability. Women used cultural channels to emphasize class, gender, and racial identities and to accentuate the separation of public and private worlds.

White women from the elite rarely took part in public life, but they used public and private social, religious, and cultural events to highlight their privileged social position. Elite white women presented themselves publicly as feminine and virtuous in order to demonstrate their superiority to women of other class and ethnic groups.[1] Middle-class women, who were often of mixed European and African parentage, chose dress styles, religious affiliations, and social pursuits that conveyed their acquisition of European-Christian values. They often devoted time to charitable works and regularly attended religious services. Through their deportment and manners, they presented themselves as moral and decorous. The relationships between class, wealth, power, and gender all shaped elite and middle-class women's decisions to adopt respectable, feminine behavior. Women who deviated from this demure form of public behavior could lose standing among their social peers.[2]

The restricted social activities of middle-class and elite women contrasted with the cultural world of poor women. While elite and middle-class women used public spheres to emphasize their accommodation of European-Christian values of femininity, many of the poorest women used entertainment to show their rejection of class, race, and gender prescriptions. The lives of working-class women spilled out onto the streets. Poor and overcrowded housing meant that poor women often had to perform household chores in public areas. They also used the roads and lanes around their homes to meet friends and socialize. Therefore, the poor were highly visible, and the elites expressed contradictory attitudes in their detailed observations and discussions of the dress, demeanor, and entertainment of poor women.[3]

The determined retention of African Caribbean traditions by poor men and women revealed the strength of their challenge to European cultural hegemony. Both during and after slavery, the street entertainment of the poor became the focus of social tensions, which occasionally resulted in violence. When slavery was abolished in 1838, African Caribbean people struggled to retain traditions such as carnivals and parties that they had created under slavery. However, it was these customs that the authorities most wanted to eradicate. The visible nature of masquerades and street dances undermined the authorities' attempts to control public space and bring about their own expectations of public behavior. Therefore, these public spaces, appropriated by the lower classes for entertainments that affirmed their freedom and heritage, became contested sites of cultural expression.

Entertainment for the Elites

Like other small Caribbean islands in the nineteenth century, St. Vincent had few elite European families because of the high percentage of absentee plantation owners.[4] In Kingstown, the capital, there were a small number of elite families who socialized together; according to one visitor, they were wary of outsiders. Within colonial societies, white women had limited social and economic authority. As members of the elite, they had some cultural privileges, but they were outside of the spheres of political influence.[5]

During slavery, white women had been further marginalized because of white men's sexual control over enslaved and free women of color. Many European men lived openly with African Caribbean or colored mistresses and attended parties for these women which excluded white females. The social and intimate relations between enslaved and free women of color and white men of all social classes emphasized white women's lack of autonomy over public space and their inability to control white male sexuality. However, the familial bonds between white women and women of color also emphasize the ambiguities of colonial relations. Publicly, white women condemned the sexual mores of enslaved women and free women of color. In private, while they may have felt humiliated by the actions of European men, some women also colluded with men's extramarital domestic relations by developing personal relations and friendships with people of color.[6]

When Caribbean societies adopted a more prurient attitude toward sexuality after the abolition of slavery, and upper-class men were no longer open about their extramarital sexual relations, white women from the elite gained more control over domestic and social arrangements. In this new era, white women organized and ran many social gatherings. While elite white men still had intimate ties with women of color, these women lost their ascendancy in publicly entertaining men from the white elite, and there were no longer descriptions of parties held exclusively for white men and colored women.[7]

In the years before the abolition of slavery, the elite's entertainment was transformed. The financial decline within the planter class in St. Vincent reduced the scale of public and private parties. As the nineteenth century progressed, power shifted and positions of influence were no longer the exclusive domain of the white elite. Colored men also held political office, and some achieved wealth and education, which necessitated the removal of barriers to many official social functions. To counter this, white men emphasized the separation between their public and private worlds.[8]

As women belonged to the private world, they became part of this demarcation. As in other colonial societies, white women in St. Vincent endorsed this separation, but they did not create it. Some elite women may have still retained family and patronage bonds with people of color privately. In addition, it was not uncommon for elite women to have close personal ties with long-standing domestic servants.[9] However, in their public social world they emphasized their exclusivity. In a world where their influence was limited, and where the mixed-race community was a constant reminder of their tenuous hold over their male peers' domestic and sexual behavior, white women opposed social interplay with nonwhites as a means of protecting their own narrow authority. This diminished their access to wider society and in some cases limited their interaction with other class groups to their domestic workers.[10]

The limited access of urban elite women to public space markedly contrasts with poor women's use of the streets as a space for public interaction. While women from the lower classes worked, danced, socialized, and sometimes even slept in the streets, young women from the elite rarely entered the streets alone. For elite girls and women, the towns were often places to fear. This disparity between the two groups of women was illustrated in 1850, when a group of angry male and female protesters confronted the chief justice and his daughters when they were on an evening ride. While women from the poor could roam and protest in the streets, the justice's daughters were chaperoned and on horseback. Their father accompanied them as protection. Elite white women continued to present themselves as delicate and sensitive to emphasize their difference from women of lower classes. As a result, restraint and boredom characterized the day-to-day social life of elite young women. They endured what special magistrate John Anderson described as "a death of life."[11]

Respectability, Culture, and Womanhood among the Middle Classes

Class positions in nineteenth-century St. Vincent were complex, rarely falling neatly into upper-, middle-, and lower-class demarcations. Class structures in the postemancipation era were influenced by several factors. Income, employment, and inherited social rank helped determine class. The institution of slavery and plantation life also created some class affiliations based on skin color, the acquisition of skills, and sexual relationships. Invariably, lighter-skinned people were more likely to belong to higher-status social positions. African Caribbean people, no matter how wealthy or educated, did not gain political office in St. Vincent during this period.

Notions of respectability also influenced membership in a social group. Religious connections, with the established church, nonconformists, or locally generated religious groups, influenced a person's social position. In addition, a greater access to education and the growing number of urban-based artisans and entrepreneurs changed the dynamics of social formation. In order to achieve social status, people displayed their acceptance of European-Christian morals and manners and adhered to certain patterns of behavior.

Susan Lowes's categories of a first and second middle class in Antigua are useful descriptors of the wide range of people between the elite white families who formed the "Upper Ten" and the laborers and unemployed in St. Vincent. Predominantly born in the Caribbean, often of mixed European and African heritage, and educated on the island, the first middle class ranged from the wealthy to those who struggled financially and socially to maintain their public standing. Men among this class were members of the professions, civil servants, and entrepreneurs. Some owned shops and stores; others were artisans. Single women from this class sometimes survived through property speculation, owning boardinghouses, or buying and reselling or renting land or houses. The second middle class was far more diverse. Schoolteachers, craftsmen and women, and the upper echelons of domestic workers formed part of this group. Within the second middle class, there were both mixed-parentage and African Caribbean families. While often very poor, they were distinct from the laboring classes both by their involvement in European-Christian churches and their adoption of European family structures.[12]

The wealthiest members of this class formed their own elite. Their shared cultural activities were usually of a literary or artistic nature, offering self-improvement as well as entertainment. Local newspapers often advertised and recorded these events. A wide range of entertainers and speakers gave lectures on diverse subjects. Theater, both amateur and professional, was also popular. Newspaper reporters gave fulsome praise to local entertainments and the efforts of the participants. For example, in one edition of the *Royal St. Vincent Gazette*, a reader calling himself "Gumble Gumption" boasted of the wide range of amusements on offer to the inhabitants of St. Vincent, comparing it favorably to life in Britain.[13]

Claiming an affiliation with European-Christian respectability was one means for women from different social groups to engage in public activities. The Methodist and Anglican churches in St. Vincent provided many women with communal activities. Leading Bible classes offered women the oppor tunity to help improve the social, educational, and physical welfare of the community. It also gave them positions of authority among the newly con-verted. Female class leaders oversaw both the religious and secular transfor-mations of new recruits. They could often determine who became a full mem-ber of the Church and who was expelled.[14]

Women from the first middle classes also formed committees to improve educational and moral conditions on the island, which they used as a social outlet that gave them wider access to the outside world. Through "good works," usually involving the sale of crafts or refreshments, exclusive and well-presented social gatherings, and an emphasis on restrained and refined activities, women of the middle classes met socially away from their domestic spheres and still remained grounded in a world of respectability. Presenta-tion was paramount, and newspapers publicized the various attempts by the "ladies" of the island to raise funds for a library, an orphanage, improved welfare and educational facilities, places of worship, and other causes. With the patronage of a few women from the elite, charity work enabled women from different social groups to meet but maintain their separateness.[15]

For many of the second middle class, respectability was also expressed through an outward appearance of propriety. Through church membership and adherence to rigid dress codes, those with a low income expressed their detachment from the lowest classes. European-Christianity became the antithesis of slavery and Africanness. Religious affiliation became synonymous with moral, educational, and social advancement. Colonial officials and missionaries encouraged the belief that people progressed into European Christianity and retreated into African cultural forms. African Christianity, polygamy, and illegitimacy, for example, were all portrayed as symptoms of a moral regression to slave culture. Membership in a European Christian church, therefore, was equated with social elevation, and participation in communal church work gave women avenues for social, educational, and religious experiences.[16]

The Poor and the Gendered Public Sphere: Street Entertainment

Poor women, who were largely excluded from institutional cultural life, often utilized the streets as their sites of identity building and resistance. While women from the elite and middle classes tended to use either private homes or public buildings as entertainment places, the poor held many of their social events in the open air. Following emancipation, the streets were frequently the focus of class tensions as ex-slaves tested the boundaries of their freedom, and the authorities attempted to limit and curtail the newly emancipated.

Before emancipation in many British Caribbean towns, slaves and lower-class free people shared similar working and living conditions. The bonds that they developed extended to family relations and to shared cultural events. Poorer free people of color often lived on the outskirts of the towns, where they held parties and dances, which were attended by slaves, free blacks and coloreds, sailors, and other lower-class men of different nationalities. During the apprenticeship period, from 1834 to 1838, urban apprentices and free people continued to socialize together. They organized weekly, commercial dances in the main towns, usually in the home of a freedman.

These dances uncover a duality of conformity and rejection of European norms. Within the dances were exaggerated adaptations of colonial manners and styles. For example, at one dance, the attendants were issued cards and invitations and, according to the proprietress, who was a free woman, the dances were very exclusive and only "young ladies" were invited, not married women. The women, who were probably domestic workers, dressed in expensive European clothes. Some wore new shoes and stockings, and the organizer was dressed in "a white Satin gown, trimmed with white and corresponding finery." At this ball, the police found a dozen and a half empty champagne bottles as well as spirits and a table spread with food served on silver plates. However, the fine clothes, food, silverware, and wine were stolen from the employers of the participants. As well as purloining the actual materials of the elite, the apprentices were also claiming rights to the elite's styles and symbols of superiority.[17]

During their working lives, domestic apprentices were reminded of their inferior social and legal positions and expected to carry out undignified tasks, but in their private lives, these apprentices dressed in borrowed finery, ate rich food, and drank the best wine. The dances also enabled them to enact clearly defined gender roles, which were often denied them during their working lives. They stressed the femininity of the "young ladies" and the gallantry of the sword-carrying men. They danced the Quadrilles, with elaborate slow movements and choreographed presentations of chivalry. The parties also included a degree of hierarchy and exclusivity, with host, hostess, and stewards, while the guests could attend by invitation only.

Although these dances revealed a desire to emulate the entertainments of the rich, they also revealed a refusal to conform to authority. African Caribbean women frequently crossed the boundaries of acceptable class behavior in their dress. Their adoption of often-luxurious European dress styles was not simply a form of acculturation. By wearing clothes that seemed expensive and grand, working-class Caribbean women defied society and the prescriptions imposed on them. The dances also revealed a disregard for authority. As well as supplying the affairs with stolen goods, the dance organizers sometimes neglected to obtain the necessary permission from the magistrates to hold a public gathering. Like the illegal parties held by slaves and free people, these events were organized outside of the authorities' control and could be broken up by police raids.[18]

The taste for fine clothes and refined etiquette also indicated their struggle for respectability. Domestic and skilled workers sequestered the dress and manners of the elite in an attempt to gain respect and status among their peers. This was noticeable not only in their choice of entertainment, but also in their strict adherence to titles and expressions of respect. People addressed each other using formal designations such as Miss and Mr. They also employed terms of deference such as Uncle and Aunt for senior acquaintances and friends. These terms enabled the poor to "rehumanize" themselves. Accordingly, the poor in the Caribbean appeared to invert the elite social norms of

Victorian Britain through their insistence on outward displays of communal regard.[19]

The refined social gatherings of the upper echelons of the urban poor in St. Vincent contrasted with the actions of those at the bottom of society. For the very poor in Kingstown, and other colonial towns, housing consisted of shared rooms and barracks in dilapidated crowded yards. Privacy was minimal. The homes were health and fire hazards and the boundaries between private and public space were blurred. Hence, the entertainment and cultural activities of the very poor occurred on the streets, occasionally spilling out into middle-class residential areas. This resulted in friction, which sporadically led to confrontations with the authorities. As a result, town residents complained at the police's inability to suppress the often rowdy entertainment of the poor.[20]

Men and women from the poorest sections of the town rejected European dress, dances, and manners for their own forms of leisure activity. In the suburbs of Kingstown, the poor danced, drank, swore, and gambled around the local rum shops. Women participated in these boisterous scenes. During drunken sessions, using almost ritualistic insults and taunting, women from the poorer sections of town chose to enhance their reputations rather than their respectability. Their choice of language and use of obscenities revealed both their rhetorical skills and their rejection of European gender behaviors. Yet the language of the very poor still contained symbols of respectability, such as the titles of deference used with their peers. Thus, although the very poor may not have always displayed the reserve that constrained European Christian polite manners, they also emphasized the importance of showing respect and deference to the elders in their community.[21]

In the years immediately after the termination of apprenticeship, freed slaves tested the limits of their freedom in a variety of ways. They not only experimented with new working patterns, but they also claimed the streets as their own. When apprenticeship ended, employers and the authorities could no longer control the movement of freed slaves, or their nighttime activities. Much of the information on entertainment organized by the poor remains hidden. Colonial officials, missionaries, newspaper editors, and travel writers rarely chose to describe these events unless they precipitated violence. However, Charles Day described several festivities that he attended while in St. Vincent, events that revealed a deep-rooted sense of fun, as well as a love of display, elaborate costume, and dance. Street entertainment also formed part of an alternative economy. While legislators attempted to control the sale of alcohol by imposing liquor licenses on rum shops, the illegal retail of spirits continued in the homes and shops of the poor. In addition, others used their entertainment skills to earn money.[22]

Kingstown's poor organized and staged elaborate entertainments for each other. In these more coordinated occurrences, enterprise, performance, and enjoyment merged. Day described a "Joe and Johnny" dance on the streets of Kingstown during the Christmas holidays. The dance was held outside and was open to everyone. Those who attended the dance had dual roles of spectator and performer. Dancers paid the musicians around three pennies per dance and were then able to perform in front of the rest of the revelers. Day claimed that a wide variety of people attended the dance, including young African Caribbean women wearing their everyday working clothes, finely dressed colored men, and elderly people. Again, the participants emphasized hierarchy. The dance organizers offered seating and refreshments to those they considered important, while other observers and dancers stood. Elite women were not present at this dance, even as observers.

The dance gave participants the chance to demonstrate their prowess in front of an audience, which acted as a judge. Day stated that the young women in particular used these dances as a way of exhibiting their sexuality through their dancing skills in order to attract the men in the audience. The description of these performances implied that these young women chose to enhance their public reputation through their interactions on the street. It suggested that they rejected the linking of femininity to demure behavior and instead adopted their own standards of feminine deportment, celebrating strength, suppleness, vivacity, and sensuality.[23]

Masquerading and carnival notably embody the play element of Caribbean culture. During slavery, planters sanctioned masquerade carnivals as a customary celebration during the Christmas period. Slaveholders believed that by permitting their slaves a few days of self-rule, they would conform more readily to servitude. During these celebrations, slaves often produced elaborate costumes and worked in teams, holding dance competitions and street parades. Slaves portrayed and mocked figures of authority, created their own kings and queens, and had control of the streets for a few days each year. Masquerade carnivals had a great significance for slaves, allowing them to comment on society and express social discontent. Furthermore, carnivals enabled slaves to celebrate their own cultural creativity and emphasize their separateness from the ruling Europeans.[24]

In postemancipation Kingstown, carnivals continued as a popular form of entertainment for the poor. Masked dances were staged at crop over (when the harvesting of sugar was completed), Christmas, before Lent, and at Easter.

They could also be performed spontaneously by small bands of professional performers. Again, participants took on the roles of competitor, performer, and spectator as they danced in the street parades. Europeans and people of color lined the streets when the masqueraders danced within the towns, and Caribbean travel accounts celebrated the masquerades as exciting and fun.[25]

For many of the poor, masquerades were the cultural highlights of each year. However, after emancipation, the poor had to struggle to retain this custom, which came under attack from the authorities. Since the dances in St. Vincent were an example of the self-created culture of the ex-slaves, they threatened the Europeans as both potential physical disturbances and particularly as representations of sensuality. Masquerades also graphically inverted the island's communities, in mocking disregard of hierarchies and conventions. Local governing bodies attempted to ban masquerades during Christmas and Lent holidays in Kingstown, leading to riots in 1850, 1851, 1871, and 1879. In 1850 and 1851 the chief justice was attacked, and in 1879 the chief of police was seriously beaten in some of the most serious urban unrest that had been experienced since emancipation. Clearly, masquerading was central in the lives of the poor, who were determined to control their cultural expressions.[26]

Representations of the Poor

After emancipation, colonial leaders and other Europeans in the Caribbean began to express a distinct anxiety about the culture of the former slaves. The elite viewed the poor's public entertainments with a mixture of indulgence and suspicion. Many of the social events took place outside of the law. For example, the quadrille dances during the apprenticeship period represented a threat to the policing powers of the authorities because they were held without permission and the apprentices had acquired stolen goods. The freed slaves' requisition of European styles of entertainment also made the authorities uneasy. The acts of gallantry performed by male attendants at the quadrille dances, and the emphasis on elegance and femininity by the female dancers, were both flattering and threatening. The poor did not merely emulate the elite; they seemed to mock them by appropriating the symbols and attributes of colonial authority. In accentuating these characteristics and claiming that they were ludicrous, the colonial authorities sought to discredit the dancers' claims to elite attributes.[27]

Dress was an important class symbol, and women often used public entertainment to show off their (or their employer's) best clothes. However, clothes worn by women from the lower classes were subjected to explicit censure. The appearance of African Caribbean women was carefully observed and recorded by European men and women. In particular, the elite expressed unease at the fondness of ex-slaves for expensive and fashionable clothes. For example, according to rumors circulating on the island during a period of social unrest, in 1862, Mrs. Cowie, the wife of one of St. Vincent's wealthiest attorneys, allegedly demanded that wages be reduced so that black women could no longer afford fine clothes. These clothes could then be reserved exclusively for white women. For white women, it seemed intolerable that symbols of European femininity should be paraded on the bodies of African Caribbean women. Elite women were also uncomfortably aware of African Caribbean women's careful observation and discussion of white women's appearance. The desire to see African Caribbean women dressed more humbly was rooted in a belief that the difference between white and black women should be manifest.[28]

Europeans found African Caribbean women's wearing of silk stockings particularly offensive. Stockings represented sensuality, status, wealth, and luxury, all seen as unsuitable for poor and especially nonwhite women. This discomfort appears to have been universal. During slavery, Mrs. A. C. Carmichael, a slaveholder in St. Vincent and Trinidad, complained that slaves saw cotton stockings as unladylike and insisted on wearing silk. During apprenticeship, Stipendiary Magistrate Anderson claimed that many Vincentian women wore kid shoes, silk stockings, bonnets, and smart parasols. He asked: "When would an English peasant's wife come so attired?"[29]

Some writers expressed their discomfort through mockery. For example, in Barbados, Stipendiary Magistrate John Colthurst publicly scorned an apprentice who bought some elegant clothes with money stolen from her employer. "She had bought wearing apparel fine enough for a Princess," he wrote. "Their colours vied with those of the rainbow, first a flaming bright yellow bonnet, flashy dresses without number, necklaces and earrings without end, rose colored silk stockings and two pairs of pink satin shoes." He ordered the woman to try on the shoes. "This was done before a very crowded court who shouted when the pink satins were placed upon the hoofs of Duchess. In truth I never saw anything as unsuitable as the satins to such feet."[30]

Consequently, through their dress, working-class women were derided for attempting (and, in the eyes of Europeans, failing) to achieve femininity. Both Anderson and Day ridiculed working-class women in St. Vincent who refused to go out if they had no stockings. Day further illustrated his disapproval when writing about women in Trinidad. "Those ladies who aimed at the superior civilization of shoes and stockings, invariably clothed their pedal extremities in pink silk stockings and blue, white or yellow kid shoes, sandaled up their sturdy legs."[31] African Caribbean women were seen as unable to achieve true standards of femininity. Their choices of colors were "flaming" and "flashy," underscoring their lack of refinement. Day described the women in Trinidad in masculine terms, contrasting the kid shoes with the women's "sturdy legs." Colthurst likened Duchess to an animal, by choosing to portray her feet as "hoofs."

Yet, middle-class observers also faulted African Caribbean women for not adopting European middle-class norms. Europeans believed that African Caribbeans should be as uncomfortable with nudity as they were, and they criticized poor women for rejecting appearances of decorum. Stipendiary Magistrate Anderson was horrified by the "spectacle of African skins" when he came across bare-breasted laundresses washing clothes in a river in Kingstown. When describing an elderly woman who came to court half naked he stated: "I question if there can be on earth so perfectly hideous a spectacle, as one of these beldames exhibiting her bare and wrinkled breasts."[32]

The middle classes shared this distaste for public displays of immodesty and also saw dress as a symbol of civilization. In 1839, some inhabitants of Kingstown complained to the Court of Grand Sessions about the ineffectual organization of the police as well as the "riotous, noisy behaviour" and "obscene language, disorderly conduct and drunkenness" of the newly freed. In addition, they complained that the town was "a scene of rioting and fighting among the lower classes." Newspapers also complained about the appearance of working-class women, their proficiency at swearing, fighting, and arguing, implicitly or explicitly contrasted with the behavior of elite and middle-class women. For example, one paper reported that during a drunken disturbance "the majority of the belligerents were women and it may therefore at once be inferred that the epithets plentifully bestowed upon each other were distinguished for their obscenity." The police also blamed women for the "gross nuisances and vicious practices" that disturbed the residents of New Edinburgh, a suburb of Kingstown. Despite these complaints, the police appeared powerless to constrain these women, who continued to perform public and personal exchanges in the streets.[33]

Poor women were more visible when they acted counter to the expectations of the male middle class. Impoverished urban women's lack of private space meant that they were frequently in public view. Thus, poor women were also stereotyped as unfeminine. Victorians believed that civilized societies had marked physical and behavioral variances between men and women. The portrayal of African Caribbean women as physically masculine (with "sturdy legs") as well as violent, unrestrained, and indelicate was part of a discourse that contrasted Europeans with Africans. By highlighting this supposed parity between African Caribbean men and women, Europeans and middle-class coloreds illustrated and affirmed their own superiority.[34]

The establishment expressed greatest concern for masquerading, which it feared would lead to disruptions because large numbers of primarily lower-class people took part. In St. Vincent in the early 1850s, the chief justice, Henry Sharpe, claimed that masquerading resulted in the "demoralisation of the lower classes," and to "other excesses." He understood that his efforts to prohibit masquerading had made him "obnoxious" to some classes on the island.[35] In addition, the authorities were clearly affected by the issues of gender and class that the masquerades exposed. The dancers, hidden in their disguises, were able to act in opposition to social prescriptions. While the gender of the participants in the masquerades or the riots that followed in 1850 and 1879 were not mentioned, the authorities were concerned with the sexual content of the dances. In 1850, Chief Justice Sharpe, for example, stated that "Amusements of an unchaste, or at least of irregular tendency ought not to be encouraged." Furthermore, in 1879, Acting-Administrator Edward Laborde expressed his unease with the disrespect that the dances generated among the "lower orders." The use of masks was particularly disturbing. Laborde claimed that masqueraders used their disguises to insult and threaten people, frighten horses, and encourage large "mobs of idle followers."[36]

Thus, following emancipation, attempts by the elite to retain control of public space and curtail the cultural activities of the poor were part of a wider struggle for authority. The colonial authorities' attempts to punish masqueraders and dancers underscore the important divisions in society. Anderson, for example, not only mocked the attendants of the quadrille parties for dressing and dancing like the elite, he also ensured that those who were arrested were humiliated, sentencing them to have their heads shaved and to work the treadmill. But these conflicts also reveal the tenuous hold that the authorities had over the poor. Sharpe was unable to prosecute the masqueraders who confronted him in the early 1850s. In 1879, Laborde reacted against the illegal masked carnival by recruiting 124 special constables in an unsuccessful bid to control the streets.[37] Thus, despite their use of police raids, legislation, and the force of the militia, the authorities were unable to quell popular forms of culture.

Conclusions

Women's access to public entertainment and other communal activities in Kingstown depended on their social position. Those who belonged to the European elite enjoyed "respectable" forms of entertainment, connected to the Anglican Church or limited to a select few families sharing similar class and color backgrounds. While they may have had private associations with a wider circle of people, European women imposed their own boundaries on their public social connections and submitted to restrictions imposed on them by elite men. In addition to occasional trips to the theater, maroon parties and balls were the principal forms of entertainment open to European women of the upper class, since expectations of behavior and association curtailed their access to public space. As the century progressed a dwindling number of white elite families remained ensconced in their privileged position, and interracial marriages remained rare.[38]

Among the middle classes, wealth and color determined female participation in cultural events. By the end of the nineteenth century, the increasingly numerous wealthy colored families had formed their own elite. Richer colored women also had limited access to public entertainment. The public demeanor of wealthy colored women usually emphasized their incorporation of Christian values and gendered behavior. Their involvement in churches and charity work exemplified their belief in self-improvement through education and religious faith. The cultural activities of these women suggest that they, like their elite white peers, were immersed in the inside world of respectability. However, within this accommodation of elite values, middle-class women also represented their rejection of European stereotypes by creating an autonomous and alternative cultural arena. Their adherence to European Christian values showed their renunciation of the sexual roles imposed on colored women during slavery.

Among the lower classes, dual influences were at work as women simultaneously asserted their similarity to and difference from elite women. For example, the formal ticket parties described by Anderson in St. Vincent and Lanaghan in Antigua combined adaptations of the dress and dance styles of the elite while remaining subversive. The distorted and exaggerated styles of dress and manners employed by the female participants in these dances parodied those of the elite. They articulated a yearning for acceptance and cultural parity while emphasizing the participants' own tastes, designs, and individuality. Women at these social functions made themselves conspicuous rather than modest.

Poor women took an active role in organizing and protecting cultural entertainment. Street dances and masquerading enabled the poor to control the streets and, for a short while, to intimidate and mock the authorities. These amusements helped to alleviate the stresses of low wages, demeaning work, and poor housing. In addition, they provided participants with a forum to express discontent and celebrate their own cultural heritage. Women's participation in these street dances and masquerades contrasted with the activities of middle-class and elite women. In the streets, poor women had a far greater freedom of movement and self-expression. Elite and middle-class women could rarely express joy, despair, or frustration without losing social respect and position among their peers. In contrast, poor women earned additional admiration from their peers when they engaged in public displays of dissent.

However, most poor African Caribbean women were unable to acquire a respectable status outside of their class group. Notions of race and gender obscured the views of those in authority. In the eyes of the elite, poor women, through their dress, demeanor, dance styles, and language remained dissolute rather than ladylike.[39]

The predominantly European authors who described the lives of the urban poor in St. Vincent employed contradictory and confused stereotypes. Women were noted for tastes for feminine, delicate clothes, yet they were described as masculine. The elite derided poor women for adopting airs of gentility, but their dancing was noted for being vigorous and their passions were portrayed as animal. Above all, throughout the nineteenth century, observers alluded to the sexuality of African Caribbean women. Anderson, for example, suggested that the "young ladies" attending the ticket parties were prostitutes. Newspapers stressed the "lewd" behavior of "dissolute" women on the streets at night. In the 1870s, the dancing and music of masquerades were also noted for their "unchaste" and sexual qualities.[40]

This correlation between the street lives of poor men and women and sexual laxity remained part of a colonial discourse that emphasized and sustained social and gender boundaries. Gendered expectations and judgments, highly determined by color and class position, were thus crucial to maintaining social boundaries in postemancipation society. In St. Vincent, an individual's relationships to the private and public sphere, relationships themselves shaped by racial histories and class hierarchies, was a key determinant in the maintenance and production of cultural identity. More studies of postemancipation in the urban areas of the Caribbean are needed to explore the degree to which the architecture of urban spaces helped mold different groups' cultural and gendered expressions of freedom.

Notes

1 In St. Vincent, newspaper reports began to stress the accomplishments and refinements of elite women after emancipation. See, e.g., *Royal St. Vincent Gazette*, 7 Jan. 1843, 10 Jan. 1846, 20 May 1854. Visitors to the Caribbean also noted this new morality; see Roderick A. McDonald, ed., *Between Slavery and Freedom: Special Magistrate John Anderson's Journal of St. Vincent during the Apprenticeship* (Kingston: University of the West Indies Press, 2000), 150. See also Susan Lowes, " 'They Couldn't Mash Ants': The Decline of the White and Non-white Elites in Antigua, 1834–1900," in *Small Islands, Large Questions: Society, Culture and Resistance in the Post-emancipation Caribbean*, ed. Karen Fog Olwig (London: Frank Class, 1995), 41–43, for a discussion on the new morality among elites in postemancipation Antigua. Diane J. Austin, *Urban Life in Kingston, Jamaica: The Culture and Class Ideology of Two Neighborhoods* (New York: Gordon and Breach, 1984), 150–57; and Lisa Douglass, *The Power of Sentiment: Love, Hierarchy, and the Jamaican Elite* (Boulder, Colo.: Westview, 1992), 242–44, 258, examine the development of elite female attitudes in twentieth-century Jamaica.

2 Jean Besson, "Reputation and Respectability Reconsidered: A New Perspective on Afro-Caribbean Women," in *Women and Change in the Caribbean*, ed. Janet H. Momsen (London: James Currey, 1993), 26–27.

3 See Homi Bhabha, "Of Mimicry and Man: The Ambivalence of Colonial Discourse," in *Tensions of Empire: Colonial Cultures in a Bourgeois World*, ed. Frederick Cooper and Ann Laura Stoler (Berkeley: University of California Press, 1997), 152–60.

4 John Davy, *The West Indies before and since Slave Emancipation* (rpt., London: Frank Cass, 1971 [1854]), 179–81. Public Record Office, Colonial Office (hereafter PRO CO) 260/82, Colebrook to Russell, no. 28, 19 May 1855, Eyre's report accompanying the Blue Book; Charles Day, *Five Years' Residence in the West Indies* (London: Colburn, 1852), 2 vols., 1:81, 2:124.

5 Ann Stoler, "Carnal Knowledge and Imperial Power: Gender, Race and Morality in Colonial Asia," in *Gender at the Crossroads of Knowledge*, ed. Michaela di Leonardo (Berkeley: University of California Press, 1991), 51; Ann Stoler, "Rethinking Colonial Categories: European Communities and the Boundaries of Rule," *Comparative Studies in Society and History* 31, no. 1 (1989): 148. Anderson claimed that it was very difficult to gain entrance into elite society without introductions. McDonald, *Between Slavery and Freedom*, 145.

6 McDonald, *Between Slavery and Freedom*, 101, 167; A. C. Carmichael, *Domestic Manners and Social Conditions of the White, Coloured and Negro Populations of the British West Indies* (rpt., New York: Negro University Press, 1969 [1833]), 2 vols., 1:71; John Stewart, *A View of the Past and Present State of the Island of Jamaica* (rpt., New York: Negro University Press, 1979 [1823]), 175.

7 Visitors to the Caribbean during slavery commented on the dances held for

colored women and white men. J. Moreton, *West Indian Customs and Manners* (London: Parsons, Richardson et al., 1798), 74; William Hickey, *Memoirs of William Hickey*, ed. Alfred Spencer (London: Hurst and Blackett, 1919), 75. According to Frances Lanaghan of Antigua, after emancipation open displays of interracial concubinage ceased. Anon. [Frances Lanaghan], *Antigua and the Antiguans: A Full Account of the Island and Its Inhabitants from the Time of the Caribs to the Present Day* (rpt., London: Macmillan, 1991 [1884]), 2 vols., 2:181–82. Anderson concurred that this was also the case in St. Vincent during apprenticeship among the elites. However, he noted that lower-class white men continued to associate freely with colored women. McDonald, *Between Slavery and Freedom*, 143, 189–90.

8 Carmichael, *Domestic Manners*, 1:41; PRO CO 260/98, Walker to Newcastle, no. 66, 15 Sept. 1862; PRO CO 260/112, Rawson to Grey, no. 21, 28 April 1870; PRO CO 260/111, Rawson to Grey, no. 662, 8 July 1869, enclosure: Half-yearly returns; McDonald, *Between Slavery and Freedom*, 98.

9 McDonald, *Between Slavery and Freedom*, 100, 101, 102. While there is very little evidence of private interactions between elite white women and others in society, Yseult Bridge's account of her childhood in late nineteenth-century Trinidad suggests that her only close contact or friendships with people of African descent were with her servants. Bridget Brereton, "Text, Testimony and Gender: An Examination of Some Texts by Women on the English-speaking Caribbean from 1770 to the 1920s," in *Engendering History: Caribbean Women in Historical Perspective*, ed. Verene Shepherd, Bridget Brereton, and Barbara Bailey (Kingston: Ian Randle, 1995), 71, 78. Descriptions of social events throughout the Caribbean attended by J. A. Froude only mention one party that included white women and a man of color. J. A. Froude, *The English in the West Indies* (London: Longmans, Green and Co., 1888), 70, 73, 82, 99, 109, 188, 310. See also the *Liberal*, 29 June 1844, for an example of a decision to prevent white and colored women from attending the same ball in British Guiana.

10 Ann Stoler suggests that white women "were committed to racial segregation for their own reasons and in their own right," and that this was linked to their attempts to curtail their husbands' sexual activities; quoted in Lowes, " 'They Couldn't Mash Ants,' " 42. Anderson claimed that colored women had "no pretensions to the society of the ladies, no matter how respectable," McDonald, *Between Slavery and Freedom*, 101.

11 *Royal St. Vincent Gazette and Weekly Advertiser*, 9 Feb., 11 May 1850; *Witness*, 24 June 1880; quoted in McDonald, *Between Slavery and Freedom*, 104, 145; see also Brereton, "Text, Testimony and Gender," 66.

12 Both St. Vincent and Antigua had small populations and a diminishing class of elites during the postemancipation era. Lowes, " 'They Couldn't Mash Ants,' " 7–8, 145, 175.

13 *Royal St. Vincent Gazette and Weekly Advertiser*, 30 July 1842.

14 Sheena Boa, " 'Walking on the Highway to Heaven': Religious Influences and

Attitudes Relating to the Freed Population of St. Vincent, 1834–1884," *Journal of Caribbean History* 35, no. 2 (2001): 189–90.

15 McDonald, *Between Slavery and Freedom*, 154; *Royal St. Vincent Gazette and Weekly Advertiser*, 9 Oct. 1841, 24 Dec. 1842, 10 Jan. 1846.

16 Diane Austin-Broos, "Redefining the Moral Order: Interpretations of Christianity in Postemancipation Jamaica," in *The Meaning of Freedom: Economics, Politics, and Culture after Slavery*, ed. Frank McGlynn and Seymour Drescher (Pittsburgh, Penn.: University of Pittsburgh Press, 1992), 225–26.

17 McDonald, *Between Slavery and Freedom*, 189–90.

18 Ibid., 116–17, 148, 158, 189–90; Lanaghan's account of dances in Antigua stressed the use of formal language. [Lanaghan], *Antigua and the Antiguans*, 2:108–14; Bhabha, "Of Mimicry and Man," 153–54, discusses the uncertainties created by the "excess or slippage produced by the ambivalence of mimicry."

19 Day, *Five Years' Residence*, 1:21; Richard D. E. Burton, *Afro-Creole: Power, Opposition, and Play in the Caribbean* (Ithaca, N.Y.: Cornell University Press, 1997), 44; McDonald, *Between Slavery and Freedom*, 159.

20 *Royal St. Vincent Gazette and Weekly Advertiser*, 18 July 1846, 23 Oct. 1847, 6 Aug. 1853; Day, *Five Years' Residence*, 2:106.

21 *St. Vincent Chronicle and Public Gazette*, 14 May 1839; *Royal St. Vincent Gazette and Weekly Advertiser*, 29 Aug. 1840, 10 Feb. 1844; *St. Vincent Chronicle and Public Gazette*, 12 Nov. 1839, 26 Nov. 1839. Day, *Five Years' Residence*, 1:22; McDonald, *Between Slavery and Freedom*, 68; Besson, "Reputation and Respectability Reconsidered," 17–19.

22 In St. Vincent, the smuggling of alcohol from the French islands was reputedly an important part of the alternative economy. PRO CO 260/89, 6 May 1857, no. 50, Hinks to Labouchere, enclosure, Smith to Hinks, 25 Jan. 1857; Day, *Five Years' Residence*, 1:46–50, 85.

23 Day, *Five Years' Residence*, 1:46–50; Burton, *Afro-Creole*, 161; Besson, "Reputation and Respectability Reconsidered," 17–19.

24 Natalie Zemon Davis, *Society and Culture in Early Modern France* (Cambridge, U.K.: Polity, 1965), 97–103; Burton, *Afro-Creole*, 161ff.

25 Day, *Five Years' Residence*, 2:120–24.

26 *Royal St. Vincent Gazette and Weekly Advertiser*, 9 Feb., 11 May 1850, 8 Feb. 1851; *Witness*, 22 Dec. 1871; PRO CO 321/30, Dundas to Hicks Beach, no. 20, 22 Feb. 1879, Laborde to Dundas, 15 Feb. 1879.

27 Bhabha, "Of Mimicry and Man," 153. Bhabha suggests that colonial authorities expressed ambivalence toward mimicry because, while mimicry provides "a desire for an approved revised other," it is also menacing, revealing the colonized subjects' awareness of the inauthenticity of colonial rule.

28 *British Parliamentary Papers* 509 (1863), xxxviii, 166; Day, *Five Years' Residence*, 1:14, 2:131; McDonald, *Between Slavery and Freedom*, 87–88. Carmichael, *Domestic Manners*, 1:46; [Lanaghan], *Antigua and the Antiguans*, 2:101. Rebecca Earle has explored

how nineteenth-century European attitudes toward the clothing of non-European women in the Americas contrasted with more favorable descriptions written in the seventeenth and eighteenth centuries. See Rebecca Earle, " 'Two Pairs of Pink Satin Shoes!!' Race, Clothing and Identity in the Americas (Seventeenth–Nineteenth Centuries)," *History Workshop Journal* 52 (2001): 175–93. This antagonism against finely dressed nonwhite women was also prevalent in the United States after the Civil War; bell hooks, *Ain't I a Woman? Black Women and Feminism* (London: Pluto, 1982), 55–56; Jacqueline Jones, *Labor of Love, Labor of Sorrow: Black Women, Work and the Family from Slavery to the Present* (New York: Vintage, 1985), 69. See also Homi Bhabha, *Locations of Culture* (London: Routledge, 1993), 90.

29 Carmichael, *Domestic Manners*, 1:75, 84; McDonald, *Between Slavery and Freedom*, 125; see also Joseph Sturge and Thomas Harvey, *The West Indies in 1837* (rpt., London: Frank Cass, 1969 [1838]), 18; James Thome and J. Horace Kimball, *Emancipation in the West Indies* (rpt., New York: Aran, 1969 [1837]), 8.

30 Woodville Marshall, ed., *The Colthurst Journal: Journal of a Special Magistrate in the Islands of Barbados and St. Vincent, July 1835–September 1838* (Millwood, New York: KTO Press, 1977).

31 McDonald, *Between Slavery and Freedom*, 81, 125; Day, *Five Years' Residence*, 2:121.

32 McDonald, *Between Slavery and Freedom*, 66, 81.

33 *Royal St. Vincent Gazette and Weekly Advertiser*, 29 Aug. 1840, 10 Feb. 1844; *St. Vincent Chronicle and Public Gazette*, 12 Nov. 1839, 26 Nov. 1839, 14 May 1839.

34 Charles Kingston, *At Last! A Christmas in the West Indies* (London: McMillan, 1871), 50–51; Jane Lewis, "Reconstructing Women's Experiences of Home and Family," in *Labour and Love: Women's Experiences of Home and Family, 1850–1940*, ed. Jane Lewis (Oxford: Blackwell, 1986), 2.

35 *Royal St. Vincent Gazette and Weekly Advertiser*, 11 May 1850.

36 *Royal St. Vincent Gazette and Weekly Advertiser*, 9 Feb., 11 May 1850; *Witness*, 22 Dec. 1871, 27 Feb. 1879; PRO CO 321/30, Dundas to Hicks Beach, no. 20, 22 Feb. 1879, Laborde to Dundas, 15 Feb. 1879.

37 McDonald, *Between Slavery and Freedom*, 117; PRO CO 321/30, Dundas to Hicks Beach, no. 20, 22 Feb. 1879, Laborde to Dundas, 15 Feb. 1879.

38 According to J. J. Thomas, while marriage between white women and men of color was rare, "case upon case have occurred where social degradation of being married to Negroes has been avoided by the alternative of forming base connections even with menials of that race." J. J. Thomas, *Froudacity: West Indian Fable Explained* (rpt., London: New Beacon, 1889), 69.

39 Sander L. Gilman, "Black Bodies, White Bodies: Towards an Iconography of Female Sexuality in the Late Nineteenth-Century Art, Medicine and Literature," in *"Race," Culture and Difference*, ed. James Donald and Ali Rattanis (London: Sage, 1992), links the iconography of black women and white prostitutes with European men's fear of sexualized women.

40 McDonald, *Between Slavery and Freedom*, 190; *Royal St. Vincent Gazette and Weekly Advertiser*, 11 Oct. 1849, 11 May 1850, 10 Jan. 1852; *St. Vincent Chronicle*, 7 May 1839. PRO CO 321/30, Dundas to Hicks Beach, no. 20, 22 Feb. 1879, Laborde to Dundas, 15 Feb. 1879; Swithin Wilmot, " 'Females of Abandoned Character?' Women and Protest in Jamaica, 1838–65," in Shepherd, Brereton, and Bailey, *Engendering History*, 279, 295.

MARTHA ABREU *(translated from the Portuguese by Amy Chazkel and Junia Claudia Zaidan)*

Mulatas, Crioulos, and Morenas: Racial Hierarchy, Gender Relations, and National Identity in Postabolition Popular Song

(Southeastern Brazil, 1890–1920)

The recordings of early twentieth-century folklorists include several lyrics of a lundu—a genre of popular song from southeastern Brazil—called "Gosto de negra" [I like black women]:[1]

> I like black women
> the color of coal
> I have a great passion for them
>
> What does it matter to me
> if people talk about me
> I like black women
> just the same.
>
> Big ears,
> All torn up,
> All scratched,
> All waxy.
>
> She has a
> velvety little foot
> and on each little toe
> she has two little vermin.
>
> I like black women . . .

What does it matter to me . . .

She has a little head of hair
All curly
On each little strand
She has two little lice.[2]

These lyrics, which appear in many variations, supply a near encyclopedia of the stereotypical defects often attributed to black men and women.[3] In so doing, they articulate a discourse pervasive in southeastern Brazil at the turn of the nineteenth century.[4] This discourse was found in parliamentary debates and in newspaper articles on the abolition of slavery, proclaimed in 1888. The songs' racial stereotypes also resonate with contemporaneous debates about measures of social control such as the repression of vagrancy, taken in order to integrate freedpeople into the new rules of the free labor market.[5]

With consistent irony, the litany of defects in the various versions of "Gosto de negra"/"Gosto de negro" emphasizes the physical. There is an arresting contrast, nevertheless, between the pejorative, racist language and the proclamations of "passion" for a black woman or man. Clearly, this combination of disgust and attraction accentuated the irony and humor typical of sung lundus, because of the improbability of romantic involvement of this type. The ironic, comical edge of the lyrics of such a lundu were even more effective when they inverted the traditional racial and sexual hierarchy, as we find in one version of the song in which a woman, presumably lighter skinned, declares her "passion for a black man."

But could this lundu do more than reinforce and spread racial prejudice through its ironic and pejorative pleasure in an improbable interracial love affair? Might it also use comic language to speak of a possibility, certainly irreverent and in defiance of socioracial hierarchies, that not only makes stereotypes and prejudices explicit but also plays with them? In fact, the folklorists who studied the lundu in the early decades of the twentieth century, including Rossini Tavares de Lima and Mário de Andrade, showed that the lundus from the countryside of São Paulo state were marked by notable criticism of and irony regarding slavery.

Undoubtedly, the lundu spoke differently to largely uneducated, black people in a rural setting, on the one hand, and audiences in Rio de Janeiro theaters and salons, on the other. In Rio, the public eagerly attended shows that promised exoticism. Such variation in audience makes it impossible to identify any universal, single meaning in these songs' racialized gender roles. This material presents ambiguities and challenges for the historian, in part because of the problem of establishing authorship. For instance, Mariza Lira's claim, made in the 1930s, that the lundu is a historical example of "Brazilian racial democracy" does not allow for the ambiguities of the genre. Lira's view is based on the fact that the lyrics seem to admit the possibility of an interracial love affair. However, the same lyrics may suggest exactly the opposite due to the overwhelming number of hostile references to women of African descent. Rather than expressing a singular meaning, these lyrics, like those discussed later in this chapter, provide the means to retrieve and analyze the images and identities of men and women of African descent that were created and spread in southeastern Brazil following emancipation. My analysis is relevant to the postemancipation context when, with Brazil confronting the need to reorganize its free labor market and plunged into debate about the future of the nation, new, often racialized, definitions of gender relations and roles played a leading part in political and intellectual debates.

Sources and Songs

The late nineteenth and early twentieth centuries saw an explosion in published collections of lundus and modinhas.[6] While racialized, gendered images do not predominate in these collections, they are present. Such collections provide important indicators of the sexual and erotic identities created and disseminated about black men and women, as well as about people from a range of "mixed" racial categories, in the largest urban centers of the southeast, such as Rio de Janeiro and São Paulo.[7]

These collections claimed, often in their titles, to be committed to what they called "popular song" or "Brazilian popular song." However, many of the lyrics assembled cannot be considered "popular" if the defining criterion of the popular is that its authors represent the society at large. Some of these songs could be considered "popular" either because we lack information about their authors or because they were sung by "simple folk" of the backlands. But many others bore the signatures of famous intellectuals such as Mello Moraes Filho and Artur Azevedo or of those black or mixed-race musicians, like Laurindo Rebelo and Xisto Bahia, who had managed to gain recognition.

The concern with disseminating so-called popular song was probably connected to the growth of an urban audience (perhaps this is the meaning of "popular") interested in exotic, "earthy" styles of music and dance, such as modinhas, lundus, and serenades. This audience contributed to the growth, in late nineteenth- and early twentieth-century Rio de Janeiro and São Paulo, of theatrical spectacles, including many musicals and comedies, and of the market for sheet music and guitars.[8]

The songs discussed here derive from two sets of sources. First, there are those published by folklorists who sought to demonstrate the originality and authenticity of Brazilian national identity. These were mainly collected in the backlands of the southeast among the so-called simple people. Second are lundus published in mass-circulation books of "popular music" or "popular song," which had a more urban orientation.

Despite the qualitative differences in the authorship of these two groups of sources, for the purposes of this article I do not maintain a rigid separation between them. Many "popular songs" published in the capital were understood to derive from the interior backlands. Folklorists generally chose not to reveal the sources of the material they documented, but many songs in urban collections were similarly not credited to a named author. And even when authorship is attributed, the song may still be an adaptation of a lyric from the backlands or one that already had wide circulation in urban areas.[9] Folklorists' eagerness to define what they found in "popular music" as "Brazilian" is also apparent in the publications of urban musicians who characterized their collections as specifically "Brazilian."

My goal here is not to provide a definitive exploration of the social representativeness of all the selected lyrics. Rather, I seek to identify and analyze themes involving black men and women in songs that circulated, and were perhaps played, in the Brazilian southeast between 1890 and 1920. I demonstrate that although these songs traveled through (and indeed were often invented in) the most erudite artistic circles and in large part reproduced social and racial hierarchies, they were not mere echoes of the racist scientific thought of the era, which asserted that the black and "mixed" populations were morally and sexually degenerate. Nor do the songs fit the prejudiced judgments often made by white men in reference to what they considered the unbridled licentiousness and degenerate sexuality of slave and freedwomen, whether black or of mixed race.

The songs show that racialized gender roles could be disseminated through the humor, criticism, and irreverence characteristic of the sung lundu. They presented an ironic view of the social and cultural conflicts of a society that was reorganizing the mechanisms of domination and social control after the abolition of slavery. In some cases, by lauding the masculine role of the crioulo malandro, these songs even offered a social critique of the new form of work discipline.[10]

The Beautiful Coquettish Mulata

In 1907 Osório Duque Estrada, a writer, poet, abolitionist, and member of early twentieth-century Rio de Janeiro's intellectual and bohemian circles, published his *Trovas populares* (Popular ballads). The book records poems and songs about love, longing, and sorrows, from both the backlands and the cities. Duque Estrada aimed to document and disseminate what he understood as the wisdom and lyricism of the Brazilian "people." He claimed that an important aspect of the "Brazilian popular ballads," as with the works dedicated to "our folklore," is the "prominence and evidence" conferred on the "mixed-race women, she who calls herself a mulata." He then records several examples sung in cities by troubadours:

The little white woman is fine silver
Mulata—a string of gold
Cabocla[11]—a basket of flowers
Black woman—sack of leather[12]

The white woman, [I] eat chicken
The mulata eats turkey
The Cabocla eats partridge
The black woman eats vulture.[13]

These "popular ballads" valorize the mulata and cabocla woman. Yet more evidently, these lyrics appear to repeat a well-known racist maxim, popularized by Gilberto Freyre, that in Brazil "the white woman is for marriage, the mulata is for f . . . ing (*foder*—fuck—or fornicate), and the black woman is for work."[14] They appear to reveal a supposed Brazilian national sexual preference for mulata women.

These comic and ironic songs may represent a joke or a creative means of dealing creatively with mixed-race women's limited opportunities in a society marked by extreme hierarchies of skin color. The racialization of beauty and the possibilities of social ascent might have served not only to discriminate against those of a darker skin color but also to criticize and denounce those racialized social hierarchies. We will return later to the question of "black women." First, the valorization of the mixed-race woman requires discussion.

Popular songs generally emphasized the mulata's beauty and sensuality, frequently symbolized by the movement of her hips. Perhaps the best-known example of a lundu that represents the mulata in this way was disseminated under the assumed authorship of Mello Moraes Filho and Xisto Bahia, who was seen as mulato by his contemporaries. Undoubtedly, these two figures were profoundly linked to the construction of a supposed "Brazilian popular music" in the nineteenth century:

I am a vain mulata
Beautiful, coquettish, adorable,
How many white women are not!
I have the most beautiful swing of my hips
If the night is my hair
The day is my heart . . .

My missus (*yáyás*) at their windows
Throw me such a look,
There they are! Dead like that . . .
And I go on, prouder,
As if the angry faces
Were not directed at me.[15]

One could argue that the representation of the mulata as a coveted object of desire was the musical accompaniment to theories that had objectified female slaves and, in the postemancipation period, led to the animalization of black and mixed-race women. Racist thought understood such women to be naturally prone to unbridled, degenerate sexuality. Although praised, mulata sexuality was to be consumed and discarded. This perspective can certainly be found in these lyrics. They were, after all, written or collected and selected by men who belonged to intellectual and literary worlds where racialized sexual roles were under debate.[16]

The mulata is objectified in all varieties of popular music: anonymous lyrics, those with attributed authorship, and those selected and distributed by authors linked to folklore or involved in the urban music market. Confirming the charges of licentiousness and passivity generally attributed to mulatas, these lyrics contain references to mulata women with "gorgeous eyes, that say yes until death," and to those who provoke sin, since they were not made to marry. In some cases, the lyrics state that the mulata carries the devil in her and is extremely amorous.[17] There are also lyrics that associate mulata women with a "sweet little fruit, appetizing tidbit, better than *vatapá*,"[18] or that label them as genuine "beauties" with "the gift of divinity."[19]

On the other hand, there are also mulatas in these songs with some power or autonomy. The lyrics portray mulatas in an active role that contradicts the image of the "thing" or sexual object. Their lovers are unable to dominate them completely. Representations abound of the mulata's power "to kill, capture, and take by force,"[20] making many into prisoners.[21] At the same time, these lyrics suggest that mulatas spent much money on their lovers.[22] The mulata exercises her seductive power, takes her suitors captive, enjoys her money, and says farewell to her "missus." At times these apparently contradictory images even appear within the same song. Occasionally, as in "Mucama," attributed to the mulato author Gonçalves Crespo, these mulatas say no, responding defiantly to sexual and social exploitation.[23] Although these lyrics mock and ironize the implausibility of such situations, through their playful treatment of the power of mulata women they may also have provided a means to speak critically of these issues, inverting their reality. Whatever its meaning, this image of the mulata snubbing her nose at a gentlemen was disseminated throughout the country.

Some will argue that these representations only served to perpetuate the mulata's domination. According to this perspective, the exaltation of mulatas' sexual qualities and their captivating power served not only to excuse sexual assaults on these women but also to justify the avarice of the songs' male authors. White men of the powerful, slave-owning class denied their own responsibility for sexual violence toward mulatas, as well as black and enslaved women in general, on the grounds of these women's supposedly natural lasciviousness.[24] These songs' valorization of mulata sexuality could serve to dominate and to reproduce gender, color, and class hierarchies. At most, the historiography allows that mulatas (and the most attractive female slaves) could manipulate their physical qualities, hoping for some sort of specific gain, such as manumission or social mobility.[25]

Considering such arguments and the multiple meanings of these songs in performance, I would suggest that they demonstrate the existence of a field of representations marked by ambiguities surrounding the meanings of gender roles. They reveal conflicts and tensions between the (sexual) powers of women and the avarice of slave-owning men, the sole "victims" of the charming mulatas. Interestingly, these tensions are evident in the music despite the fact that the male subjects depicted in the lyrics were not always white, as evidenced in the examples sung by the "crioulo" Eduardo das Neves.

The images in the lyrics I analyze here do not fit the intellectual standards of the postabolition period, which regarded mulatas and morenas as signs of the evils of race mixing.[26] Despite reinforcing the stereotypical sexual features of mulatas and morenas, the lyrics do value their beauty as well as their power over men. Such valorization was much more widespread in music than in debates about the country's future. Although I was able to trace two songs that associate pride in being Brazilian with pride in the mulata, this view was not shared by those in the political and intellectual spheres who sought to construct a national identity. In one of these songs, an unknown poet wrote:

When I kindly see her
So tender, so *moreninha*,
I soon exclaim: "How beautiful
The Brazilian *mulatinha*!

Her eyes she can turn
So kind as she flirts
I wish I always could
Stand by her side[27]

Notwithstanding these words, it was only later, as a result of Gilberto Freyre's frequent references to mulatas and mixed-race people, that black and mixed-race culture were incorporated and valorized as part of Brazilian national identity.[28]

The representations of mulatas and other dark-skinned women found in these songs involve a panoply of varied and often conflicted images that highlight their sensuality, beauty, power, submission, affective sentiments, passivity, irreverence, autonomy, status as objects of sexual pleasure, and Brazilian identity, to name a few. Yet we gain a richer understanding of this imagery by examining it alongside contemporary images and norms of sexual behavior and gender roles spread by doctors and jurists. Contemporaneous attempts to consolidate a positivist ideology of work developed together with the diffusion of rules regarding social hygiene and public order. Doctors and educators developed these social norms according to their conceptions of a healthy family life.[29] More than ever, women had to assume the responsibilities of marriage, maternity, and education of children; in other words, women had to take on gender roles suitable and necessary to confronting the challenges of a modernizing Brazil. The types of behavior recommended for Brazil's better-off families, who were generally white, provided the principal model for all Brazilians in the conduct of their sex and love lives. This model provided a basis for standards of honesty and morality, and included attributes such as order, politeness, and discretion.[30]

For many jurists, doctors, and politicians concerned with the normalization of popular life, carrying out this task was an enormous challenge. It was especially daunting given that these intellectuals considered the popular classes in general, and black people in particular, to be carriers of the supposed vices of poverty and slavery, such as ill-health, financial profligacy, idleness, lack of concern with the education of one's children, and, by extension, disregard for family ties, marriage, and female honor.[31]

Amid such attempts to discipline sexual behavior, the songs discussed here invert, laugh at, and joke about ideas of beauty, honor, and purity. True, these songs reproduced many of the meanings that jurists and doctors attributed to the sexual and moral lives of black families, particularly their supposedly unbridled sexual desire. Yet the lyrics also bear witness to a broader range of representations of the sexual roles of black woman, particularly with respect to the passive and retiring role demanded of women in general.

Songs involving grossly negative images of black women, such as the lundu with which this article opens, exist alongside songs describing mulatas' charms.[32] These negative songs often employ the term crioula (Creole) for black women, a word that in Brazilian Portuguese originally simply denoted a Brazilian-born slave, but which came to take on potent derogatory racialized connotations after abolition. Such women, unlike the mulatas, were not represented as beautiful and alluring. Nevertheless, crioulas could be represented as less passive and not readily manipulated. This is demonstrated by "Vem cá, meu anjo," published in 1911 without attributed authorship by the pianist and folklorist Julia Brito Mendes. The song takes the form of a dialogue, describing the attraction that a "crioula" stimulates when she shakes her hips.[33] In this lyric-dialogue, "he," presumably a white male, affirms that "the movement of her hips grabs and kills me," and "she makes any man start to drool." In seeking to conquer the "crioula," he claims that "she" is "the twilight star," and indeed not just "a star" but a "gorgeous and beautiful saint."

In response to this conqueror, the lyrics demonstrate that it was possible to represent a crioula with some sensitivity to the conflicts involved in a romantic relationship between people of different ascribed races. In the dialogue, "she" always seeks to expose his true intentions. After "he" declares that he would marry her only if she were whiter, the disconcerting response of the "crioula" is that she has no intention of marrying a "white man."

Seeking to free herself of her seducer, the "crioula" asks "him" "to let her dance, without being bothered and with his consent." Responding to his claim that she is a "twilight star" and a "gorgeous and beautiful saint," she responds that these are "lies," since "in the sky no black stars shine, and as for saints of this color, I only know of Saint Benedict." The dialogue continues, and nothing will evoke the richness of the conversation but a lengthy quotation:

"He":
I have never before seen
my God, such a fate!
Oh, sad life
of someone in love! . . .

"She":
Please console yourself
my dear friend!
Do you want to try your luck
and marry me?

"He":
Oh, no, crioula,
I am not so crazy . . .
Only if you were
a little more white.

"She":
I also declare
Now that you're being so frank
that I don't want
to marry someone white.

"He":
In these cases
my criola friend
you can get moving
right away, belly first.

"She":
So, my white man
let me dance
for I am not beautiful enough
to get swollen.[34]

The Crioulo Malandro

The masculine counterpoint to the "beautiful and coquettish mulata" of the songs is the *crioulo malandro* (black rogue). Like that of the mulata, this was a polysemic identity. If, on the one hand, the malandro confirmed the stereotype of the freedperson as inherently indisposed to honest labor, on the other, it challenged the principles underlying late nineteenth- and early twentieth-century medical and juridical discourse, which intended to create and disseminate appropriate sexual roles for working black men.[35] The "reckless black man" or the "preto" proud of his relationship with white women and even with mulatas and other dark-skinned women appears in exemplary form in the work of the so-called crioulo Eduardo das Neves.[36]

Eduardo das Neves (1874–1919), famous singer of modinhas, lundus, and serenades, published four books of songs, most of which he is presumed to have authored.[37] He assumed the role of *trovador de malandragem* (troubador of roguery) and defined himself as "crioulo," which became the title of one of his compositions.[38] Through an examination of this formidable song, written in 1900, we can discern an autobiography of sorts. These lines suggest a "crioulo" with a great deal of self-esteem.

At the beginning of the song, the narrator affirms that since he was a "little punk," he had "a special knack with the guitar." He went on "growing" and "learning and getting involved in the life of scoundrel." His success was such that as soon as he placed his hand on his instrument, "the little morenas stayed there enjoying the sight of the crioulo singing a prelude." He eventually found work at the railway station. After a strike, however, he was "fired," since, as he explains, he had a "boss" who "did not like his swing." But his musical success must have been exceptional, since he not only attracted dark-skinned women but also pleased mulatas and brides who were about to marry:

> I went to a certain wedding . . .
> I did my thing with the guitar,
> The bride said to the maid of honor:
> This crioulo is my damnation.
>
> I am enchanted,
> Admired,
> How he has . . .
> A light touch . . .

At least tell me
what is his name?
—I am the crioulo
Dudu das Neves

Such lyrics suggest that the themes of mulatas, crioulos, and morenas also belonged to the underworlds of the malandro. They could be sung about by members of the poor, black community of the city, like Eduardo das Neves. Until he was discovered by the music publisher and recording house Casa Edison in 1906, Dudu das Neves, as he styled himself, shared the hard life of thousands of other poor workers in the city. The ability of such musicians to travel in and out of different social and cultural environments reaffirms the polysemic character of these songs, especially when presented and danced at popular balls and circuses by a renowned crioulo such as Dudu. The songs' success should be understood to lie not only in the irony of the impossibility of the situations depicted but also in the power of the mulatas and crioulos portrayed.

For our purposes, the most interesting songs recorded by Eduardo das Neves concern the love of the "Sinhazinha" ("little missus," or the young mistress of the slave plantation) and the old competition between mulatas and "little white women." First, leaving aside the question of authorship, it is significant that a black musician could be represented, even if only for comic purposes, as able to direct love songs to a "little missus." In the course of this courtship, he points out the young lady's lovely eyes and her perfume.

Another song, "Sempre chorando" (Always crying) refers to a supposed rivalry between "mulatinhas" (little mulatas) and "branquinhas" (little white women). If we consider Dudu das Neves as an interpreter or even as author of these lyrics, they again demonstrate that it was possible to represent "elegant crioulo men" playing with the hearts of "branquinhas." It is also evident that these crioulos held on to their abiding love for "mulatinhas." The story begins with the memory of an ungrateful act committed by a "branquinha," to whom the singer had given his heart. Concurrently, the same singer had been courting a mulata, who remained "firm" even after the "white woman scorned him." The protagonist considers himself "satisfied" with what he called "my mulatinha." But he became even more satisfied to "see the mulata singing," while she was

Making defiant gestures to the white woman
Who is constantly crying

Always crying she says,
Your heart is what kills me
I say, always crying,
I am not yours, I am the mulata's.[39]

In addition to Eduardo das Neves's challenges to the narrow medical and juridical canons of his age, in singing lyrics that diverged so sharply from the ideal of marriage and that valorized sexual seduction, his publications made explicit that the figure that best symbolized the troubles of the world of workers was the malandro, the object of official attempts to discipline working-class Brazilians. This character was the symbolic antithesis of the disciplined worker and the well-behaved citizen: idle, disrespectful of the law and of good habits,[40] he served to justify the police's imprisonment of innumerable people considered suspect because they were unable to provide proof of fixed employment. Indeed, Dudu represented and disseminated such a character better than anyone, losing his own stable jobs and earning a living through exceptionally unstable activities, such as writing music and singing in circuses and variety theaters.

Conversations with the Historiography

Scholars who have studied the racial and cultural construction of Brazilian national identity unanimously agree that the 1930s were a watershed. This change is represented most clearly in Gilberto Freyre's writings, which incorporated and valorized black and mixed-race culture in order to construct an idea of Brazilianness.[41] Freyre broke with racial determinism as a guiding principle in the sociological analysis of Brazil. I do not intend to downplay the importance of this moment, considering the subsequent influence of Freyre's work, in both Brazilian and international academic circles, and its contribution to the diffusion and vulgarization of a hypernationalistic image of "mixed-race Brazil."[42]

Nevertheless, these songs about mulatas and crioulos demonstrate that weighty intellectuals such as Freyre were not the first to exalt mixed-race and dark-skinned people. Prior to Freyre, the products of miscegenation, the mulata and the morena, as well as the proud crioulo, were already widely sung about and valorized in Brazil's interior backlands and southeastern cities.[43]

As I have shown, this was a highly ambiguous valorization. It can be seen as a new form of control and exploration of black and mixed-race women's bodies, reproducing old socioracial and gender hierarchies. It can be considered a way of guaranteeing a greater chance of marriage for white and lighter-skinned mulata women, casting many other women of African descent out of the supposed civilization that this social control was meant to augment.

However, the theme of race relations in these songs also marks a space where a nonwhite identity was laid out after abolition. Amid the proliferation of theories positing the natural (and cultural) inequality of black and mixed-race populations, these songs suggested, albeit ironically, the existence of other social and racial identities. These identities did not subscribe to a singular vision, although they were always distant from the ideal standards of order and morality, which were officially condoned as the most civilized. Moreover, these identities do not project onto themselves the classic racial divisions approved by scientific discourse and found in the official documentation: preto, pardo, and white.[44]

Let us turn now to the historiography about mulatas and the stereotypes and prejudices surrounding them. In general, such studies have correctly denounced these women's sexual exploitation by men and women of the slave-owning classes throughout Brazilian history. Using examples from "high" literary genres, such as romanticism, naturalism, and modernism, as well as "common sense" drawn from popular proverbs, these analyses affirm the development of a highly sensual image of the mulata. This image, scholarly consensus holds, was "exalted only for its exceptional physical attributes and for its excellence in all things sexual."[45] In this approach, the analysis of the (re)creation and dissemination of "the mulata" in this period may serve as just another example of her sad destiny.

Teófilo de Queiroz Junior shows that mulatas were depicted as irresponsible, unfaithful, lazy, averse to work, and incapable of mothering.[46] The description of the mulata's charms justified the violation of the interdiction against unions between whites and blacks. In addition, the mulata's exalted sensuality placed the blame for masculine extramarital impulses on the mulatas themselves.[47]

Such reasoning contains many problems, arising primarily from the difficulty of understanding the relationship between these images of mulatas and the historical conjuncture in which they were produced and which conferred meaning on them. For example, how can we think about the continuity, if there was any, of such racial stereotypes after the 1930s, when theories hostile to miscegenation were discredited? How could these stereotypes have been associated with the political strategy of the Estado Novo (the period of authoritarian rule under President Getúlio Vargas), which consecrated racial mixing, *feijoada*, capoeira, Afro-Brazilian religions, samba, and mulatas into official national symbols?[48] How can we understand these racial stereotypes vis-à-vis the themes that authors of so-called popular music, especially samba, would privilege in their compositions, such as the malandro, workers, mulatas, mulatos, and morenas?[49]

A second recurring problem in such studies is their conviction, developed through a less-than-systematic analysis of carnival music and popular proverbs, that high culture's stereotypes of mulata women would be reiterated among the popular classes and the black population in general.[50] This logic suggests that the dominant ideology among the slave-owning classes, and later among jurists and doctors, was passed to the dominated classes, forming yet another level of domination. Such arguments require us to conclude that the black and poor population in general as well as their anonymous and renowned artists reproduced, without questioning, these judgments about themselves.

For some time, studies of slave culture in the Americas and of Brazilian popular culture have demonstrated the importance of considering the possibility of cultural autonomy in terms of the vitality of family values and social practice. Similarly, scholarship has asked just how much we can talk about a common repertoire on the theme of mulatas—in saints' festivals and in carnival, for example—when each of these different contexts could have completely different meanings if executed by different social actors.[51]

In the spirit of these debates, I want to emphasize that these songs' images of mulatas, morenas, and crioulos might signify more than the reiteration and reproduction of inequalities. Indeed, by resorting to jokes and irony, these lyrics conveyed irreverence and challenged the measures of social control, particularly when sung by unknown authors or by a "crioulo malandro." The songs also imply a plea for autonomy, equality, and freedom of choice in relationships and sexual partners for men and women of African descent. The songs not only played a crucial part in valorizing Afro-Brazilians, they also expressed a demand for equality and freedom in behaviors and desires. These songs, therefore, take on an unquestionably political tone in the postslavery context.

There is something disconcerting about these songs, something rarely encountered in nineteenth- and early-twentieth-century romantic or naturalist literature: free relationships between the sexes. Interethnic sexual or romantic relationships in the erudite literature almost always involve a white man and a nonwhite woman. There is no space in which a white woman might seek a partner outside her own class or caste, as this act might disturb the code of patriarchal domination and the reproduction of slavery and socioracial hier-archies.[52] Even though the inversion of the gender hierarchy in these lundus results from the comic nature of the genre, which plays with the impossibility of situations, we must not dismiss other possible meanings. These lyrics may also represent and disseminate alternative identities, particularly if performed by a "crioulo malandro" during an age when intellectual and political elites sought to harness the country to one common path to "civilization," a path which sought to moralize behavior and impose free labor according to a narrowly defined white, educated, European model. The musical world indi-cated the existence of other possibilities.

The political tone of the lundus can be even better understood if we consider particular features of the musical world in the late nineteenth and early twen-tieth centuries, when the songs analyzed here started to figure prominently in theaters, circuses, studios, and popular festivals. These represented one of the few possibilities for social mobility for Afro-Brazilians in the postslavery pe-riod, as well as an efficient means to establish their presence in society.[53] Despite continuing racial inequality, the musical world created concrete possi-bilities for Afro-Brazilians to express their hopes and desires.[54]

Taking account of the meanings conveyed by the music and dance present in African-descended communities in America allows us to better understand the dimensions of love songs in the postabolition period. Much research draws at-tention to the presence of satire, mockery, insults, and irony in Afro-American songs, poems, and tales, both in the United States and in the Caribbean. Some scholars attribute these features to African, and particularly West African heri-tage, where songs very often involved personal, social, and political criticism of dominant classes. In African communities, it is argued, satire minimized collective frustrations and united communities. In the Americas, in turn, satire was targeted at slave masters and thus worked as a sophisticated weapon of resistance. In common with the conclusions of my own research, the historian William Piersen states that many songs composed by Afro-Americans from the southern United States and the Caribbean used irony and humor as a way to defend black people from their slave masters.[55] In addition, by ironically and humorously dealing with the issues posed by relationships between slaves and masters, the songs criticized the masters' power to attract black women. As an example, the author points to songs which show black men's lust for their mistresses. The songs also include lyrics implying that white men were inevita-bly convinced of the superiority of colored women. In these songs, the explana-tion of the master's and white men's interest might not be in the weakness of black men but in the strength of women of African descent.

In southeastern Brazil, the ironic and satirical character of the lundus was not a mere white intellectual strategy to take these songs to refined salons and theaters. I hope the lundus and songs analyzed here, despite their ambiguities, have allowed us to identify possible ways chosen by people of African descent to participate in building the identity of a nation which was not receptive to them. In so doing, they were able to project their dreams and to criticize the social and racial disparities that continued to abound after the end of slavery.

Notes

1 The song probably originated in the nineteenth century, a period during which lundu is difficult to define. It took multiple forms and emerged in varied locations, performed by simple folk in rural areas and on city streets, but also in more upscale venues like the theaters and salons of Rio de Janeiro, then Brazil's capital. Mário de Andrade describes lundu as a song and dance style deeply embedded in all of Brazilian culture. Probably originally developed by Angolan slaves, it began as a dance characterized by abdominal movements accompanied by guitar. It arrived in Brazil's salons as a song form rather than a dance, although it retained its characteristic syncopation. See Andrade, *Dicionário musical brasileiro* (Belo Horizonte: Itatiaia, 1989), 292; Martha Abreu, *O império do divino: Festas religiosas e cultura popular no Rio de Janeiro, 1830–1900* (Rio de Janeiro: Nova Fronteira, 1999).

2 The innumerable versions of these lyrics were each adjusted to local situations and tastes. Some portrayed a black man rather than a black woman (in which case it was of course titled "Gosto de negro"), employing more vulgar language: "they stink," "dirty armpit," "stinking like onion." See Mário de Andrade, *Ensaio sobre a música brasileira*, 3rd ed. (São Paulo: Martins Fontes, n.d.), 143; Rossini Tavares de Lima, *Da conceituação do lundu* (São Paulo: n.p., 1953), document 16. The material cited by Andrade and Tavares de Lima was recorded in the interior of São Paulo state, where slavery predominated in the nineteenth century.

3 The use of *negros* in reference to the African-descended population is a part of the nomenclature of that historical moment. [The term, used by Abreu here, is translated throughout this essay as "black men," "black men and women," or "blacks" (translators' note).]

4 Southeastern Brazil encompasses the present-day states of Rio de Janeiro, São Paulo, and Minas Gerais. In the nineteenth century, due to the expansion of coffee, these provinces were the ones most heavily dominated by slavery.

5 See Celia Azevedo, *Onda negra, medo branco: O negro no imaginário das elites* (Rio de Janeiro: Paz e Terra, 1987), 223; Lilia Schwarcz, *O espetáculo das raças* (São Paulo: Companhia das Letras, 1996); Hebe Castro, *Das cores do silêncio: Os significados da liberdade no sudeste escravista—Brasil, século XIX* (Rio de Janeiro: Nova Fronteira, 1998).

6 Lundu also existed during slavery. While it would be interesting to chart the genre's evolution during the transition from slavery to postslavery society, this is not possible, as very few sources exist for the study of slavery-era lundus. From around 1880 on, published lundus proliferated as part of a more general expansion of commercial popular culture.

7 These collections included dozens of songs on mainly sentimental topics, and some reached fifteen editions. For example, *O Trovador Popular Moderno*, 16a. edição, de Eduardo das Neves e Bahiano, São Paulo, C. Teixeira e Cia. ed., 1923. There are also collections that do not treat the theme in question here. From sixteen publications, I selected sixty-four songs for closer analysis.

8 See Fernando Antonio Mencarelli, *Cena aberta: A absolvição de um bilontra e o teatro de revista de Arthur [sic] Azevedo* (Campinas: Editora UNICAMP, 1999); Hermano Viana, *Os mistérios de samba* (Rio de Janeiro: Editora UFRJ/Jorge Zahar, 1995); Santuza Cambraia Naves, *O violão azul: modernismo e música popular* (Rio de Janeiro: Editora Fundação Getúlio Vargas, 1998).

9 For further discussion of the issue of authorship in the earliest songs acknowledged as samba in Rio de Janeiro, see Carlos Sandroni, *Feitiço decente: Transformaçoes do samba no Rio de Janeiro (1917–1933)* (Rio de Janeiro: Zahar/Ed. UFRJ, 2001), 143–55.

10 The implications of "crioulo malandro" are impossible to translate into English. *Crioulo* originally meant "Creole" (i.e., born in Brazil) and was applied particularly to slaves. Sometimes it was a more pejorative term than *negro*. *Malandro* is usually translated as "scoundrel" or "rogue," but it has connotations of malice not always implied by these English terms. We leave these untranslatable terms in the original Portuguese. (Translators' note.)

In the period following abolition (1888) and the intimately related proclamation of the republic (1889), the republican municipal and federal governments, located in the city of Rio de Janeiro, attempted to inculcate a new work ethic in the laboring class. This disciplinary project primarily targeted freed slaves, who found themselves the principle targets of police and judicial repression of "idleness," vagrancy, and moral offenses.

11 The term *cabocla* in Brazilian Portuguese refers to a woman of mixed indigenous and European origin. (Translator's note.)

12 The last line reads, "A negra—surrão de couro." A *surrão* is a leather sack often used by rural people, but the word also has the proverbial meaning of a wayward woman. (Translators' note.)

13 Osório Duque Estrada, *Trovas populares* (Petrópolis: Tipografia Moderna, 1907), 32.

14 This sentence, according to Gilberto Freyre, is an adage recorded by H. Handelmann in his *História do Brasil* (Rio de Janeiro: n.p., 1931). See Gilberto Freyre, *Casa grande e senzala*, 18th ed. (Rio de Janeiro: José Olympio, 1977), 10.

15 Other lyrics of this song praise the Bahian mulata. They have been traced in

compilations by Mello Moraes Filho, *Cantares brasileiros: Cancioneiro fluminense* (Rio de Janeiro: Cruz, 1900), 95; Julia Brito Mendes, *Canções populares do Brasil* (Rio de Janeiro: Cruz Coutinho, 1911), 184; *O trovador moderno* (Rio de Janeiro: Quaresma, n.d.), 19; *Trovador popular moderno*, from Eduardo das Neves's and Bahiano's collection, 16th ed. (São Paulo: C. Teixeira, 1925).

16 This erotic representation of black and mixed-race women's bodies in love songs was not exclusive to this period. These representations, often conveyed by the theater, records, and published songs, gained new meaning in the postabolition context in which discussion about a national identity took place. In printed nineteenth-century lundus studied by Carlos Sandroni at Brazil's Biblioteca Nacional, black women, as well as mulatas, are seduced by their slave masters. Sandroni, *Feitiço decente*. Also cf. Rachel Soihet, "A sensualidade em festa: Algumas representações do corpo feminino nas festas populares no Rio de Janeiro—séculos XIX e XX," *Diálogos latinoamericanos* (Arhus, Denmark: CLAS—Centro de Estudios Latinoamericanos, University of Aarhus, Feb. 2000). The association of the mulata with Brazilianness continued in twentieth-century literature. Cf. M. Seigel and T. de Melo Gomes, "Sabina das Laranjas: Gênero e nação na trajetória de um símbolo popular, 1889–1930," *Revista brasileira de história* 22, no. 43 (2002): 171–93.

17 For these expressions, see the lundu "Mulatinha do caroço no pescoço" [Little mulata with the pit on her neck], in Brito Mendes, *Canções populares do Brasil*, 97, and in Eduardo das Neves, *O cantor* (Rio de Janeiro: Laemmert, 1895), 376. Another example from the interior backlands is "Sambalêlê," recorded by Alvarenga Oneyda in 1935 in Varginha, Minas Gerais. Oneyda, *Música popular brasileira* (Rio de Janeiro: Globo, 1950), 238. Also see the anonymous "A mulata da Bahia," in José de Souza Conegundes, *Serenatas e fadinhos* (Rio de Janeiro: Quaresma, 1914), 131.

18 *Vatapá* is a Brazilian stew. See Santana Nery, *Folclore brasileiro* (Recife: Fundação Joaquim Nabuco, 1992), 60; and Mello Moraes Filho, *Serenatas e saraus* (Rio de Janeiro: Garnier, 1902), 109–10. Eduardo das Neves, a black musician discussed below, also published these lyrics as an anonymous lundu in *Cantor de modinhas brasileiras: Coleção completa de lindas modinhas, lundus, recitativos, etc.* (Rio de Janeiro: Laemmert, 1895), 344.

19 See "A mulata" (1899) and "Quando vejo a mulata" (1902), in Eduardo das Neves, *O trovador da malandragem* (Rio de Janeiro: Quaresma, 1926), 71, 72, 120. These songs were presumably written by Neves.

20 See the anonymous "Mulatinha do caroço no pescoço."

21 Conegundes, *Serenatas e fadinhos*, 131 (no author specified).

22 "Quando vejo uma mulata," supposedly authored by Eduardo das Neves, *Trovador*, 72. The image of the woman who lavishly spends money also features in "Isto é bom," a song attributed to Xisto Bahia but also recorded by Oneyda in the interior of the state of Minas Gerais in 1935. Oneyda, *Música popular brasileira*, 154.

23 This song, attributed to Gonçalves Crespo in the collections consulted for this study, recounts the story of a slave driver in love with a "gorgeous mixed-race

woman with a vivacious gaze." He ends up "wasting away with a lost love" because his mulata runs away, abandoning him forever. A mucama was a slave or black servant who served as a personal or lady's maid, chambermaid, or wet nurse.

24 Sônia Maria Giacomini, "Ser escrava no Brasil," Estudos afro-asiáticos 15 (1988): 154.

25 Freyre, Casa grande, 373; and Teófilo de Queiroz Junior, Preconceito de cor e a mulata (São Paulo: Ática, 1975).

26 Morena means "dark-skinned" or "brown-skinned" woman, as distinct from a preta or black woman.

27 See O trovador moderno (Rio de Janeiro: Quaresma, n.d.), 25.

28 After 1930, "popular music" became an effective vehicle for the dissemination of antiracist ideology. Brazilian popular music was proudly defined as mestiça and, in essence, valorized mixed-race people and things. During this period, black and mixed-race culture started to be acknowledged and valued in the Brazilian cultural world.

29 See J. F. Costa, Ordem médica e norma familiar (Rio de Janeiro: Graal, 1977); Magali Engel, Meretrizes e doutores: O saber médico e a prostituição na cidade do Rio de Janeiro, 1845–1890 (São Paulo: Brasiliense, 1989); Rachel Soihet, "Mulheres pobres e violência no Brasil urbano," and Joana Maria Pedro, "Mulheres no Sul," in Mary del Piore, História das mulheres no Brasil (São Paulo: Contexto, 1997), 362–400; 278–321.

30 Maria Ângela d'Incao, "Mulher e família burguesa," in del Piore, História das mulheres, 224. See also Thales Azevido, Regras de namoro à antiga (São Paulo: Ática, 1986).

31 See Martha de Abreu Esteves, Meninas perdidas: Os populares e o cotidiano de amor no Rio de Janeiro da belle époque (Rio de Janeiro: Paz e Terra, 1989); and Sueann Caufield, In Defense of Honor, Sexual Morality, Modernity, and Nation in Early-Twentieth-Century Brazil (Durham, N.C.: Duke University Press, 2000).

32 See "Recorte da negra," in Cornélio Pires, Sambas e cateretês (São Paulo: Unitas, 1933).

33 Brito Mendes, Canções populares do Brasil, 50–53.

34 In the lines "que eu não sou bela / para engrossar," engrossar means "to thicken" or "to swell up," and here appears to refer to pregnancy, as well as to the suitability of a black woman to carry the child of a white man. (Translators' note.)

35 The theme of resistance to labor is not exclusive to songs of the postabolition period, but the term malandro, which became widespread in the late 1920s and is directly related to samba, first appeared in popular songs in "Trovador da malandragem," by Eduardo das Neves. Cf. Sandroni, Feitiço decente, 159.

36 Preto or preta in Brazilian Portuguese means a black man or woman. It was used frequently during slavery to mean African slave or simply slave. (Translators' note.)

37 In his first book, O cantor de modinhas brasileiras [The singer of Brazilian modinhas] (Rio de Janeiro: Laemmert, 1895), Eduardo das Neves published widely

distributed songs about mulatas and some others about irresistible, dark-skinned women. His later books, *Mistérios do violão* (Rio de Janeiro: Quaresma, 1905), and *Trovador da malandragem*, 33, pursue the same themes.

38 See das Neves, *Trovador da malandragem*, 64.

39 Das Neves, *Mistérios do violão*, 57–58. My ongoing research has revealed other popular lyrics, collected originally by folklorists, in which black men try to seduce the "sinha."

40 On the "malandro," see Claudia Matos, *Acertei no milhar: Samba e maladragem no tempo de Getúlio* (Rio de Janeiro: Paz e Terra, 1982).

41 See Lilia Schwarcz, "Questão racial no Brasil," in *Negras imagens*, ed. L. Schwarcz and L. V. de Souza Reis (São Paulo: Edusp, 1996), 153–78.

42 This statement does not seek to invalidate the critiques of the ideas of racial democracy that spread following the publication of Freyre's *Casa grande*.

43 The preeminence and valorization of dark skin color in these types of songs deserves a more in-depth study, due to the broad spectrum of possibilities brought together by this category. Women with dark skin are described with various adjectives: "Dark-colored" or "brown" skin (*cor morena*) has today reached a surprising level of acceptance: for instance, 43% of all Brazilians polled by the *Jornal folha de São Paulo* in 1990 classified themselves as moreno. See Schwarcz, "Questão racial," 173.

44 *Pardo* means dark-skinned, but not quite black. The strategy of valorizing the woman of African descent in black people's struggle for equality can also be detected in other periods of Brazilian history, as well as in other societies. In Brazil, however, this did not mean black people's subordination to faith in racial democracy. See mulata's beauty contest in the 1940s, in the publication *O quilombo*, discussed in M. A. de Motta Maués, "Entre o branqueamento e a negritude: O TEM e o debate da questão racial," *Dionysios* 28 (1988): 92, which is cited in Antônio Sergio A. Guimarães, *Classes, raças e democracia* (São Paulo: Ed. 34, 2002), 145. Maxine Leeds Craig's study of African American beauty contests, as depicted in early twentieth-century U.S. black publications, demonstrates the significance of their deliberate emphasis on black women's beauty as a way of voicing opposition to segregationist policies. As in Brazil, the standards of black women's beauty emerged out of this construction. For Craig, the beauty contests, seen as a legitimate expression of black people's identity, were neither totally dominated by nor completely free from ideological aesthetic values. Craig, *Ain't I a Beauty Queen? Black Women, Beauty and the Politics of Race* (Oxford: Oxford University Press, 2002), 45–64.

45 Queiroz Junior, *Preconceito de cor*, 111. Gilberto Freyre cites numerous sources of that era, such as travelers and literary writers, who accuse female slaves and mulatas of being lascivious. Freyre, *Casa grande*, 378.

46 Queiroz Junior, *Preconceito de cor*, 118.

47 See Giacomini, "Ser escrava no Brasil," 155; and Queiroz Junior, *Preconceito de cor*, 26. Gilberto Freyre also develops these hypotheses; *Casa grande*, 378.

48   Feijoada is the black bean stew associated with Afro-Brazilian culture. Capoeira is an Afro-Brazilian martial art dance form, originally developed by slaves.

49   See Schwarcz, "Questão racial," 164; and Caetana Maria Damasceno, "República das moscas," Estudos afro-asiáticos 21 (1991): 136–39.

50   See Queiroz Junior, Preconceito de cor, 83.

51   On this debate, see Robert Slenes, Na senzala uma flor: Esperanças e recordações na formação da família escrava: Brasil, Sudeste, século XIX (Rio de Janeiro: Nova Fronteira, 1999); and Abreu, O império do divino.

52   See Jean M. Carvalho França, "O negro no romance urbano oitocentista," Estudos afro-asiáticos 29 (1996): 111; and Heloisa Toller Gomes, As marcas de escravidão: O negro eo discurso oitocentista no Brasil e nos Estados Unidos (Rio de Janeiro: Ed. da UFRJ, 1994), 144. Toller Gomes highlights the fact that novels only rarely showed this racial inversion. Even when they did, the white woman would be sickly, or the situation would end in tragedy, as in, e.g., Aluísio de Azevedo's O mulato (1881) and the play O escravocrata (1884) by Artur Azevedo and Urbano Duarte.

53   Some late nineteenth- and early-twentieth-century attempts by important conductors to describe what Brazilian music ought to be like recognized and valued African and Afro-Brazilian influences. Resulting from miscegenation among Indians, Portuguese, and Africans, those songs that were considered "Brazilian popular music" were acknowledged as the most authentic national art after 1930. Cf. Martha Abreu, "Histórias da música popular brasileira: Uma análise da produção sobre o período colonial," in Festa, cultura e sociabilidade na América portuguesa, ed. L. Jancsó and I. Kantor (São Paulo: Imprensa Oficial, Hucitec, EDUSP, FAPESP, 2001).

54   Micol Seigel and Tiago de Melo Gomes also identify Afro-Brazilians' desire and hope for harmony in dramatic productions by the Companhia Negra de Revistas in the 1920s. See their article "Sabina das Laranjas: Gênero, raça e nação na trajetória de um símbolo popular, 1889–1930," Revista brasileira de história 22, no. 43 (2002): 171–93, esp. 187. The same issue is discussed in relation to the 1950s Teatro Experimental Negro (Black experimental theater) in Guimarães, Classes, raças e democracia, esp. chap. 3, 146, 147.

55   William Piersen, "A Resistance Too Civilized to Notice," in Signifyin(G), Sanctifyin', & Slam Dunking: A Reader in African American Expressive Culture, ed. Gena Dagel Caponi (Amherst: University of Massachusetts Press, 1999), 359.

 HANNAH ROSEN

The Rhetoric of Miscegenation and the Reconstruction of Race: Debating Marriage, Sex, and Citizenship in Postemancipation Arkansas

In January 1868 at a constitutional convention in Little Rock, Arkansas, a debate took place that laid bare the connections between postemancipation politics, racial formation, and discourses of gender and sexuality. In order for Arkansas to regain its status as a state in the Union, after having seceded from the United States and joining the Confederacy six years earlier, this convention was obliged to design a new constitution meeting the requirements of the Reconstruction Acts passed by the U.S. Congress the previous March. The most revolutionary of these requirements was that the new constitution institute universal male suffrage (excluding former U.S. officials who gave aid to the Confederacy as specified under the Fourteenth Amendment), and thus extend previously denied voting rights to African American men.[1] But on the eighteenth day of the gathering, a moderate white southern delegate named John Bradley took the floor and argued that the revolutionary threat of Reconstruction lay elsewhere. He claimed that "the great question that is agitating Arkansas from centre to circumference" was interracial marriage, and thus proposed that the new constitution also contain a clause "forbidding any officer, either civil or ecclesiastical, to solemnize the rites of matrimony between a white person and a person of African descent."[2]

William Henry Grey, a black Republican delegate and a leading advocate for African American citizenship rights in the state, immediately mocked Bradley's seeming diversion from the more important tasks at hand: "I have no particular objection to the resolution. But I think that in order to make the law binding, there should be some penalty attached to its violation—kill them, quarter them, or something of that kind." Sarcasm aside, Grey quickly followed with a more serious response. He contended that the provision was "superfluous," as demonstrated by the fact that such prohibitions were not seen as necessary in the northern states where interracial marriage was nonetheless rare. Furthermore, he challenged the proposal's exclusive focus on marriage, rather than on cross-racial sexual relations outside of marriage where African American women in particular had suffered a long history of abuse and exploitation: "I know that such provisions have heretofore more or less obtained; but while the contract has been kept on our part, it has not been kept upon the part of our friends; and I propose, if such an enactment is to be inserted in the Constitution, to insist, also, that if any white man shall be found cohabitating with a negro woman, the penalty shall be death."[3] Grey's words were followed by applause from like-minded delegates and parties, many of them former slaves, observing the convention from the galleries above.[4]

Bradley, feigning surprise that there should be any opposition to his resolution, responded by implying that Grey's resistance to the measure raised questions about his own intentions toward white women: "If such a provision as I propose is not necessary, if you do not mean to rush into these practices, I ask, in all candor, why, in the name of God, do you object to having a line established, and to saying, to the white race and to the black,—'Thus far shalt thou go, and no farther?'" Bradley also offered his rationale for why an interracial marriage prohibition was indeed relevant to the task assigned to this convention: "As to the idea that no such difficulty exists in the Northern States, I am only able to use this argument in reply,—that there is no negro suffrage in the Northern States."[5]

Packed into this small exchange, the beginning of a debate over marriage and sexual relations that would occupy more than two days of Arkansas's constitutional convention, is evidence of an increasing recourse to discourses of gender and sexuality in battles over citizenship and the meaning of race following emancipation in the southern United States. Bradley's defense of his proposal—that interracial marriage prohibitions were needed where there was black male suffrage—presumed a direct connection between political authority and domestic relationships, a presumption at the heart of an ever widening discourse of "miscegenation" circulating throughout Reconstruction-era political debates and struggles. Rhetoric surrounding the Civil War–era neologism *miscegenation*, and its companion terms *amalgamation* and *social equality*, entailed the persistent conflation of the political empowerment of black men with "race mixing," particularly the idea that enfranchised black men would seek sex and marriage with white women.[6]

As we will see, though, measures such as Bradley's proposed constitutional ban were designed not so much to prevent white-black unions as to permanently identify them as illegitimate. Despite the image of biological mixture invoked by the term *miscegenation*, the issue driving this discourse was not in fact concern about the physical amalgamation of what were imagined to be two distinct races, but rather what emancipation and the enfranchisement of black men would mean for the future significance of race as a social and political category. The postemancipation years were a time of profound social change and political uncertainty. Slavery had been abolished, but what freedom for former slaves was to mean, what sort of citizenship African Americans would possess, what power they would hold relative to other free people, remained open questions. Still undetermined was whether a republic that offered nominal equality in civil and political rights to former slaves would nonetheless affirm racial difference and inequality in other ways. Were there realms outside of political and civil life where difference and inequality would continue to be legitimated and racial hierarchy reinscribed? Although racial slavery was ultimately succeeded in the United States by racial segregation and disfranchisement, racially unequal citizenship and rigidly separated racial communities were not legally consolidated until the late nineteenth century. The discourse of miscegenation reveals, though, that white southerners began envisaging such a society during the era of Reconstruction. They responded to the instability of race as a politically significant category by turning to gender and domestic relations to carve out a supposedly legitimate space for codifying difference and separation.

This putatively legitimate sphere of difference, identified as the "social," was not, in fact, distinguishable from the "political" and the "civil." In white southern political culture, white men's exclusive claims to political authority had long been predicated on claims to domestic roles and identities as responsible and honorable patriarchs. The rhetoric of miscegenation, with its implications of an unrestrained and unruly sexuality among former slaves, was in the end a protest against representing African American men as similarly legitimate patriarchs and hence as independent men worthy of full citizenship and a voice in public affairs. It was also a protest against depicting black women as "virtuous" and deserving state protection from sexual abuse. In its inscription of difference through gendered representations of race, the discourse of miscegenation would ultimately serve to rationalize the perpetuation of white men's political privileges even in a society of supposedly equal rights.

To investigate the politics of "miscegenation" during Reconstruction, this essay closely examines the debate—similar to contests occurring throughout the southern states at this time—that followed Bradley's proposed prohibition of interracial marriage.[7] Rarely would white southern politicians again be obliged to explain their alarm over the possibility of marriage and sex between black and white people, nor to reveal why they believed that political equality between men would impel these cross-racial sexual relations. But post–Civil War political conditions—which gave African Americans as well as white supporters of a race-blind republic considerable influence over the requisites and parameters of political discourse—allowed opponents of an interracial marriage ban to directly challenge the measure. Thus its advocates were forced to articulate in its defense what would subsequently be accepted without explication, that is, the mechanisms connecting this supposed social taboo with political power. The debates over race, sex, and marriage that resulted highlight how gender and sexuality became instruments for constructing racial difference and inequality despite universal male suffrage, and how this gendered discourse of race shaped profound dilemmas and perilous political terrain for black leaders as they approached demands for equality.

Citizenship and Suffrage

Arkansas was a relatively young state at the outbreak of the Civil War, having joined the Union only in 1836. Its first constitution, which enfranchised all "free white male citizens," reflected a trend in the United States in the 1830s toward removing property restrictions on voting while imposing racial ones.[8] As suffrage in many states was simultaneously broadened to include all white men and narrowed to exclude all those considered nonwhite, citizenship became increasingly associated with white manhood and political enfranchisement became a crucial component of many white men's identities. In states such as Arkansas, where for much of the antebellum era land was inexpensive and abundant, almost all white men shared the privilege not only of suffrage, but also of being independent producers.[9] Thus most white men were, in historian Stephanie McCurry's phrase, "masters of small worlds," wherein they controlled the lives and labor of their dependents, white women, children, and, in some cases, slaves.[10] This common patriarchal experience, in turn, shaped the meaning of white men's citizenship. It was primarily those who were masters at home who came together to exercise civic rights and duties. In fact, white men's exclusive claim to political power was justified through their authority in, and responsibilities to, their households. Fulfillment of roles as benevolent patriarchs providing for and protecting virtuous wives and chaste daughters supposedly both required and warranted a voice in public affairs.[11] Whiteness, independent manhood, and domestic authority constituted what it meant to be a citizen in antebellum Arkansas, and exclusive citizenship as well as domestic authority constituted what it meant to be a white man. A cross-class community of white men was constituted through patriarchy, slavery, and racism, and through white men's domination in both civic and domestic realms.

This exclusive political community of supposedly independent men was fractured by the Civil War and emancipation. The war destroyed the state's economy and resultant class tensions among whites disrupted their ante-bellum alliance.[12] At the same time, former slaves began demanding a place in politics. Immediately after emancipation, African Americans formed public forums for political discussion in churches and on individual plantations. And as soon as the opportunity arose under the Reconstruction Acts, they seized the right to speak and to vote in existing white-controlled public arenas. In Little Rock, freedmen and freedwomen crowded the galleries during politi-cal conventions at the state capitol and held speaking events on the capitol steps. Throughout the state, freedpeople formed Republican clubs, attended political meetings and demonstrations, and traveled great distances to hear speeches. On Election Day, they gathered in large groups and marched in long processions to the polls. Both urban and rural classes embraced liberal politi-cal rights as a sign of freedom and as an important tool in ongoing economic and social struggles.[13] African Americans thus presented in the public spaces of politics a vision for political community very different from the exclusively white male citizenship of antebellum southern society. Former slaves becom-ing citizens, and particularly African American men obtaining and exercising the franchise, fundamentally challenged the significance of race as a social and political category in a society that had previously excluded all black people from the rights, liberties, and identities accorded to "citizens." Their action posed a formidable challenge to antebellum constructions of citizenship, which had presupposed that those speaking and voting in public would be white men.

Many former Confederate leaders responded to this challenge to a white-male monopoly on political power and to the disruption of political unity among white men by asserting that former slaves were not fit to be citizens, and that black men were not fit to vote. Jesse Cypert, for instance, offered clear expressions of this position while serving as a delegate to the Arkansas Con-stitutional Convention in 1868. "The highest judicial authority in the land has decided that the negro cannot be a citizen," Cypert told his fellow delegates on the eighth day of the convention, invoking the 1857 Dred Scott decision of the U.S. Supreme Court in defense of his opposition to extending suffrage to black men. Calling "the elective franchise . . . not a universal right, but a class right," Cypert continued, "it was only reasonable that the privilege of the ballot should be withheld, from negroes, or from any other class, not citizens of the United States, destitute of a knowledge of the principles and working of our government, and not by nature qualified to exercise with sufficient judgment the privilege of the ballot." Most importantly, Cypert claimed that black men were not in possession of an independent manhood comparable to that of white men that would qualify them for suffrage or citizenship. Black men, rather, were in a position of dependency: "Let us afford them the same protection that our wives and our daughters have,—the right of liberty, the right of property, and of the pursuit of happiness. Let us afford to them the same rights enjoyed by the white man under the age of twenty-one. Let them be as minors." Cypert concluded, "Let us not attempt to render homogeneous races essentially dissimilar and unequal. Our fathers made a government for the white man. Let us govern it."[14]

In an attempt to reclaim for white men the sole position of those worthy of political power and to repair their antebellum political alliance, Cypert drew on notions of independent manhood to resignify race as a significant marker of inequality between men. However, the makeup of delegates to Arkansas's convention guaranteed a rejection of Cypert's views. Due to federal restrictions on participation of the state's former political leadership, only twelve white southern conservatives who consistently opposed black male suffrage were elected to the convention. These twelve faced a pro-Reconstruction alliance affiliated with the Republican Party that included eight African American delegates (seven of whom were southern-born and six of whom had been slaves prior to the Civil War); seventeen white delegates of northern origin (having moved to Arkansas some time after 1860); and thirty-two white southern delegates, some of whom were veteran unionists and others of whom were simply making peace with Reconstruction for the sake of returning their state to the Union.[15] Together, these three groups produced a franchise article for the new constitution that established universal male suffrage (excluding those men who were disqualified from office by the Fourteenth Amendment as well as any who persisted in opposing Reconstruction) and required electors to take an oath endorsing the "civil and political equality of all men."[16] Yet the future of racial difference in spaces other than those defined as the "civil and political," such as one increasingly named the "social," remained an open question. Indeed, the political chasm between these temporary pro-Reconstruction allies was brought to the surface by the issue of "social equality" and specifically interracial marriage.

Sex and Marriage

John Bradley was one of the white southern delegates tenuously allied with Republicans for political expediency, and he would seek to stake out a middle ground between conservative opposition to the enfranchisement of black men and radical Republican visions for a race-blind republic. He would claim to support universal male suffrage but would seek other ways to mark racial difference between men. Early in life a "humble mechanic," subsequently a minister, and practicing law at the time of the convention, Bradley had come to Little Rock an opponent of the planter and professional elite which had ruled Arkansas before the war—those whom he labeled "vile intriguing demagogues" for having led his state into, and persisted in, a disastrous civil war. Like many white southern men of modest means, Bradley saw in the defeat of the Confederacy and the exclusion from office of the state's former political leadership an opportunity to take political control away from the antebellum elite. Yet his distaste for this elite was matched only by his disdain for former slaves and, increasingly, his resentment of the new Republican "dynasty in Little Rock" that had recently repaid his offer of affiliation by denying him a nomination for a seat in Congress. Soon thereafter, when it became clear that the radical wing of the Republican Party, dominated by northern-born whites and African Americans, would interfere with his political ambitions, he introduced his proposed ban. Reflecting the complexity of the post–Civil War political landscape and its shifting political alliances, it was this former opponent of the Confederacy and former Freedmen's Bureau agent who threatened to stymie the process of Reconstruction in Arkansas by making interracial marriage a contentious political issue.[17]

Despite Bradley's claim that marriage was "the great question . . . agitating Arkansas," emancipation had not yet presented any serious challenge to the state's 1838 statute declaring marriages between "whites" and "Negroes or mulattoes" to be "illegal and void."[18] Nonetheless, Bradley's call for a constitutional clause prohibiting the marriage of "a white person and a person of African descent" was strongly supported by many of his fellow white southerners—both moderate and conservative. It was also vigorously opposed by black and northern white delegates. The first reaction to Bradley's resolution came from James Hodges, a white Union Army veteran from New York who settled in Arkansas during the war: "If persons want to intermarry in this way, they ought certainly to have the privilege. . . . I, for one, am entirely opposed to legislation, or Constitutional enactment, upon any such subject."[19] Straightforward objections to legal intervention into domestic life and assertions of the acceptability of cross-racial marriages, however, would prove politically unfeasible and were eschewed even by most who opposed the provision. Instead, many followed the approach introduced by William Henry Grey, who appeared willing to accept racial separation but pointed out the hypocritical character of a ban only on interracial marriage (implicitly relations between black men and white women) that ignored illicit sexual relations across racial lines (often exploitative ones between white men and black women). In fact, at the end of two days of contentious debate, the convention approved a compromise resolution proposed by James Hinds, another white New York native who came to Arkansas with the Union Army, that was clearly influenced by Grey's approach.[20] The compromise read: "Resolved: That this Convention is utterly opposed to all amalgamation between the white and colored races, whether the same is legitimate or illegitimate. We would therefore recommend that the next General Assembly enact such laws as may effectually govern the same."[21] The conservatives were joined by John Bradley and another white southern Republican in opposition to this compromise. They argued that recommendations to the legislature carried no legal force and continued to push for a constitutional prohibition of only marriage. Nonetheless, the resolution secured sufficient support, including the vote of every black delegate, to pass the convention.[22]

What did the original proposal and the final compromise mean to the various parties involved in Arkansas's constitutional convention? Why did Bradley and his supporters so vehemently endorse a constitutional ban on interracial marriage and then refuse to support an instruction to the legislature to prevent "amalgamation" of all kinds? And why were Grey and other black delegates willing to support the latter measure? Given that the existing interracial marriage prohibitions faced no current legal challenge,[23] it seems that Bradley's, Hinds's, and other related proposals were largely symbolic, allowing their proponents to map out broader visions for postemancipation political community in terms of race. Underlying debates about interracial marriage and sex was a political struggle over the contours of African American citizenship and the meaning of race in this postemancipation world.

"Let us build a wall"

The importance of the future meaning of race to John Bradley's proposal for a constitutional ban on interracial marriage was made evident in the arguments he offered in its defense. When Grey first objected to Bradley's resolution as "superfluous," Bradley's response was telling. He began by affirming his commitment to what he understood to be the rights of African Americans: "[I intend] to give the negro every right that God in heaven . . . has assigned him. I am ready to recognize his civil and political rights." "But sir," he quickly added, "I am a white man."[24] Bradley thus coupled his endorsement of the civil and political rights of African Americans with an invocation of his own racial and gender identity. While ostensibly accepting political equality he called for the preservation of race.

What was the meaning of "race" that Bradley sought to preserve? Bradley first articulated an essentialized notion of racial difference, representing his proposal as a principled stance against interracial sexual relations of all kinds and professing to offer it in the interests of maintaining two physically distinct "races." Echoing common nineteenth-century understandings of race—as the characteristics and developments of a particular "civilization" carried from generation to generation through "blood"[25]—he called for a vote on his proposal in order to show where each delegate "stood . . . upon the idea of keeping his own blood and race pure and unadulterated from an inferior race." Though he clearly believed white "blood" to be superior, Bradley assured his audience that he was nonetheless equally concerned about preserving black uniqueness: "I do not mean to infringe upon the pure blood of the African race. . . . I do not want it adulterated with the blood of the white man." In fact, Bradley thought it an indication of his own honor that he himself had neither any history of nor desire for sex with black women. Regarding Grey's suggestion that "any white man . . . found cohabiting with a negro woman" be punished by death, Bradley proudly proclaimed, "I can say, sir, it will not circumscribe me in any of my social enjoyments or privileges. Thank God, I have no seed, to-day, that has germinated in human form, but is of my own color."[26]

Yet at other moments, Bradley revealed that his concerns focused far more on marriage than on sex and procreation, and thus that his visions for race were more social and political than physical. In frustration at objections to his resolution, Bradley at one point declared, "If men are so much alarmed about having a barrier in the way—why, if you want to, scratch under, and get to the other race; but for God's sake let us build a wall! Let it be understood as the organic law of the land that a white man shall be a white man, and a black man a black man, and that each shall have their rights in their respective spheres."[27] "Keeping . . . race pure," in Bradley's mind, was threatened more by a lack of racial distinction in social worlds and legitimate relationships than by sexual intercourse or reproduction by people of different races. To engage in illicit forms of interracial sex, or "scratch under" in Bradley's phrase, did not portend for him the same disruption of racial difference and social order as long as legal norms kept this kind of crossing of racial boundaries illicit and the resultant relationships illegitimate. It was not the crossing but rather the representation of that crossing that concerned him. The rhetoric of miscegenation, then, was first and foremost about marriage, not because marriage involved sex—which in the end was not of much concern to Bradley—but because marriage was a means of organizing legitimate social relationships.

Bradley further explained that his primary motive for insisting that the constitution establish segregation in social relationships was to clarify the implications of racial equality in civil and political realms. "There is no limitation and distinction, there is no fixed determined meaning, to 'civil rights,' and 'equality before the law,'" he argued, "and so long as these terms stand undefined and uninterpreted, so long will this remain a vexed question for future generations to fight and war over." Bradley recognized emancipation as a critical juncture, a moment of potentially revolutionary change in racial meanings, and he feared that the establishment of political and civil equality in this moment might level and even erase racial difference and hierarchy. He emphasized the convention's responsibility "when we are launching out upon a new era" to "establish . . . a line between the races,—one that shall be recognized by all future generations." This responsibility he felt would be met through his proposed interracial marriage ban: "When the Constitution goes before [the people], let us not leave them in doubt whether that Constitution is susceptible of the interpretation of social equality and amalgamation. Let us plant it upon the ground that each race shall move in its own sphere." Through his interracial marriage ban and its establishment of a society without social integration and "social equality," Bradley sought, as he said, "to fix the true status of the two races." In other words, he sought to fix a hierarchical meaning for racial difference despite the creation of formal political equality.[28]

What did "social equality" signify to Bradley and his audience? Its specific referent opaque yet often employed with a presumption of transparency (even before emancipation), "social equality" referred broadly to forms of association between white and black people that did not convey a hierarchical meaning for race and that did not serve to mark racial difference.[29] As used by white southern opponents of racial equality during Reconstruction, it referred both to integrated access to public spaces and facilities, and to access to the "private" spaces of society and domestic life; in fact the latter was presumed to follow from the former. It drew on the general concept of "the social," which emerged in the mid-nineteenth century (for instance in "social science" or "social reform") to delineate an imagined realm that was distinct from the political yet not entirely private.[30] And it seems to have evoked for men such as Bradley specifically public manifestations of private relations, the spaces where the contours of legitimate private relationships were visible in public and where they in turn produced meanings of legitimacy. Who attended the theater or sat in a streetcar with whom, which women were escorted to public events by which men, who was invited into whose home, who married whom, were important indicators of socially legitimate interactions. Courtship and marriage across racial lines could be particularly powerful signs of a society organized without racial difference or hierarchy. Alternatively, legislating racial separation in this social sphere would help to consolidate a racially hierarchical society by making visible and meaningful distinct racial groups and by marking black manhood and womanhood as inferior to those of whites.

Bradley was not alone in his desire to preserve racial inequality through an idiom of the social, nor in justifying social segregation through a logic that conflated political empowerment with cross-racial sexual relations. One colleague at the convention, Gayle Kyle, proclaimed, "I have said it was right to make [African Americans] equal in the courts of the country. I have said,— Give them their political rights. . . . But as for saying that they must be brought up upon an equality, socially, with the white race, I never will give my assent to it." As evidence that "it is the highest climax of [former slaves] aspiration, to come up socially, on an equal footing with the white race," he recounted how, "in my own neighborhood . . . a negro . . . misled an unfortunate step-daughter of his employer. . . . This negro started to run away with the unhappy girl, and did actually take her from her father's home." When pressed by opponents of the proposed ban to explain why state intervention was necessary to prevent respectable white women from making such choices, he explained that especially poor whites would be increasingly vulnerable to "social degradation" as former slaves gained wealth and status: "These colored people will acquire . . . money, they will acquire lands, after a while, and position in society . . . and they can insidiously make their advances to these unfortunate and helpless persons, and, by the use of their power, can mislead and misguide them, into error and folly."[31] Kyle employed common antebellum imagery of depraved and desperate poor white women to help him out of a tight spot in a debate.[32] But he simultaneously revealed that lurking behind his opposition to cross-racial sexual relations was the specter of black economic mobility and its consolidation, through racial integration, of a world in which race had no visible significance.

Such discourse opposing social equality, with its implications of inferior black culture, civility, status, and personal restraint, would inevitably redound to white men's political power. By focusing on the danger of newly empowered black men's supposedly misleading white women into domestic and sexual relations, and of the necessity of an outside force, the law, to restrain black men from seeking cross-racial sexual relationships, was also to imply that black men were dishonorable, if honor was measured as Bradley contended by concern with keeping one's race "pure." Thus the debate itself circulated images of black men as less willing and able than white men to act in the interest of a supposed common good and the good of their "race." This discourse not only disparaged the manhood and worthiness for citizenship of black men. It also imputed by contrast virtue and honor to an abstract white manhood now called on to protect its "race" by protecting white women and white homes from black men's putative transgressions. Like Cypert's earlier critique of black male suffrage, this discourse ultimately depicted white men as alone capable of governing themselves and thus fit for a role in governing the republic.

"A place among men"

African American delegates to the Arkansas Constitutional Convention recognized in the proposed constitutional ban on interracial marriage and in its broader discourse opposing "social equality" the potential for insidiously promoting racial inequality in political and civil realms. The black delegates who spoke out against the measure denounced it as an effort to enshrine racial inequality in the very document intended to produce equality, the state's new postemancipation constitution. William Henry Grey, a minister born in Washington, D.C., who came to Arkansas during the war and the delegate who first rejected Bradley's proposal as "superfluous," led the way in formulating arguments in opposition.[33] In his most impassioned appeal to the convention to reject the resolution, Grey—like Bradley—implored his audience to recognize the importance of the formative political moment in which they stood. Why was it, Grey asked rhetorically, that "men of proved valor, and patriotism, approved on many a well-contested field," who had lived in close proximity to black men for generations, were "now afraid of miscegenation from four million negro slaves?" "Because," he hypothesized, "in the progress of the nineteenth century, the negro has come up from the substratum, and claims, in the sentiment of the world, a place among men, [you] propose to log off, little by little, here and there, those rights which they have at length obtained!"[34] Grey perceived that the impetus to regulate domestic relations by race reflected a desire to limit the meaning of emancipated black manhood and black men's equal place in public, their "place among men." Grey's primary objective was the opposite, to assure black men a voice in public on an equal footing with all other men, and this required precluding any representation of African American manhood and thus black men's worthiness for citizenship as subordinate to that of whites. Grey sought to establish in the constitution the basis for a society in which, "in the sentiments of the world," black men would have a place among—not beneath—other men. The real questions raised by the proposed constitutional ban for Grey and his supporters was how former slaves were to be represented as citizens; what model the new constitution would put forth for race in a republic without slavery; and what kind of freedom this revolutionary constitution would envisage.

The constitution was of particular importance to Grey, who emphasized the perils of legitimating illiberal distinctions between racial groups in what was to be the voice of authority for the principles of a new supposedly liberal republic. "When you place in your Constitution a provision of this nature," Grey told the convention, "you at once create an inequality." "Why is it necessary that the organic law of the land should contradict the very purpose for which we are assembled?" he asked. Grey refuted the notion that the social could be bracketed off as a space of inequality not touching on the civil and political. Indeed, he dismissed the claim that this was his opponents' intention. He saw in any constitutional reference to social difference the production of inequality in a broader sense. He thus accused his opponents of promoting "a piece of prejudice" that would undermine the constitution, and pleaded, "Do not touch that sacred instrument by inserting anything that indicates class legislation."[35]

Grey also criticized the notion that the law could "fix" race, a malleable social phenomenon, as if it were a transparent reflection of distinct types of "blood." He stated, "If we are to adopt this proposition, the Legislature will have to pass an act creating a board of scientific physicians, or professors of anatomy, to discover who is a negro. There is the trouble. The purity of blood, of which [Mr. Bradley] speaks, has already been somewhat interfered with." Even though Grey claimed that "if you can show where the line can be drawn, I am perfectly willing," in fact he was advising against drawing any lines in the law that would enshrine essentialized notions of race. Not only would a constitutional ban on cross-racial marriage harden and legitimate prejudicial racial constructs, but it would also be ineffective, simply forcing certain relationships underground. To Bradley's plea for building a "wall" even if some men would "scratch under," Grey responded with outrage, "I propose that we shall stop this crawling under the fence. I propose that if persons desire intermarriage with the other race, it shall be done honorably and above-board."[36]

Grey thus opposed reinscribing in the constitution racial difference and false notions of distinct physical races. He also favored measures granting legitimacy and security to black women involved in relationships with white men over laws that made these relationships and their offspring illegitimate. And yet he also revealed ambivalence about asserting this position as force-fully as had, say, James Hodges, who had objected to any state regulation of marriage choice immediately after Bradley offered his proposal. Instead, Grey repeatedly proclaimed that he shared white southern men's opposition to miscegenation, though he wished it to be recognized in all forms. "It does seem strange to me that gentlemen oppose [amalgamation] only when it takes place in a legitimate form," Grey told the convention. "They make no opposi-tion to it when manifesting itself in an illegitimate form. They do not propose to punish anybody for illegitimate intercourse. Is that fair? . . . Surely the latter is just as vicious and harmful." He also sought, as in his initial retort to Bradley's plan, to place blame for "illegitimate intercourse" on white men and to establish for the record that his constituency was not responsible for "race mixing": "The census of the United States shows that forty per cent of us, already, have crossed the line. It is no fault of ours. No gentleman will lay it to our door. The intermixture has taken place illegitimately. Those gentlemen who so place themselves upon a pedestal of virtue, will not deny that this was wrong. Their own race has thus created the difficulty."[37] It was these critiques that were embodied in Hinds's compromise resolution declaring opposition to "all amalgamation . . . legitimate or illegitimate," which Grey and the other seven black delegates to the convention would ultimately endorse. Certainly, the resolution's call for future legislation in place of a constitutional ban preserved the constitution as a race-blind document, heeding Grey's forceful plea. But why would such legislation not have been viewed by Grey and others as having the same pernicious effects of reinscribing racial inequality as Bradley's original proposal did?

On the one hand, African American support for Hinds's resolution seems to have been perceived as a necessary compromise. The resolution offered a measure acceptable to most southern white men at the convention that also avoided corrupting with inevitably invidious racial distinctions the document on which citizenship in a postemancipation republic would be based. On the other hand, it protected black leaders and other Republicans from potentially damaging charges that they were promoting miscegenation. These charges threatened to split the pro-Reconstruction coalition at the convention. Approval of a constitution enfranchising all of the state's male citizens depended on the survival of this coalition.[38]

Statements made by other delegates in response to the proposed ban suggest that clear acknowledgment of the history of rape of black women by white men was also at stake for Grey and the other black men at the convention. Late in the debate, Robert Gantt, a leading white southern conservative delegate, conceded that sexual relations outside of marriage between white men and black women had occurred. But he implicitly attributed such relationships to black women's supposed lack of "virtue." "Whilst I sincerely and honestly believe that the virtuous and upright black woman should never consent to cohabit with a white man, such intercourse does take place," he said. "Affections may grow up between [black women and white men] . . . that would bring them together. But . . . I believe it would be better for both, and for the country at large, that the law should put its condemnation upon such marriages, even if it thus sacrifice an individual affection."[39] Gantt did not oppose the relationships themselves, and in fact argued that the law could do nothing to prevent them, but he did oppose legitimating them with marriage as too detrimental to "the country at large." He also implied that the desire and "affection" of those black women who were not "virtuous and upright" were at least equally responsible for these relationships as were white men.

A free-born black delegate named James T. White subsequently took the floor, claiming that he had been compelled to speak by such conservative insinuations: "I did not think that I would have anything to say upon this subject—that of amalgamation;—but the gentlemen on the other side of the house have forced me to say a few words." Responding both to the implications of Gantt's comments and to charges of black men's dishonorable conduct in matters of cross-racial sex, White declared, "Gentlemen, the shoe pinches on the other foot. The white men of the South have been for years indulging in illicit intercourse with colored women, and in the dark days of slavery this intercourse was in a great majority of cases forced upon the innocent victims; and I think the time has come when such a course should end."[40] White thus forcefully protested the long history of sexual exploitation of black women by white men, in essence calling it rape. And he turned charges of dishonorable manhood back onto white men, framing the question of preventing amalgamation as one of righting a past and extant wrong—the rape of black women by white men—rather than addressing a current and future possibility—newly empowered black men courting white women. Supporting Hinds's compromise condemning "all amalgamation" similarly allowed him and his colleagues to protest a long-silenced history of sexual violence and the hypocrisy of white men on the issue of cross-racial sex. This in turn affirmed honorable gender identities for black men and women, which were important signifiers of their worthiness for citizenship. In this way black delegates to Arkansas's constitutional convention were ultimately drawn into endorsing measures that affirmed that all racial mixture was detrimental to society and thus into hardening racial boundaries in the law in ways to which Grey had originally indicated he was opposed. The ambivalence that Grey must have felt about Hinds's resolution was evidently shared by another black delegate to the convention. Henry Rector, a twenty-two-year-old former slave, asked to abstain from voting on the part of the resolution that opposed all "amalgamation." When his request was denied, however, Rector joined the other black men in voting for the entire measure.[41] Working under extraordinary political constraints and facing multiple challenges, African American delegates to the Arkansas Constitutional Convention agreed to a compromise that achieved some of their aims while jeopardizing others.

On the other hand, black delegates' acceptance of the resolution may also reflect their own experimentation with the future meaning of race, and with the possibility of a social separation on equal footing as opposed to one implying inequality. Indeed, in this moment, they could perhaps hardly envisage a racially integrated domestic and social world of equality, all the more so in the face of white delegates' degrading representations of African Americans and their disavowals of the history of the rape of black women. Throughout, Grey himself had spoken in two different voices on the matter of legally prohibiting cross-racial sex. Provided that they were fairly and equitably imposed, restrictions on interracial sexual relationships may have been seen as offering some protection to black women and their communities from the inequities of what were likely to remain extramarital sexual relationships with white men and resultant "illegitimate" children. More broadly, the idea of drawing boundaries around black communities in general may have held certain appeal, if it could be done in such a way as to avoid representing African American manhood and womanhood as somehow less than that of whites. No doubt the black delegates at the convention would have preferred that racial separation in social life be voluntarily rather than legally established.[42] However, given the strategic utility of endorsing a legal—but not constitutional—prohibition, recommending future legislation was evidently not seen as too costly. Racial separatism in social and domestic life—but not public life—was not seen as inherently objectionable to these black leaders or irreconcilable with their visions of freedom.

In the days following the final vote on Hinds's compromise resolution, a constitution was drafted and approved by the convention and then one month later (narrowly) ratified by popular vote.[43] The new constitution extended suffrage to black men and contained no prohibition on interracial marriage.[44] Twenty-one white southern delegates to the convention opposed the final document—including Bradley, who called it a "damnable instrument of ruin that proposes to crush my race"—but they were outvoted.[45] In the early postemancipation years, opposition to social equality and interracial marriage—which responded to political more than visceral concerns for white men—was still far from hegemonic, inevitable, or uncontested. Alternative visions for racial organization were possible and even held sway.

And yet, simply by participating in debates over the constitutional ban on interracial marriage, white southern men helped establish a pernicious segregationist discourse that would gain ground in coming years, as political conditions shifted and federal support for full citizenship and suffrage for African American men waned. When the antebellum link between white manhood and an exclusive voice in the public sphere was severed by emancipation, some white southern men nonetheless fashioned a distinct, racially superior manhood for themselves through a rhetoric of miscegenation that drew on gender to signify race. This rhetoric sutured some of the tears in the antebellum political alliance between moderates (like Bradley) and conservatives (like Cypert) by promoting political identities as "white men." It also obliged black leaders to endorse problematic legislative action that legitimated legally enforced racial separation and had dangerous implications for extending segregation beyond the realm of sex and marriage. This rhetoric both helped lay the ideological groundwork for the establishment of Jim Crow and set the stage for decades to come in which African Americans would be forced to maneuver through a minefield of politicized gender discourses, identities, and violence as they struggled for equality.[46]

The discourse of miscegenation offers a window onto an important question for the comparative study of emancipation in the Atlantic world: the making of race and, specifically, gender's place in the formation of and contest over race and racism following the abolition of slavery. Postemancipation moments represent critical junctures in the histories of race, moments when competing visions were made explicit, and certain key trajectories—as well as potential alternatives—in forms of racism, racial meanings, and racial organization emerged. If we are to understand the similarities as well as the divergences between the postemancipation path ultimately followed in the United States—that of legally enforced racial separation and African American disfranchisement—and those taken elsewhere, it may well be useful to consider the various similar and divergent ways each was consolidated on gendered terrain.

Notes

I would like to thank Leora Auslander, Cynthia Blair, John Carson, George Chauncey, Matthew Countryman, Thomas Holt, Linda Kerber, James McIntosh, Pamela Scully, Carroll Smith-Rosenberg, and the participants in the American Culture Workshop at the University of Michigan for their comments on versions of this essay, and Richard Turits for his crucial contributions to its formulation and analysis.

1 The Reconstruction Acts applied to all former Confederate states except Tennessee.

2 *Debates and Proceedings of the Convention Which Assembled at Little Rock, January 7th, 1868, under the Provision of the Act of Congress of March 2d, 1867, and the Acts of March 23d and July 19th, 1867, Supplement thereto, to Form a Constitution for the State of Arkansas* (Little Rock: J. G. Price, 1868), 363, 365.

3 *Debates and Proceedings*, 363.

4 Ibid., 363, 371, 373, and *Weekly Arkansas Gazette*, 14 Jan. 1868, p. 2, col. 3, for reference to freedpeople observing the convention's proceedings.

5 *Debates and Proceedings*, 364. Bradley was mistaken; in 1860, black men voted equally with white men in five northern states, and, by 1868, this was the case in eight. He was no doubt referring to post–Civil War rejection of black male suffrage in other northern states. See Leon F. Litwack, *North of Slavery: The Negro in the Free States, 1790–1860* (Chicago: University of Chicago Press, 1961), 263; Eric Foner, *Reconstruction: America's Unfinished Revolution, 1863–1877* (New York: Harper and Row, 1988), 223, 448.

6 On the origin of the term *miscegenation*, see Sidney Kaplan, "The Miscegenation Issue in the Election of 1864," in *American Studies in Black and White: Selected Essays*, ed. Allan D. Austin (Amherst: University of Massachusetts Press, 1991), 47–100. See also Martha Hodes, *White Women, Black Men: Illicit Sex in the Nineteenth-Century South* (New Haven: Yale University Press, 1997), esp. 143–48, 151–54, 165–69, 171–74.

7 See also Hannah Rosen, "The Gender of Reconstruction: Rape, Race, and Citizenship in the Postemancipation South" (PhD diss., University of Chicago, 1999), chap. 4; Richard L. Hume, "The Arkansas Constitutional Convention of 1868: A Case Study in the Politics of Reconstruction," *Journal of Southern History* (1973): 191; Paul C. Palmer, "Miscegenation as an Issue in the Arkansas Constitutional Convention of

1868," *Arkansas Historical Quarterly* 24 (1965): 99–119; Peter Wallenstein, *Tell the Court I Love My Wife: Race, Marriage, and Law—An American History* (New York: Palgrove Mac-Millan, 2002), 62–63. For an overview of similar contests in other states, see Peter W. Bardaglio, " 'Shameful Matches': The Regulation of Interracial Sex and Marriage in the South before 1900," in *Sex, Love, Race: Crossing Boundaries in North American History*, ed. Martha Hodes (New York: New York University Press, 1999), 121–28.

8 Cal Ledbetter Jr., "The Constitution of 1836: A New Perspective," *Arkansas Historical Quarterly* 41 (1982): 215–52.

9 Carl H. Moneyhon, *The Impact of the Civil War and Reconstruction on Arkansas: Persistence in the Midst of Ruin* (Baton Rouge: Louisiana State University Press, 1994), 38–58.

10 Stephanie McCurry, *Masters of Small Worlds: Yeoman Households, Gender Relations, and the Political Culture of the Antebellum South Carolina Low Country* (New York: Oxford University Press, 1995).

11 See, e.g., Nancy F. Cott, "Marriage and Women's Citizenship in the United States, 1830–1934," *American Historical Review* 103 (1998): 1440–74; Laura F. Edwards, *Gendered Strife and Confusion: The Political Culture of Reconstruction* (Urbana: University of Illinois Press, 1997); Linda K. Kerber, "The Meanings of Citizenship," *Journal of American History* (1997): 833–54; Amy Dru Stanley, *From Bondage to Contract: Wage Labor, Marriage, and the Market in the Age of Slave Emancipation* (New York: Cambridge University Press, 1998).

12 See Carl H. Moneyhon, "Disloyalty and Class Consciousness in Southwestern Arkansas, 1862–1865," *Arkansas Historical Quarterly* 52 (1993): 223–43; Moneyhon, *Impact of the Civil War*, 101–23, 179.

13 On Arkansas, see Randy Finley, *From Slavery to Uncertain Freedom: The Freedmen's Bureau in Arkansas, 1865–1869* (Fayetteville: University of Arkansas Press, 1996); Hannah Rosen, "Gender of Reconstruction," chap. 3. See also Julie Saville, *The Work of Reconstruction: From Slave to Wage Laborer in South Carolina, 1860–1870* (New York: Cambridge University Press, 1994), esp. chap. 5; Elsa Barkley Brown, "To Catch the Vision of Freedom: Reconstructing Southern Black Women's Political History, 1865–1880," in *African American Women and the Vote, 1837–1965*, ed. Ann D. Gordon with Bettye Collier-Thomas, John H. Bracey, Arlene Voski Avakian, and Joyce Avrech Berkman (Amherst: University of Massachusetts Press, 1997), 66–99; and Brown, "Negotiating and Transforming the Public Sphere: African American Political Life in the Transition from Slavery to Freedom," *Public Culture* 7 (1994): 107–46.

14 *Debates and Proceedings*, 89, 91, 146, 152.

15 Joseph M. St. Hilaire, "The Negro Delegates in the Arkansas Constitutional Convention of 1868: A Group Profile," *Arkansas Historical Quarterly* 33 (1974): 38–39; Richard L. Hume, "The 'Black and Tan' Constitutional Conventions of 1867–1869 in Ten Former Confederate States: A Study of Their Membership" (PhD diss., University of Washington, 1969), 269–324; and Hume, "Arkansas Constitutional Convention of 1868," 185, 192–205.

16 *Debates and Proceedings*, 599.

17 Information on Bradley from *Weekly Arkansas Gazette*, 24 Sept. 1867, p. 1, cols. 3–4 and 21 Jan. 1868, p. 2, cols. 6–7; Hume, " 'Black and Tan,' " 307–8; Finley, *From Slavery to Uncertain Freedom*, 46; Thomas S. Staples, *Reconstruction in Arkansas: 1862– 1874* (Gloucester, Mass.: Peter Smith, 1964 [1923]).

18 *Debates and Proceedings*, 365; Arkansas, *Revised Statutes* (1838), 536; Staples, *Reconstruction*, 83–84.

19 Hume, " 'Black and Tan,' " 318; *Debates and Proceedings*, 363.

20 Hume, " 'Black and Tan,' " 318.

21 *Debates and Proceedings*, 489.

22 Ibid., 507.

23 Many may have feared, though, that future ratification of the Fourteenth Amendment would undermine existing laws. Reconstruction-era miscegenation laws were struck down in Alabama, Texas, and Louisiana on the grounds that they violated the equal protection clause. However, they were upheld in Georgia and reinstated throughout the South in the 1870s as subsequent courts decided they were not discriminatory. See Peggy Pascoe, "Miscegenation Law, Court Cases, and Ideologies of 'Race' in Twentieth-Century America," *Journal of American History* (1996): 50–51.

24 *Debates and Proceedings*, 364.

25 On the influence of Lamarckian theories on racial ideology in the United States, see, e.g., Gail Bederman, *Manliness and Civilization: A Cultural History of Gender and Race in the United States, 1880–1917* (Chicago: University of Chicago Press, 1995), 29, 92. Pascoe writes about nineteenth-century understandings of race, "the important point was not that biology determined culture (indeed, the split between the two was only dimly perceived), but that race, understood as an indivisible essence that included not only biology but also culture, morality, and intelligence, was a compellingly significant factor in history and society." Pascoe, "Miscegenation Law," 47–48.

26 *Debates and Proceedings*, 371, 365.

27 Ibid., 365. Bradley would repeatedly use the term *spheres* to describe the social segregation he envisioned, perhaps drawing on the presumed legitimacy of separation conveyed in the mid-nineteenth-century notion of "separate spheres" for men and women.

28 *Debates and Proceedings*, 370, 369, 490. See also Hodes, *White Women, Black Men*, 147, 157–59, 173–74, 199–200, 202.

29 See, e.g., Martha Hodes, *White Women, Black Men: Illicit Sex in the Nineteenth-Century South* (New Haven, Conn.: Yale University Press, 1997), 166; Nell Irvin Painter, " 'Social Equality,' Miscegenation, Labor, and Power," in *The Evolution of Southern Culture*, ed. Numan V. Bartley (Athens: University of Georgia Press, 1988), 47–67.

30 See Denise Riley, *"Am I That Name?" Feminism and the Category of "Women" in*

History, chap. 3; Leora Auslander, *Taste and Power: Furnishing Modern France* (Berkeley: University of California Press, 1996), 143–44, 185, 194, 212; Nancy Fraser, *Unruly Practices: Power, Discourse and Gender in Contemporary Social Theory* (Minneapolis: University of Minnesota Press, 1989), 156–58, 162 n32.

31 *Debates and Proceedings*, 494–95.

32 See Victoria E. Bynum, *Unruly Women: The Politics of Social and Sexual Control in the Old South* (Chapel Hill: University of North Carolina Press, 1992), 6–7; Hodes, *White Women*, 5; Diane Sommerville, "The Rape Myth Reconsidered: The Intersection of Race, Class, and Gender in the American South, 1800–1877" (PhD diss., Rutgers University, 1995).

33 St. Hilaire, "Negro Delegates," 43, 60–61; Hume, " 'Black and Tan,' " 321.

34 *Debates and Proceedings*, 493.

35 Ibid., 375, 492.

36 Ibid., 366.

37 Ibid., 498–99, 366. On similar responses of other black leaders, see, e.g., Hodes, *White Women, Black Men*, 145, 167–68.

38 Hume argues that Hinds "realized that the debate . . . had created serious divisions within the ranks of the assembly's 'reconstructionists' " and introduced his compromise resolution "to regain the support of the gathering's Southern whites" (" 'Black and Tan,' " 285–87).

39 *Debates and Proceedings*, 385, 388.

40 Ibid., 501.

41 Ibid., 507.

42 This sentiment was expressed by James W. Hood at North Carolina's Constitutional Convention, when he endorsed racial separation "whenever it is possible, not by written law, but by mutual consent and the law of interest." Quoted in Hume, " 'Black and Tan,' " 491, 683. See also Peter W. Bardaglio, *Reconstructing the Household: Families, Sex, and the Law in the Nineteenth-Century South* (Chapel Hill: University of North Carolina Press, 1995), 178.

43 Hume, " 'Black and Tan,' " 296.

44 Arkansas's Reconstruction-era legislators ignored the convention's recommendation that they design laws to "govern" amalgamation. Nonetheless, the 1838 statute was resurrected in 1884; Arkansas, *Digest of the Statutes* (1884), 911; Bardaglio, "Shameful Matches," 135 n62.

45 *Debates and Proceedings*, 656, 661.

46 See, e.g., Jacquelyn Dowd Hall, " 'The Mind That Burns in Each Body': Women, Rape, and Racial Violence," in *Powers of Desire: The Politics of Sexuality*, ed. Ann Snitow, Christine Stansell, and Sharon Thompson (New York: Monthly Review Press, 1983), 328–49; Glenda Elizabeth Gilmore, *Gender and Jim Crow: Women and the Politics of White Supremacy in North Carolina, 1896–1920* (Chapel Hill: University of North Carolina Press, 1996).

MAREK STEEDMAN

Gender and the Politics of the Household in Reconstruction Louisiana, 1865–1878

To the men who heard her testimony, Eliza Pinkston's wounds appeared to speak for themselves. From 20 November 1876, the Louisiana Returning Board had been holding hearings on various allegations of vote fraud, intimidation, and violence in the presidential and gubernatorial election held on 7 November of that year.[1] Charged with recording and deciding any controversies over the electoral returns sent in by parish supervisors of registration, the Returning Board had the power to throw out returns from entire parishes. The election had failed to produce a clear outcome at either the state or national level, and Louisiana was one of three states whose electoral votes would decide the presidency—putting the Returning Board in the eye of an intense political storm. As November slipped into December, the Returning Board listened to testimony and tried to determine whether the state's electoral votes should go to Republican Rutherford Hayes or Democrat Samuel Tilden. Turning to the returns from Ouachita Parish, located in the north of the state close to the Arkansas border, the Returning Board began to listen to Eliza Pinkston. Carried into the room on a chair, and attended by a nurse, Eliza recounted to the board the details of her rape, and the murder of her husband and baby, by a group of armed men on the night of 4 November. She was to tell and retell this story in the weeks ahead—to the Returning Board, in a court case she brought against two of her attackers, and to a committee of U.S. Senators who came to New Orleans to investigate the election in Louisiana. As she did so, she told not simply of a violent, and particularly brutal, attack. Eliza also spoke of her life with her husband Henry, of her relations with the white family on whose rented land Eliza and her husband had lived, and of the enormous pressures felt by freedpeople in the context of the violent termination of Reconstruction in Louisiana. Her testimony, I suggest, illuminates three propositions. First, that in defending the integrity of their households freedpeople were also aware of the social stakes involved in the proper performance of gender roles. Second, that southern white men perceived a threat to their own social standing in the ability of freedpeople to successfully assume these gender roles. Third, that the eclipse of the legal autonomy of the slave-owner household meant that these questions of household authority, race, and gender were directly implicated in, and in turn implicated, national electoral politics.

Eliza was "bred and born a slave in Canton, Mississippi."[2] At some point before the Civil War, she had been sold to a Colonel Morrison in Alabama. "At the surrender," Eliza was still "not big enough to work, no more than just to nurse a baby that was about a year old or two years old." Like many slave girls she had cared for young children (whether the baby of her master or of a slave woman she does not say) but "never worked until three years after the surrender." After the war, Eliza said, Charles Tidwell (she calls him "Master Charley"), a white farmer who rented land from Morrison, "bound me over to him until I was come to be of age." It is unclear precisely what Eliza meant to convey by this phrase—was her obligation to Tidwell legal, or merely social? If legal, did Tidwell have legal custody of Eliza, or was she somehow contractually bound to work for him? But perhaps it wasn't merely the words that were unclear—her relationship to the Tidwell family was from the start ambiguous, an unsettled halfway house between slavery and freedom. In any case, Eliza, who was probably about nine or ten years old, remained with the Tidwell family and was "raised up together" with Tidwell's son David "Sonny" Tidwell. Eliza told the committee of U.S. Senators that she and Sonny had been sexually intimate (had "taken up with each other") "since we was little children." Eliza indicated some ambivalence about this relationship (she "was getting big enough to know right from wrong," she said)—but Sonny "got so he did not want to twist or turn without" her. Charles Tidwell, Sonny's father, soon intervened and "runned Sonny off to school" saying that Sonny "would ruin his character" if the relationship continued. In 1870, after Sonny had been sent away and when Eliza was thirteen, Eliza married a schoolteacher named Adam Finch—but here again "Master Charlie" intervened, this time having Finch jailed for marrying an underage girl. In Eliza's words, "he had him bound over not to go with me till I came of age." When Adam Finch posted his own bond and was released from jail, however, Eliza began to meet him secretly. On the last day of September 1870, Eliza gave birth to a daughter, Ida. Adam Finch died soon after Ida's birth, seemingly of natural causes, and in 1872 the Tidwell family moved to Ouachita Parish, Louisiana. Eliza remained in Alabama working for Colonel Morrison. Morrison also owned land in Morehouse Parish, Louisiana, not far from Ouachita, and soon Eliza and some other laborers moved to this plantation. Not long after this Sonny's sister, who lived in Morehouse, told Sonny that Eliza was in Louisiana. According to Eliza, Sonny came to Morehouse and "stole me away at night," taking her to the Tidwell's rented farm in Ouachita.

By 1873 Eliza and Sonny were lovers again, now living in Ouachita, and Eliza gave birth to twin boys later in the year (both subsequently died). But Sonny would not marry her, and Eliza began to feel that she was "scorned" by other people "of my color." When Eliza met Henry Pinkston, who worked as a sharecropper on the land Tidwell rented, she decided to end her relationship with Sonny and marry Henry. Henry Pinkston had also been born a slave and apparently grew up in Ouachita parish. He had continued working as a laborer since the war, at one time working for Charles Tidwell to bring in his cotton crop. Sonny was determined that Eliza should not marry Henry, and threatened both of them until Henry moved across the river into Union Parish. Eliza soon joined Henry and they were married there by an itinerant preacher. Henry worked at a sawmill in Union Parish, but the Tidwells encouraged him to move back with Eliza and work as a sharecropper for them again.

Henry Pinkston was, by all accounts, not deeply involved in politics. But in the week before the November 1876 election even small actions could be threatening to Democrats, who sought complete control of Ouachita Parish, after eight years of Republican dominance. Henry had voted Democratic in 1874 and, perhaps regretting this, was determined to vote for the Republicans this time. This alone was sufficient to draw him to the attention of parish Democrats. The Democrats had organized armed militia "clubs" in Ouachita and other parishes, one of which Sonny Tidwell joined, and these groups were very active in the weeks leading up to the election. Riding around the parish, they threatened and intimidated acknowledged Republicans by day, and murdered, whipped, and assaulted them and their families by night. Eliza told the Senate committee investigating the election that in 1874 she threatened to "quit him" if Henry voted Democratic again, but she now argued that Henry was foolhardy to publicly support the Republicans. His attempts to attend Republican Party meetings and cheer on Republican speakers drew the attention of the group Sonny had joined and, Eliza told the senators, she had seen one of them "set [Henry's] name down."

On Saturday night, 4 November 1876, just a day after Eliza had observed the Democrats taking Henry's name down, the attack came. Woken by the sound of horses approaching the house, Eliza and Henry got out of bed. Almost immediately someone knocked on the door. Eliza tried to convince the men outside, who asked for Henry, that he was not at home. But somebody kicked in the door and a number of men rushed into the house. Sonny, according to Eliza, was not among them but she did recognize many who were there. Most were young white men, sons of local planters, lawyers, and farmers. There were also two "colored" men present—"old democrats" as Eliza called them. The men rushed into the house and grabbed Henry, gagging him with a handkerchief. Eliza tried to stop them but she was knocked aside with the butt of a pistol and lay stunned for some moments. The attackers mutilated Henry's body and castrated him before finally dragging him outside and shooting him several times. After they had killed Henry, the men came back into the house. One white man told Eliza to give him her baby, and when she refused, he slit its throat. The men then told Eliza to "take her rigging off" and marched her around the front room of her house, before two of the men raped her. They then shot her at least twice, leaving her for dead.[3]

But Eliza, though very seriously wounded, was not dead. Along with her daughter Ida, who had been hiding under the bed during the incident, she escaped into the fields before her attackers returned. Over the next two weeks Eliza hid in various places and slowly made her way to Monroe, the parish seat, where she told her story to a U.S. marshal. From Monroe, Eliza took a steamer down to New Orleans where she testified to the Returning Board, persuading them that the overwhelming vote for the Democrats in Ouachita parish should be thrown out. When she realized that two of her attackers had also made the journey to New Orleans, she immediately took her case to court, charging George Phillips, the son of a planter, and Tom Lyons, a "colored democrat," with the murder of her husband.[4]

Eliza's testimony was relayed to Washington by observers of the Returning Board's proceedings and was picked up by many northern papers, which found in it clear evidence of southern barbarity.[5] But Eliza revealed more than the details of her harrowing ordeal, and her testimony was almost unique in the voluminous congressional record from Louisiana, which centered on the increasingly violent election campaigns of the middle to late 1870s. Testimony from freedwomen rarely ran to more than a few pages, and was usually narrowly focused on events related to the election. Eliza Pinkston, by contrast, discussed her childhood, her relationship with Sonny and the Tidwell family, and her relationship with her husband Henry. As such her account, which runs to over a hundred pages, affords an unusually detailed look at the life of a rural Louisiana freedwoman in the decade following emancipation, and at the political conflict that engulfed her.

Law and Politics

Charles Tidwell, though he had apparently never owned slaves himself and did not own any land, had difficulty seeing Eliza Pinkston as a free person. Called by Democrats to testify against Eliza Pinkston before the Louisiana Returning Board, he was cross-examined by J. Madison Wells, the board's Republican president. Though Wells was now a Republican he had been governor of the state between 1865 and 1868, before people of African descent exercised the vote in Louisiana. During this period the planter-dominated legislature had reacted to emancipation by passing a series of laws known as the "Black Code" because they were directed at sharply constraining the rights of freed-people through mandated labor contracts, vagrancy laws, and similar provisions.[6] When Wells asked Charles Tidwell how Eliza came to Alabama, then, it is perhaps not surprising that they shared a common language:

> WELLS: How did she come from Alabama?
> TIDWELL: Colonel Morrison imported her to the State.
> WELLS: He imported her with laborers he was bringing over?
> TIDWELL: Yes. She lived on his plantation in Gum Swamp, Alabama; in that neighborhood.[7]

Except that we know this conversation took place in 1876, these men could have been talking about slaves. It is not just that Eliza's agency disappeared from view as they talked—we cannot tell how she felt about making the trip to Louisiana, or whom she might have left behind—the terminology used was more specific than that. Eliza was simply a laborer, belonging to a particular planter, who might be transported or "imported" along with other laborers according to the needs of that planter.

In continuing to think of freedpeople as primarily a labor force under the control of white planters and farmers, Charles Tidwell was also continuing to think about his own authority over Eliza in patriarchal terms. Examining legal decisions in southern courts in the years before the Civil War, Peter Bardaglio argues that southern elites saw the antebellum household as a patriarchal structure that mediated the relation between the governed and institutions of governance. Political rights, on this view, were vested in male heads of households who both exercised authority over a discrete set of dependents and acted as the legal representative of those dependents. In antebellum court decisions, the legal person of the male head of household was invested with familial authority, control of property, and the exercise of legal rights. In Louisiana and elsewhere, even wage laborers fell under the household authority of their employers. Control over production and reproduction, as well as the exercise of legal and political rights, were thus legally structured through relations of dependence within the household. This conception implied that "the state supported the family in the person of its male head, and state power flowed through the network of patriarchs who ruled over their households," while "subordinate members of the household, according to this ideal, were connected to the state only through the patriarch."[8] This view, while perhaps never wholly accurate, informed state Supreme Court decisions throughout the South and, in Louisiana, also shaped the Civil Code and statute law. It also informed the everyday understandings of many white southerners, particularly planters who saw themselves as patriarchs.

In terms of codified law, emancipation and Reconstruction in Louisiana did not alter this basic framework. In the main the Revised Code of 1870 retained intact those articles that established the authority of the head of household over familial dependents. More surprisingly, given that Republicans were largely responsible for this revision, the Code also retained provisions that established this authority over economic dependents. Wage laborers were, as they had been before the war, classed as a form of "free servant."[9] Louisiana law, like that of other southern states, continued to locate control of both production and reproduction in the "private dominion" of male heads of households.[10] Court decisions which affirmed that sharecropping itself was a wage-labor relationship, and not a form of partnership, therefore pointed to unresolved questions about the social status of freedpeople.[11]

In the decade after the war, former slaves and former masters struggled to find a new modus vivendi based on their own answers to those questions. But while freedpeople sought increased autonomy in their daily lives, planters were determined to retain as much control as possible. One indication of this was the "Black Code" laws themselves, which not only required freedpeople to contract as laborers, but also specified the duration of those contracts and the time of year when they should be made, as well as forbidding laborers from leaving a contract with one planter in order to make another. They also established vagrancy provisions that could be used against freedmen who did not enter into labor contracts. This created a labor system based on wages, but one closer to southern planters' views of wage labor than to "free labor." [12] In the eyes of most Republicans, it was simply an attempt to reimpose slavery.[13]

But in fact, however much this system was intended by legislators to create mechanisms for planters to control their labor, it was importantly different from slavery. For while the legal structure of the antebellum household had been intended to contain relations of production (and reproduction) by placing them under the authority of the white planter, the "Black Code" recognized the new relation between landowner and laborer as a contractual one. As such it opened the way for questions of the relative rights and obligations of each party to be resolved in court, and not by planters. This in itself entailed a role for the state in the resolution of conflicts which would previously have been left to the planter's discretion.

The Reconstruction Acts passed by the U.S. Congress ended this particular attempt to preempt a struggle between landowners and laborers, between former patriarchs and dependents. Of course, nothing in the Reconstruction Acts, or in the amended U.S. Constitution, determined the outcome of this struggle. But insofar as the national state had embarked on the project of ensuring civil, and then political, rights to freedpeople, violence directed against them had ceased to be merely a private concern of planters (to the extent that it had ever been). It was now a matter for congressional investigation, federal-level legal intervention, court cases, front-page news in Chicago, Boston, and New York, and party political campaigns. In this sense (and perhaps in this sense only) the Reconstruction Acts had in fact deepened the logic of the "Black Codes": the state was now directly involved in regulating the previously private relations among former masters and former slaves.

The Politics of Gender

Eliza Pinkston was often caught in the middle of this ongoing struggle, as Charles Tidwell and other employers continued to try to exercise control over the time and resources of freedpeople. In the week before the 1876 election, Charles Tidwell pressured Henry Pinkston to attend Democratic Party meetings, or "speakings," as they were called, and to bring Eliza with him.[14] On 1 November, Charles Tidwell came to Henry while he was at work in his fields. Eliza described the encounter for the U.S. senators:

> Mr. Tidwell says, "Come Henry; come out to Grady's school-house today to the speakin'." Henry said, "Mr. Tidwell I hain't got time; I want to make a living for my family. Lize is a fine woman, and always wants to be dressy, and I hain't got time."

Charles Tidwell then offered to pay Henry two dollars for the day if he would go to the meeting, saying, "You and Lize don't make but two dollars a day." Eliza was in fact already getting ready to go. "I was done already dressed up and at the quarters waiting to get in my wagon," she said, "I was in the wagon, and Henry made me get out. I commenced snuffing like I was going to cry." At this Charles Tidwell lost his temper, yelling, "I'll be damned if she shan't go. I can make her go. Come and get a flask and get a quart of whiskey, and let us go." But, according to Eliza, "Henry said, 'I don't drink whiskey, I don't want no whiskey. I don't want to go.' [Charles] says, 'Come on; you had better go. If you know what is good for yourself you had better go.' Henry said, 'Well, I will go.' "[15]

One can characterize this encounter as a struggle of wills between two men, each of whom was trying to exert authority over a woman he saw as his dependent. On this reading, Charles Tidwell "won." And, indeed, for both men Eliza was central. Henry invoked his role as male head of household, explaining that he needed to support Eliza's desire to be a "fine woman." Perhaps by cavalierly offering a full day's wages, Charles Tidwell was attempting to belittle this role—obviously he was better placed than Henry to provide for Eliza. Certainly Henry's assertion of authority over Eliza was maddening to the man who had raised her—when Henry told Eliza to get out of the wagon Charles Tidwell exploded with anger, declaring that he could "make" her go to the meeting.

But while Eliza was central to the two men involved, reading this as a simple battle of wills which Charles Tidwell won is insufficient. First, Charles Tidwell's frustration when Eliza got out of the wagon came after a series of failed attempts to influence Henry. He was unable to use his economic position, either as employer or as provider of whiskey and other articles to sharecroppers. Charles Tidwell in fact misunderstood himself as supporting the Pinkstons economically. This was made clear by his reaction when Henry left the Democratic meeting early. Henry Pinkston did not stay at the meeting long, telling Eliza that the music being played there was "nothing but to entice me back to slavery," and returned to his fields. Charles Tidwell was furious— hurling abuse at Henry, he shouted, "You is a God damned, thieving, sly, undermining God damned son of a bitch, and you won't get no more meat out of my smokehouse." But Henry quickly reminded him, "Mr. Tidwell, you don't give me no meat. I works for all I gets. I pays you for every pound of meats, every spoonful of meats I gets. . . . you never been the gentleman to give me anything but a quart of whiskey, and that's only when I started to the meeting to please you."[16] To which Charles Tidwell responded, rather lamely, "No, God damn you; you'll never get another mouthful from me." Henry was aware that wage labor was not simply an extension of slavery—while legally a dependent, Henry could successfully thwart Tidwell's exercise of authority to the degree that he could exercise economic control over his own resources.[17]

Reading this encounter as a clash between Henry and Charles also obscures Eliza's experience. It is not simply that we fail to see Eliza's agency—but rather that we misconstrue her agency. For it is clear that Eliza wanted to go to the Democratic meeting. She got dressed and ready to go, even while Henry was insisting that they would not go. And when Henry told her to get out of the wagon she "commenced snuffing" in apparent protest. At the same time, Eliza's language here suggests that in part she is concerned with acting, and especially dressing, in an appropriate way. Eliza puts the words into Henry's mouth, but there is no reason to doubt that she did indeed wish to be, and appear to be, "dressy." This suggests, further, that it would be wrong simply to note that the transition from the slave household to legal marriage entailed, for freedwomen, a shift in the terms of their subordination to men (though doubtless it was this as well).[18] For Eliza the ability to act out the role of a "fine woman" was itself a way of securing a higher social status.

The next day, 2 November, was to be the Republican speaking. Henry and Eliza set out for the speaking, but as they were leaving they ran into a group of about thirty or forty white men—"young Tidwell and all of them." Telling Henry, "There ain't going to be a speakin here today," they tried to get both Henry and Eliza to go back home. When Henry insisted on going on, Sonny called Eliza over to him: "Sonny Tidwell says, 'Come here, Lize.' Henry didn't speak but looked at me. He gave me the eye like so (imitating with a movement of her eyes), and I didn't know whether to go or not. At last I said, 'What must I do, go to Sonny, or go on?' " Henry was unequivocal: "He says, 'Come on here.' He had the baby, and he taken me by the shoulders and snatched me around plumb to go on."

Like his father on the previous day, Sonny was furious at Henry's assertion of authority over Eliza. "Sonny says, 'Hold on, God damn you. When I call her she's got to come. That's the rule of this parish, by God. Come here to me.' I went to him."[19] The parish, like Louisiana as a whole, had been under Republican control for the past eight years, and it is highly unlikely that there was any formal rule of this kind.[20] But Sonny was not invoking the letter of the law. Instead his "rule" was simply a condensed version of a conception of authority that still drew, for its sense, on the ideal boundaries of the antebellum household. The structure of this encounter was quite similar to that of the previous day—and again it seems that Sonny "won." But in Eliza's telling of the story, Sonny's anger burst out at precisely the same point as his father's—when Henry asserted authority over Eliza. Sonny's frustration again indicates a presumption of authority, and a certain failure to exercise it successfully.

Understanding Eliza Pinkston's actions in these scenes, however, requires seeing the complicated relationship she had to these men. The white men involved were men she had been raised by, or raised with, one of whom she had had a sexual relationship with. The point is not to suggest that Eliza had split loyalties, but rather that each of these encounters was shaped by the personal relationships she had developed with all the men involved, and by what those relationships meant to each one. Asked by a member of the Senate investigating committee if she and Sonny had lived together "as man and wife," Eliza replied that they "lived like black wimens and white mans usually take up with each other." Eliza went on, "I never was sot up as a mistress, I worked; but when nighttime came I done duty too."[21] Eliza and Sonny had had a sexual relationship while still children in Alabama, and this had continued when Sonny learned that Eliza had also moved to Louisiana. Indeed, Sonny was the father of twins whom Eliza gave birth to a year before she married Henry, though both subsequently died. But Eliza clearly understood that she was neither Sonny's mistress nor his future wife. When Eliza met Henry Pinkston, therefore, she decided to end the relationship with Sonny and marry Henry. Sonny opposed this marriage and tried to convince her that she was better off with him. "He always told me that I was doing well there with him and his pa," Eliza said, "that I got everything I wanted to eat and to drink and to wear." But this did not convince Eliza. She explained, "People looked on me with such scorn, no matter if I was well dressed. Wherever I would go they would say, 'That's David Tidwell's piece.' " Eliza understood that the reason for this was Sonny's refusal to marry her. "I could not be called 'Mrs. Tidwell' it was always 'Eliza Finch.' " But after her marriage to Henry Pinkston, her standing in the community changed, "After I married my color I went everywhere, and I had a name."[22]

Sonny did not see his relationship with Eliza as equivalent to marriage. Although opposition to "social equality" among white southerners was apparently motivated by fear of racial "mixing" or "miscegenation," this fear was itself modulated by the assumption of continued patriarchal authority over freedwomen.[23] Sonny provided Eliza with "everything [she] wanted to eat and to drink and to wear" and he expected Eliza to sleep with him. To Sonny the relationship was not similar to a marriage, and it did not require legal ratification. Instead, it was the exercise of the same prerogative his father had exercised—to sexual relations with women who were his economic dependents. Epsy, possibly the sister who told Sonny that Eliza was in Louisiana, was "the daughter of [Charles] Tidwell that he had with a black woman," and Sonny was well aware this—indeed according to Eliza he called Epsy "sister."[24]

Sonny grew up in a household in which his father had claimed sexual access to black women, and he intended to live in the same way. Sonny himself planned to marry in March of 1877; he did not see his relationship with Eliza as an obstacle to that marriage but rather as a prerogative, another "rule" of the parish. "Look at the thousands of colored women who has got white men and who is glad to get them," he told Eliza.[25] By implication, Eliza should be equally "glad" to "get" Sonny.

It is not completely clear that Eliza wanted to marry Sonny, but it is clear that she felt considerable social pressure on account of her relationship with him. As Eliza had once tried to explain to Sonny, "my color didn't look on me with honor." Sonny hoped to convince Eliza that he could provide for her in a way that Henry never could. But, Eliza told him, "that was not it; that I was looking on principle, and I wanted people to say Mrs. something else besides Eliza Finch."[26] To be called "Eliza Finch," she said, "didn't sound pretty, and it didn't look upright and honest." Freedpeople looked with "scorn" on a relationship that reproduced the structure of those between antebellum planters and slave women. Rather than simple opposition to "race mixing," freedpeople looked down on relationships that reproduced race as a relation of dependence. When Eliza decided she agreed, Sonny tried to prevent her from marrying Henry, and his threats forced Henry to go to neighboring Union Parish, where Eliza joined him.

If for Sonny his relationship with Eliza was an exercise of prerogative, Eliza saw her marriage to Henry as a way of achieving "honor." For Eliza this was a clear move out of the world of the white tenant farmers with whom she had grown up, and into the world of the black community. But Eliza's relationship with the Tidwells continued to be a source of friction—which the election contest, proving as it did that Eliza was more comfortable than Henry among white Democrats, only served to heighten. When Henry left the Democratic meeting Eliza stayed, and Henry chided her, "You are ignorant; you stay and enjoy yourself, and eat dinner if you want to and come on home when you get through." That Eliza might be able to enjoy listening to music and eating at a Democratic meeting was only a reminder to Henry of her closer connection to that world.

Perhaps as a result, Henry often cast disputes over whether to go to Republican and Democratic meetings in terms of Eliza's obligations as his wife. Eliza herself reiterated these obligations to the Senate investigating committee. Asked whether she lived with Henry, she replied, "you know wherever Henry stay, of course, if I am his wife I am there too. I always put him in the head." And though they both worked in the fields, at the end of the day, Eliza said, she left before Henry and "got dinner and fixed things up for him." But in practice Eliza did not always put Henry in the head—as when she got dressed and ready to go to the Democratic meeting while Henry was determined not to go.

Eliza had initially refused to go to the 2 November Republican meeting, but Henry insisted: "Says he, 'You must go. If you call yourself a wife of mine, you've got to go. You was anxious to go yonder the other day, and you shall be anxious today.'" Henry invoked his authority as husband and also reminded Eliza of her challenge to that authority the day before, but Eliza argued that Henry was being foolhardy: "'O, Henry, you called me ignorant, but you are the ignorant one.' Says I, 'The white folks are watching you. You see everyone is gone democratic on this river, that is bigger men than you is, and smarter men than you is, and they has done it to save their lives, and it seems like you don't care no more for your life than you do for a rabbit's life.'" Eliza, whatever her own politics, had no illusions about the realities of the dangers Henry was running. But Henry probably saw his political participation, as well as his authority over Eliza, as integral to his masculinity. Like many black men in Reconstruction, Henry connected his political rights to his manhood, and so the issue was not simply his own personal safety but his status. As Henry put it, "I is not a man having a thing in him without speaking of it out. I will go yonder if I get killed."[27] And this exchange suggests that Henry saw a connection between this status and his authority over Eliza, "He says, 'Then you want to part this morning?' Says I, 'No, I don't. I loves you and I loves you with all my heart.' Says he, 'Well, fix up and go to that speakin'.'"[28] For Henry, therefore, the marriage itself was at stake in Eliza's refusal to go to the Republican speaking.

Eliza's realization that many people, white and black, were turning to the Democrats out of fear suggests that perhaps this was all that motivated her in the altercations she described. Perhaps she simply saw, rightly, that force was on the side of the white men. But though this was undoubtedly part of the story, her experience was more complicated than this. On 3 November, a Republican meeting finally took place. Again, Henry was determined to go, and again Eliza initially refused: "Henry said, 'Fix yourself and come on and go.' I said, 'Oh no, I can't.' He said, 'Fix yourself and I am going to carry you. You don't believe and I want you to go and hear for yourself.'" Henry, then, was aware that Eliza was not convinced by the political message of the Republicans. Eliza was not simply a radical Republican who was intimidated into supporting the Democrats. Instead she was genuinely conflicted. Going to the meeting did not obviously convince her to publicly support the Republicans. When "the damn lie was given," as Eliza put it, and Henry began to cheer, Eliza noticed the white Democrats take Henry's name down and she "dashed off from him and didn't go no more to him."[29] Her connections to the Tidwells led her both to a clear-sighted view of the violent threat white men posed to freedpeople and to rely on some of those white men nonetheless. Thus, after the attack on her family, Eliza immediately went to Charles Tidwell's house for help—though it appears that he did very little, and very possibly alerted the armed men to her presence there.[30]

The attack itself had been carried out by local men (two of whom were described by Eliza as "colored"), and Eliza recognized and could name many of them. As Jacqueline Jones suggests, such violence was often personal, "carried out face-to-face by men who knew their victims and their families."[31] In this instance many were friends and acquaintances of the Tidwell family, whom Eliza had seen drinking and dining in the Tidwell house. They tended to be in their mid- to late twenties and were sons of local notables. A Democratic report to the U.S. House described them as "among the first young men of the parish, moving in the best circles of society."[32] Organized into "militia companies" in the early to mid-1870s, they had set about "regulating," as they put it, the local community.

The sheer brutality of the attack produced shocked comments from even Democratic observers of the Returning Board's proceedings.[33] But the violence was quite different from other, equally brutal, forms of racial violence. Lynchings, for example, which began to be almost bimonthly events in some Louisiana communities in the 1890s and early twentieth century, were usually targeted specifically at black men. Further, in contrast to the attacks of the 1870s, lynchings were generally public and ritualistic, involving whole communities of white spectators. So-called militia groups, on the other hand, generally carried out attacks—like the one on Henry and Eliza Pinkston—on horseback, at night, and in the homes of freedpeople.[34]

The attack on Henry and Eliza was specifically directed at their physical integrity—both their bodies and their house. The men burst in through the door of the Pinkston's home and immediately began mutilating Henry's body. Castrating him was part of this—but they also cut him elsewhere and broke his ribs. Similarly, two men raped Eliza, violating her sexually, but also they broke her skull, cut a long gash in her thigh, and cut the Achilles tendon of one ankle. This mutilation seems "gratuitous" if we see the violence as simply aimed at intimidating voters—as does the murder of Eliza and Henry's baby. But the men were not simply attacking Henry and Eliza as individuals, or as Republicans—they were attacking the ability of freedpeople to establish independent households, protect their own bodies, and control their own reproduction. While apparently senseless violence, the attack on Eliza and Henry involved attacking potent, and specific, symbols of autonomy for freedpeople. One of the worlds Eliza had inhabited was bent on annihilating the other.

Unhealed Wounds

Violence and cruelty were hardly new to the dynamic between southern land-owners (or tenants) and the people who actually worked the land. As Elizabeth Fox-Genovese puts it, in the experience of slave women, "random cruelty and violence were part of what whites did—part of what they were."[35] What had changed was the reaction of the state to such violence. Where before courts and legislatures had sought to contain violence against slaves within the pa-triarchal household, violence against freedpeople now represented a threat to public order and had not merely local but national implications.[36] Of course Eliza Pinkston's case was singular—her determination to tell her story, and to name the men involved, made it impossible to ignore the story she had to tell. But the numerous congressional committees that gathered testimony throughout the middle 1870s attest to the importance attached to this violence following the Reconstruction amendments to the U.S. Constitution.

The implications for freedpeople were mixed: this also made freedpeople vulnerable to fluctuations in the national mood, and, in the absence of federal oversight, to the indifference or active hostility of state governments. But, in principle, extension of political and civil rights to freedpeople had made vio-lence against them a public matter, opening the door for increased state regulation of everyday rural life but also providing freedmen and freedwomen with new resources. Eliza Pinkston could now take the stand and testify against white men, bringing a court case against them and thwarting their political ambitions, if only temporarily. Similarly, Eliza Pinkston and other freedwomen participated actively in political life throughout the 1870s—at-tending political meetings, discussing and arguing about politics with their husbands, even joining them at the polls on Election Day. Within and without the black community, freedwomen gave voice to their political demands.[37]

At the same time, the violence that became such a focus of national atten-tion was itself sparked by a partisan conflict shaped by social hierarchies of gender and race. The exchanges described in this chapter, among Charles Tidwell, Henry, and Eliza, among Sonny Tidwell, Henry, and Eliza, or between Henry and Eliza themselves, imbued partisan conflict with gendered and racial stakes. Part of what fueled the violence of this period was the specific chal-lenge white Democrats saw in the assertion by freedpeople of gender roles appropriate to freely contracted marriage, as well as of a political independence incompatible with their presumed legal dependence as laborers. National politics rarely reflected these social stakes—but through the violence of local partisan conflict, in the context of the new legal status of freedpeople, it was swept into the fray.

The stakes for freedwomen like Eliza Pinkston were very high. Eliza's desire to be a "fine woman" was painfully undermined in the course of the hearings in which she testified. A series of character witnesses testified that Eliza would have sex with any man, that she raised her skirts above her waist in public, that she often fought and had a violent temper. A House committee concluded Eliza was "ugly, vulgar, indecent and lewd beyond the worst."[38] There is no need to claim that all of these character witnesses were lying, though some clearly were. Eliza Pinkston's enemies knew that credibility was generally established through one's standing in the community—and that hierarchies of race, class, and gender made any freedwoman's standing suspect. Eliza, indeed, never returned to Ouachita Parish. Instead she went back to Canton, Mississippi, where she had been born. Though she perhaps married again, she got no peace in Canton—she was arrested in March 1883 for "petty larceny and assault and battery." Eliza Pinkston died in jail a month later—at the age of twenty-six.[39]

Notes

I would like to thank Charlene Allen, Dan Carpenter, Khristina Haddad, Don Herzog, Ryan Hudson, Harwood McClerking, Brian McKenzie, Diana Paton, Tasha Philpot, Rebecca Scott, Pamela Scully, Joan Sitomer, Lester Spence, Jackie Stevens, Elizabeth Wingrove, and the anonymous reviewer for Duke University Press, for invaluable comments on earlier drafts.

1 For Democratic and Republican reports of the Louisiana Returning Board's proceedings, see U.S. Congress, Senate, *Memorial on Counting Vote of People of Louisiana for the Appointment of Presidential Electors, November 7, 1876*, 44th Cong., 2d sess., Senate Miscellaneous Document no. 14, Washington, D.C., U.S. G.P.O., 1877; and U.S. Congress, Senate, *Message of President Accompanied by Testimony, from John Sherman and Others, on Canvass of Vote for Electors in Louisiana*, 44th Cong., 2d sess., Senate Executive Document no. 2, Washington, D.C., U.S. G.P.O., 1877, respectively.

2 U.S. Congress, Senate, *Denial of Elective Franchise in Louisiana at Election of November 7, 1876*, vol. 2, 44th Cong., 2d sess., Senate Report (hereafter SR) 701, part 2, 909–87, Washington, D.C., U.S. G.P.O., 1877, Testimony of Eliza Pinkston. The description that follows comes from that testimony.

3 Democrats disputed her account. Nevertheless, even historians generally sympathetic to the Democrats have found her credible. For Democratic testimony, see, e.g., SR 701, 517–36; and U.S. Congress, House, *Denial of Elective Franchise in Louisiana at Election of November 7, 1876*, 44th Cong., 2d sess., House Report (hereafter HR) 156, 44–46, Washington, D.C., U.S. G.P.O., 1877. For previous historiography mentioning the Pinkstons, see Ella Lonn, *Reconstruction in Louisiana after 1868* (New York: G. Putnam and Sons, 1918), 433–35; Paul Leland Haworth, *The Hayes-Tilden Disputed Presidential Election of 1876* (Cleveland: Burrows Brothers, 1906), 105–8; and Ted Tunnell, "The Negro, the Republican Party, and the Election of 1876 in Louisiana," in *Louisiana History* 7, no. 2 (1966): 104–5n. I have found no later treatments of this case.

4 A partial transcript is reproduced in SR 701, 961–77.

5 See, e.g., *New York Times*, 29 Nov. and 30 Nov. 1876.

6 Joe Gray Taylor, *Louisiana Reconstructed, 1863–1877* (Baton Rouge: Louisiana State University Press, 1974), 58. Wells was a Unionist, not a Democrat.

7 Senate Ex. Doc. no. 2, 120.

8 Peter W. Bardaglio, *Reconstructing the Household: Families, Sex, and the Law in the Nineteenth-Century South* (Chapel Hill: University of North Carolina Press, 1995), 24–29. See also Elizabeth Fox-Genovese, *Within the Plantation Household: Black and White Women of the Old South* (Chapel Hill: University of North Carolina Press, 1988); and James Oakes, *Slavery and Freedom: An Interpretation of the Old South* (New York: Alfred A. Knopf, 1990). On the gap between the authority accorded heads of households in law and its exercise in practice, see Laura F. Edwards, "Law, Domestic Violence, and the Limits of Patriarchal Authority in the Antebellum South," in *Gender and the Southern Body Politic*, ed. Nancy Bercaw (Jackson: University Press of Mississippi, 2000), 63–86.

9 *Revised Civil Code of the State of Louisiana* (New Orleans, n.p.: 1870), 4, 22. See also Title 6, chap. 5, "Of the Respective Rights and Duties of Married Persons," and Title 7, "Of Father and Child." Cf. *Civil Code of the State of Louisiana with the Statutory Amendments from 1825 to 1866 Inclusive*, ed. James O. Fuqua (New Orleans: B. Bloomfield, 1867 [1825]), 24, 29–33.

10 Laura F. Edwards, *Gendered Strife and Confusion: The Political Culture of Reconstruction* (Urbana: University of Illinois Press, 1997).

11 On the distinction between sharecropping and tenancy, see Harold Woodman, *New South—New Law: The Legal Foundations of Credit and Labor Relations in the Postbellum Agricultural South* (Baton Rouge: Louisiana State University Press, 1995), 68–69 and 76–77.

12 On the transition from slavery to free labor, see Ira Berlin, Barbara J. Fields, Steven F. Miller, Joseph P. Reidy, and Leslie S. Rowland, *Slaves No More: Three Essays on Emancipation and the Civil War* (Cambridge: Cambridge University Press, 1992). For Louisiana, see Paul Eiss, "A Share in the Land: Freedpeople and the Government of Labour in Southern Louisiana, 1862–1865," *Slavery and Abolition* 19, no. 1 (April

1998): 46–89; C. Peter Ripley, *Slaves and Freedmen in Civil War Louisiana* (Baton Rouge: Louisiana State University Press, 1974), chap. 8, esp. 153–59; Ronald L. F. Davis, *Good and Faithful Labor: From Slavery to Sharecropping in the Natchez District, 1860–1890* (Westport, Conn.: Greenwood, 1982), 63ff.; and Noralee Frankel, *Freedom's Women: Black Women and Families in Civil War Era Mississippi* (Bloomington: Indiana University Press, 1999).

13 Taylor, *Louisiana Reconstructed*, 99–103.

14 These events combined music, barbeques, and partisan speeches, and were thrown by both political parties. See Lonn, *Reconstruction in Louisiana*, 419–20.

15 SR 701, 915–16.

16 Ibid., 916.

17 Of course, the power of Henry's position partly depended on his ability to exercise meaningful choice: if there were no other merchants from whom Henry could buy his provisions, then his options were rather limited.

18 I do not intend to commit Carole Pateman to the position described here, but for the argument that contractual marriage is, necessarily, a form of patriarchal control of women, see her *The Sexual Contract* (Oxford, U.K.: Polity, 1988).

19 SR 701, 917.

20 *Report from the Subcommittee on Privileges and Elections of the U.S. Senate*, in SR 701, vol. 1, part 1, ix–x. The parish went Republican in 1868.

21 SR 701, 932.

22 Ibid., 937.

23 For a particularly insightful treatment of the "discourse of miscegenation" in this period, see Hannah Rosen's essay in this volume.

24 SR 701, 933.

25 Ibid., 937.

26 Ibid.

27 Ibid., 918. See also Martha Hodes, *White Women, Black Men: Illicit Sex in the Nineteenth-Century South* (New Haven, Conn.: Yale University Press, 1997), 167; and Edwards, *Gendered Strife and Confusion*.

28 SR 701, 916.

29 Ibid., 918. The phrase "giving the damn lie" generally referred to Republican claims that the Democrats sought to revive slavery.

30 Senate Exec. Doc. no. 2, 119–20.

31 Jacqueline Jones, *Labor of Love, Labor of Sorrow: Black Women, Work and the Family from Slavery to the Present* (New York: Vintage, 1995), 71–72. See also Dorothy Sterling, ed., *We Are Your Sisters: Black Women in the Nineteenth Century* (New York: W. W. Norton, 1984); and Nell Painter, *Exodusters: Black Migration to Kansas after Reconstruction* (New York: Alfred A. Knopf, 1977), 97.

32 HR 156, 45.

33 See *New York Times*, 29 Nov.; but see also Lonn, *Reconstruction in Louisiana*, 434n.

34 Hodes, *White Women, Black Men*, 176. Hodes compares lynchings to Klan violence. In Louisiana, the men were rarely disguised.

35 Fox-Genovese, *Within the Plantation Household*, 154.

36 Hodes, *White Women, Black Men*, esp. chap. 7.

37 Elsa Barkley Brown, "To Catch the Vision of Freedom: Reconstructing Southern Black Women's Political History, 1865–1880," in *African American Women and the Vote, 1837–1965*, ed. Ann D. Gordon et al. (Amherst: University of Massachusetts Press, 1997), 66–87. In 1875, the Louisiana Republican party created Councils of Freedom in which women were nonvoting members. See also Julie Saville, "Rites and Power: Reflections on Slavery, Freedom and Political Ritual," *Slavery and Abolition* 20, no. 1 (April 1999), 81–102.

38 HR 156, 45.

39 *Ouachita Telegraph*, 1 June 1877; *Canton Picket*, 24 March, 21 April 1883. Thanks to Jennifer A. Smith, branch coordinator/genealogy librarian, Madison County Library System, Madison County, Miss., for locating the *Picket* articles. See also *New York Times*, 26 April 1883. One of the men Eliza accused of raping her became sheriff of Ouachita Parish in 1878; *Louisiana State Commission Books*, reel no. 2.003, Nov. 1876–May 1884, Louisiana State Archives, Baton Rouge.

🪷 DIANA PATON

Bibliographic Essay

This essay provides a selective guide to the historiography on slavery, slave emancipation, postemancipation societies, and abolitionism insofar as the scholarship attends to women, gender, and/or masculinity. Some nongendered material on slave emancipation and postemancipation societies is also included, especially where it has been particularly influential or in areas where little work has been done that explicitly focuses on gender. We generally have not included quantitative studies of the slave trade, population structure, or manumission patterns even though these typically cover such topics as sex ratios and differential access to manumission, except where these are integrated into larger analyses of slavery/emancipation and gender, nor have we included published versions of primary sources such as letters, diaries, and memoirs. We have included work in English, French, Spanish, and Portuguese, while emphasizing English-language material. Further references may be found in a series of bibliographies produced by Joseph C. Miller which, while not specifically focusing on gender or emancipation, include material on both: *Slavery: A Worldwide Bibliography, 1900–1982* (White Plains, N.Y.: Kraus International, 1985); *Slavery and Slaving in World History: A Bibliography, 1900–1991* (Millwood, N.Y.: Kraus International, 1993); *Slavery and Slaving in World History: A Bibliography* (Armonk, N.Y.: M. E. Sharpe, 1999); and the annual updates published in the journal *Slavery and Abolition*. Rebecca J. Scott, Thomas C. Holt, Frederick Cooper, and Aims McGuinness, eds., *Societies after Slavery: A Select Annotated Bibliography of Printed Sources on Cuba, Brazil, British Colonial Africa, South Africa, and the British West Indies* (Pittsburgh, Penn.: University of Pittsburgh Press, 2002), focuses specifically on emancipation and postemancipation society, although not especially on gender.

This essay is organized geographically. General works are followed by sections on the Caribbean (divided according to colonizing power), mainland

Spanish America, Brazil, North America, the Cape Colony, and the rest of Atlantic Africa. The final section deals with abolitionism.

General Works

David Barry Gaspar and Darlene Clark Hine have edited two important collections bringing together essays on a wide range of New World societies, one on women and slavery, the other on free women of color: *More Than Chattel: Black Women and Slavery in the Americas* (Bloomington: Indiana University Press, 1996), and *Beyond Bondage: Free Women of Color in the Americas* (Urbana: University of Illinois Press, 2004). Darlene Clark Hine and Jacqueline McLeod, eds., *Crossing Boundaries: Comparative History of Black People in Diaspora* (Bloomington: Indiana University Press, 1999), includes a number of essays on emancipation. Examinations of women and slavery from an international point of view include Dorothy C. Wertz, "Women and Slavery: A Cross-Cultural Perspective," *International Journal of Women's Studies* 7, no. 4 (1984): 372–84; Rosalyn Terborg-Penn, "Women and Slavery in the African Diaspora: A Cross-Cultural Approach to Historical Analysis," *Sage: A Scholarly Journal on Black Women* 3, no. 2 (1986): 11–15; and Terborg-Penn, "Black Women in Resistance: A Cross-Cultural Perspective," in *In Resistance: Studies in African, Caribbean and Afro-American History*, ed. Gary Y. Okihiro (Amherst: University of Massachusetts Press, 1986), 188–209. Teresita Martínez-Vergne, "The Liberation of Women in the Caribbean: Research Perspectives for the Study of Gender Relations in the Post-emancipation Period," *Caribbean Studies* 27, nos. 1–2 (1994): 5–36, is a suggestive article on approaches to studying gender and slave emancipation, using examples from across the Caribbean.

Important comparative or Atlantic-focused studies of emancipation include Eric Foner, *Nothing but Freedom: Emancipation and Its Legacy* (Baton Rouge: Louisiana State University Press, 1983), and Robin Blackburn, *The Overthrow of Colonial Slavery, 1776–1848* (London: Verso, 1988), neither of which pay substantive attention to gender. Two edited volumes are more concerned with gender: Frank McGlynn and Seymour Drescher, eds., *The Meaning of Freedom: Economics, Politics, and Culture after Slavery* (Pittsburgh, Penn.: University of Pittsburgh Press, 1992), especially the essays by Raymond Smith, Jean Besson, and Diane Austin-Broos; and Frederick Cooper, Thomas C. Holt, and Rebecca J. Scott, *Beyond Slavery: Explorations of Race, Labor, and Citizenship in Postemancipation Societies* (Chapel Hill: University of North Carolina Press, 2000).

British Caribbean

For historiographical essays on gender, slavery, and emancipation in the Anglophone Caribbean, see Bridget Brereton, "Gender and the Historiography of the English-Speaking Caribbean," in *Gendered Realities: Essays in Caribbean Feminist Thought*, ed. Patricia Mohammed (Mona, Jamaica: University of the West Indies Press, 2002), 129–44; and Hilary Beckles, "Sex and Gender in the Historiography of Caribbean Slavery," in *Engendering History: Caribbean Women in Historical Perspective*, ed. Verene Shepherd, Bridget Brereton, and Barbara Bailey (New York: St. Martin's, 1995), 125–40. The pioneering work on women in British Caribbean slave society is Lucille Mathurin, "A Historical Study of Women in Jamaica from 1655 to 1844" (PhD diss., University of the West Indies, 1974), which remains unpublished, although some of the author's arguments are presented in Lucille Mathurin Mair, *The Rebel Woman in the British West Indies during Slavery* (Kingston: Institute of Jamaica Publications, 1995 [1975]), aimed at school students, and her Elsa Goveia Memorial Lecture, "Women Field Workers in Jamaica during Slavery," in *Slavery, Freedom and Gender: The Dynamics of Caribbean Society*, ed. Brian L. Moore et al. (Mona, Jamaica: University of the West Indies Press, 2001), 183–96.

In the late 1980s, three books published in quick succession established the importance of the topic of women and slavery for Anglophone Caribbean history, and they remain key works in the field: Hilary McD. Beckles, *Natural Rebels: A Social History of Enslaved Black Women in Barbados* (New Brunswick, N.J.: Rutgers University Press, 1989); Barbara Bush, *Slave Women in Caribbean Society, 1650–1838* (London: James Currey, 1990); and Marietta Morrissey, *Slave Women in the New World: Gender Stratification in the Caribbean* (Lawrence: University Press of Kansas, 1989). See also Bush's essays "White 'Ladies,' Coloured 'Favourites' and Black 'Wenches': Some Considerations on Sex, Race, and Class Factors in Social Relations in White Creole Society in the British Caribbean," *Slavery and Abolition* 2, no. 3 (1981): 245–62; and " 'The Family Tree Is Not Cut': Women and Cultural Resistance in Slave Family Life in the British Caribbean," in *In Resistance: Studies in African, Caribbean and Afro-American History*, ed. Gary Y. Okihiro (Amherst: University of Massachusetts Press, 1986), 117–32; and two further works by Beckles, *Afro-Caribbean Women and Resistance to Slavery in Barbados* (London: Karnak House, 1988); and *Centering Women: Gender Discourses in Caribbean Slave Society* (Kingston: Ian Randle, 1999). The latter, made up of revised versions of the author's previously published essays, presents a gendered interpretation of Anglophone Caribbean slave society, weighted toward Barbados.

Shorter discussions of women in Caribbean slavery include Richard S. Dunn, "Sugar Production and Slave Women in Jamaica," in *Cultivation and Culture: Labor and the Shaping of Slave Life in the Americas*, ed. Ira Berlin and Philip D. Morgan (Charlottesville: University Press of Virginia, 1993), 49–72; Stella Dadzie, "Searching for the Invisible Woman: Slavery and Resistance in Jamaica," *Race and Class* 32, no. 2 (1990): 21–38; and Lucille Mathurin, "The Arrivals of Black Women," *Jamaica Journal* 9, nos. 2–3 (1975): 2–7, 49. Michael Mullin, "Women, and the Comparative Study of American Negro Slavery," *Slavery and Abolition* 6, no.1 (1985): 25–40, is based primarily on Jamaican advertisements for fugitive women slaves. The main contribution of Maureen G. Elgersman, *Unyielding Spirits: Black Women and Slavery in Early Canada and Jamaica* (New York: Garland, 1999), is to the study of enslaved and freedwomen in British Canada (1760–1834), although it also draws on secondary sources to discuss enslaved women in Jamaica. Mary Turner, "The Eleven O'clock Flog: Women, Work, and Labour Law in the British Caribbean," *Slavery and Abolition* 20, no.1 (1999): 38–58, examines enslaved women's experience of law in the context of the "amelioration" of slavery in the 1820s and 1830s, focusing particularly on Berbice. Rhoda E. Reddock, "Women and Slavery in the Caribbean: A Feminist Perspective," *Latin American Perspectives* 12, no.1 (1985): 63–80, while mainly concerned with slavery, includes some discussion of the post-emancipation period.

Since the 1970s, demographic data has provided new understanding of enslaved people's family lives. Barry W. Higman, "The Slave Family and Household in the British West Indies, 1800–1834," *Journal of Interdisciplinary History* 6, no. 2 (1975): 261–87, and Michael Craton, "Changing Patterns of Slave Families in the British West Indies," *Journal of Interdisciplinary History* 10, no. 1 (1979): 1–35, discuss enslaved people's family structures, while Orlando Patterson, "Persistence, Continuity, and Change in the Jamaican Working-Class Family," *Journal of Family History* 7, no. 2 (1982): 135–61, includes discussion of family life in both slavery and the postemancipation period.

Women as slave owners in the British Caribbean are considered in Hilary McD. Beckles, "White Women and Slavery in the Caribbean," *History Workshop Journal* 36 (1993): 66–82; and Trevor Burnard, "Inheritance and Independence: Women's Status in Early Colonial Jamaica," *William and Mary Quarterly*, 3rd ser., 48, no.1 (1991): 93–114. Kathleen Mary Butler, *The Economics of Emancipation: Jamaica and Barbados, 1823–1843* (Chapel Hill: University of North Carolina Press, 1995), includes discussion of the position of female slave owners in the emancipation process. On free women of color, see Pedro L. V. Welch with Richard A. Goodridge, *"Red" and Black over White: Free Coloured Women in*

Pre-emancipation Barbados (Bridgetown, Barbados: Carib, 2000); and Sheena Boa, "Urban Free Black and Coloured Women: Jamaica, 1760–1834," *Jamaican Historical Review* 18 (1993): 1–6.

Good general histories of emancipation in the British Caribbean, although relatively unconcerned with gender, include William A. Green, *British Slave Emancipation: The Sugar Colonies and the Great Experiment, 1830–1865* (Oxford: Clarendon, 1991); Douglas Hall, *Free Jamaica, 1838–65: An Economic History* (New Haven, Conn.: Yale University Press, 1959); and Hall, *Five of the Leewards, 1834–1870: The Major Problems of the Post-emancipation Period in Antigua, Barbuda, Montserrat, Nevis, and St. Kitts* (St. Laurence, Barbados: Carib University Press, 1971). Thomas C. Holt, *The Problem of Freedom: Race, Labor, and Politics in Jamaica and Britain, 1832–1938* (Baltimore: Johns Hopkins University Press, 1992), pays more attention to gender, as do Diana Paton, *No Bond but the Law: Punishment, Race, and Gender in Jamaican State Formation, 1780–1870* (Durham, N.C.: Duke University Press, 2004), and many of the articles in Karen Fog Olwig, ed., *Small Islands, Large Questions: Society, Culture and Resistance in the Post-emancipation Caribbean* (London: Frank Cass, 1995).

Women's experience of the apprenticeship period (1834–38) is discussed in Henrice Altink, "Slavery by Another Name: Apprenticed Women in Jamaican Workhouses in the Period, 1834–1838," *Social History* 26, no. 1 (2001): 40–59; and Sheena Boa, "Experiences of Women Estate Workers during the Apprenticeship Period in St. Vincent, 1834–1838: The Transition from Slavery to Freedom," *Women's History Review* 10, no. 3 (2001): 381–407.

Diana Paton, "The Flight from the Fields Reconsidered: Gender Ideologies and Women's Labor after Slavery in Jamaica," in *Reclaiming the Political in Latin American History: Essays from the North*, ed. Gilbert M. Joseph (Durham, N.C.: Duke University Press, 1999), 175–204, examines labor and gender in the immediate aftermath of slavery in Jamaica. Women's political participation in the postemancipation period is the concern of Mimi Sheller, "Quasheba, Mother, Queen: Black Women's Public Leadership and Political Protest in Post-emancipation Jamaica, 1834–65," *Slavery and Abolition* 19, no. 3 (1998): 90–117; while women's position as workers after emancipation is discussed in Richard Lobdell, "Women in the Jamaican Labour Force, 1881–1921," *Social and Economic Studies* 37, nos. 1–2 (1988): 203–40. Melanie Newton, " 'New Ideas of Correctness': Gender, Amelioration and Emancipation in Barbados, 1810s–50s," *Slavery and Abolition* 21, no. 3 (2000): 94–124, examines the gendering of slavery and postslavery society in Barbados. Persis Charles, "The Name of the Father: Women, Paternity, and British Rule in Nineteenth-Century Jamaica," *International Labor and Working-Class History* 41 (1992): 4–22, and respondents Catherine Hall, Thomas Holt, and Dale Tomich debate the significance of law regarding "illegitimacy" in postemancipation Jamaica. Women's lives in postemancipation Jamaica are the subject of Erna Brodber, "Afro-Jamaican Women at the Turn of the Century," *Social and Economic Studies* 35, no. 3 (1986): 23–50. Edith Clarke's classic ethnographic study, *My Mother Who Fathered Me: A Study of the Families in Three Selected Communities in Jamaica* (London: George Allen and Unwin, 1957; rpt. Mona, Jamaica: University of the West Indies Press, 1999), while conducted in the 1930s, has been drawn on by historians of the immediate postslavery period in the Caribbean. Jack Alexander, "Love, Race, Slavery, and Sexuality in Jamaican Images of the Family," in *Kinship Ideology and Practice in Latin America*, ed. Raymond T. Smith (Chapel Hill: University of North Carolina Press, 1984), likewise draws on twentieth-century ethnographic evidence, but includes reflection on Jamaican narratives about enslaved women's sexual interactions with white masters. Helen I. Safa, "Economic Autonomy and Sexual Equality in Caribbean Society," *Social and Economic Studies* 35, no. 3 (1986): 1–21, discusses women's position in the postemancipation Caribbean. Rhoda E. Reddock's *Women, Labour and Politics in Trinidad and Tobago: A History* (London: Zed, 1994), focuses mainly on the twentieth century but includes some material on slavery and the immediate postemancipation period. About half of Eugenia O'Neal, *From the Field to the Legislature: A History of Women in the Virgin Islands* (Westport, Conn.: Greenwood Press, 2001), is devoted to slavery and the early postemancipation period. Diane J. Austin-Broos, *Jamaica Genesis: Religion and the Politics of Moral Order* (Chicago: University of Chicago Press, 1997), investigates the gender dynamics of Jamaican religious practice, including sections on slavery and the early postemancipation period as a backdrop to the contemporary anthropological account.

Anthropologists may have been more willing than historians to use gender analysis, in part because of the long-standing debates about the Afro-Caribbean family. Caribbean postemancipation studies have been dominated by an anthropological framework which sees Afro-Caribbean culture dominated by twin poles of "reputation" and "respectability." In its initial formulation in Peter J. Wilson, *Crab Antics: The Social Anthropology of English-Speaking Negro Societies in the Caribbean* (New Haven, Conn.: Yale University Press, 1973), this paradigm linked men to the autonomous culture of "reputation" and women to that of Eurocentric "respectability," and suggested that women's concern for the latter led to greater social and political conservatism on their part. This framework remains significant, although it has been significantly revised by feminist scholars who challenge the gendered binary and the denial of gender hierarchy which underlie it. Most significant in this regard is the work of Jean Besson, whose many important articles have been incorporated into her book-length study, *Martha Brae's Two Histories: European Expansion and Caribbean Culture-Building in Jamaica* (Chapel Hill: University of North Carolina Press, 2002). See also Roger D. Abrahams, *The Man-of-Words in the West Indies: Performance and the Emergence of Creole Culture* (Baltimore: Johns Hopkins University Press, 1983), which focuses primarily on men and masculinity. Karen Fog Olwig's study of Nevis, *Global Culture, Island Identity: Continuity and Change in the Afro-Caribbean Community of Nevis* (Chur, Switzerland: Harwood Academic, 1993), emphasizes the gender dimensions of class and race difference. Janet Henshall Momsen's work, while mainly focused on the contemporary Caribbean, provides important insights into the postemancipation period in relation to gender and land. See her "Gender Roles in Caribbean Agricultural Labour," in *Labour in the Caribbean: From Emancipation to Independence*, ed. Malcolm Cross and Gad Heuman (London: MacMillan, 1988), 141–58, and "Gender Ideology and Land," in *Caribbean Portraits: Essays on Gender Ideologies and Identities*, ed. Christine Barrow (Kingston: Ian Randle, 1998), 115–32.

Studies of women's position in the postemancipation indenture system include Rhoda E. Reddock, "Indian Women and Indenture in Trinidad and Tobago, 1845–1917: Freedom Denied," *Caribbean Quarterly* 32, nos. 3–4 (1986): 27–49; and Jeremy Poynting, "East Indian Women in the Caribbean: Experience and Voice," in *India in the Caribbean*, ed. David Dabydeen and Brinsley Samaroo (London: Hansib/University of Warwick, Centre for Caribbean Studies, 1987), 231–63. Verene Shepherd, *Maharani's Misery: Narratives of a Passage from India* (Mona, Jamaica: University of the West Indies Press, 2002), investigates the experience of an indentured woman who died during the voyage from India to Guyana. Shepherd has also published several essays on Indian women in Jamaica, including "Emancipation through Servitude: Aspects of the Condition of Indian Women in Jamaica, 1845–1945," *Bulletin of the Society for the Study of Labour History* 53, no. 3 (1988): 13–19, reprinted in *Caribbean Freedom: Economy and Society from Emancipation to the Present: A Student Reader*, ed. Hilary Beckles and Verene Shepherd (Kingston: Ian Randle, 1993), 245–50; "Gender, Migration and Settlement: The Indentureship and Post-indentureship Experience of Indian Females in Jamaica, 1845–1943," in *Engendering History: Caribbean Women in Historical Perspective*, ed. Verene Shepherd, Bridget Brereton, and Barbara Bailey (New York: St. Martin's, 1995), 233–57; "Indian Females in Jamaica: An Analysis of the Population Censuses, 1861–1943," *Jamaican Historical Review* 18 (1993): 18–30; and "Constructing Visibility: Indian Women in the Jamaican Segment of the Indian Diaspora," in *Gendered Realities: Essays in Caribbean Feminist*

Thought, ed. Patricia Mohammed (Mona, Jamaica: University of the West Indies Press, 2002), 107–28. Studies of the indenture system that use gender as a category of analysis include Verene A. Shepherd, *Transients to Settlers: The Experience of Indians in Jamaica, 1845–1950* (Leeds, U.K.: Peepal Tree, 1994); Madhavi Kale, *Fragments of Empire: Capital, Slavery, and Indian Indentured Labor Migration in the British Caribbean* (Philadelphia: University of Pennsylvania Press, 1998); and Prabhu P. Mohapatra, " 'Restoring the Family': Wife Murders and the Making of a Sexual Contract for Indian Immigrant Labour in the British Caribbean Colonies, 1860–1920," *Studies in History* 11, no. 2 (1995): 227–60. Like Mohapatra and Kale, Basdeo Mangru, "The Sex-Ratio Disparity and Its Consequences under the Indenture in British Guiana," in *India in the Caribbean*, ed. David Dabydeen and Brinsley Samaroo (London: Hansib, 1987), 211–30, deals with the question of the uneven sex ratio in Indian communities and the prevalence of wife murder within these communities; however, unlike Mohapatra and Kale, Mangru does not critique the colonial framework of morality within which the sex-ratio "problem" was initially framed. Patricia Mohammed, *Gender Negotiations among Indians in Trinidad, 1917–1947* (Basingstoke, U.K.: Palgrave, 2002), while primarily concerned with the period after the abolition of the indenture system, includes substantial discussion of indenture.

French Caribbean

The pioneering monograph on enslaved women in the French colonies was Arlette Gautier, *Les soeurs de Solitude: La condition féminine dans l'esclavage aux Antilles du XVIIe au XIXe siècle* (Paris: Caribéennes, 1985), which has recently been joined by Bernard Moitt, *Women and Slavery in the French Antilles, 1635–1848* (Bloomington: Indiana University Press, 2001). See also Gautier, "Les esclaves femmes aux Antilles françaises, 1635–1848," *Historical Reflections* 10, no. 3 (1983): 409–33. Myriam Cottias, "La séduction coloniale: Damnation et stratégies—Les Antilles, XVIIe–XIXe siècle," in *Séduction et sociétés: Approches historiques*, ed. Cécile Dauphin and Arlette Farge (Paris: Seuil, 2001), 125–40, focuses specifically on issues of "seduction," a topic that in Anglophone literature is more likely to appear as sexual violence. See also Cottias's essay "Mariage et citoyenneté dans les Antilles françaises (XVIIe–XXe): De l'esclave à la femme 'poto mitan,' " in *Construire l'histoire antillaise: Mélanges offerts à Jacques Adélaide-Merlande*, ed. Lucien Abenon, Danielle Bégot, and Jean-Pierre Sainton (Paris: Comité des Travaux Historiques et Scientifiques, 2002), 319–34. A gendered analysis of slave society in Saint-Domingue may be found in John Garrigus,

"Redrawing the Color Line: Gender and the Social Construction of Race in Pre-revolutionary Haiti," *Journal of Caribbean History* 30, nos. 1–2 (1996): 28–50.

The classic account of the Haitian Revolution is C. L. R. James, *The Black Jacobins: Toussaint L'Ouverture and the San Domingo Revolution* (New York: Vintage, 1963). For more recent important studies of the Haitian revolution, see Franklin W. Knight, "The Haitian Revolution," *American Historical Review* 105, no. 1 (2000): 103–15; Laurent Dubois, *Avengers of the New World: The Story of the Haitian Revolution* (Cambridge, Mass.: Harvard University Press, 2004); and Carolyn E. Fick, *The Making of Haiti: The Saint Domingue Revolution from Below* (Knoxville: University of Tennessee Press, 1990). Judith Kafka has studied women's role in the revolutionary process in "Action, Reaction and Interaction: Slave Women in Resistance in the South of Saint Domingue, 1793–94," *Slavery and Abolition* 18, no. 2 (1997): 48–72. Jacques Adelaïde-Merlande, *La Caraïbe et la Guyane au temps de la Révolution et de 1'Empire (1789–1804)* (Paris: Karthala, 1992), provides an overview of the French Caribbean as a whole, including Saint-Domingue, during the revolutionary period. Laurent Dubois, *A Colony of Citizens: Revolution and Slave Emancipation in the French Caribbean, 1787–1804* (Chapel Hill: University of North Carolina Press, 2004), focuses on Guadeloupe in the revolutionary period, during which slavery was first overthrown, then restored.

David Nicholls, *From Dessalines to Duvalier: Race, Colour and National Independence in Haiti* (London: Macmillan, 1996), is an important account of the postrevolutionary period in Haiti which pays little attention to gender. Mimi Sheller, *Democracy after Slavery: Black Publics and Peasant Radicalism in Haiti and Jamaica* (London: Macmillan, 2000), integrates gender with other categories of analysis in its comparison of the two nations, while the same author's "Sword-Bearing Citizens: Militarism and Manhood in Nineteenth-Century Haiti," *Plantation Society in the Americas* 4, nos. 2–3 (1997): 233–78, focuses on issues of masculinity. For another gendered analysis of Haitian society, see Carolle Charles, "Sexual Politics and the Mediation of Class, Gender and Race in Former Slave Plantation Societies: The Case of Haiti," in *Social Construction of the Past: Representation as Power*, ed. George Clement Bond and Angela Gilliam (London: Routledge, 1994), 44–58. John Garrigus, "Race, Gender, and Virtue in Haiti's Failed Foundational Fiction: *La mulâtre comme il y a peu de blanches* (1803)," in *The Color of Liberty: Histories of Race in France*, ed. Sue Peabody and Tyler Stovall (Durham, N.C.: Duke University Press, 2003), 73–94, examines a rare Haitian novel that attempted to reimagine black and brown women "as virtuous wives and loving mothers" (74).

For an important general study of the process of emancipation that took place in the French Caribbean in the wake of the 1848 revolution, see Nelly

Schmidt, *Victor Schoelcher et l'abolition de l'esclavage* (Paris: Fayard, 1994). On women and emancipation in Martinique, see Gilbert Pago, *Les femmes et la liquidation du système esclavagiste à la Martinique, 1848–1852* (Petit-Bourg, Guadeloupe: Ibis Rouge, 1998).

Danish West Indies

Karen Fog Olwig, *Cultural Adaptation and Resistance on St. John: Three Centuries of Afro-Caribbean Life* (Gainesville: University of Florida Press, 1985), includes substantial discussion of gender in the slavery and postslavery periods. Sandra Greene, "From Whence They Came: A Note on the Influence of West African Ethnic and Gender Relations on the Organizational Character of the 1733 St. John Rebellion," in *The Danish West Indian Slave Trade: Virgin Islands Perspectives*, ed. Arnold R. Highfield and George F. Tyson (St. Croix: Virgin Islands Humanities Council, 1994), 47–67, argues that the rebellion involved a radical shift in gendered patterns of behavior for enslaved Africans. Karen Fog Olwig's article in the same volume, "African Culture in the Danish West Indies: The Slave Trade and Its Aftermath," discusses kinship and other aspects of gender relations. Eddie Donoghue, *Black Women/White Men: The Sexual Exploitation of Female Slaves in the Danish West Indies* (Trenton, N.J.: Africa World Press, 2002), is a more wide-ranging study of women and slavery than its title suggests. For general studies of emancipation in the Danish West Indies, see Neville A. T. Hall, "The Victor Vanquished: Emancipation in St. Croix: Its Antecedents and Immediate Aftermath," *New West Indian Guide/Nieuwe West-Indische Gids* 58 (1984): 3–36, reprinted in Hall, *Slave Society in the Danish West Indies: St. Thomas, St. John and St. Croix*, ed. B. W. Higman (Mona, Jamaica: University of the West Indies Press, 1992), 208–27.

Dutch West Indies

Slave family structure in Suriname is discussed in Humphrey E. Lamur, "The Slave Family in Colonial Nineteenth-Century Suriname," *Journal of Black Studies* 23, no. 3 (1993): 371–81. Rosemary Brana-Shute emphasizes the gendered difference in access to manumission among Surinamese slaves in "Approaching Freedom: The Manumission of Slaves in Suriname, 1760–1828," *Slavery and Abolition* 10, no. 3 (1989): 40–63. On female maroons, see Silvia W. de Groot, "Maroon Women as Ancestors, Priests and Mediums in Surinam,"

Slavery and Abolition 2, no. 7 (1986): 160–74. Emancipation in Suriname is considered along with the other Dutch Caribbean colonies as part of Cornelis Ch. Goslinga's eight-hundred-page history, The Dutch in the Caribbean and in Surinam, 1791/5–1942 (Assen, the Netherlands: Van Gorcum, 1990), and more succinctly in Alex van Stipriaan, "Suriname and the Abolition of Slavery," in Fifty Years Later: Antislavery, Capitalism and Modernity in the Dutch Orbit, ed. Gert Oostindie (Leiden, the Netherlands: KITLV Press, 1995), 117–41; and Pieter Emmer, "Between Slavery and Freedom: The Period of Apprenticeship in Suriname (Dutch Guiana), 1863–1873," Slavery and Abolition 14, no.1 (1993): 87–105, reprinted in Emmer, The Dutch in the Atlantic Economy, 1580–1880: Trade, Slavery and Emancipation (Aldershot, U.K.: Ashgate, 1998), 227–54. However, gender has surfaced more in discussions of the postemancipation indenture system than in studies of slavery and emancipation themselves. In "The Great Escape: The Migration of Female Indentured Servants from British India to Surinam, 1873–1916," in Abolition and Its Aftermath: The Historical Context, 1790–1916, ed. David Richardson (London: Frank Cass, 1985), 245–66, Emmer interprets the experience of Indian indentured women in Suriname as "a vehicle of female emancipation," an interpretation challenged by Rosemarijn Hoefte, "Female Indentured Labor in Suriname: For Better or Worse?" Boletín de estudios latinoamericanos y del Caribe 42 (1987): 55–70. The debate continues in Emmer, "The Position of Indian Women in Suriname: A Rejoinder," and Hoefte's "The Position of Female British Indian and Javanese Contract Laborers in Suriname: A Last Word," Boletín de estudios latinoamericanos y del Caribe 43 (1987): 115–20 and 121–23, respectively. See also Hoefte, In Place of Slavery: A Social History of British Indian and Javanese Laborers in Suriname (Gainesville: University Press of Florida, 1998).

Spanish Caribbean

There is little work on emancipation in the Dominican Republic, where slavery was relatively insignificant, but for an article on the transition to free labor there, see Frank Moya Pons, "The Land Question in Haiti and Santo Domingo: The Sociopolitical Context of the Transition from Slavery to Free Labor, 1801–1843," in Between Slavery and Free Labor: The Spanish-Speaking Caribbean in the Nineteenth Century, ed. Manuel Moreno Fraginals, Frank Moya Pons, and Stanley L. Engerman (Baltimore: Johns Hopkins University Press, 1985), 181–214.

More work has been done on Puerto Rico. Félix V. Matos Rodríguez, Women in San Juan, 1820–1868 (Princeton, N.J.: Markus Wiener, 1999), explores the lives of women in Puerto Rico's capital as the city underwent an elite-driven process of "modernization." Teresita Martínez-Vergne, *Shaping the Discourse on Space: Charity and Its Wards in Nineteenth-Century San Juan, Puerto Rico* (Austin: University of Texas Press, 1999), analyzes bourgeois attempts to discipline a variety of "unruly" populations, including "disorderly" women, during the periods of late slavery and emancipation. In both books, enslaved and freed women receive some attention, although the emphasis is on the urban free population. Jay Kinsbruner, *Not of Pure Blood: The Free People of Color and Racial Prejudice in Nineteenth-Century Puerto Rico* (Durham, N.C.: Duke University Press, 1996), a demographic study focused on San Juan, includes extensive discussion of family form and gender-related opportunities for free people of color during the late period of slavery. Ivette Pérez Vega, "Juana María Escobales, liberta 'liberada,' " *Homines* 11, nos. 1–2 (1987–88): 397–402, discusses the life of a nineteenth-century free woman of color. Eileen J. Suárez Findlay, *Imposing Decency: The Politics of Sexuality and Race in Puerto Rico, 1870–1920* (Durham, N.C.: Duke University Press, 1999), undertakes a gendered analysis of race and sexuality in Puerto Rico in the postemancipation transition from Spanish to U.S. colonial rule, attending in particular to questions of marriage, divorce, prostitution, and the labor movement. Rural developments in postemancipation Puerto Rico are addressed in Teresita Martínez-Vergne, "New Patterns for Puerto Rico's Sugar Workers: Abolition and Centralization at San Vicente, 1873–92," *Hispanic American Historical Review* 68, no. 1 (1988): 45–74; and in Martínez-Vergne, *Capitalism in Colonial Puerto Rico: Central San Vicente in the Late Nineteenth Century* (Gainesville: University Press of Florida, 1992). Félix V. Matos Rodríguez and Linda C. Delgado, eds., *Puerto Rican Women's History: New Perspectives* (Armonk, N.Y.: M. E. Sharpe, 1998), deals with the twentieth century, with the exception of Matos Rodríguez's essay " 'Quién Trabajará?': Domestic Workers, Urban Slaves, and the Abolition of Slavery in Puerto Rico," 62–82, reprinted in *Slavery without Sugar: Diversity in Caribbean Economy and Society since the Seventeenth Century*, ed. Verene A. Shepherd (Gainesville: University Press of Florida, 2002), 248–71.

Women slaves in Cuba are one concern of Manuel Moreno Fraginals, "Peculiaridades de la esclavitud en Cuba," *Islas: Revista de la Universidad de Las Villas*, Santa Clara, no. 85 (1986): 3–12; and they are the main subject of Digna Castañeda, "The Female Slave in Cuba during the First Half of the Nineteenth Century," in *Engendering History: Caribbean Women in Historical Perspective*, ed. Verene Shepherd, Bridget Brereton, and Barbara Bailey (New York: St. Martin's, 1995), 141–54. Verena Martinez-Alier (Stolcke), *Marriage, Class, and Colour in Nineteenth-Century Cuba: A Study of Racial Attitudes and Sexual Values in* a *Slave Society* (rpt., Ann Arbor: University of Michigan Press, 1989 [1974]), presents a gendered analysis of Cuban slave society, focusing particularly on marital and kinship relationships among the free population. Martinez-Alier's emphasis on ideologies of bloodlines and racial mixing has been influential in studies of other colonial societies. María Elena Díaz, *The Virgin, the King, and the Royal Slaves of El Cobre: Negotiating Freedom in Colonial Cuba, 1670–1780* (Stanford, Calif.: Stanford University Press, 2000), presents an excellent gendered study of a special group of Cuban slaves, the Royal slaves of El Cobre, and the intertwined histories of slavery and forms of manumission before emancipation. Luz Adriana Maya Restrepo's article "Paula de Eguiluz y el arte del bien querer: Apuntes para el estudio de la sensualidad y el cimarronaje feminino en el caribe, siglo XVII," *Historia Crítica* (Revista del Departamento de Historia de la Facultad de Ciencias Sociales de la Universidad de los Andes) 24 (2002):101–24 uses the case of Paula de Eguilez, a female slave who spent most of her life in Cuba before being tried by the Inquisition for witchcraft, to investigate enslaved women's specific modes of resistance or *cimarronaje*.

Major studies of Cuban slave emancipation include Rebecca J. Scott, *Slave Emancipation in Cuba: The Transition to Free Labor, 1860–1899* (Princeton, N.J.: Princeton University Press, 1985); María del Carmen Barcia, *Burguesía esclavista y abolición* (Havana: Ciencias Sociales, 1987); and the classic study by Raúl Cepero Bonilla, *Azúcar y abolición: Apuntes para una historia crítica del abolicionismo* (Havana: Cenit, 1948). For gendered analyses of the struggle for independence, see Ada Ferrer, *Insurgent Cuba: Race, Nation, and Revolution, 1868–1898* (Chapel Hill: University of North Carolina Press, 1999); and Ferrer, "Raza, region y género en la Cuba rebelde: Quintín Bandera y la cuestión del liderazgo politico," in *Espacios, silencios y los sentidos de la libertad: Cuba entre 1878 y 1912*, ed. Fernando Martínez Heredia, Rebecca J. Scott, and Orlando F. García Martínez (Havana: Unión, 2001), 141–62. Joan Casanovas, *Bread, or Bullets! Urban Labor and Spanish Colonialism in Cuba, 1850–1898* (Pittsburgh, Penn.: University of Pittsburgh Press, 1998), focuses on labor in the context of the decline and abolition of slavery. It includes brief discussions of gender politics in the labor movement, referring to the participation of freedwomen within associational life. Aline Helg, *Our Rightful Share: The Afro-Cuban Struggle for Equality, 1886–1912* (Chapel Hill: University of North Carolina Press, 1995), is concerned mainly with black politics, especially the 1912 massacre of the Partido Independiente de Color. For a narrative history of Cuba in the emancipation and postemancipation period, see Louis A. Pérez Jr., *Cuba between Empires, 1878–1902* (Pittsburgh, Penn.: University of Pittsburgh Press, 1983).

Mainland Spanish America

Studies of slavery in mainland Spanish America which study women's lives include Miguel Acosta Saignes, *Vida de los esclavos negros en Venezuela* (Valencia, Venezuela: Vadell Hermanos, 1984 [1967]), which discusses family life, marriage, and sexual abuse, among other topics. On the slave family, see David L. Chandler, "Family Bonds and the Bondsman: The Slave Family in Colonial Colombia," *Latin American Research Review* 16, no. 2 (1981): 107–31. María Eugenia Chaves, "Slave Women's Strategies for Freedom and the Late Spanish Colonial State," in *Hidden Histories of Gender and the State in Latin America*, ed. Elizabeth Dore and Maxine Molyneux (Durham, N.C.: Duke University Press, 2000), 108–26, uses a late eighteenth-century case from Guayaquil, New Granada, to examine enslaved women's attempts to become free.

For an overview of emancipation processes in Latin America as a whole, see Hebe Clementi, *La abolición de la esclavitud en América Latina* (Buenos Aires: La Pléyade, 1974). A starting point on legal abolition in Colombia, Venezuala, and Ecuador is Harold A. Bierck, "The Struggle for Abolition in Gran Colombia," *Hispanic American Historical Review* 33, no. 3 (1953): 365–86, which, although written without attention to gender or women, includes quotations exemplifying the gendered liberalism of Simón Bolívar's emancipation policies. The major study of emancipation in Venezuela remains John V. Lombardi, *The Decline and Abolition of Negro Slavery in Venezuela* (Westport, Conn.: Greenwood, 1971), which pays little attention to women or gender. On the abolition process in Colombia, see Jorge Castellanos, *La abolición de la esclavitud en Popayán, 1832–1852* (Cali, Colombia: Universidad del Valle, 1980). Claudia Mosquera, Mauricio Pardo, and Odile Hoffmann, eds., *Afrodescendientes en las américas: Trayectorias sociales e identitarias—150 años de la abolición en Colombia* (Bogotá: Universidad Nacional de Colombia, 2002), includes essays dealing with Colombian emancipation. For a primarily political history of Chilean emancipation, see Guillermo Feliú Cruz, *La abolición de la esclavitud en Chile* (Santiago: Universitaria, 1973). There is a growing literature on abolition in Peru. Peter Blanchard, *Slavery and Abolition in Early Republican Peru* (Wilmington, Del.: Scholarly Resources, 1992), and Carlos Aguirre, *Agentes de su propia libertad: Los esclavos de Lima y la desintegración de la esclavitud, 1821–1854* (Lima: Fondo Editorial de la Pontifica Universidad Católica del Perú, 1993), include scattered references to the differences in men's and women's experience of the emancipation process, while Christine Hünefeldt, *Paying the Price of Freedom: Family and Labor among Lima's Slaves, 1800–1854* (Berkeley: University of California Press, 1994), is more focused on family and gender.

North America

There is a large literature on women, gender, slavery, and emancipation in the
United States and the colonies that preceded it. For historiographical over-
views, see Darlene Clark Hine, "Lifting the Veil, Shattering the Silence: Black
Women's History in Slavery and Freedom," in The State of Afro-American History:
Past, Present and Future, ed. Darlene Clark Hine (Baton Rouge: Louisiana State
University Press, 1986), 223–49, reprinted in Hine Sight: Black Women and the
Reconstruction of American History (Bloomington: Indiana University Press, 1994),
3–26. Hine Sight also includes Hine's essays "Female Slave Resistance: The
Economics of Sex," 27–36, and "Rape and the Inner Lives of Black Women:
Thoughts on the Culture of Dissemblance," 37–48. See also Hine's reader,
edited with Wilma King and Linda Reed, We Specialize in the Wholly Impossible: A
Reader in Black Women's History (New York: Carlson, 1995); and her series Black
Women in American History: From Colonial Times to the Nineteenth Century (New
York: Carlson, 1990) and Black Women's History: Theory and Practice (New York:
Carlson, 1990), which between them reprint more than 120 articles, including
many cited in this essay. Darlene Clark Hine and Earnestine Jenkins, eds., A
Question of Manhood: A Reader in U.S. Black Men's History and Masculinity, vol. 1,
"Manhood Rights": The Construction of Black Male History and Manhood, 1750–1870
(Bloomington: Indiana University Press, 1999), reprints essays that approach
the history of black men during slavery and the Civil War from a gendered
perspective. Two collections of essays focusing predominantly on women and
slavery or the immediate postemancipation period are Virginia Bernard, Betty
Brandon, Elizabeth Fox-Genovese, and Theda Perdue, eds., Southern Women:
Histories and Identities (Columbia: University of Missouri Press, 1992); and Patricia Morton, Discovering the Women in Slavery: Emancipating Perspectives on the
American Past (Athens: University of Georgia Press, 1996).

Kenneth E. Marshall, "Work, Family and Day-to-Day Survival on an Old
Farm: Nance Melick, a Rural Late Eighteenth- and Early Nineteenth-Century
New Jersey Slave Woman," Slavery and Abolition 19, no. 3 (1998): 22–45, uses
one woman's life history to explore the gendering of slavery in the Northern
United States. For another study of Northern enslaved women, see Debra L.
Newman, "Black Women in the Era of the American Revolution in Pennsylva-
nia," Journal of Negro History 61, no. 3 (1976): 276–89. On abolition during the
revolutionary period in the Northern United States, see Joanne Pope Melish,
Disowning Slavery: Gradual Emancipation and "Race" in New England, 1780–1860
(Ithaca, N.Y.: Cornell University Press, 1998).

For an important gendered analysis of the development of slave society in colonial Virginia, see Kathleen M. Brown, *Good Wives, Nasty Wenches, and Anxious Patriarchs: Gender, Race, and Power in Colonial Virginia* (Chapel Hill: University of North Carolina Press, 1996). On enslaved women in early Barbados and South Carolina, see Jennifer L. Morgan, *Laboring Women: Reproduction and Gender in New World Slavery* (Philadelphia: University of Pennsylvania Press, 2004. Other studies of the colonial South include Catherine Clinton and Michele Gillespie, eds., *The Devil's Lane: Sex and Race in the Early South* (Oxford: Oxford University Press, 1997); and Carole Shammas, "Black Women's Work and the Evolution of Plantation Society in Virginia," *Labor History* 26, no. 1 (1985): 5–28.

On women and slavery in the antebellum South, see Deborah Gray White, *Ar'n't I a Woman? Female Slaves in the Plantation South* (New York: Norton, 1985); Elizabeth Fox-Genovese, *Within the Plantation Household: Black and White Women of the Old South* (Chapel Hill: University of North Carolina Press, 1988); Victoria E. Bynum, ed., *Unruly Women: The Politics of Social and Sexual Control in the Old South, 1840–1865* (Chapel Hill: University of North Carolina Press, 1992); Stephanie M. H. Camp, *Closer to Freedom: Enslaved Women and Everyday Resistance in the Plantation South* (Chapel Hill: University of North Carolina Press, 2004); and Marli F. Weiner, *Mistresses and Slaves: Plantation Women in South Carolina, 1830–1880* (Urbana: University of Illinois Press, 1997).

Much work on U.S. black women's history has involved refutation of the "black matriarchy" thesis popularized by Daniel Moynihan's 1965 report, "The Negro Family." See for instance Herbert G. Gutman, *The Black Family in Slavery and Freedom, 1750–1925* (New York: Pantheon, 1976). Gutman's acceptance of Moynihan's fundamental premise, that female-headed households and female power within the household are social problems, has been challenged in feminist studies of African American family life under slavery, including Suzanne Lebsock, "Free Black Women and the Question of Matriarchy: Petersburg, Virginia, 1784–1820," *Feminist Studies* 8, no. 2 (1982): 271–92; Christie Farnham, "Sapphire? The Issue of Dominance in the Slave Family, 1830–1860," in *"To Toil the Livelong Day": America's Women at Work, 1780–1980*, ed. Carol Groneman and Mary Beth Norton (Ithaca, N.Y.: Cornell University Press, 1987), 68–83; and Ann Patton Malone, *Sweet Chariot: Slave Family and Household Structure in Nineteenth-Century Louisiana* (Chapel Hill: University of North Carolina Press, 1992). Malone argues that historians have exaggerated the stability and the patriarchal nature of the slave family, but she agrees with Gutman that the two-parent nuclear family was the preferred form among slaves. Brenda E. Stevenson, *Life in Black and White: Family and Community in the Slave South* (New York: Oxford University Press, 1996), examines black and white families, arguing that for enslaved people, extended families and wide kin networks were more significant than nuclear family groups. Endorsing Stevenson's work and focusing on small plantations in the Mountain South, Wilma A. Dunaway, *The African-American Family in Slavery and Emancipation* (Cambridge: Cambridge University Press, 2003), argues that recent historiography has underestimated the threats to enslaved people's families and overemphasized their commitment to the nuclear family. Wayne K. Durrill, "Slavery, Kinship and Dominance: The Black Community at Somerset Place Plantation, 1786–1860," *Slavery and Abolition* 13, no. 2 (1992): 1–19, argues that men were able to attain a position of patriarchal dominance within the antebellum slave community. Other studies of family life under slavery include Cheryll Ann Cody, "Naming, Kinship, and Estate Dispersal: Notes on Slave Family Life on a South Carolina Plantation, 1786 to 1833," *William and Mary Quarterly* 39, no.1, 3rd serv. (1982): 192–211; Cody, "There Was No 'Absalom' on the Ball Plantations: Slave-Naming Practices in the South Carolina Low Country, 1720–1865," *American Historical Review* 92, no. 3 (1987): 563–96, reprinted in *The Slavery Reader*, ed. Gad Heuman and James Walvin (London: Routledge, 2003), 300–331; and Loren Schweninger, "A Slave Family in the Ante Bellum South," *Journal of Negro History* 60, no.1 (1975): 29–44. Thelma Jennings, " 'Us Colored Women Had to Go through a Plenty': Sexual Exploitation of African-American Slave Women," *Journal of Women's History* 1, no. 3 (1990): 45–74, focuses specifically on sexual exploitation, as do Catherine Clinton, "Caught in the Web of the Big House: Women and Slavery," in *The Web of Southern Social Relations: Women, Family, and Education*, ed. Walter J. Fraser Jr., R. Frank Saunders Jr., and Jon L. Waklyn (Athens: University of Georgia Press, 1985), 19–34; and Melton A. McLaurin, *Celia: A Slave* (New York: Avon, 1991). Many of the essays (reprinted from earlier publication) in Nell Irvin Painter, *Southern History across the Color Line* (Chapel Hill: University of North Carolina Press, 2002), address the issue of the psychic impact of sexual exploitation on all members of southern society during slavery.

Betty Wood, *Women's Work, Men's Work: The Informal Slave Economies of Lowcountry Georgia* (Athens: University of Georgia Press, 1995), emphasizes the sexual division of labor within enslaved communities, as embodied in slaves' "independent" or "informal" economies, as does Larry E. Hudson Jr., *To Have and To Hold: Slave Work and Family Life in Antebellum South Carolina* (Athens: University of Georgia Press, 1997). For a discussion of slave women's role in resistance, see Elizabeth Fox-Genovese, "Strategies and Forms of Resistance: Focus on Slave Women in the United States," in *In Resistance: Studies in African, Caribbean and Afro-American History*, ed. Gary Y. Okihiro (Amherst: University of Massachusetts Press, 1986), 143–65. On slave-owning women, see Anne Firor Scott, *The*

Southern Lady: From Pedestal to Politics (Chicago: University of Chicago Press, 1970); Catherine Clinton, The Plantation Mistress: Woman's World in the Old South (New York: Pantheon, 1982); Kirsten E. Wood, Masterful Women: Slaveholding Widows from the American Revolution through the Civil War (Chapel Hill: University of North Carolina Press, 2004); and Jane Turner Censer, North Carolina Planters and Their Children, 1800–1860 (Baton Rouge: Louisiana State University Press, 1984). For a gendered interpretation of antebellum culture and politics, see Stephanie McCurry, Masters of Small Worlds: Yeoman Households, Gender Relations, and the Political Culture of the Antebellum South Carolina Low Country (New York: Oxford University Press, 1995).

Kimberly S. Hanger, Bounded Lives, Bounded Places: Free Black Society in Colonial New Orleans, 1769–1803 (Durham, N.C.: Duke University Press, 1997), includes substantial discussion of the situation of free women of color, in particular in relation to property and family life. Free women of color are also discussed in Adele Logan Alexander, Ambiguous Lives: Free Women of Color in Rural Georgia, 1789–1879 (Fayetteville: University of Arkansas Press, 1991); Loren Schweninger, "Property Owning Free African-American Women in the South, 1800–1870," Journal of Women's History 1, no.3 (1990): 13–44; Suzanne Lebsock, The Free Women of Petersburg: Status and Culture in a Southern Town, 1784–1860 (New York: Norton, 1984), which discusses black and white free women; and James O. Horton, Free People of Color: Inside the African-American Community (Washington, D.C.: Smithsonian Institution, 1993).

On black women during and immediately after the U.S. Civil War, see Noralee Frankel, Freedom's Women: Black Women and Families in Civil War Era Mississippi (Bloomington: Indiana University Press, 1999); Leslie A. Schwalm, A Hard Fight for We: Women's Transition from Slavery to Freedom in South Carolina (Urbana: University of Illinois Press, 1997); Tera W. Hunter, To 'Joy My Freedom: Southern Black Women's Lives and Labors after the Civil War (Cambridge, Mass.: Harvard University Press, 1997); Jacqueline Jones, Labor of Love, Labor of Sorrow: Black Women, Work, and the Family from Slavery to the Present (New York: Basic, 1985); and Carolyn E. Wedin, "The Civil War and Black Women on the Sea Islands," in Southern Women, ed. Caroline Matheny Dillman (New York: Hemisphere, 1988), 71–80, a collection which also includes some articles on women in antebellum slave society. Elizabeth Leonard, Yankee Women: Gender Battles in the Civil War (New York: W. W. Norton, 1994), and Jeanie Attie, Patriotic Toil: Northern Women and the American Civil War (Ithaca, N.Y.: Cornell University Press, 1998), focus on Northern women in the Civil War. Catherine Clinton and Nina Silber, eds., Divided Houses: Gender and the Civil War (New York: Oxford University Press, 1992), presents a gendered analysis of the Civil War, as do LeeAnn

Whites, *The Civil War as a Crisis in Gender: August, Georgia, 1860–1890* (Athens: University of Georgia Press, 1995); and Stephanie McCurry, "Citizens, Soldiers' Wives and 'Hiley Hope Up' Slaves: The Problem of Political Obligation in the Civil War South," in *Gender and the Southern Body Politic*, ed. Nancy Bercaw (Jackson: University Press of Mississippi, 2000), 95–129. Drew Gilpin Faust, *Mothers of Invention: Women of the Slaveholding South in the American Civil War* (Chapel Hill: University of North Carolina Press, 1996), analyzes planter-class women during the war.

Peter W. Bardaglio, *Reconstructing the Household: Families, Sex, and the Law in the Nineteenth-Century South* (Chapel Hill: University of North Carolina Press, 1995), and Carol Bleser, ed., *In Joy and in Sorrow: Women, Family and Marriage in the Victorian South, 1830–1900* (New York: Oxford University Press, 1991), draw attention to the importance of the household in both slave and postslave society. In the latter, Brenda Stevenson's essay, "Distress and Discord in Virginia Slave Families, 1830–1860," 103–24, focuses on the havoc the peculiar institution created within slave families, including alcoholism and abuse. Martha Hodes, *White Women, Black Men: Illicit Sex in the Nineteenth-Century South* (New Haven, Conn.: Yale University Press, 1997), examines the changing meaning of and response to "interracial" sex before and after the end of slavery. Kimberly Schreck, "Her Will against Theirs: Eda Hickam and the Ambiguity of Freedom in Postbellum Missouri," in *Beyond Image and Convention: Explorations in Southern Women's History*, ed. Janet L. Coryell, Matha H. Swain, Sandra Gioia Treadway, and Elizabeth Hayes Turner (Columbia: University of Missouri Press, 1998), 99–118, explores the shifting and complex meanings of "household" demonstrated by an 1890 legal case in which a woman sued for the freedom that had been denied her since the legal abolition of slavery in 1865, while Elizabeth Regosin, *Freedom's Promise: Ex-Slave Families and Citizenship in the Age of Emancipation* (Charlottesville: University Press of Virginia, 2002), uses pension records to examine the meaning and experience of family for former slaves.

Gendered analyses of Reconstruction include Laura F. Edwards, *Gendered Strife and Confusion: The Political Culture of Reconstruction* (Urbana: University of Illinois Press, 1997); Karin L. Zipf, " 'The Whites Shall Rule the Land or Die': Gender, Race, and Class in North Carolina Reconstruction Politics," *Journal of Southern History* 65, no. 3 (1999): 499–534; Elsa Barkley Brown, "Negotiating and Transforming the Public Sphere: African American Political Life in the Transition from Slavery to Freedom," *Public Culture* 7, no. 1 (1994): 107–46; Brown, "To Catch the Vision of Freedom: Reconstructing Southern Black Women's Political History, 1865–1880," in *African American Women and the Vote*,

1837–1965, ed. Ann D. Gordon with Bettye Collier-Thomas, John H. Bracey, Arlene Voski Avakian, and Joyce Avrech Berkman (Amherst: University of Massachusetts Press, 1997), 66–99; and Martha Hodes, "The Sexualization of Reconstruction Politics: White Women and Black Men in the South after the Civil War," *Journal of the History of Sexuality* 3, no.3 (1993): 402–17. Amy Dru Stanley, *From Bondage to Contract: Wage Labor, Marriage, and the Market in the Age of Slave Emancipation* (Cambridge: Cambridge University Press, 1998), includes important discussion of the gendered nature of contracting in the transition from slavery, an argument pursued in Stanley, " 'We Did Not Separate Man and Wife, but All Had to Work': Freedom and Dependence in the Aftermath of Slave Emancipation," in *Terms of Labor: Slavery, Serfdom, and Free Labor*, ed. Stanley L. Engerman (Stanford, Calif.: Stanford University Press, 1999). Eve-lyn Nakano Glenn, *Unequal Freedom: How Race and Gender Shaped American Citizen-ship and Labor* (Cambridge: Harvard University Press, 2002), includes a chapter on gender, race, and labor in the Reconstruction and post-Reconstruction South. The gendering of work after slavery is the focus of Sharon Ann Holt, "Making Freedom Pay: Freedpeople Working for Themselves, North Carolina, 1865–1900," *Journal of Southern History* 60, no. 2 (1994): 228–62; and Susan A. Mann, "Slavery, Sharecropping, and Sexual Inequality," *Signs* 14, no. 4 (1989): 774–98. On family during Reconstruction, see Karin L. Zipf, "Reconstruct-ing 'Free Woman': African-American Women, Apprenticeship, and Custody Rights during Reconstruction," *Journal of Women's History* 12, no. 1 (2000): 8–31; and Ira Berlin, Steven F. Miller, and Leslie S. Rowland, "Afro-American Families in the Transition from Slavery to Freedom," *Radical History Review* 42 (1988): 89–121, which contains reprints of primary documents alongside sev-eral pages of interpretation.

Brazil

The founding study of Brazilian slavery, Gilberto Freyre's *Casa grande e senzala*, published in English as *The Masters and the Slaves: A Study in the Development of Brazilian Civilization*, trans. Samuel Putnam (New York: Alfred A. Knopf, 1946), celebrated black and white racial "intermixture" under slavery in decidedly problematic ways. Nevertheless, this initial emphasis on sexuality and women has produced a historiography which has placed at its center questions of women's role in slave society, in particular the patriarchal nature of slavery and the role of sexual interaction between black women and white men. On women and slavery in Brazil, see Sônia Maria Giacomini, *Mulher e escrava: Uma introdução* histórica ao estudo da mulher negra no Brasil (Petrópolis: Vozes, 1988); Eni de Mesquita Samara and Horacio Gutiérrez, "Mujeres esclavas en el Brasil del siglo XIX," in *Historia de las mujeres en occidente*, ed. Georges Duby and Michelle Perrot, vol. 4, *El siglo XIX*, ed. Geneviève Fraisse, Michelle Perrot, and María José Rodríguez Galdo (Madrid: Taurus, 1993), 643–51 (this chapter does not appear in the non-Spanish versions of this multinational collaboration); and a short book, aimed at undergraduates, by Maria Lucia de Barros Mott, *Submissão e resistência: A mulher na luta contra a escravidão* (São Paulo: Contexto, 1988). Luciano Figueiredo, *O avesso da memória: cotidiano e trabalho da mulher em Minas Geras no século XVIII* (Rio de Janeiro: José Olympio Editora, 1993) integrates the histories of free and enslaved women in the gold-producing slave society of eighteenth-century Minas Gerais, while Kathleen J. Higgins, *"Licentious Liberty" in a Brazilian Gold-Mining Region: Slavery, Gender, and Social Control in Eighteenth Century Sabará, Minas Gerais* (University Park: Penn State University Press, 1999), pays particular attention to enslaved women's use of their sexuality to achieve emancipation. Elizabeth K. C. Magalhães and Sônia Maria Giacomini, "A escrava ama-de-leite: Anjo ou demônio?," in *Mulher, mulheres*, ed. Carmen Barroso and Albertina Oliveira Costa (São Paulo: Cortez / Fundação Carolos Chagas, 1983), 73–89, examines the role and representation of enslaved wet nurses.

Sandra Lauderdale Graham, *Caetana Says No: Women's Stories from a Brazilian Slave Society* (Cambridge: Cambridge University Press, 2002), takes a microhistorical approach to women and slavery, contrasting the experiences of enslaved and slaveowning women. Also taking a microhistorical approach is Júnia Ferreira Furtado, *Chica da Silva e o contrador dos diamantes: O outro lado do mito* (São Paulo: Companhia das Letras, 2003), which reexamines the much-mythologized life of Chica da Silva, a freedwoman born during Brazil's eighteenth-century diamond fever. Keila Grinberg, *Liberata—A lei da ambigüidade: As ações de liberdade da Corte de Apelação do Rio de Janeiro no século XIX* (Rio de Janeiro: Relume Dumará, 1994), is a study of a woman's lawsuit for freedom that sheds light on manumission law and gender in nineteenth-century Brazil. Maria Isaura P. de Queiroz, "Viajantes, século XIX: Negras escravas e livres no Rio de Janeiro," *Revista do Instituto de estudos brasileiros: Edição comemorativa do centenário da abolição da escravatura* 28 (1988): 53–76, uses travel writing to analyze relationships between free and enslaved black and mulatto women in Rio. Maria Pessoa Monteiro, "A mulher negra escrava no imaginário das elites do século XIX," *Clio: Revista de pesquisa histórica (série História do Nordeste)* 12 (1989): 93–102, examines elite representations of enslaved women. Several of the essays in Luiz Mott, *Escravidão, homossexualidade e demonologia* (São Paulo: Ácone, 1988), deal with sexuality in Bahian slave society.

There has been an outpouring of work on family life under slavery in Brazil. Notable works include Robert W. Slenes, *Na senzala, uma flor: Esperanças e recordações na formação da família escrava, Brasil Sudeste, século XIX* (Rio de Janeiro: Nova Fronteira, 1999); Alida C. Metcalf, *Family and Frontier in Colonial Brazil: Santana de Parnaíba, 1580–1822* (Berkeley: University of California Press, 1992); Manolo Florentino and José Roberto Góes, *A paz das senzalas: Famílias escravas e tráfico atlântico, Rio de Janeiro, c. 1790–1850* (Rio de Janeiro: Civilização Brasileira, 1997); and Richard Graham, "Slave Families on a Rural Estate in Colonial Brazil," *Journal of Social History* 9, no.3 (1976): 382–402; and José Flávio Motta, "A família escrava e a penetração do café em Bananal, 1801–1829," *Revista brasileira de estudos de população* 5, no. 1 (1988): 71–101. Sandra Lauderdale Graham, *House and Street: The Domestic World of Servants and Masters in Nineteenth-Century Rio de Janeiro* (Austin: University of Texas Press, 1992), focuses on women as slaves and servants in pre- and postemancipation Rio, while Kátia M. de Queirós Mattoso, *Família e sociedade na Bahia do século XIX* (São Paulo: Corrupio, 1988), for a similar period, examines the familial strategies and structure of enslaved and freedpeople alongside those of free Bahians. Queirós Mattoso's longer work, *Bahia, século XIX: Uma província no Império* (Rio de Janeiro: Nova Fronteira, 1992), offers an extensive exploration of family and marriage strategy. Sheila de Castro Faria, *A colônia em movimento: fortuna e família no cotidiano colonial* (Rio de Janeiro: Nova Fronteira, 1998) examines the family strategies and experiences of slaves and free people in colonial Brazil, shifting the research focus away from the traditional historiographical concern with the plantation.

Emília Viotti da Costa's important assessment of nineteenth-century Brazilian society, *The Brazilian Empire: Myths and Histories*, pays sustained attention to slavery and emancipation; the revised edition (Chapel Hill: University of North Carolina Press, 2000), includes a chapter on women. Viotti da Costa, *Da senzala à colônia* (São Paulo: Ciencias Humanas, 1982), focuses specifically on the process of emancipation. Sexuality and the body during late slavery and the early postemancipation period are among the concerns of Martha Abreu, *O império do divino: Festas religiosas e cultura popular no Rio de Janeiro, 1830–1900* (Rio de Janeiro: Nova Fronteira, 1999).

Important general analyses of Brazilian emancipation and postemancipation society include Robert Conrad, *The Destruction of Brazilian Slavery, 1850–1888* (Berkeley: University of California Press, 1972); Rebecca J. Scott, Seymour Drescher, Hebe Maria Mattos de Castro, George Reid Andrews, and Robert M. Levine, *The Abolition of Slavery and the Aftermath of Emancipation in Brazil* (Durham, N.C.: Duke University Press, 1988), originally published as *Hispanic*

American Historical Review 68, no. 3 (1988); Ciro Flamario Cardoso, ed., Escravidão e abolição no Brasil: Novas perspectivas (Rio de Janeiro: Jorge Zahar, 1988); Robert Brent Toplin, The Abolition of Slavery in Brazil (New York: Atheneum, 1972); and Florestan Fernandes, A integração do negro na sociedade de classes, 2 vols. (São Paulo: Ática, 1978). Fernandes's attention to the "social disorganization" of urban black life after slavery raises important questions about gender. Regional studies include Vilma Paraíso Ferreira de Almada, Escravismo e transição: O Espírito Santo (1850/1888) (Rio de Janeiro: Graal, 1984); Manoel Correia de Andrade, Escravidão e trabalho "livre" no nordeste açucareiro (Recife: ASA Pernambuco, 1985); Peter L. Eisenberg, The Sugar Industry in Pernambuco, 1840–1910: Modernization without Change (Berkeley: University of California Press, 1974); Hebe Maria Mattos, Das cores do silêncio: Os significados da liberdade no Sudeste escravista, Brasil século XIX (Rio de Janeiro: Nova Fronteira, 1998); Théo Lobarinhas Piñeiro, Crise e resistência no escravismo colonial: Os últimos anos da escravidão na província do Rio de Janeiro (Passo Fundo, Brazil: Editora Universidade de Passo Fundo, 2002); and Maria Helena Machado, O plano e o pânico: Os movimentos sociais na década da abolição (Rio de Janeiro: Editor UFRJ, EDUSP, 1994), which focuses on the Southeast.

Studies of Brazilian emancipation that include gender as a key category of analysis include Sandra Lauderdale Graham, "Slavery's Impasse: Slave Prostitutes, Small-Time Mistresses, and the Brazilian Law of 1871," Comparative Studies in Society and History 33, no. 4 (1991): 369–94; and Martha Abreu, "Slave Mothers and Freed Children: Emancipation and Female Space in Debates on the 'Free Womb' Law, Rio de Janeiro, 1871," Journal of Latin American Studies 28, no. 3 (1996): 567–80. José Oscar Beozzo, "A família escrava e imigrante na transição do trabalho escravo para o livre," in Família, mulher, sexualidade e igreja na história do Brasil (São Paulo: CEDHAL/CEHILA/Loyola, 1993), 29–100, compares family structures among enslaved people and the immigrant workers who largely replaced them after emancipation. George Reid Andrews, Blacks and Whites in São Paulo, Brazil, 1888–1988 (Madison: University of Wisconsin Press, 1991), includes a short discussion of freedpeople's gendered choices regarding labor, arguing that liberto families' withdrawal of women from the labor market encouraged employers to import migrant workers.

Sidney Chalhoub's books about Rio de Janeiro during the emancipation period, Trabalho, lar, e botequim: o cotidiano dos trabalhadores no Rio de Janeiro da Belle Époque (São Paulo: Brasiliense, 1986) and Visões da liberdade: uma história das últimas décadas da escravidão na corte (São Paulo: Companhia das Letras, 1992) both include some attention to gender.

Gender relations among freedpeople are considered in Maria Inês Côrtes de

Oliveira, O liberto: Seu mundo e os outros (São Paulo: Corrupio, 1988). Kim D. Butler's Freedoms Given, Freedoms Won: Afro-Brazilians in Post-abolition São Paulo and Salvador (New Brunswick, N.J.: Rutgers University Press, 1998), makes some use of gender analysis in its comparison of Afro-Brazilian political and cultural activism in the two cities studied. Martha de Abreu Esteves, Meninas perdidas: Os populares e o cotidiano do amor no Rio de Janeiro da belle époque (Rio de Janeiro: Paz e Terra, 1989), and Sueann Caulfield, In Defense of Honor: Sexual Morality, Modernity, and Nation in Early-Twentieth-Century Brazil (Durham, N.C.: Duke University Press, 2000), include gendered analyses of the postemancipation moral panic regarding the urban poor. Ruth Landes, The City of Women (Albuquerque: University of New Mexico Press, 1995 [1947]), based on ethnographic research conducted in Bahia in the 1930s, was a pioneering analysis of the importance of women and the role of gender in candomblé with relevance to the slavery and early postemancipation periods. The gendered nature of postemancipation Brazilian agriculture is addressed in Verena Stolcke, Coffee Planters, Workers, and Wives: Class Conflict and Gender Relations on São Paulo Coffee Plantations, 1850–1980 (Basingstoke, U.K.: Macmillan, 1988).

The Cape Colony

Studies of slavery have largely sought to identify the mechanisms of control and resistance under Dutch slavery and have rarely focused on gender. Landmark books on slavery include Nigel Worden, Slavery in Dutch South Africa (Cambridge: Cambridge University Press, 1985); and Robert Ross, The Cape of Torments: Slavery and Resistance in South Africa (Boston: Routledge and Kegan Paul, 1983). Robert C.-H. Shell, Children of Bondage: A Social History of the Slave Society at the Cape of Good Hope, 1652–1838 (Hanover, N.H.: Wesleyan University Press published by the University Press of New England, 1994), presents a paternalist model of Cape slavery, arguing that it was sustained through the integration of slaves into masters' households, and downplaying violence and direct domination. John Edwin Mason, Social Death and Resurrection: Slavery and Emancipation in South Africa (Charlottesville: University of Virginia Press, 2003), which focuses on the late period of slavery and the apprenticeship period, makes use of gender analysis, in particular in his discussion of the slaveholding household and enslaved people's family lives. Mason's epilogue on the post-slavery period emphasizes the reshaping of gender as a critical aspect of emancipation. Patricia van der Spuy has focused on women and the slave experience in articles including "Slave Women and the Family in Nineteenth-

Century Cape Town," *South African Historical Journal* 27 (1992): 50–74; and "'What, Then, Was the Sexual Outlet for Black Males?' A Feminist Critique of Quantitative Representations of Women Slaves at the Cape of Good Hope in the Eighteenth Century," *Kronos* 23 (1996): 43–56.

The multiple emancipations in the Cape, which freed both enslaved people and those living under other forms of servitude, are discussed in Clifton C. Crais, *White Supremacy and Black Resistance in Pre-industrial South Africa: The Making of the Colonial Order in the Eastern Cape, 1770–1865* (Cambridge: Cambridge University Press, 1991); Robert Ross, "Emancipations and the Economy of the Cape Colony," *Slavery and Abolition* 14, no. 1 (1993): 131–48; and Nigel Worden and Clifton Crais, eds., *Breaking the Chains: Slavery and Its Legacy in the Nineteenth-Century Cape Colony* (Johannesburg: Witwatersrand University Press, 1994), a volume that includes several essays attentive to gender.

On gender and slave emancipation, see Pamela Scully, *Liberating the Family? Gender and British Slave Emancipation in the Rural Western Cape, South Africa, 1823–1853* (Portsmouth, N.H.: Heinemann, 1997). Gender in the postemancipation Cape is also discussed in two articles by Scully: "Rape, Race and Colonial Culture: The Sexual Politics of Identity in the Nineteenth-Century Cape Colony, South Africa," *American Historical Review* 100, no. 2 (1995): 335–59, and "Narratives of Infanticide in the Aftermath of Slave Emancipation in the Nineteenth-Century Cape Colony, South Africa," *Canadian Journal of African Studies/Revue canadienne des études africaines* 30, no. 1 (1996): 88–105.

Subsaharan Africa, Excluding the Cape Colony

Analysis of women and slavery in other parts of Africa is often integrated into larger studies of African women, as is the case with Niara Sudarkasa, "The 'Status of Women' in Indigenous African Societies," in *Women in Africa and the African Diaspora*, ed. Rosalyn Terborg-Penn, Sharon Harley, and Audrea Benton Rushing (Washington, D.C.: Howard University Press, 1987), 25–41; Sandra Greene, *Gender, Ethnicity and Social Change on the Upper Slave Coast: A History of the Anlo-Ewe* (Portsmouth, N.H.: Heinemann, 1996); and Edna G. Bay, *Wives of the Leopard: Gender, Politics, and Culture in the Kingdom of Dahomey* (Charlottesville: University of Virginia Press, 1998). For specific attention to enslaved women, see the influential collection edited by Claire C. Robertson and Martin A. Klein, *Women and Slavery in Africa* (Madison: University of Wisconsin Press, 1983); and Beverley B. Mack, "Women and Slavery in Nineteenth-Century

Hausaland," *Slavery and Abolition* 13, no.1 (1992): 89–110; and, particularly, Marcia Wright, *Strategies of Slaves and Women: Life Stories from East/Central Africa* (New York: Lillian Barber, 1993). In his influential work on African slavery, Claude Meillassoux devotes substantial attention to the position of enslaved women, arguing that they were not used to reproduce the captive population; see, especially, *The Anthropology of Slavery: The Womb of Iron and Gold*, trans. Alide Dasnois (London: Athlone, 1991).

For overviews of the protracted end of slavery in Africa, see Suzanne Miers and Richard Roberts, eds., *The End of Slavery in Africa* (Madison: University of Wisconsin Press, 1988); and Suzanne Miers and Martin A. Klein, eds., *Slavery and Colonial Rule in Africa* (London: Frank Cass, 1998), also published as a special issue of *Slavery and Abolition* 19, no.2 (1998). Other important studies of emancipation in Africa include Frederick Cooper, *From Slaves to Squatters: Plantation Labor and Agriculture in Zanzibar and Coastal Kenya, 1890–1925* (New Haven, Conn.: Yale University Press, 1980); and Paul Lovejoy and Jan Hogendorn, *Slow Death for Slavery: The Course of Abolition in Northern Nigeria, 1897–1906* (Cambridge: Cambridge University Press, 1993).

Susan Martin, "Slaves, Igbo Women and Palm Oil in the Nineteenth Century," and Robin Law, " 'Legitimate' Trade and Gender Relations in Yorubaland and Dahomey," in *From Slave Trade to "Legitimate" Commerce: The Commercial Transition in Nineteenth-Century West Africa*, ed. Robin Law (Cambridge: Cambridge University Press, 1995), 172–94 and 195–214, respectively, examine the impact of the ending of the Atlantic slave trade (in which by the nineteenth century the captives were predominantly men) and the shift to palm oil production on African gender relations and the gender division of labor. Richard Roberts, "Representation, Structure, and Agency: Divorce in the French Soudan in the Early Twentieth Century," *Journal of African History* 40, no. 3 (1999): 389–410, emphasizes the important relationship between colonialism, shifts in marriage policy and practice, and the end of slavery. Elias Mandala, "Capitalism, Kinship and Gender in the Lower Tchiri (Shire) Valley of Malawi, 1860–1960: An Alternative Theoretical Framework," *African Economic History* 13 (1984): 137–69, examines how gender relations changed as slavery and slave trading declined. Martin Klein and Richard Roberts, "The Banamba Slave Exodus of 1905 and the Decline of Slavery in the Western Sudan," *Journal of African History* 21, no. 3 (1980): 375–94, includes discussion of the slave family in the emancipation process. The greater difficulty for women in achieving free status under British colonial rule is emphasized in Ahmad Sikainga, "Shari'a Courts and the Manumission of Female Slaves in the Sudan, 1898–

1939," International Journal of African Historical Studies 28, no.1 (1995): 1–24, and Sikainga, Slaves into Workers: Emancipation and Labor in Colonial Sudan (Austin: University of Texas Press, 1996).

For gendered perspectives on African societies after slavery, see Barbara M. Cooper, Marriage in Maradi: Gender and Culture in a Hausa Society, 1900–1989 (Portsmouth, N.H.: Heinemann, 1997); and Jean Allman, Susan Geiger, and Nakanyike Musisi, eds., Women in African Colonial Histories (Bloomington: Indiana University Press, 2002). Two articles by Paul Lovejoy, "Concubinage in the Sokoto Caliphate (1804–1903)," Slavery and Abolition 11, no. 2 (1990): 158–89, and "Concubinage and the Status of Women Slaves in Early Colonial Northern Nigeria," Journal of African History 29, no. 2 (1988): 245–66, emphasize the sexual exploitation of women slaves in the Islamic Sokoto Caliphate and its successor state, the British colony Northern Nigeria.

Abolitionism

The historiography of abolitionism and metropolitan debates over slavery has become increasingly concerned with questions of gender. In addition to her book Women against Slavery: The British Campaigns, 1780–1870 (London: Routledge, 1992), Clare Midgley has published a number of important articles on women, gender, and British abolitionism, including "Anti-slavery and Feminism in Nineteenth-Century Britain," Gender and History 5, no. 3 (1993): 343–62, and "Slave Sugar Boycotts, Female Activism and the Domestic Base of British Anti-slavery Culture," Slavery and Abolition 17, no. 3 (1996): 137–62. See also Henrice Altink, " 'An Outrage on All Decency': Abolitionist Reactions to Flogging Jamaican Slave Women, 1780–1934," Slavery and Abolition 23, no.2 (2002): 107–22. For the gendering of slavery in wider British culture, see Catherine Hall, "Missionary Stories: Gender and Ethnicity in England in the 1830s and 1840s," in White, Male and Middle Class: Explorations in Feminism and History (Cambridge: Polity, 1992), 205–54; Hall, Civilising Subjects: Metropole and Colony in the English Imagination, 1830–1867 (Cambridge: Polity, 2002); and Diana Paton, "Decency, Dependence, and the Lash: Gender and the British Debate over Slave Emancipation, 1830–1834," Slavery and Abolition 17, no. 3 (1996): 162–84.

Much historiography on women's role in U.S. abolitionism stresses the connections between abolitionism and feminism. For scholarship along these lines, see Blanche Glassman Hersh, The Slavery of Sex: Feminist-Abolitionism in America (Chicago: University of Illinois Press, 1978); Shirley J. Yee, Black Women

Abolitionists: A Study in Activism, 1828–1860 (Knoxville: University of Tennessee Press, 1992); Kathryn Kish Sklar, Women's Rights Emerges within the Anti-slavery Movement, 1830–1870 (New York: Bedford, 2000); and Susan Zaeske, Signatures of Citizenship: Petitioning, Antislavery, and Women's Political Identity (Chapel Hill: University of North Carolina Press, 2003). Scholarship which places less emphasis on abolitionism's connection to feminism includes Debra Gold Hansen, Strained Sisterhood: Gender and Class in the Boston Female Anti-slavery Society (Amherst: University of Massachusetts Press, 1993); Julie Roy Jeffrey, The Great Silent Army of Abolitionism: Ordinary Women in the Antislavery Movement (Chapel Hill: University of North Carolina Press, 1998); Michael D. Pierson, "Gender and Party Ideologies: The Constitutional Thought of Women and Men in American Anti-slavery Politics," Slavery and Abolition 19, no. 3 (1998): 46–67; and Deborah Van Broekhoven, "'Better Than a Clay Club': The Organization of Women's Anti-slavery Fairs, 1835–60," Slavery and Abolition 19, no. 1 (1998): 24–45. The essays in Jean Fagan Yellin and John C. Van Horne, eds., The Abolitionist Sisterhood: Women's Political Culture in Antebellum America (Ithaca, N.Y.: Cornell University Press, 1994), study both feminist and nonfeminist abolitionist women, as does Lori D. Ginzburg, Women and the Work of Benevolence: Morality, Politics, and Class in the Nineteenth-Century United States (New Haven, Conn.: Yale University Press, 1990). For studies of individual abolitionist women, see Dorothy Sterling, Ahead of Her Time: Abby Kelley and the Politics of Antislavery (New York: W. W. Norton, 1991); Carolyn L. Karcher, The First Woman in the Republic: A Cultural Biography of Lydia Maria Child (Durham, N.C.: Duke University Press, 1995); Jane Rhodes, Mary Ann Shadd Cary: The Black Press and Protest in the Nineteenth Century (Bloomington: Indiana University Press, 1998); and Nell Irvin Painter, Sojourner Truth: A Life, A Symbol (New York: Norton, 1996). Donald R. Kennon, "'An Apple of Discord': The Woman Question at the World's Anti-slavery Convention of 1840," Slavery and Abolition 5, no.3 (1984): 244–65, demonstrates the tension around the participation of women in transatlantic abolitionism. On abolitionist women during the Civil War, see Wendy Hamand Venet, Neither Ballots nor Bullets: Women Abolitionists and the Civil War (Charlottesville: University of Virginia Press, 1991). For a gendered approach to U.S. antislavery, rather than a consideration of women antislavery activists per se, see Michael D. Pierson, Free Hearts, Free Homes: Gender and American Antislavery Politics (Chapel Hill: University of North Carolina Press, 2003).

Some of the most important work on gender and abolitionism has been done by literary scholars: see Moira Ferguson, Subject to Others: British Women Writers and Colonial Slavery, 1670–1834 (New York: Routledge, 1992); Charlotte

Sussman, *Consuming Anxieties: Consumer Protest, Gender, and British Slavery, 1713–1833* (Stanford, Calif.: Stanford University Press, 2000); and, on U.S. abolitionism, Jean Fagan Yellin, *Women and Sisters: The Antislavery Feminists in American Culture* (New Haven, Conn.: Yale University Press, 1989); Karen Sánchez-Eppler, *Touching Liberty: Abolition, Feminism, and the Politics of the Body* (Berkeley: University of California Press, 1993); and Kristin Hoganson, "Garrisonian Abolitionists and the Rhetoric of Gender, 1850–1860," *American Quarterly* 45, no. 3 (1993): 558–95.

Women's participation in the Brazilian abolitionist movement is considered in Roger A. Kittleson, " 'Campaign All of Peace and Charity': Gender and the Politics of Abolitionism in Porto Alegre, Brazil, 1879–88," *Slavery and Abolition* 22, no. 3 (2001): 83–108. Much less work has been done on French antislavery, and the main studies remain unconcerned with gender. See, for instance, Lawrence C. Jennings, *French Anti-slavery: The Movement for the Abolition of Slavery in France, 1802–1848* (Cambridge: Cambridge University Press, 2000).

Note

This essay could not have been written without the help of many colleagues who supplied me with references. Thanks especially to Martha Abreu, Carol Faulkner, Sue Peabody, Pamela Scully, Marek Steedman, and Michael Zeuske. Responsibility for errors and omissions remains with me.

Contributors

MARTHA ABREU is a professor at the Universidade Federal Fluminense, Rio de Janeiro, Brazil. She is the author of *Meninas perdidas: Os populares e o cotidiano do amor no Rio de Janeiro da belle époque* (1989) and *O império do divino: Festas religiosas e cultura popular no Rio de Janeiro, 1830–1900* (1999).

SHEENA BOA has a PhD in history from Warwick University, where she teaches Caribbean and North American history. Her research interests include gender issues in postemancipation St. Vincent and childhood experiences in the nineteenth-century Caribbean.

BRIDGET BRERETON is a professor of history at the St. Augustine, Trinidad, campus of the University of the West Indies. She is the author or editor of several books on the history of the Caribbean and of Trinidad and Tobago, as well as numerous articles and book chapters. She is a past president of the Association of Caribbean Historians and the editor of volume 5 of the UNESCO *General History of the Caribbean.*

CAROL FAULKNER received her PhD from the State University of New York, Binghamton. She held a National Historical Publications and Records Commission Editing Fellowship at the Lucretia Mott Project and was assistant editor of *The Selected Letters of Lucretia Coffin Mott* (2001). She is currently assistant professor of history at the State University of New York College, Geneseo, and is working on a book manuscript titled, "Women's Radical Reconstruction: The Freedmen's Aid Movement, 1862–1876."

ROGER A. KITTLESON is an associate professor at Williams College, where he teaches Latin American history. His book, *A New Regime of Ideas: Transformations of Political Culture in Porto Alegre, Brazil, 1845–1895*, will be published by the University of Pittsburgh Press in fall 2005. His current research focuses on race, region, and masculinity in Brazilian soccer.

MARTIN KLEIN is retired from teaching history at the University of Toronto. He has written extensively on West African slavery. He is the editor (with Claire Robertson) of *Women and Slavery in Africa* (1983) and *Breaking the Chains: Slavery,*

Bondage and Emancipation in Modern Africa and Asia (1993) and the author of *Slavery and Colonial Rule in French West Africa* (1998).

MELANIE NEWTON completed her doctorate at Oxford University and is an assistant professor of Caribbean history at the University of Toronto. She is currently working on a manuscript titled "The Children of Africa in the Colonies: Free People of Color in Barbados in the Age of Emancipation, 1790–1860."

DIANA PATON is a senior lecturer in history at the University of Newcastle upon Tyne. She is the author of *No Bond but the Law: Punishment, Race, and Gender in Jamaican State Formation, 1780–1870* (2004) and editor of *A Narrative of Events since the First of August, 1834, by James Williams, an Apprenticed Labourer in Jamaica* (2001).

SUE PEABODY is an associate professor of history at Washington State University, Vancouver. Her publications include *"There Are No Slaves in France": The Political Culture of Race and Slavery in the Ancien Régime* (1996) and articles on colonial citizenship, religious culture, and slavery in the first French empire. She is currently writing on slavery, freedom, and the law in the Atlantic world.

RICHARD ROBERTS is a professor of history at Stanford University. He has published extensively on the history of West Africa. His books include *Warriors, Merchants, and Slaves: The State and the Economy in the Middle Niger Valley, c. 1700–1914* (1987).

ILEANA RODRÍGUEZ-SILVA is an assistant professor of Latin American history at the University of Washington. She received her PhD in Latin American history at the University of Wisconsin, Madison. Her dissertation was titled "A Conspiracy of Silence: Blackness, Class, and National Identities in Post-emancipation Puerto Rico (1850–1920)."

HANNAH ROSEN is an assistant professor at the University of Michigan. She received her doctorate in history from the University of Chicago. She is currently completing a manuscript titled "The Gender of Reconstruction: Race, Citizenship, and Sexual Violence in the Postemancipation South."

MIMI SHELLER is a visiting associate professor in the Department of Sociology and Anthropology at Swarthmore College and visiting senior fellow in the Centre for Mobilities Research, Lancaster University. She is the author of *Democracy after Slavery: Black Publics and Peasant Radicalism in Haiti and Jamaica* (2000) and *Consuming the Caribbean: From Arawaks to Zombies* (2003).

PAMELA SCULLY holds a joint appointment in the Department of Women's Studies and the Institute of African Studies at Emory University. She is the author of *Liberating the Family? Gender and British Slave Emancipation in the Rural Western Cape, South Africa, 1823–1853* (1997) and *The Bouquet of Freedom: Social and Economic Relations in the Stellenbosch District, South Africa, c. 1870–1900* (1990).

MAREK STEEDMAN is an assistant professor of political theory at the University of Southern Mississippi. He received his PhD from the University of Michigan with a focus in political theory. His dissertation was a historically grounded examination of representations of race, and the social hierarchies they partly constitute, in North Louisiana, 1870–1913.

MICHAEL ZEUSKE is a professor of Iberian and Latin American history at the University of Cologne. His works on Cuba include *Kleine Geschichte Kubas* [A short history of Cuba] (2000) and *Insel der Extreme: Kuba im 20. Jahrhundert* [Island of extremes: Cuba in the twentieth century] (2000).

Index

Abolition Act for Puerto Rico, 202, 208

Abolitionism: appeals to morality in, 109–12; associating with femininity, 113–14; in Brazil, 21, 99–114; charity and, 105–6; family relations and, 110–11; femininity and, 109; French, 164; gender politics and, 2–3; philanthropy and, 225, 230–33; political power and, 106–7, 230; practice of, 105–6; process of, 10; resistance to, 201; in United States, 21; U.S. Civil War and, 122–23; womanhood and, 108–12; women in, 21, 102–5. See also Women abolitionists

Abolitionism (Nabuco), 111

Abolitionist Center of Fortaleza, 109

Abolitionist Center of Porto Alegre (Centro Abolicionista de Porto Alegre), 102–4

Abolitionist groups, 103–4

Abolitionists, Puerto Rican, 204–5

Abolitionists, women. See Women abolitionists

Abreu, Luciana de, 112–13

Abreu, Martha, 23

Activism, antislavery, 102, 104. See also Women abolitionists

Africa: emancipation in, 10; experiences in, 25; slavery in, 6–7

African Caribbean traditions, 248

African Caribbean women, 253

African migrants, 88–89

Allen, J. A., 147

Almiroti, Santos, 208

Amaral Lisboa, Ana Aurora do, 112

American Freedmen's Aid Commission, 126, 129

Anderson, John, 250, 257–60

Ando, Petrona, 184

Andrade, Mário de, 268

Andrea (enslaved man in Puerto Rico), 208

Anguilla, 154

Anthony, Susan B., 134

Antigua, 146–47, 250–52

Antiracism, and philanthropy, 230–33

Antislavery activism, 102, 104

Antislavery coalition building, 100–101, 105–6, 113–14

Apprenticeship: attempts at exemption from, 216–17; in Cape Colony, 37–38; and dances, 252–53, 256–57; domestic, 253; emancipation through, 9; of free children, 145; freedpeople challenging, 213–14; "indulgences" to women and, 144; in Puerto Rico, 199, 202–4; responses to, 208. See also Occupations, for freedpeople

Arango y Parreño, Francisco de, 181

Archives, as colonizers' accounts, 40–42; as contested site, 51–52

Freed communities, 14–16, 22

Freedmen: apprenticeship system and, 208; autonomy of, 14–15; caring for children, 212, 215; citizenship for, 182, 190; employment opportunities for, 57, 69–70; as estate laborers, 146–47, 153–54; as heads of household, 17–18, 87, 155; invoking status as Christians, 46; lineage of masculinity, 42–45; as main producers, 204–5; marriage for, 17, 39, 44–45, 49–51; masculine identity of, 90, 93; in military service, 3; philanthropic activity of, 240–41; political agency of, 41, 45–49, 52, 92–94; in postemancipation societies, 1; power of, over wives, 15, 17–18, 44–45; in public spheres, 293; right of, to land, 45–48, 192; speech acts of, 41–42, 90–91; suffrage for, 18, 289; as threat to white men's power, 293, 300, 311; using language of labor, 200–201; and women abolitionists, 128–29. *See also* Men

Freedmen's Bureau, 21, 122; assistance offered by, 126; closing of, 131–32, 134; freedpeople and, 14, 128; as source of political power for women, 132; and women abolitionists, 123–24. *See also* Women abolitionists

Freedom: manhood and, 79; meanings of, 143; race and, 49–51; rights inherent in, 48

Freedpeople: adaptations of, 13–14; apprentice system and, 213–14; autonomy of, 5, 14–15, 315; citizenship for, 19–20; contractual relations of, 22; employment opportunities for, 211–12; entertainment for, 255–56; European gender norms influencing, 156–57; forced work of, 130–31; gender roles for, 214, 311; households of, 310–11; identity of, 169–70; leisure activities of, 254–55; manhood for, 8–9; mobility of, 208–11; objectives of, 152–53; planters and, 8, 145; policing of, 206–7; political activity for, 19–20; Reconstruction Acts and, 323; representations of, 228; U.S. policy toward, 121–35; womanhood for, 8–9; work for, 19–20. *See also* Apprenticeship; Family and families, freedpeople's; Freedmen; Freedwomen; Reconstruction

Freedwomen: and abolitionist women, 124–25; apprenticeship system and, 208; autonomy of, 14–15; citizenship for, 182, 190; contracts of, 200–201; divorces granted to, 162–63, 172–74; in domestic service, 153–54, 206–7, 210–12, 214–15, 253; family responsibilities of, 217–18; in field labor, 146–47; gender experience of, 24–25; as housewives, 155–56; labor of, 143, 150–51, 181, 205–6; marriage for, 17, 44–45, 324; native courts and, 171–75; in notarial records, 183–88; opportunities for, 57, 67, 69–70; political activity of, 18–19; in postemancipation societies, 1; power of husbands over, 15, 17–18, 44–45; property ownership among, 191, 228; public role of, 232–33; respectability of, 23, 232–33, 250–52, 253–54; rights of, 93–94; status of, 59; suffrage and, 18; testimony by, 313; wage labor and, 19; withdrawal of, from estate labor, 143, 146–48, 150–54, 157–58; in working class,

Marriage (*continued*)
freedwomen, 44–45, 324; interracial, 23–24, 289–306; meanings of, 44–45; in postemancipation Arkansas, 289–306; redefining relationships, 17; and respectability of women, 232–33, 320, 324; reverence of, 238–39; sex and, 295–96; *signares* (temporary marriages) and, 165; of slaves, 65, 164–65, 170–71, 175; symbolism of, 44–45. *See also* Divorces, for freedwomen

Marshall, W. K., 148

Martín (son of Celedonio), 215

Martinique: citizenship in, 70; emancipation in, 9, 69; free status in, 61; history of women in, 56–57; maintenance of slavery in, 67; manumission in, 68–69; promoting religiosity in, 13–14; racial segregation in, 62; sex ratio among slaves in, 57; society in, 60–61

Más, Salvador, 209

Masculinity: black, 80–81; citizenship and, 11–12, 37–52, 79–94; emancipation and, 21; expression of, in terms of family, 38–39; of freedmen, 44–45, 90; in Haiti, 80; identity of free workers and, 206; lineages of, 42–45; nationalism and, 11; philanthropy and, 22; poor women and, 258–59; slaves' understanding of, 3, 42–44; white, 80–81; working class, 81–82

Masquerading, 255–56, 259, 261

Massiah, Mrs. Benjamin, 232

McArthur, Ronald, 84, 85

McCurry, Stephanie, 292

McKim, J. Miller, 126

McLaren, James, 90

Meers (widow), 37–38, 40, 42, 49–51

Meillassoux, 164

Men: as category, 26; reconstructing categories of, 2; roles of, 5–6, 189; slavery denying recognition as, 43–44. *See also* Freedmen; White men

Mendes, Joana Emília da Costa, 102

Mendes, Julia Brito, 275

Middle-class women: charitable work of, 251–52; entertainment for, 260; respectability of, 250–52; social activities of, 247–48. *See also* Class; Elite, nonwhite; Elite, white

Midgley, Clare, 99

Migration, 4, 170–71, 209–10

Military service, 3, 11–12, 64–65, 167–68

Mintz, Sidney, 157

"Miscegenation," discourse of, 290–91, 298, 305–6

Missionaries, 171, 230–31, 242. *See also* Christians; Protestant areas

Mithon, Jean Jacques, 58

Mobility, of freedpeople, 208–11

Modinhas (songs), 269

Montefiore, Joseph, 232

Montefiore, Mary, 232

Montejo, Esteban, 188, 190, 192

Montserrat, 154

Moraes Filho, Mello, 269, 272

Morality: abolitionists' appeals to, 110–12, 125; charity and, 236, 242; estate labor as dangerous to female, 156; public debate on, 237

Morant Bay Rebellion, 90, 92

Moré (exslave family), 186–87

Morenas (blacks), 184–85, 267–83

Moret Law, 202

Morisseau, Philippe, 61

Morisseau, Sieur d'Ester, 61–63

Morrison, Coloniel, 311

Morúa Delgado, Martín, 190

Mozambique, slaves from, 43

"*Mucama*" (song), 273

Mulatas (mixed-race women): in popular song, 267–83; representations of, 23, 271–76; stereotypes of, 280–81

Mulâtresse, 56–70

"Mulatto dance," 232

Muni Sarni, 87–88

Music, popular, 267–83

Muslims, manumissions by, 163–64

Nabuco, Joaquim, 110–11, 113

Napoleon Bonaparte, 66–67

National Freedmen's Relief Association of Washington, 130

Nationalism, and masculinity, 11

National Woman Suffrage Association, 134

Nation building, 4

Négresse, 56–70

Neves, Eduardo das, 273, 277–79

Newton, Melanie, 22

Nonwhite, elite. *See* Elite, nonwhite

North Carolina, 15

Notarial records, 183–88, 191

Núñez, Manuel, 185

O mulato (Azevedo), 111

Obeso y Robles, Felipe, 184

Obligations, male, 81–82

Occupations, for freedpeople: domestic-related, 206–7, 210–12, 214–15, 253; restricted to women, 218; skilled trades, 153–54. *See also* Apprenticeship; Estate labor; Labor

Ordinance 50 (Cape Colony), 38, 47–48

Ortiz, Fernando, 181

Otero, Benigno, 212

Otero, Juan Pedro, 212

Otero, Manuel Ríos, 212

Ouachita Parish, 310

Pago, Gilberto, 18–19

Paraguayan War, 100, 106

Participation, political, 48

Pateman, Carol, 17

Patriarchal households, 5, 82, 229–30. *See also* Households

Patrocíno, José do, 94, 104

Patterson, Orlando, 42

Peabody, Sue, 20–21

Pérez, Barbara, 189

Pérez, Eusebio, 186

Pétion, Alexandre, 11

"Petition of Coolies," 87–88

Petitions, family, 86–89

Phélypeaux, Raimond Balthazar, 59–60

Philanthropy: abolitionism and, 104–5, 225, 230–33; civil rights and, 229–30; domesticity and, 241–42; masculinity and, 22; morality and, 236; of planter class, 226–27; and production of public life, 225–42; public roles of women through, 232–35. *See also* Charity; Elite, nonwhite

Philip, John, 38

Phillippo, J. M., 155

Phillips, George, 313

Phipps, Mrs. Charles, 232

Picó, Fernando, 206

Piersen, William, 282

Pinkston, Eliza, 23, 310–14, 316, 318–23

Pinkston, Henry, 312–13, 316–17, 319–23

Pinkston, Ida, 311, 313

Plantation work. *See* Estate labor

Planter class: allowances for free children by, 144–45; emergence of nonwhite elites and, 227–28; employment choices for, 82–83, 85; on loss of female labor, 149–50; opposing missionary societies, 230–31; philanthropic work of, 226–27; racial segregation and, 234; reinventing public image of, 236–37; relations of, with freedpeople, 145, 315

dle class and, 250–52; struggle of
nonwhites for, 253–34
Revolution of 1848, 69
Reyes Castillo Bueno, María de los
(Reyita), 189
Ribalta, Tomás, 185
Rights: to accumulate wealth, 174–
75; Christianity as basis for, 85; to
citizenship, 90–91; family as basis
for, 89; freed status as basis for,
48; patriarchy and, 229–30; to
political activity, 92–93, 241. *See
also* Suffrage
Rio de Janeiro, Brazil, 102–3, 268–70
Rivera, Catalina, 203–4
Rivera, María Francisca, 213
RLASS. *See* Rochester Ladies' Anti-
slavery Society (RLASS)
Robert, Richard, 22
Rochester Ladies' Anti-slavery Society
(RLASS), 122–24, 126, 132
Rodríguez-Silva, Illena, 22
Romaní, Elvira, 216
Rosen, Hannah, 23
Roume, Ernest, 168, 169
Rousseau, Jean Jacques, 64

Sagua la Grande, Cuba, 184–85
Saint-Christophe, 57
Saint-Domingue: citizenship in, 70;
emancipation in, 10–12, 65–67;
former slave owners in, 8; history
of women in, 56–57; racial segre-
gation in, 62; sex ratio among
slaves in, 57, 64; slave insurrec-
tions in, 64; society in, 60–61
Sale, Maggie, 81–82
Samake, Karounga, 173
Samaritan Charitable Society of the
Free People of Color, 229
San Juan, Puerto Rico, 210–14
Santa Clara, Cuba, 181–93
Santo, Qorpo, 107–8

São Paolo, Brazil, 270
Schwartz, Stuart, 182
Scoble, John, 151
Scott, Rebecca, 79, 181–82
Scully, Pamela, 20
Self-purchase, of slaves, 191–92
"Sempre chorando" (song),
278–79
Sena (slave of Marais), 37–38
Senegal, 165–66, 169
Servatius, René, 166
Seven Years' War, 61
Sewell, W. G., 143, 146
Sex: marriage and, 295–96; in post-
emancipation Arkansas, 289–306;
violence and, 304, 322. *See also*
Rape
Sexual abuse, risks of, 156–57
Sexuality: of freedpeople, 228; in
political debates, 23–24; politics
of, 20; poor women and, 261
Sharpe, Henry, 259
Sheller, Mimi, 18, 21, 39, 68, 70, 150
Shepherd, Verene, 149
Shipherd, Jacob R., 129, 131
Shurland, Mrs. Joseph, 232
Signares (temporary marriages), 165
"Sinhazinha" (little missus), 278
Skilled trades, freedmen working in,
153–54
Slave children, 57–58. *See also* Chil-
dren; Freedchildren
Slave flight, 166–67
Slaveholders' families, 43, 111–12
Slave insurrections, 64
Slave marriages, 164–65
Slave men: opportunities of, to
achieve freed status, 58; on planta-
tions, 144; resistance of, to slavery,
43. *See also* Freedmen
Slave owners, former, 8,
Slave revolts, 202
Slavery: in Africa, 6–7; gendering of

Underhill, Edward Bean, 91, 156
United States: abolitionism in, 21, 99–100; Arkansas, 289–306; Christianity in, 7; emancipation in, 9; freedpeople in, 14–15, 121–35; Louisiana, 8, 79, 310–24; militia act in, 64–65; women abolitionists in, 125–26. See also Reconstruction; Women abolitionists
Urban areas, labor in, 210
Urban audiences, of popular songs, 268–70
Urban women, entertainment of, 247

Vagrancy Act (Cape Colony), 47
Vagrancy Law (Puerto Rico), 205
Vagrancy laws, 206
Valorization, of mixed-races, 279–80
Values, women's, and abolitionists, 124–25
Varela, Bibiana, 184
Vaucresson, Nicolas-François Amoult de, 58
Velázquez, Simplicia, 213
"Vem ça, meu anjo" (song), 275
Verissimo, José, 106
Vieira, Damasceno, 110–11
Violence: landowners and, 323, against men, 24, slave uprisings and, 10, against women, 23. See also Rape
Voting rights. See Suffrage

Wage labor, 143–57. See also Labor
Wealth, slaves' right to, 174–75
Wells, Henry H., 126–27
Wells, J. Madison, 314
Wells, Marshal, 127
Welter, Barbara, 238
West Africa. See French West Africa
Western Anti-slavery Society, 122–23
West Indies, 9, 230
White, James T., 303

White elite. See Elite, white
White Fathers, 167–68
White men: abuse black women, 303–4; claims of, to political authority, 291–93; masculinity of, 80–81; philanthropic work of, 226; power of, threatened by freedmen, 38, 300, 311; sexual control of, over slaves, 248–49
Whiteness, privileges of, 51, 61–62
Whites, impoverished, 226–27
White womanhood, ideal of, 2–3
White women: avoidance of non-domestic labor by, 19; charitable work by, 241; freedmen's affront to, 37–38; interracial marriage and, 23–24, 39; involvement in government, 121; marginalization of, 248–49; as part of private world, 249; philanthropic work of, 226; public role of, 234–35; social activities of, 247–48. See also Charity; Philanthropy; Wives; Women; Women abolitionists
Wilbur, Julia, 21, 122; background of, 122; Freedmen's Bureau and, 123–24, 131, 135; on Reconstruction policy, 126–28; women's values and, 124–25
Wilmot, Swithin, 149
Windward Islands, 147, 150, 153
Wives, 43–44, 64–65; freedmen's power over, 15, 17–18, 44–45; freedwomen as, 155–56. See also Husbands; Marriage
Womanhood: abolitionism and, 108–12; in Brazil, 99–114, 106–8; freedpeople's vision of, 8–9; ideal of white, 2–3
Women: abolitionism and, 102–5; as category, 26; emancipation reconstructing categories of, 2; household and, 21; negative implications

Women (continued)
of emancipation for, 65–66; political activity of, 121; roles of, 5–6, 189, 200; in West Africa, 43. See also Freedwomen; White women; Women abolitionists

Women, white. See White women

Women abolitionists, 121; appeal of, on behalf of freedmen, 128–29; in Britain, 99–100; former slaves portrayed by, 133; on Freedmen's Bureau, 123–24; opposed by male abolitionists, 131, 135; opposition of, to Reconstruction policy makers, 126–27; political power for, 132; pushing government policy, 125–26; in the United States, 99–100, 122; women's values and, 124–25

Woodhull, Victoria, 107

Work, meaning of, for freedpeople, 19–20

Worker, political identities of, 199

Workers, indentured ("Coolies"), 21, 80, 82–89, 94

Working-class freedmen, 90–93

Working-class freedwomen, 19, 93–94, 257–58

Yoruba, social organization among, 5

Ysabel, Doña, 215–16

Zeuske, Michael, 11, 22

Library of Congress

Cataloging-in-Publication Data

Gender and slave emancipation in the
Atlantic world / edited by Pamela Scully
and Diana Paton.

p. cm.

Includes bibliographical references and
index.

ISBN 0-8223-3581-6 (cloth : alk. paper)

ISBN 0-8223-3594-8 (pbk. : alk. paper)

1. Slaves—Emancipation—America.

2. Slaves—Emancipation—Caribbean
Area. 3. Sex role—America—History.

4. Sex role—Caribbean Area—
History. I. Scully, Pamela.

II. Paton, Diana, 1969-

HT1050.G45 2005

306.3'62'097—dc22

2005010057